DIGITAL SIGNAL PROCESSING

DIGITAL SIGNAL PROCESSING

William D. Stanley
Professor of Engineering
Old Dominion University

RESTON PUBLISHING COMPANY, INC., Reston, Virginia

Prentice-Hall Company

Library of Congress Cataloging in Publication Data
Stanley, William D
Digital signal processing.

Includes bibliographical references.
1. Signal processing. 2. Digital electronics.
3. Digital filters (Mathematics) I. Title.
TK5102.5.S69 621.38'043 75-6992
ISBN 0-87909-199-1

RESTON PUBLISHING COMPANY, INC.
A Prentice-Hall Company
Reston, Virginia 22090

10 9 8 7

Printed in the United States of America.

To my daughter,
Karen Louise

PREFACE

The use of digital techniques for various signal processing applications has increased tremendously in the last few years, and this trend is expected to continue in the years ahead. Systems that previously consisted only of analog circuits now have incorporated digital circuits to do many of the functions required. Engineering personnel at all levels are now required to deal with such systems, and the impact on electronic hardware development and design is most significant.

The major objective of this book is to provide an introductory treatment of the concepts of digital signal processing with suitable supporting work in linear system concepts and filter design. It was motivated by the recognition by this author that there was a need for such a book at the introductory level. Most of the journal articles and textbooks having direct application to digital processing are written at a higher level and with stronger assumptions on the part of the reader's mathematical background. Thus, this book will have served one of its purposes if it provides enough background to prepare readers with little or no background in discrete system theory to understand some of the many fine references in this field. However, it is also felt that sufficient information will be given to enable the reader to actually specify or design significant portions of digital signal processing systems.

The first chapter provides a qualitative discussion of digital signal processing and an overview of some of the applications. A review of some of the important fundamentals of continuous-time linear system theory is given in Chapter 2. The techniques of Fourier series and spectral analysis are discussed in Chapter 3, and the concept of the sampled signal and its spectrum are developed. The basic theory of discrete-time systems is developed in Chapter 4. The realization process for discrete-time systems and the concept of the frequency response of such systems are discussed in Chapter 5. A survey of the major types of analog filters is given in Chapter 6. A comprehensive treatment of infinite-duration impulse response digital filter design is given in Chapter 7, and the treatment of finite-duration impulse response digital filter design is given in Chapter 8. The properties of the fast Fourier transform are presented in Chapter 9, and various applications of this concept are discussed in Chapter 10.

The actual details of the digital processing modules such as adders, multipliers, etc., are not considered in this book. There are many good books available on the subject of digital hardware design. Furthermore, this is a field which is changing so rapidly that it is almost impossible to provide the latest state of the art techniques of this type in a textbook. Many digital functions that required discrete implementation by the systems designer only a short while ago may now be found "on-the-shelf" in the form of integrated circuits. Thus, the concentration in this book has been on the theory and development of appropriate algorithms and signal processing layouts which will probably not become obsolete as quickly.

It is felt that this book can be used for the following purposes: (a) a textbook for formal college courses in digital signal processing at either the advanced undergraduate or beginning graduate levels, (b) a textbook or reference book for non-credit professional courses in the same area, and (c) a self-study book for practicing engineers who wish to learn the fundamentals of digital signal processing. The large number of example problems and exercises should enhance its value in the third category.

The material has been organized toward a gradual development of the concepts of digital signal processing with the assumption that many readers will need to review and strengthen their understanding of continous-time system theory as they progress. However, the reader having a reasonable background in these fundamentals should be able to advance to any appropriate section of the book without any significant difficulty.

The original source of inspiration for this book was a series of lectures which the author gave while on a temporary appointment at the Naval Underwater Systems Center, New London, Conn., during the summer of 1971. The author wishes to express his deep appreciation to that organization for their help in this matter and, in particular, to Mr. Harold J. Morrison, Head of the Design Review Division. Last, but certainly not least, the author wishes to thank Mrs. Ann Reid for patiently typing the manuscript.

William D. Stanley

CONTENTS

Chapter 1 **GENERAL CONCEPTS OF DIGITAL SIGNAL PROCESSING** **1**

1-0 Introduction, 1
1-1 General Discussion, 1
1-2 Types of Processing, 7
References, 9

Chapter 2 **CONTINUOUS-TIME SYSTEM ANALYSIS** **11**

2-0 Introduction, 11
2-1 Time-Domain Description, 11
2-2 Laplace Transform Methods, 16
2-3 Transfer Function, 19
2-4 Poles, Zeros, and Stability, 22
2-5 Steady-State Frequency Response Concepts, 28
Problems, 32
References, 35

Chapter 3 **FOURIER ANALYSIS AND SAMPLED-DATA SIGNALS** **37**

3-0 Introduction, 37
3-1 Fourier Series, 37
3-2 Fourier Transform, 41
3-3 Sampled-Data Signals, 44
3-4 Ideal Impulse Sampling, 48
3-5 Holding Circuit, 51
Problems, 54
References, 57

Chapter 4 **DISCRETE-TIME SYSTEM ANALYSIS** **59**

4-0 Introduction, 59
4-1 Discrete-Time Signals, 60
4-2 Z-Transform, 61
4-3 Transfer Function, 66
4-4 Inverse Z-Transform, 69
4-5 Response Forms and Stability, 77
4-6 Discrete-Time Convolution, 79
Problems, 81
References, 83

Chapter 5 **REALIZATION AND FREQUENCY RESPONSE OF DISCRETE-TIME SYSTEMS** **85**

5-0 Introduction, 85
5-1 Discrete-Time System Operations, 85
5-2 Direct Realizations Forms, 88
5-3 Parameter Quantization Effects, 91
5-4 Cascade and Parallel Realization Forms, 93
5-5 Steady-State Frequency Response Concepts, 101
5-6 Properties of the Amplitude Response, 110
Problems, 114
References, 115

Chapter 6 **PROPERTIES OF ANALOG FILTERS** **117**

6-0 Introduction, 117
6-1 Ideal Frequency-Domain Filter Models, 117
6-2 General Approaches, 122
6-3 Butterworth Approximation, 126
6-4 Chebyshev Approximation, 128
6-5 Survey of Other Approximations, 133
6-6 Filter Design Data, 136
6-7 Low-Pass to Band-Pass Transformation, 139
6-8 Low-Pass to Band-Rejection Transformation, 144
6-9 Low-Pass to High-Pass Transformation, 148
6-10 Filter Response Curves, 151
Problems, 157
References, 160

Chapter 7 **INFINITE IMPULSE RESPONSE DIGITAL FILTER DESIGN** 163

7-0 Introduction, 163
7-1 General Considerations, 164
7-2 Discussion of Notation, 168
7-3 Bilinear Transformation Method, 168
7-4 Bilinear Transformation Design Examples, 176
7-5 Numerical Interpretation of Bilinear Transformation, 185
7-6 Impulse-Invariance Method, 187
7-7 Step-Invariance Method, 190
7-8 Band-Pass Digital Filter Design, 194
7-9 Band-Rejection Digital Filter Design, 202
7-10 High-Pass Digital Filter Design, 205
Problems, 206
References, 209

Chapter 8 **FINITE IMPULSE RESPONSE DIGITAL FILTER DESIGN** 211

8-0 Introduction, 211
8-1 General Discussion, 211
8-2 Fourier Series Method, 213
8-3 Window Functions, 221
Problems, 235
References, 237

Chapter 9 **BASIC PROPERTIES OF DISCRETE AND FAST FOURIER TRANSFORMS** 239

9-0 Introduction, 239
9-1 Forms of the Fourier Transform, 239
9-2 Discrete Fourier Transform, 245
9-3 Even and Odd Properties of the DFT, 249
9-4 Functional Operations with the DFT, 253
9-5 Fast Fourier Transform, 256
9-6 Survey of Algorithms, 261
Problems, 273
References, 274

Chapter 10 **APPLICATIONS OF THE DISCRETE FOURIER TRANSFORM** **277**

10-0 Introduction, 277
10-1 Approximation of Continuous-Time Transforms with the DFT, 277
10-2 Selection of DFT (or FFT) Parameters, 282
10-3 Convolution with the FFT, 284
10-4 Power Spectrum, 294
10-5 Correlation and Statistical Analysis, 295
10-6 Frequency Sampling Filters, 301
Problems, 305
References, 306

Appendix **APPENDIX A** **309**

INDEX **317**

CHAPTER ONE

GENERAL CONCEPTS OF DIGITAL SIGNAL PROCESSING

1-0 Introduction

In recent years, there has been a tremendous increase in the use of digital computers and special purpose digital circuitry for performing varied signal processing functions that were originally achieved with analog equipment. The continued evolution of relatively inexpensive integrated circuits has led to a variety of microprocessing units and minicomputers which can be used for various signal processing functions. It is now possible to build special purpose digital processors within the same size and cost constraints of systems previously all analog in nature.

This chapter will provide a general discussion of a few of the basic concepts associated with digital signal processing. The major intent is to provide the reader with a brief overview of the subject before developing the concepts in detail in later chapters.

1-1 General Discussion

At the beginning of this work, it is appropriate to discuss a few of the common terms that will be used and some of the assumptions that will be made. Wherever possible, the definitions and terminology will be established in accordance with the 1972 recommendations of the IEEE Group on Audio and Electroacoustics (ref. 1).

An *analog* signal is a function that is defined over a continuous range of time and in which the amplitude may assume a continuous range of values. Common examples are the sinusoidal function, the step function, the output of a microphone, etc. The term "analog" apparently originated from the field of analog computation, in which voltages and currents are used to represent physical variables, but the term has been extended in usage.

A *continuous-time* signal is a function that is defined over a continuous range of time, but in which the amplitude may either have a continuous range of values or a finite number of possible values. In this context, an analog signal could be considered as a special case of a continuous-time signal. In practice, however, the terms "analog" and "continuous-time" are interchanged casually in usage and are often used to mean the same thing. Because of the association of the term "analog" with physical analogies, a statement of preference has been made for the term "continuous-time" (ref. 1), and this practice will be followed for the most part in this text. Nevertheless, there will be places in which the term "analog" will be used for clarity, particularly where it relates to the term "digital".

The term *quantization* describes the process of representing a variable by a set of distinct values. A *quantized variable* is one that may assume only distinct values.

A *discrete-time* signal is a function that is defined only at a particular set of values of time. This means that the independent variable time is quantized. If the amplitude of a discrete time signal is permitted to assume a continuous range of values, the function is said to be a *sampled-data* signal. A sampled-data signal could arise from sampling an analog signal at discrete values of time.

A *digital* signal is a function in which both time and amplitude are quantized. A digital signal may always be represented by a sequence of numbers in which each number has a finite number of digits.

The terms "discrete-time" and "digital" are often interchanged in practice and are often used to mean the same thing. A great deal of the theory underlying discrete-time signals is applicable to purely digital signals so it is not always necessary to make rigid distinctions. The term "discrete-time" will more often be used in pursuing theoretical developments, and the term "digital" will more often be used in describing hardware or software realizations.

A system can be described by any of the preceding terms according to the type of hardware or software employed and the type of signals present. Thus, reference can be made to "analog systems", "continuous-time systems", "discrete-time systems", "digital systems", etc.

A *linear* system is one in which the parameters of the system are not dependent on the nature or the level of the input excitation. This statement is equivalent to the fact that the principle of superposition applies. A linear system can be described by linear differential or difference equations. A *time-invariant* linear system is one in which the parameters are fixed and do not vary with time.

A *lumped* system is one that is composed of finite non-zero elements satisfying ordinary differential or difference equation relationships (as opposed to a distributed system satisfying partial differential equation relationships).

Very little reference will be made in this text to distributed systems, so it will be implied that all systems considered will be lumped unless otherwise noted.

In carrying out various theoretical developments, it will frequently be necessary to refer to systems that are either (a) continuous-time, linear, and time-invariant, or (b) discrete-time, linear, and time-invariant. For conciseness, we will designate (a) as a CTLTI system and (b) as a DTLTI system.

The standard form for numerical processing of a digital signal is the binary number system. The binary number system makes use only of the values 0 and 1 to represent all possible numbers. The number of levels m that can be represented by a number having n *bi*nary dig*its* (bits) is given by

$$m = 2^n \tag{1-1}$$

Conversely, if m is the number of possible levels required, the number of bits required is the smallest integer greater than or equal to $\log_2 m$.

The process by which digital signal processing is achieved will be illustrated by a simplified system in which the signal is assumed to vary from 0 to 7 volts and in which 8 possible levels (at 1 V increments) are used for the binary numbers. A block diagram is shown in Fig. 1-1, and some waveforms of interest are shown in Fig. 1-2. The signal is first passed through a continuous-time pre-sampling filter whose function will be discussed later. The signal is then read at intervals of T seconds by a sampler. These samples must then be quantized to one of the standard levels. Although there are different strategies employed in the quantization process, one common approach, which will be assumed here, is that a sample is assigned to the *nearest* level. Thus, a sample of value 4.2 V would be quantized to 4 V, and a sample of value 4.6 V would be quantized to 5 V.

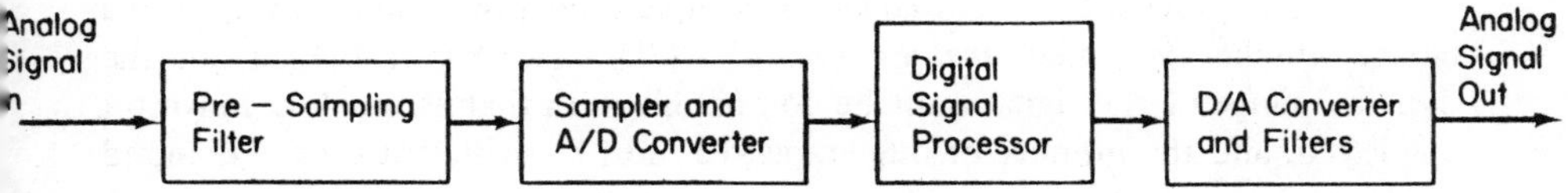

Figure 1-1 Block diagram of a possible digital processing system.

This process for the signal given is illustrated in Fig. 1-2, a and b. The pulses representing the signal have been made very narrow to illustrate the fact that other signals may be inserted or *multiplexed* in the empty space. These pulses may then be represented as binary numbers as illustrated in (c). In order that these numbers could be seen on the figure, each has been shown over much of the space in a given interval. In practice, if other signals are to be inserted, the pulses representing the bits of the binary numbers could be made very short. A given binary number could then be read in a very short interval at the beginning of a sampling period, thus leaving most of the time available for other signals.

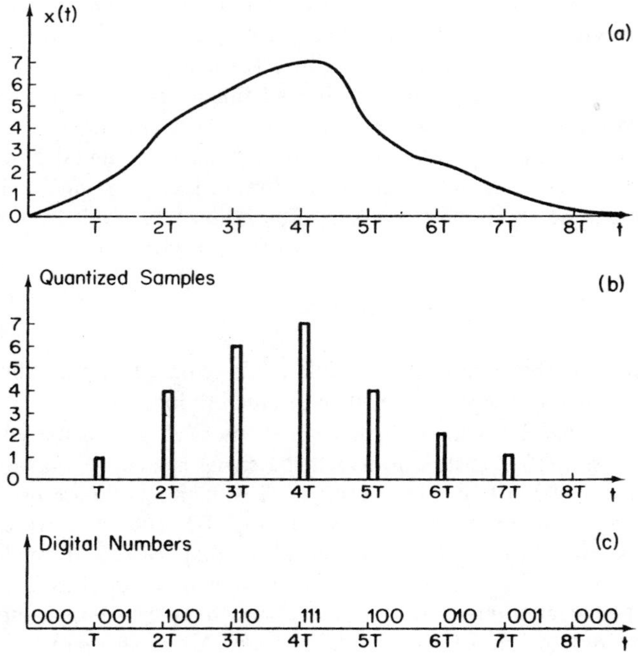

Figure 1-2 Sampling and digital conversion process.

The process by which an analog sample is quantized and converted to a binary number is called *analog-to-digital (A/D) conversion*. In general, the dynamic range of the signal must be compatible with that of the A/D converter employed, and the number of bits employed must be sufficient for the required accuracy.

The signal can now be processed by the type of unit appropriate for the application intended. This unit may be a general purpose computer or minicomputer, or it may be a special unit designed specifically for this purpose. At any rate, it is composed of some combination of standard digital circuits capable of performing the various arithmetic functions of addition, subtraction, multiplication, etc. In addition, it has logic and storage capability.

At the output of the processor, the digital signal can be converted to analog form again. This is achieved by the process of *digital-to-analog (D/A) conversion*. In this step, the binary numbers are first successively converted back to continuous-time pulses. The "gaps" between the pulses are then filled in by a *reconstruction filter*. This filter may consist of a holding circuit, which is a special circuit designed to hold the value of a pulse between successive sample values. In some cases, the holding circuit may be designed to extrapolate the output signal between successive points according to some prescribed curve-fitting strategy. In addition to a holding circuit, a basic continuous-time filter may be employed to provide additional smoothing between points.

A fundamental question that may arise is whether or not some information has been lost in the process. After all, the signal has been sampled only at discrete intervals of time; is there something that might be missed in the intervening time intervals? Furthermore, in the process of quantization, the actual amplitude is replaced by the nearest standard level, and this means there is a possible error in amplitude.

In regard to the sampling question, it will be shown in Chapt. 3 that if the signal is bandlimited, and if the sampling rate is greater than or equal to twice the highest frequency, the signal can theoretically be recovered from its discrete samples. This corresponds to a minimum of two samples per cycle at the highest frequency. In practice, this sampling rate is usually chosen to be somewhat higher than the minimum rate (say three or four times the highest frequency) in order to ensure practical implementation. For example, if the highest frequency of the analog signal is 5 kHz, the theoretical minimum sampling rate is 10,000 samples per second, and a practical system would employ a rate somewhat higher. The input continuous-time signal is often passed through a low-pass analog *pre-sampling filter* to ensure that the highest frequency is within the bounds for which the signal can be recovered.

If a signal is not sampled at a sufficiently high rate, a phenomenon known as *aliasing* results. This concept results in a frequency being mistaken for an entirely different frequency upon recovery. For example, suppose a signal with frequencies ranging from dc to 5 kHz is sampled at a rate of 6 kHz, which is clearly too low to ensure recovery. If recovery is attempted, a component of the original signal at 5 kHz now appears to be at 1 kHz, resulting in an erroneous signal. A common example of this phenomenon is one we will call the "wagon wheel effect", probably noticed by the reader in western movies as the phenomenon in which the wheels appear to be rotating backwards. Since each individual frame of a film is equivalent to a discrete sampling operation, if the rate of spokes passing a given angle is too large for a given movie frame rate, the wheels appear to be turning either backwards or at a very slow speed. The effect of a pre-sampling filter removes the possibility that a spurious signal whose frequency is too high for the system will be mistaken for one in the proper frequency range.

With respect to the quantization error, it can be seen that the error can be made as small as one chooses if the number of bits can be made arbitrarily large. Of course, there is a practical maximum limit, so it is necessary to tolerate some error from this phenomenon. Even in continuous-time systems, there may be noise present which would introduce uncertainty in the actual magnitude. In fact, the uncertainty present in the digital sampling process is called *quantization noise*.

Let E_{max} and E_{min} represent the maximum and minimum values of the signal, and let q represent the vertical distance between successive quantum levels. Using n and m as previously defined, we have

$$q = \frac{E_{max} - E_{min}}{2^n} = \frac{E_{max} - E_{min}}{m} \tag{1-2}$$

Assuming that a sample between two successive quantum levels is assigned to the nearest quantum level, the peak quantization noise and peak percentage quantization noise values are

$$\text{Peak Quantization Noise} = \frac{q}{2} \tag{1-3}$$

$$\text{Peak Percentage Quantization Noise} = \frac{100\%}{2m} \tag{1-4}$$

In many cases, the *variance* of the quantization noise is more important than the maximum value. The variance is directly proportional to the *average power* associated with the noise. If the signal is assumed to be uniformly distributed between quantum levels, it can be shown by statistical analysis that the noise variance σ^2 is

$$\sigma^2 = \frac{q^2}{12} \tag{1-5}$$

The *root-mean-square (RMS)* (or *standard deviation*) value of this noise component is

$$\sigma = \frac{q}{2\sqrt{3}} \tag{1-6}$$

Comparing (1-6) with (1-3), it is seen that the RMS noise component is $1/\sqrt{3}$ times the peak noise component.

In view of the preceding discussion, it appears that no information is lost in the sampling operation provided that the sampling rate is high enough, and the quantization error can be reduced to an insignificantly small level by choosing a sufficient number of bits to represent each binary number. These concepts then permit us to represent a continuous-time signal in terms of a series of discrete binary numbers, which may be processed directly with digital circuits.

The rather involved procedure of A/D conversion, processing, and final D/A conversion may seem like a lot of effort in order to handle one signal channel. Indeed, in many cases such a complex process may not be economically feasible for a single signal. One of the great advantages of the digital concept is the possibility of processing a number of channels with the same arithmetic unit. This process can be achieved by a process called *time-division multiplexing (TDM)*. It was observed in the sampled signal shown in Fig. 1-2 that there was a relatively long period between successive samples of the signal. During this period, samples of additional signals are fed into the processor.

This concept is illustrated in Fig. 1-3. Each channel is read in a sequential order, and the corresponding values are converted into binary numbers in the same sequence. These numbers enter into the processing unit and, after suitable processing, appear at the output in the appropriate order. This composite digital signal must first be separated into the original different channels by means of a *demultiplexer*, which is synchronized with the input sampling signal. The channels then undergo the D/A conversion required for output.

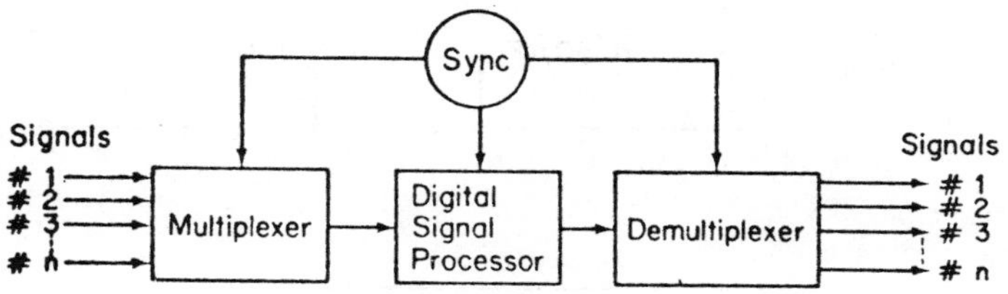

Figure 1-3 Multiplexed digital processing system.

In the preceding discussions, we have assumed that both the starting and final signals in the system are in continuous-time forms. Actually, there are many systems in which one or both are already digital in form. In such cases the A/D conversion and/or the D/A conversion may not be required, thus simplifying the system. For example, assume that a number of continuous-time telemetry signals is to be processed by a digital unit, but the output data is to be kept in digital form for scientific data reduction and computation. In this case, the A/D unit at the input is required, but no conversion is needed at the output.

1-2 Types of Processing

This textbook will be devoted primarily to the development of two important tools for modern digital signal processing: (a) *digital filters* and (b) *fast Fourier transforms (FFT)*.

A digital filter is a computational process in which the sequence of input numbers is converted into a sequence of output numbers representing the alteration of the data in some prescribed manner. A common example is the process of filtering out a certain range of frequencies in a signal while rejecting all other frequencies, which is one of the foremost classical approaches to analog filter design. In the classical continuous-time case, this filtering is achieved by a suitable choice of inductors, capacitors, and resistors arranged to provide the required transmission characteristics. However, in the digital case, this can be achieved completely by the process of digital addition, multiplication by constants, and delay.

To present an example which the reader is not expected to understand at this point, but which is shown for motivation, consider the circuits in Fig. 1-4. A certain low-pass analog filter having a 3 dB cutoff frequency of 50 Hz is shown in (a). A digital filter having approximately the same frequency response from dc to five times cutoff (250 kHz) is shown in (b). The various units in the filter correspond to addition, multiplication, and delay, as indicated on the figure.

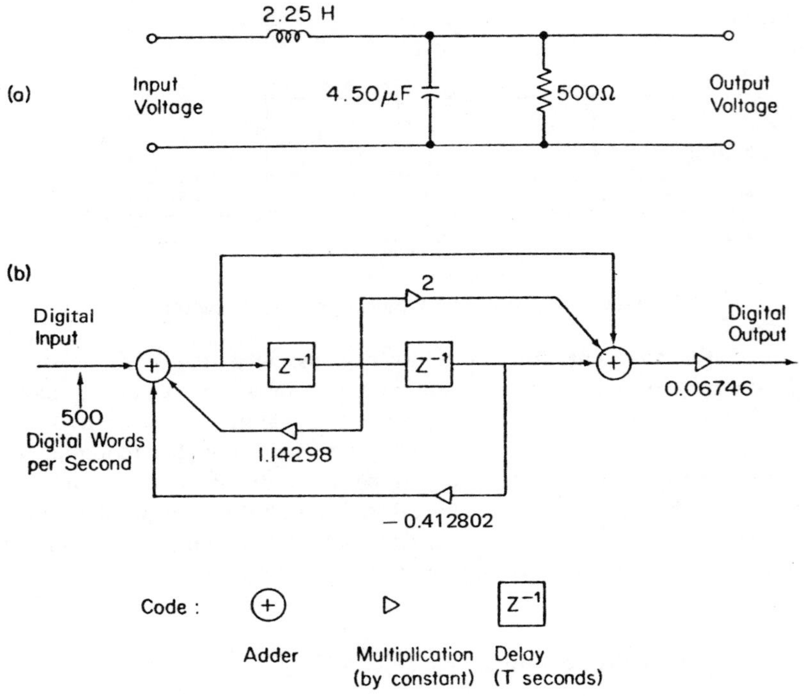

Figure 1-4 Analog and digital filters having similar characteristics.

The second method that we will consider is that of the fast Fourier transform (FFT) concept. The techniques of spectral analysis employing Fourier transforms and series have long represented an important area of application in continuous-time signal processing. The development in 1965 of the Cooley-Tukey algorithms for rapid computation of the approximate spectrum paved the way for new and varied applications of spectral analysis. With this approach, the spectrum of signals containing many thousands of sample points can be achieved in a matter of milliseconds. In fact, it has become quite feasible to filter signals by FFT transformation, numerical alteration of the spectrum, and inverse FFT computation.

There are many varied scientific disciplines that utilize spectral analysis in one form or another and in which the FFT has opened new potential applications. Among these are communications signal analysis, solution of boundary value problems in heat and electricity, statistical analysis, oceanographic wave analysis, spectroscopy, and vibrations. There are available special FFT processors which may be used for real-time processing in many applications. In addition, many computers have FFT subroutines available in their libraries.

REFERENCE

1. L. R. Rabiner *et al*, "Terminology in Digital Signal Processing", *IEEE Trans. Audio and Electroacoustics*, vol. AU-20, pp. 323-337, Dec. 1972.

CHAPTER TWO

CONTINUOUS-TIME SYSTEM ANALYSIS

2-0 Introduction

As a basis for developing the concepts of digital signal processing and simulation, it is highly desirable that the fundamentals of classical continuous-time linear system theory be understood and utilized extensively in the development process. This body of material has been widely used in the analysis of electric circuits, communications systems, control systems, vibration systems, and many other areas of scientific endeavor.

The treatment of continuous-time linear system theory given in this chapter is intended to summarize only some of the more basic concepts essential to our primary goal, since many complete textbooks have been written on the subject. It is assumed that most readers will have been previously exposed to the subject in one form or another, so that many of the concepts presented are necessarily abbreviated. Readers who require more extensive background may wish to consult one of the references given at the end of this chapter.

2-1 Time-Domain Description

Consider a continuous-time, linear, time-invariant (CTLTI) system with a single input $x(t)$ and a single output (response) $y(t)$ as illustrated in block form in Fig. 2-1. The output-input relationship of such a system can always be described by a differential equation of the form

$$b_k \frac{d^k y}{dt^k} + b_{k-1} \frac{d^{k-1} y}{dt^{k-1}} + \cdots + b_0 y = a_\ell \frac{d^\ell x}{dt^\ell} + a_{\ell-1} \frac{d^{\ell-1} x}{dt^{\ell-1}} + \cdots + a_0 x \tag{2-1}$$

In most cases of interest here, $k \geqslant \ell$, and we will assume this inequality unless otherwise stated. In this case, the integer k specifies the *order* of the system. For any arbitrary input $x(t)$, the solution of the resulting kth order differential equation will yield the output $y(t)$. Various classical procedures for solving differential equations are available, and they may be found in both linear system and differential equation textbooks.

Figure 2-1 Input-output form for CTLTI system.

The output may also be expressed in terms of the *convolution integral* and the *impulse response*. The impulse response $g(t)$ is the response of the system when the input is a unit impulse function $\delta(t)$. Assuming that the impulse response is known, the response due to any input $x(t)$ can be expressed as

$$y(t) = x(t)^*g(t) = \int_{-\infty}^{\infty} x(\tau)g(t-\tau)d\tau \tag{2-2}$$

or

$$y(t) = \int_{-\infty}^{\infty} g(\tau)x(t-\tau)d\tau \tag{2-3}$$

where τ is a dummy variable of integration, and the symbol * denotes convolution. Some examples will now be given to illustrate the relationships of this section.

Example 2-1

Obtain a differential equation of the form of (2-1) for the circuit of Fig. 2-2. The input is v_1 and the output is v_2.

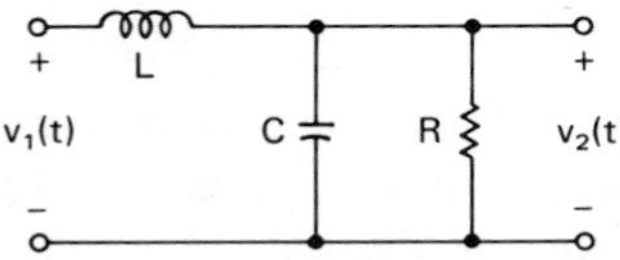

Figure 2-2 Circuit of Ex. 2-1.

Solution

A node voltage equation written at the output node will accomplish the goal. This equation results from the application of Kirchhoff's Current Law at this node, which states that the sum of the currents leaving the node is zero. We have

$$i_L + i_C + i_R = 0$$

or

$$\frac{1}{L}\int_{-\infty}^{t}(v_2 - v_1)dt + C\frac{dv_2}{dt} + \frac{v_2}{R} = 0 \tag{2-4}$$

Differentiation of all terms of (2-4) and rearrangement yield

$$\frac{d^2 v_2}{dt^2} + \frac{1}{RC}\frac{dv_2}{dt} + \frac{1}{LC}v_2 = \frac{1}{LC}v_1 \tag{2-5}$$

The form of (2-5) indicates that the circuit represents a second-order system. Note that there are no derivative terms on the right in this particular case.

Example 2-2

Obtain a differential equation of the form of (2-1) for the circuit of Fig. 2-3. The input is v_1 and the output is v_2.

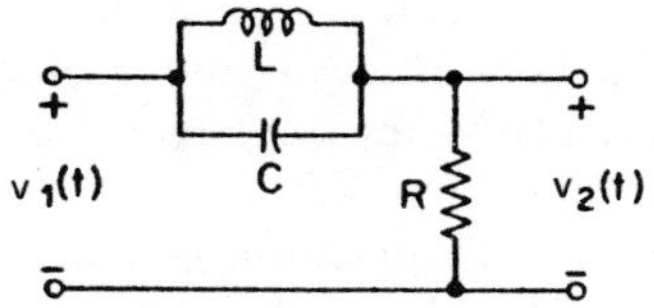

Figure 2-3 Circuit of Ex. 2-2.

Solution

Proceding as in Ex. 2-1, we sum the currents leaving the output node to obtain

$$C\frac{d}{dt}(v_2 - v_1) + \frac{1}{L}\int_{-\infty}^{t}(v_2 - v_1)dt + \frac{v_2}{R} = 0 \tag{2-6}$$

Differentiation of all terms and rearrangement yield

$$\frac{d^2 v_2}{dt^2} + \frac{1}{RC}\frac{dv_2}{dt} + \frac{1}{LC}v_2 = \frac{d^2 v_1}{dt^2} + \frac{1}{LC}v_1 \tag{2-7}$$

Note that the order of the highest derivative on the right is the same as the order of the highest derivative on the left in this case.

Example 2-3

The impulse response of a certain CTLTI system is given by

$$\begin{aligned} g(t) &= 0 \quad \text{for } t < 0 \\ &= \epsilon^{-2t} \quad \text{for } t \geqslant 0 \end{aligned} \tag{2-8}$$

By means of the convolution integral, determine the response $y(t)$ due to the ramp input

$$\begin{aligned} x(t) &= 0 \quad \text{for } t < 0 \\ &= 4t \quad \text{for } t \geqslant 0 \end{aligned} \tag{2-9}$$

Solution

Although the form of either (2-2) or (2-3) could be used, we will arbitrarily select (2-3) in this case. It is highly recommended that a series of sketches depicting the various quantities within the integrand be made before actually performing any convolution integration. Such sketches serve to precisely define the actual integration limits required in the integral. The determination of these limits is often a source of difficulty in applying the convolution process, particularly for functions having different forms over different intervals.

Referring to Fig. 2-4, the functions $g(t)$ and $x(t)$ are first shown in (a) and (b) with the actual time variable t replaced by the dummy variable τ. Hence, the functions shown are $g(\tau)$ and $x(\tau)$. The dummy variable τ in $x(\tau)$ is replaced by $-\tau$ in (c). This results in a new function, which is the mirror image of the original function about the vertical axis. When $-\tau$ is replaced by $t-\tau$, where t is any arbitrary positive value of time, the function shifts to the right by an amount t as shown in (d). Note that for integration purposes, t is considered as a parameter rather than a variable. The form of the product of $g(\tau)$ and $x(t-\tau)$ is shown in (e). This is the integrand of the convolution integral, so the area under this curve must be determined as a function of the parameter t.

In this problem, we will use analytical methods for the integration due to the nature of the functions involved. For problems in which one or both of

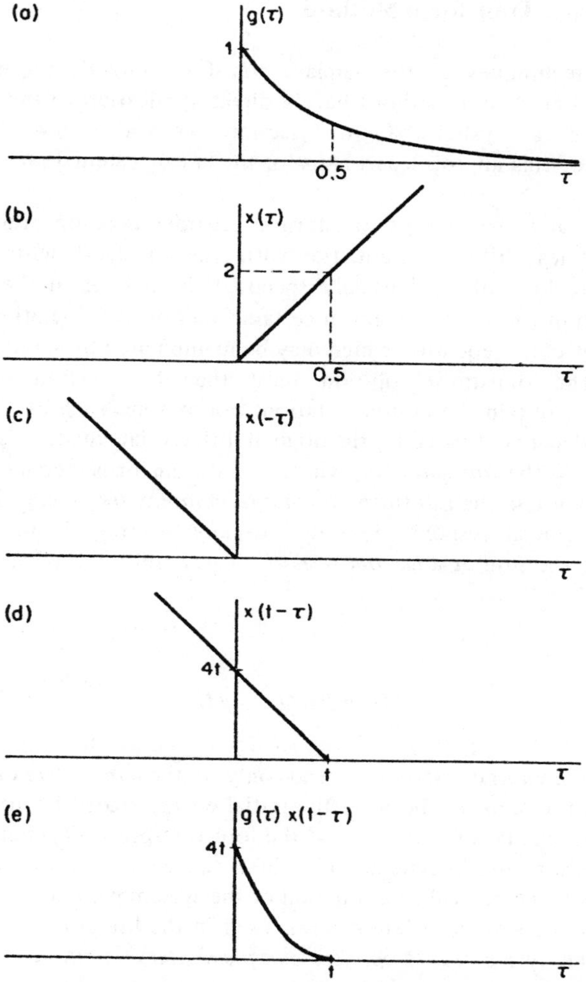

Figure 2-4 Convolution operations for Ex. 2-3.

the functions have constant values over specific intervals, the convolution integral is often easier to evaluate by direct graphical methods. (See Prob. 2-4.) In the present case, the actual limits of integration are seen to be from 0 to t. Substitution of these limits and the appropriate functions in (2-3) results in

$$y(t) = \int_0^t \epsilon^{-2\tau} 4(t-\tau) d\tau = 4t \int_0^t \epsilon^{-2\tau} d\tau - 4 \int_0^t \tau \epsilon^{-2\tau} d\tau$$
$$= \epsilon^{-2t} + 2t - 1 \quad \text{for } t \geq 0 \tag{2-10}$$

2-2 Laplace Transform Methods

The techniques of the Laplace transform provide certain powerful conceptual and analytical methods having direct application to the analysis and synthesis of linear systems. In this section, we will review some of the fundamentals of this approach as a basis for the linear system developments that follow.

Classically, the Laplace transform is regarded as an operational method for solving a linear differential equation with constant coefficients such as was described in (2-1), with $x(t)$ usually specified. Both sides of the differential equation are transformed by means of certain function and operation pairs. This results in an algebraic equation which may be manipulated by standard algebraic operations. The transform solution must then be inverted (or inversely transformed) to obtain the desired solution. For systems such as (2-1) in which time is the independent variable, the original differential equation is said to be a representation in the *time domain*; whereas, the transformed equation is said to be a representation in the *transform domain* or *complex frequency domain*.

The general response $y(t)$ due to any arbitrary input $x(t)$ can be represented as the sum of a *natural response* $y_n(t)$ and a *forced response* $y_f(t)$; i.e.,

$$y(t) = y_n(t) + y_f(t) \tag{2-11}$$

The *form* of the natural response depends only on the *parameters* of the system, but its magnitude depends both on the initial energy stored in the system and the form of the excitation. The form of the forced response depends only on the type of excitation, and in general will exhibit the same form as the excitation. Its magnitude, however, will be a function of the system parameters.

There are several different terms used in the literature to denote these quantities. The terms *free response, complementary solution,* and *transient response* are used synonymously with *natural response*. Likewise, the terms *particular solution* and *steady-state* are used synonymously with *forced response*. Strictly speaking, the terms *transient* and *steady-state* in this context are descriptively correct only when the system is stable. In this case, these latter terms are widely used in engineering problems to describe the system behavior. (More will be said about these points later.)

The treatment of the Laplace transform in this text will be limited to the *one-sided* form, which is the most widely employed form in engineering applications. The actual definition of the one-sided Laplace transform is given by

$$X(s) = \mathcal{L}[x(t)] = \int_0^\infty x(t)\epsilon^{-st}\,dt \tag{2-12}$$

subject to certain mathematical restrictions on $x(t)$. (These restrictions rarely cause difficulty in most engineering applications and will not be discussed here.) The inverse Laplace transform is given by the complex inversion integral

$$x(t) = \mathcal{L}^{-1}[X(s)] = \frac{1}{2\pi j} \int_C X(s)\epsilon^{st}\,ds \tag{2-13}$$

where C is a contour chosen to include all singularities of $X(s)$. Many transforms can be inverted with the aid of a few standard pairs, so it is not often necessary to employ (2-13) in routine transform problems.

$x(t)$	$X(s) = \mathcal{L}[x(t)]$	
$\delta(t)$	1	(LT-1)
1 or $u(t)$	$\frac{1}{s}$	(LT-2)
t	$\frac{1}{s^2}$	(LT-3)
$\epsilon^{-\alpha t}$	$\frac{1}{s+\alpha}$	(LT-4)
$\sin \omega t$	$\frac{\omega}{s^2+\omega^2}$	(LT-5)
$\cos \omega t$	$\frac{s}{s^2+\omega^2}$	(LT-6)
$\epsilon^{-\alpha t} \sin \omega t$	$\frac{\omega}{(s+\alpha)^2+\omega^2}$	(LT-7)
$\epsilon^{-\alpha t} \cos \omega t$	$\frac{s+\alpha}{(s+\alpha)^2+\omega^2}$	(LT-8)
t^n	$\frac{n!}{s^{n+1}}$	(LT-9)
$\epsilon^{-\alpha t} t^n$	$\frac{n!}{(s+\alpha)^{n+1}}$	(LT-10)

Table 2-1 Some common Laplace transform function pairs.

Using the transform definition, various pairs can be derived and tabulated. A list of the most common transform pairs encountered in CTLTI system analysis is given in Table 2-1. It is also convenient to employ certain operation pairs in manipulating transforms. A list of some of the most common operation pairs is given in Table 2-2. Many of the more complex function and operation pairs can be derived by application of these basic pairs.

The actual transforms of most desired response waveforms will normally be more complex than the functions given in the tables. However, such transforms can usually be decomposed into a sum of terms of the forms given in the tables by means of partial fraction expansion methods.

$x(t)$	$X(s) = \mathcal{L}[x(t)]$	
$ax_1(t) + bx_2(t)$	$aX_1(s) + bX_2(s)$	(LO-1)
$\frac{d^n x(t)}{dt^n}$	$s^n X(s) - \sum_{i=0}^{n-1} s^{n-1-i} \frac{d^i x(o)}{dt^i}$	(LO-2)
$\int_{-\infty}^{t} x(\tau)d\tau$	$\frac{X(s)}{s} + \frac{1}{s}\int_{-\infty}^{o} x(\tau)d\tau$	(LO-3)
$x(t-a)\,u(t-a)$	$\epsilon^{-as} X(s)$	(LO-4)
$\epsilon^{-\alpha t} x(t)$	$X(s+\alpha)$	(LO-5)
$x(at)$	$\frac{1}{a} X(\frac{s}{a})$	(LO-6)
$tx(t)$	$-\frac{dX(s)}{ds}$	(LO-7)
$x(0^+)$	$\lim_{s\to\infty} sX(s)$	(LO-8)
$x(\infty)$	[1] $\lim_{s\to 0} sX(s)$	(LO-9)
$\int_{-\infty}^{\infty} x_1(\tau)x_2(t-\tau)d\tau$	$X_1(s)X_2(s)$	(LO-10

[1] This theorem is valid only if the poles of sX(s) are located in the left-hand half-plane.

Table 2-2 Some common Laplace transform operation pairs.

Example 2-4

The input-output relationship of a certain system is described by the differential equation

$$\frac{d^2y}{dt^2} + 3\frac{dy}{dt} + 2y = x \tag{2-14}$$

Find the response when $x(t)$ is a step function of 10 units applied at $t = 0$, i.e. $x(t) = 10\,u(t)$. The initial conditions are $y(0) = 2, y'(0) = -10$.

Solution

Application of the Laplace transformation to both sides of the equation and utilization of pairs (LT-2), (LO-1), and (LO-2) yield

$$s^2 Y(s) - 2s - (-10) + 3[sY(s) - 2] + 2Y(s) = \frac{10}{s} \tag{2-15}$$

$$(s^2 + 3s + 2)Y(s) = \frac{10}{s} + 2s - 4 \tag{2-16}$$

$$\begin{aligned} Y(s) &= \frac{10}{s(s^2 + 3s + 2)} + \frac{2s - 4}{s^2 + 3s + 2} \\ &= \frac{10}{s(s+1)(s+2)} + \frac{2s - 4}{(s+1)(s+2)} \end{aligned} \tag{2-17}$$

Individual partial fraction expansion of the preceding terms yields

$$Y(s) = \frac{5}{s} - \frac{10}{s+1} + \frac{5}{s+2} - \frac{6}{s+1} + \frac{8}{s+2} \tag{2-18}$$

Inversion yields

$$y(t) = 5 - 16\epsilon^{-t} + 13\epsilon^{-2t} \tag{2-19}$$

The reader is invited to verify that the initial conditions are satisfied.

2-3 Transfer Function

Consider a CTLTI system as described by (2-1), and assume that the system is initially *relaxed*; i.e., no energy is stored in the system. Under these conditions, it can be shown that all initial condition terms resulting from application of the Laplace transform to (2-1) cancel on both sides of the equation. Making use of this fact, the transformed equation is

$$(b_k s^k + b_{k-1} s^{k-1} + \cdots + b_0)\, Y(s) = (a_\ell s^\ell + a_{\ell-1} s^{\ell-1} + \cdots + a_0)\, X(s) \tag{2-20}$$

Solving for $Y(s)$ we obtain

$$Y(s) = \frac{(a_\ell s^\ell + a_{\ell-1} s^{\ell-1} + \cdots + a_0)}{(b_k s^k + b_{k-1} s^{k-1} + \cdots + b_0)} X(s) \tag{2-21}$$

We may now define a *transfer function* (or *system function*) $G(s)$ as

$$G(s) = \frac{N(s)}{D(s)} = \frac{a_\ell s^\ell + a_{\ell-1} s^{\ell-1} + \cdots + a_0}{b_k s^k + b_{k-1} s^{k-1} + \cdots + b_0} \tag{2-22}$$

where $N(s)$ is the numerator polynomial and $D(s)$ is the denominator polynomial. Using the transfer function, the input-output relationship simply becomes

$$Y(s) = G(s)X(s) \tag{2-23}$$

The time-domain response $y(t)$ can then be determined by inversion of $Y(s)$.

The impulse response can now be readily determined by letting $x(t) = \delta(t)$ or $X(s) = 1$. In this case the output transform is identical with the transfer function, so we have for the impulse response

$$g(t) = \mathcal{L}^{-1}[G(s)] \tag{2-24}$$

In later chapters, we will deal with transfer functions of discrete-time systems as well as those of continuous-time systems. When it is necessary to distinguish between these different functions, a transfer function of a CTLTI system as described by (2-22) will be denoted simply as a *continuous transfer function*.

Example 2-5

(a) Determine the transfer function of the circuit in Ex. 2-1. (b) Determine the impulse response for $L = 2\text{H}$, $C = 1/10\text{F}$, and $R = 5\Omega$.

Solution

(a) We may transform (2-4) directly and obtain

$$\left(\frac{1}{sL} + sC + \frac{1}{R}\right)V_2(s) = \frac{1}{sL} V_1(s) \tag{2-25}$$

or

$$\frac{V_2(s)}{V_1(s)} = G(s) = \frac{\frac{1}{LC}}{s^2 + \frac{s}{RC} + \frac{1}{LC}} \tag{2-26}$$

As an alternate approach, we may replace the resistor, inductor, and capacitor by their *transform impedances* as shown in Fig. 2-5. This circuit may now be manipulated by any standard circuit method without going through the differential equation at all. (Note that if a system is not initially relaxed, a transform circuit model would have to contain one or more fictitious generators to take care of the initial energy stored.)

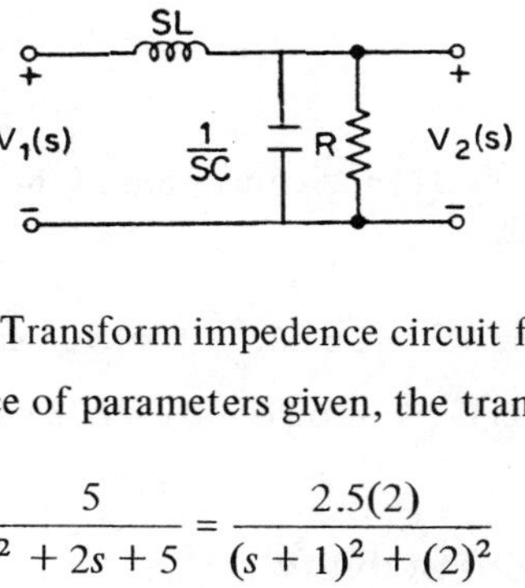

Figure 2-5 Transform impedence circuit for Ex. 2-5.

(b) For the choice of parameters given, the transfer function is

$$G(s) = \frac{5}{s^2 + 2s + 5} = \frac{2.5(2)}{(s+1)^2 + (2)^2} \tag{2-27}$$

which has been put in the form of (LT-7) in Table 2-1 due to the presence of complex roots. The impulse response is then

$$g(t) = 2.5\epsilon^{-t} \sin 2t \tag{2-28}$$

Example 2-6

Determine the response of the system considered in Ex. 2-5 when the input is a sinusoidal function $x(t) = 40 \sin t$.

Solution

The transform of the input signal is

$$X(s) = \frac{40}{s^2 + 1} \tag{2-29}$$

The output transform is

$$Y(s) = \frac{200}{(s^2 + 2s + 5)(s^2 + 1)} \tag{2-30}$$

Although there are various approaches to inverting (2-30), we will use a standard partial fraction expansion with the quadratic polynomials factored in the forms displaying their natural roots. (We will also choose to express the angles of complex exponentials in degrees for convenience.) We have

$$\frac{200}{(s+1-j2)(s+1+j2)(s-j)(s+j)} =$$

$$\frac{11.18\epsilon^{j26.565^\circ}}{s+1-j2} + \frac{11.18\epsilon^{-j26.565^\circ}}{s+1+j2} + \frac{22.361\epsilon^{-j116.565^\circ}}{s-j} + \frac{22.361\epsilon^{j116.565^\circ}}{s+j} \tag{2-31}$$

Inversion of the terms in (2-31) and conversion of the two complex exponential pairs to real functions yield

$$\begin{aligned} y(t) &= 22.361\epsilon^{-t}\cos(2t + 26.565^\circ) + 44.721\cos(t - 116.565^\circ) \\ &= 22.361\epsilon^{-t}\sin(2t + 116.565^\circ) + 44.721\sin(t - 26.565^\circ) \end{aligned} \tag{2-32}$$

2-4 Poles, Zeros, and Stability

Consider the transfer function

$$G(s) = \frac{N(s)}{D(s)} \tag{2-33}$$

The following definitions are given:

(a) *Poles (finite).* The k roots of $D(s)$ are called the *finite poles* of the transfer function.

(b) *Zeros (finite).* The ℓ roots of N(*s*) are called the *finite zeros* of the transfer function.

(c) *Critical Frequencies.* All the poles and zeros are said to be the complex critical frequencies of the function.

The finite poles and zeros of a transfer function may be plotted in the *complex s-plane* as illustrated in Fig. 2-6 for a particular case. The zeros are represented as O's and the poles as X's.

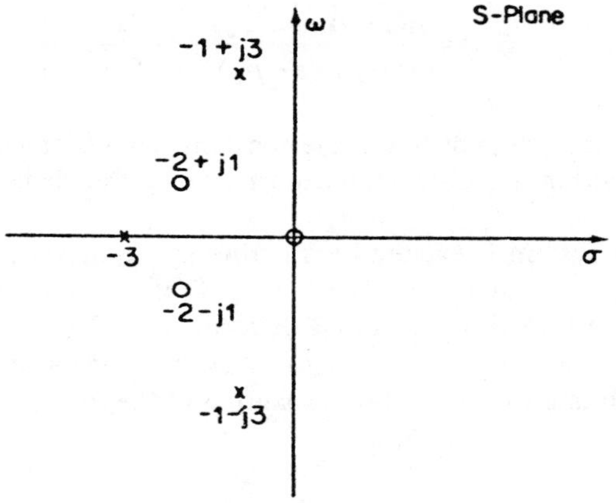

Figure 2-6 Pole-zero plot for a typical CTLTI transfer function.

In the analysis of filter responses, it is desirable to refer to *zeros at* ∞, (as contrasted from finite zeros). Assuming that the degree of the denominator polynomial k is larger than the degree of the numerator polynomial ℓ, we define an integer r to represent the *number of zeros at* ∞. The quantity r is given by

$$r = k - \ell \tag{2-34}$$

It can be shown that for large s, the function G(*s*) becomes asymptotic to

$$G(s) \approx \frac{a_\ell}{b_k s^{k-\ell}} = \frac{a_\ell}{b_k s^r} \quad \text{for } |s| \gg 1 \tag{2-35}$$

In the analysis of certain special types of functions, the degree of N(*s*) may exceed the degree of D(*s*). In this case, it is convenient to define an integer r_1 to represent the *number of poles at* ∞. It is given by

$$r_1 = \ell - k \tag{2-36}$$

In this case for large s, G(*s*) becomes asymptotic to

$$G(s) \approx \frac{a_\ell s^{\ell-k}}{b_k} = \frac{a_\ell s^{r_1}}{b_k} \quad \text{for } |s| \gg 1 \tag{2-37}$$

Using these definitions, the number of poles will always equal the number of zeros as long as we include critical frequencies at $s = \infty$.

Assume now that all the finite zeros and poles of a transfer function are known. Let us denote the ℓ finite zeros as $z_1, z_2, \cdots, z_\ell$ and the k finite poles as $p_1, p_2, \cdots, p_k$. $G(s)$ can then be expressed as

$$G(s) = \frac{A(s - z_1)(s - z_2) \cdots (s - z_\ell)}{(s - p_1)(s - p_2) \cdots (s - p_k)} \tag{2-38}$$

where $A = a_\ell / b_k$ is equivalent to a single constant. Thus, a transfer function may be determined within a constant multiplier from a knowledge of its poles and zeros.

When a system is excited by an arbitrary input $x(t)$, the transform of the output $Y(s)$ is obtained by multiplying $G(s)$ by $X(s)$. For simplicity in discussion, assume for the moment that there are no multiple-order poles in $Y(s)$ and that the denominator degree is higher than the numerator degree. $Y(s)$ may then be expanded in a partial fraction expansion of the form

$$Y(s) = \sum_{r=1}^{M} \frac{K_r}{s - p_r} \tag{2-39}$$

A given K_r represents the coefficient corresponding to the pole p_r in the partial fraction expansion. (It is also the *residue* of $Y(s)$ at $s = p_r$.) The integer M is the sum of the order of $G(s)$ and the number of poles of $X(s)$. The time response resulting from inversion of (2-39) is of the form

$$y(t) = \sum_{r=1}^{M} K_r \epsilon^{p_r t} \tag{2-40}$$

In general, a given pole p_r is complex and can be expressed as

$$p_r = \sigma_r + j\omega_r \tag{2-41}$$

where σ_r is the real part and ω_r is the imaginary part. The poles in (2-39) correspond to complex natural frequencies in the exponential terms of (2-40). A given σ_r quantity represents the damping factor for an exponential (if it is negative), and a given ω_r quantity represents the radian frequency of a sinusoidal oscillation.

The poles present in $Y(s)$ may result from two sources: (a) poles due to the transfer function $G(s)$, and (b) poles due to the input $X(s)$. The *natural response* is defined as that portion of the response due to the poles of $G(s)$. The *forced response* is defined as that portion of the response due to the poles of $X(s)$. The critical frequencies appearing in the natural response are identical with the critical frequencies appearing in the impulse response $g(t)$. For this reason, the impulse response provides a convenient means to characterize the natural response of a system without obscuring its behavior by some arbitrary forcing function.

If the *natural response* vanishes after a sufficiently long time, it is often called the *transient response*. In this case, only the *forced response* remains, and it is then often referred to as the *steady-state response*.

A system is said to be stable if every finite input produces a finite output. The properties of stability for a CTLTI system may be readily expressed by conditions relating to the impulse response $g(t)$. These conditions are:

(a) *Stable system*. A system is stable if $g(t)$ vanishes after a sufficiently long time.

(b) *Unstable System*. A system is unstable if $g(t)$ grows without bound, i.e. approaches ∞, after a sufficiently long time.

(c) *Marginally stable system*. A system is marginally stable if $g(t)$ approaches a constant non-zero value or a bounded oscillation after a sufficiently long time.

Examples of the three cases are shown in Fig. 2-7.

A stable system will have a bounded output for any bounded input. At the other extreme, an unstable system will have an unbounded output for almost any input signal. A marginally stable system may have either a bounded or an unbounded output, depending on the excitation.

Stability is best determined from the transfer function if the poles are known. A given complex pole $p_r = \sigma_r + j\omega_r$, which may be of multiple-order, can be considered to produce terms of the form

$$y_r(t) = At^i \epsilon^{\sigma_r t} \epsilon^{j\omega_r t} \tag{2-42}$$

It can be shown that the only condition required for $y_r(t)$ to eventually vanish is that $\sigma_r < 0$. Likewise, if $\sigma_r = 0$ and $i = 0$ (corresponding to a first-order pole), $y_r(t)$ will be either a constant ($\omega_r = 0$) or a constant amplitude oscillation. However, if $\sigma_r = 0$ and $i > 0$ (corresponding to a multiple-order pole on the $j\omega$-axis), $y_r(t)$ will grow without bound.

A summary of the preceding points and a few other deductions follow:

(a) Poles of a transfer function in the left-hand half-plane (LHHP) represent stable terms regardless of the order of the poles.

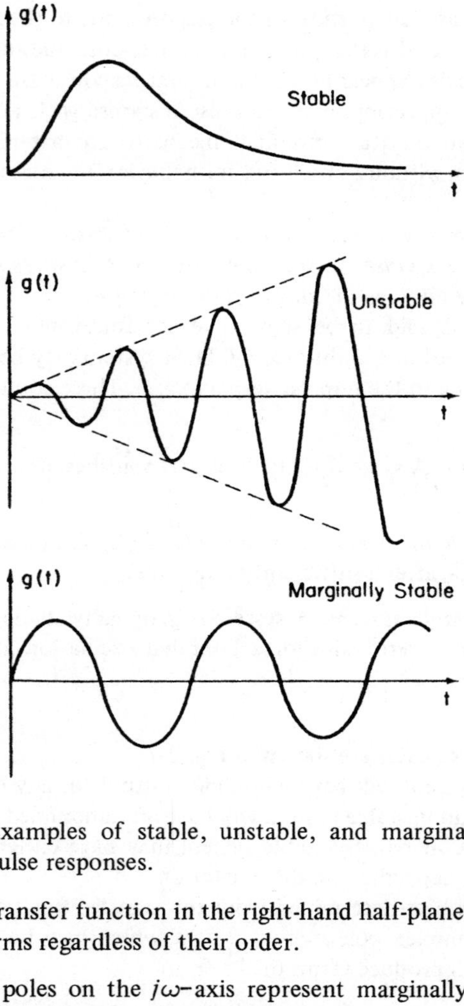

Figure 2-7 Examples of stable, unstable, and marginally stable impulse responses.

(b) Poles of a transfer function in the right-hand half-plane (RHHP) represent unstable terms regardless of their order.

(c) First-order poles on the $j\omega$–axis represent marginally stable terms, but multiple-order poles represent unstable terms.

(d) A system is only as stable as its least stable term. Thus, all poles of a perfectly stable system must lie in the LHHP.

(e) Zeros are permitted in the RHHP and/or the $j\omega$–axis of most transfer functions.

Example 2-7

Write the transfer function corresponding to the pole-zero plot of Fig. 2-6. As an additional fact, it is known that $G(\infty) = 5$.

Solution

Using the form of (2-38), we have

$$G(s) = \frac{A(s-0)[s-(-2+j1)][s-(-2-j1)]}{[s-(-3)][s-(-1+j3)][s-(-1-j3)]} \tag{2-43}$$

or

$$G(s) = \frac{As(s^2+4s+5)}{(s+3)(s^2+2s+10)} \tag{2-44}$$

Alternately, $G(s)$ could be expressed as

$$G(s) = \frac{A(s^3+4s^2+5s)}{s^3+5s^2+16s+30} \tag{2-45}$$

As $s \to \infty$, $G(s) \approx A$. Since $G(\infty) = 5$, then $A = 5$. Thus,

$$G(s) = \frac{5s(s^2+4s+5)}{(s+3)(s^2+2s+10)} \tag{2-46}$$

Example 2-8

Discuss the stability, natural response, and forced response of the system of Examples 2-5 and 2-6.

Solution

The system has a pair of complex poles at $s = -1 \pm j2$ and a zero of second-order at $s = \infty$. This means that the system is stable, and the natural response due to any input will be transient in nature. Hence, the forced response will be of a steady-state nature. This can be observed in Ex. 2-6. From (2-32), it can be seen that the first term, representing the poles of $G(s)$, vanishes after a few seconds, whereas the second term continues indefinitely. Note that the critical frequencies of the transient response are the same as in $g(t)$ of Ex. 2-5, but the amplitude and phase are different. Observe also that the steady-state response is a sinusoid with the same frequency as the input sinusoid, but with a different amplitude and phase.

2-5 Steady-State Frequency Response Concepts

A very important special case of a CTLTI system is the steady-state response due to a sinusoidal input. This type of situation is probably the most widely used condition employed in analytical and experimental studies of linear systems.

In order for the steady-state sinusoidal response to have meaning, it is necessary that the system be perfectly stable; i.e., all poles must lie in the left-hand half-plane. In this case, the steady-state response will be a sinusoid. Only two quantities are necessary to specify the steady-state output: (a) amplitude, and (b) phase.

Assume that the input is of the form

$$x(t) = X\epsilon^{j(\omega t + \phi_x)} \tag{2-47}$$

where ω is the *radian frequency* (rad/s), f is the *cyclic frequency* (Hz), and $\omega = 2\pi f$. We may specify either the real or the imaginary part in (2-47) depending on whether we desire a cosine or a sine input. Letting $y(t)$ represent the *steady-state* response in this case, it will be of the form

$$y(t) = Y\epsilon^{j(\omega t + \phi_y)} \tag{2-48}$$

We need only determine Y and ϕ_y in terms of X and ϕ_x to characterize the solution.

Taking the Laplace transforms of both sides of (2-47) and using the transfer function definition of (2-23), we have

$$Y(s) = \frac{X\epsilon^{j\phi_x}}{s - j\omega} G(s) \tag{2-49}$$

Inversion of only the steady-state portion of (2-49) yields

$$y(t) = G(j\omega)\, X\epsilon^{j(\omega t + \phi_x)} \tag{2-50}$$

Substitution of (2-48) in (2-50) and cancellation of exponential factors yield

$$Y\epsilon^{j\phi_y} = G(j\omega)\, X\epsilon^{j\phi_x} \tag{2-51}$$

The input and output variables may now be expressed as phasors.

$$\overline{X} = X\,\epsilon^{j\phi_x} \triangleq X\underline{/\phi_x} \tag{2-52}$$

$$\overline{Y} = Y\,\epsilon^{j\phi_y} \triangleq Y\underline{/\phi_y} \tag{2-53}$$

We then have

$$\overline{Y} = G(j\omega)\,\overline{X} \tag{2-54}$$

We may now define the *steady-state* or *Fourier transfer function* as

$$\frac{\overline{Y}}{\overline{X}} = G(j\omega) \tag{2-55}$$

While this development has been carried out at a single frequency, it should be readily observed that the quantity $G(j\omega)$ may be interpreted to include the behavior as a function of a variable frequency if ω is considered as a variable. In so doing, the frequency dependent behavior of the system is readily determined.

At this point, we will pause briefly to discuss some notational procedures that will be followed throughout the remainder of the book. In many analytical developments involving the steady-state frequency behavior of linear systems, the radian frequency ω appears frequently, often due to its direct link with the Laplace variable $s(s = j\omega)$. On the other hand, the cyclic frequency f is almost always the variable specified in a practical situation. Of course, the only difference is the scale factor 2π, i.e., $\omega = 2\pi f$. Nevertheless, there are times when confusion arises because of this difference.

There are certain functions that are best expressed in terms of the argument $j\omega$ (or simply ω in some cases), and there are other functions that are best expressed in terms of the argument f. In fact, some expressions may be encountered in which both the arguments ω and f appear. These should not be thought of as separate variables; rather they are different ways of expressing the same variable. The choice as to which argument is used will depend on the form of the function and its ultimate use. For example, a function like $G(j\omega)$ in (2-55) is best represented in that form since it is more easily related to the Laplace transfer function. On the other hand, some functions that will be introduced shortly are best represented as functions of the argument f, since the ultimate goal is to display their behavior as a function of frequency, and the most common way this is done in practical applications is in terms of cyclic frequency.

A related point is that we may frequently express a function on the left in terms of the argument f, while the expression on the right involving a series of calculations may remain expressed in terms of ω. This need not cause any concern, since $\omega = 2\pi f$ could be easily inserted in the equation on the right, but the expression is often less awkward if it remains in terms of ω.

Returning to the problem at hand, and with consideration of the notational policy just discussed, the complex transfer function of (2-55) can be expressed in the form

$$G(j\omega) = A(f)\epsilon^{j\beta(f)} = A(f)\underline{/\beta(f)} \tag{2-56}$$

The function $A(f)$ is called the *amplitude* or *magnitude response*, and $\beta(f)$ is called the *phase response*. Normally, $A(f)$ is simply the magnitude of the complex function $G(j\omega)$, but there are a few situations in which the amplitude response is permitted to assume negative values. (Some cases will appear later in the book.) Both $A(f)$ and $\beta(f)$ are real functions of frequency.

Although the simplest procedure for computing the amplitude response $A(f)$ is usually that of converting all factors in $G(j\omega)$ from rectangular to polar form, there is an alternate representation which will be used later in the text for deriving the transfer functions of filters. In general, the square of the magnitude of a complex number can be expressed as the product of the number and its complex conjugate. Using ~ to represent the complex conjugate, we can write

$$A^2(f) = |G(j\omega)|^2 = G(j\omega)\,\widetilde{G}(j\omega) \tag{2-57}$$

For rational functions (ratios of polynomials) with real coefficients, the conjugate of a function of a complex variable can be shown to be equivalent to the function evaluated for the conjugate of the original argument. (The interested reader may wish to verify this point.) Since $\widetilde{j\omega} = -j\omega$, (2-57) is equivalent to

$$A^2(f) = G(j\omega)G(-j\omega) \tag{2-58}$$

Since $G(j\omega)$ can be considered as $G(s)$ evaluated for $s = j\omega$, (2-58) can finally be expressed as

$$A^2(f) = G(s)G(-s)\big]_{s=j\omega} \tag{2-59}$$

The result given by (2-59) is used extensively in deriving transfer functions from specified amplitude response functions, and developments of this nature will be given in Chapt. 6. In the meantime, we do not necessarily propose that the reader use this relationship for computing $A^2(f)$ from $G(s)$, since the usual sequence of basic complex number operations is normally simpler. This form has been developed here so that we may refer to it when required later in the text.

Two additional definitions related to the phase response will now be given. They are the *phase delay* $T_p(f)$ and the *group* or *envelope delay* $T_g(f)$. The definitions are

$$T_p(f) = \frac{-\beta(f)}{\omega} = \frac{-\beta(f)}{2\pi f} \tag{2-60}$$

$$T_g(f) = \frac{-d\beta(f)}{d\omega} = \frac{-1}{2\pi}\frac{d\beta(f)}{df} \tag{2-61}$$

The significance of these definitions will be discussed in Chapt. 6.

Example 2-9

(a) For the circuit shown in Fig. 2-8, determine the following functions: $A(f)$, $\beta(f)$, $T_p(f)$, and $T_g(f)$. The input is $v_1(t)$ and the output is $v_2(t)$. (b) Determine the steady-state output $v_2(t)$ when the input is $v_1(t) = 10 \sin 1000t$.

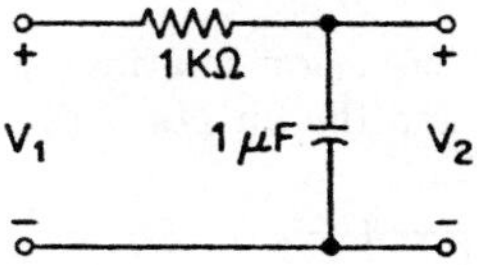

Figure 2-8 Circuit of Ex. 2-9.

Solution

(a) The Laplace transfer function is

$$G(s) = \frac{1/10^{-6}s}{10^3 + 1/10^{-6}s} = \frac{1}{1 + 10^{-3}s} \tag{2-62}$$

The steady-state transfer function is

$$G(j\omega) = \frac{1}{1 + j10^{-3}\omega} = \frac{1}{1 + j(\omega/1000)} \tag{2-63}$$

The various functions required are readily calculated from the definitions of this section.

$$A(f) = \frac{1}{\sqrt{1 + (\omega/1000)^2}} \tag{2-64}$$

$$\beta(f) = -\tan^{-1}\frac{\omega}{1000} \tag{2-65}$$

$$T_p(f) = \frac{1}{\omega}\tan^{-1}\frac{\omega}{1000} \tag{2-66}$$

$$T_g(f) = \frac{10^{-3}}{1 + (\omega/1000)^2} \tag{2-67}$$

(b) At the specific frequency ω = 1000 rad/s (≈ 159 Hz), the amplitude and phase are determined from (2-64) and (2-65) as

$$\begin{aligned} A(159) &= 1/\sqrt{2} \approx 0.7071 \\ \beta(159) &= -45^\circ \end{aligned} \tag{2-68}$$

The output steady-state sinusoid $v_2(t)$ is then given by

$$v_2(t) = 7.071 \sin (1000t - 45°) \tag{2-69}$$

PROBLEMS

2-1 Obtain a differential equation relating v_1 and v_2 in the circuit of Fig. P2-1. The input is v_1 and the output is v_2.

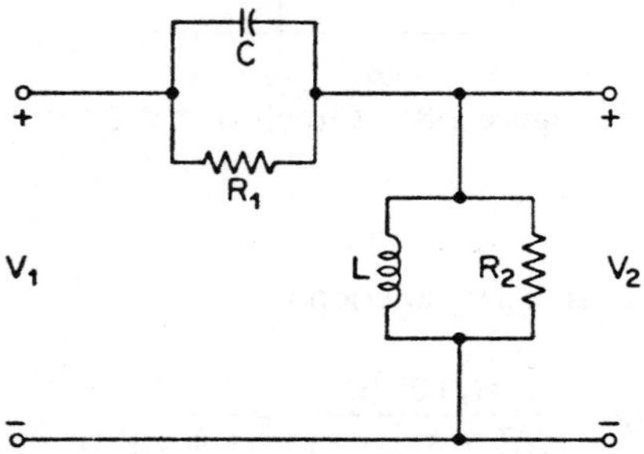

Figure P2-1

2-2 Obtain a differential equation relating v_1 and v_2 in the circuit of Fig. P2-2. The input is v_1 and the output is v_2. (Hint: Write a set of integro-differential equations and eliminate the undesired variable(s).)

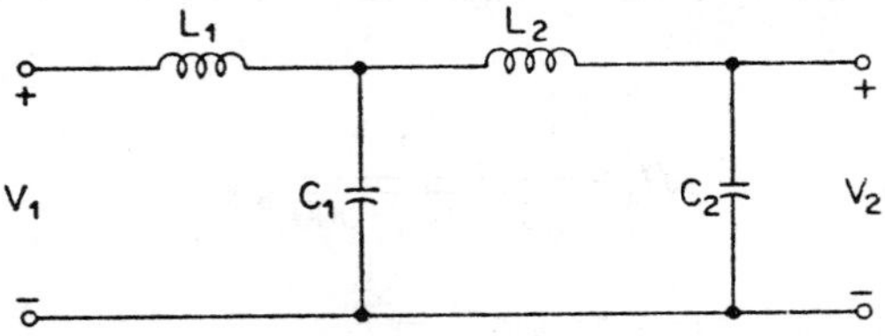

Figure P2-2

2-3 The impulse response of a certain CTLTI system is given by

$$\begin{aligned} g(t) &= 0 \text{ for } t<0 \\ &= \epsilon^{-t} - \epsilon^{-2t} \text{ for } t \geqslant 0 \end{aligned}$$

Using the convolution integral, determine the response $y(t)$ due to each of the following inputs applied at $t = 0$: (a) $x(t) = 10\,\delta(t)$, (b) $x(t) = 10$, (c) $x(t) = 10\epsilon^{-3t}$, (d) $x(t) = 10\epsilon^{-t}$.

2-4 The impulse response $g(t)$ and excitation $x(t)$ for a certain CTLTI system are shown in Fig. P2-4. Find the output $y(t)$ by use of the convolution integral. (Hint: Graphical techniques are suggested.)

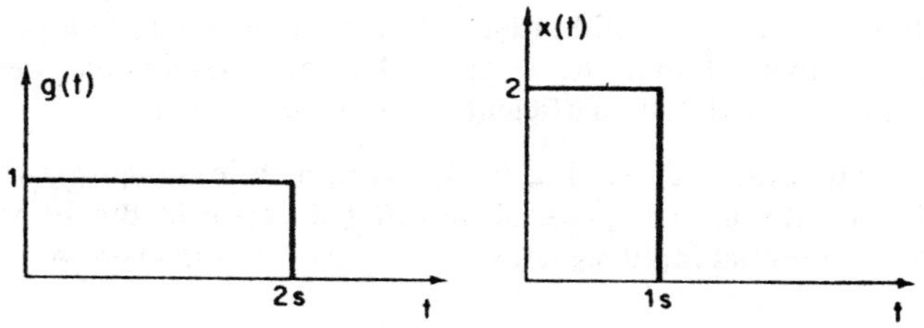

Figure P2-4

2-5 Solve the differential equation

$$4\frac{d^2y}{dt^2} + 24\frac{dy}{dt} + 32y = 800$$

with initial conditions $y(0) = 10, y'(0) = -20$.

2-6 Solve the integro-differential equation

$$2\frac{dy}{dt} + 8y + 26\int_0^t y\,dt = 200 \cos t$$

with the initial condition that $y(0) = 0$.

2-7 For the system described by the differential equation in Prob. 2-5, determine what values of $y(0)$ and $y'(0)$ would result in no transient response; i.e., the system should immediately reach its steady-state condition.

2-8 Determine the transfer function of the circuit of Prob. 2-1 two ways: (a) by transforming the differential equation, and (b) by transforming the circuit and manipulating it directly in transform form.

2-9 Determine the transfer function of the circuit of Prob. 2-2 by the two procedures stated in Prob. 2-8.

2-10 A transfer function is given by

$$G(s) = \frac{s}{s^2 + 3s + 2}$$

Determine the impulse response $g(t)$.

2-11 Using the transfer function concept, determine the response of the system of Prob. 2-10 when the input is the sinusoid

$$x(t) = 10 \sin t$$

2-12 Determine the response of the system of Ex. 2-5b to the step input $x(t) = 10u(t)$.

2-13 Discuss the stability of the system of Prob. 2-10, and identify the natural and forced responses in Prob. 2-11.

2-14 Show that for a second-order polynomial, necessary and sufficient conditions that all roots lie in the LHHP are that (a) all coefficients be non-zero and (b) all coefficients have the same sign.

2-15 Show that the circuit of Fig. P2-15 is unstable. Assume that the amplifier has infinite input impedance and that it performs the amplification of the differential input signal; i.e., $v_0 = A(v_2 - v_1)$, where $A > 1$.

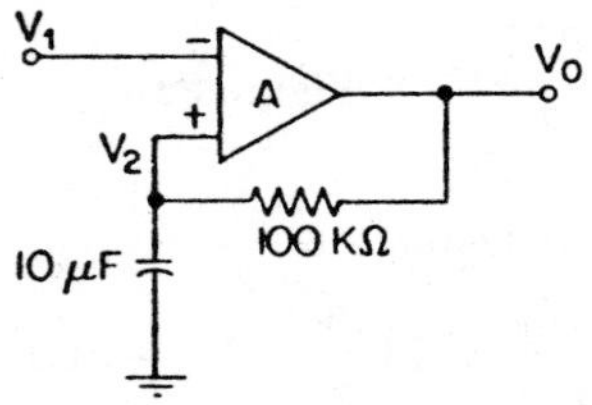

Figure P2-15

2-16 Determine the range of A in the circuit of Fig. P2-16 for which the system is stable. Assume that the amplifier has infinite input impedance and zero output impedance. (This circuit can function as an active high-pass filter.)

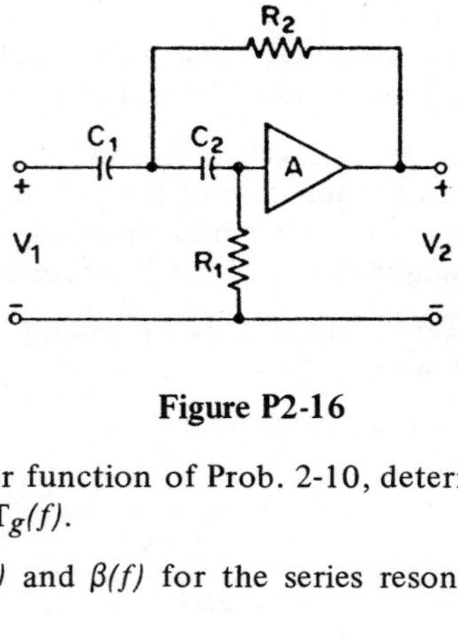

Figure P2-16

2-17 For the transfer function of Prob. 2-10, determine (a) $A(f)$, (b) $\beta(f)$, (c) $T_p(f)$, and (d) $T_g(f)$.

2-18 Determine $A(f)$ and $\beta(f)$ for the series resonant circuit shown in Fig. P2-18.

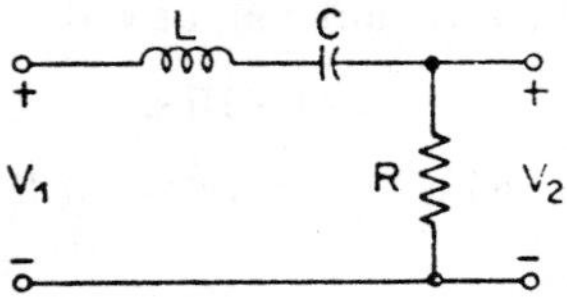

Figure P2-18

2-19 Determine $A(f)$ and $\beta(f)$ for the lead network shown in Fig. P2-19.

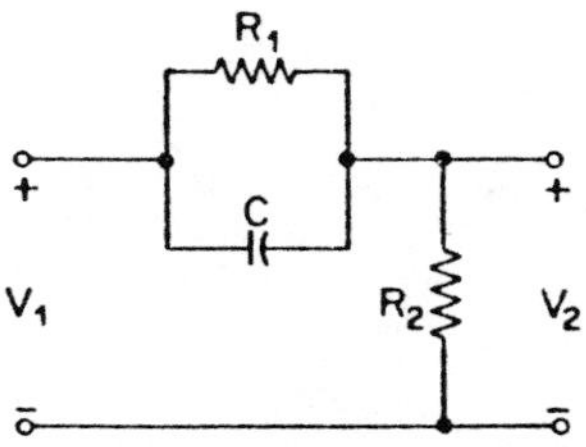

Figure P2-19

2-20 Prove that for a kth order transfer function with *all zeros at infinity*, the high-frequency amplitude response will become asymptotic to a curve with slope $-6k$ dB/octave.

2-21 Prove that for a kth order transfer function with *all zeros at the origin*, the low-frequency amplitude response will become asymptotic to a curve with slope $+6k$ dB/octave.

REFERENCES

1. G. R. Cooper and C. D. McGillem, *Methods of Signal and System Analysis*. New York: Holt, Rinehart and Winston, 1967.

2. F. F. Kuo, *Network Analysis and Synthesis*, 2nd Ed. New York: Wiley, 1966.

3. L. J. Lewis, D. K. Reynolds, F. R. Bergseth, and F. J. Alexandra, Jr., *Linear Systems Analysis*. New York: McGraw-Hill, 1969.

4. W. D. Stanley, *Transform Circuit Analysis for Engineering and Technology*. Englewood Cliffs, N. J.: Prentice-Hall, 1968.

5. M. E. Van Valkenburg, *Network Analysis*, 2nd Ed. Englewood Cliffs, N.J.: Prentice-Hall, 1964.

CHAPTER THREE

FOURIER ANALYSIS AND SAMPLED-DATA SIGNALS

3-0 Introduction

The primary purpose of this chapter is to introduce the concept of a sampled signal as considered from the continuous-time system or analog point of view. This approach enables us to establish a link between the domain of continuous-time signals and the domain of discrete-time or digital signals. Fourier analysis methods are very significant in this process. These techniques enable the concept of spectrum, a powerful mechanism for analyzing continuous-time systems, to be extended to discrete-time or digital systems.

Because of the importance of spectral analysis in this development, the first portion of the chapter will be devoted to a review and strengthening of Fourier series and transform relationships. The concept of a sampled-data signal will then be introduced by considering it as a continuous-time signal modulated by a pulse train. The Fourier techniques will then be applied to the sampled-data signal, and some powerful interpretations will be developed. A very important relationship that will be deduced from this approach is Shannon's Sampling Theorem, which provides the basic sampling requirements for all sampled-data systems.

3-1 Fourier Series

Some of the most important relationships of Fourier analysis will be reviewed in this section. Full mathematical details of the derivations of the

Fourier equations and additional properties can be found in various mathematical and engineering textbooks such as those listed in the references at the end of this chapter. It can be shown that a *periodic* function satisfying certain restrictions (usually causing no great limitations in engineering applications) can be expanded into the sum of an infinite number of harmonically related sine and cosine terms of the form

$$x(t) = \frac{a_0}{2} + \sum_{m=1}^{\infty} (a_m \cos m\omega_1 t + b_m \sin m\omega_1 t) \tag{3-1}$$

where

$$a_m = \frac{2}{T} \int_{-T/2}^{T/2} x(t) \cos m\omega_1 t \, dt \tag{3-2}$$

and

$$b_m = \frac{2}{T} \int_{-T/2}^{T/2} x(t) \sin m\omega_1 t \, dt \tag{3-3}$$

Various terms associated with the expansion are defined as follows:

T = period of waveform
f_1 = fundamental cyclic frequency = $1/T$
ω_1 = fundamental radian frequency = $2\pi f_1$
m = integer defining order of harmonic

Although the forms given in (3-1), (3-2), and (3-3) are probably the most widely employed results for practical problems, the development of many analytical and theoretical concepts is enhanced by use of the exponential Fourier series. This form reads

$$x(t) = \sum_{m=-\infty}^{\infty} c_m \epsilon^{jm\omega_1 t} \tag{3-4}$$

where

$$c_m = \frac{1}{T} \int_{-T/2}^{T/2} x(t) \epsilon^{-jm\omega_1 t} \, dt \tag{3-5}$$

It can be shown (Prob. 3-1) that the coefficients of the two forms are related by

$$c_m = \frac{a_m - jb_m}{2} \tag{3-6}$$

$$a_m = 2\, R_e[c_m] = c_m + \tilde{c}_m \tag{3-7}$$

$$b_m = -2\, I_m[c_m] = j(c_m - \tilde{c}_m) \tag{3-8}$$

where $R_e[\ ]$ represents the *real* part of the quantity in brackets, $I_m[\ ]$ represents the *imaginary* part of the same quantity, and ~ represents the complex conjugate.

It can be seen that c_m is, in general, a complex value. As such it may be written as

$$c_m = |c_m|\, \epsilon^{j\phi_m} \tag{3-9}$$

For a given periodic signal, the complex set c_m is called the *frequency spectrum* of the signal. The set $|c_m|$ specifies the *amplitude* or *magnitude spectrum*, and the set ϕ_m specifies the *phase spectrum*. A typical amplitude spectrum is shown in Fig. 3-1. Note that the horizontal axis is labeled in terms of cyclic frequency *f*.

In some cases, it is desirable to allow the amplitude spectrum to assume both positive and negative real values rather than purely positive values. This interpretation will be made in Examples 3-1 and 3-2.

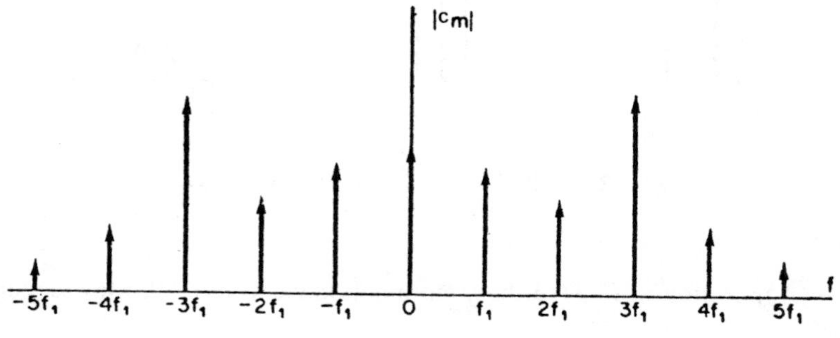

Figure 3-1 Typical discrete amplitude spectrum for a periodic signal.

A significant point to observe for the *periodic* signal is that its spectrum is *discrete*, consisting only of components at *dc*, the fundamental frequency $f_1 = 1/T$, and integer multiples of the fundamental.

Assume now that a periodic signal excites a CTLTI stable system with transfer function $G(s)$. From work covered in the previous chapter, it can be deduced that the steady-state response due to any single component of the Fourier spectrum can be obtained by weighting the amplitude and phase of that particular frequency component with the steady-state transfer function $G(j\omega)$ evaluated at the frequency in question. By superposition, the total *steady-state response* $y(t)$ can be expressed as

$$
\begin{aligned}
y(t) &= \sum_{m=-\infty}^{\infty} c_m G(jm\omega_1)\epsilon^{jm\omega_1 t} \\
&= \sum_{m=-\infty}^{\infty} |c_m| A(mf_1)\epsilon^{j[m\omega_1 t + \phi_m + \beta(mf_1)]}
\end{aligned}
\tag{3-10}
$$

where $A(mf_1)$ represents the steady-state amplitude response evaluated at the mth harmonic and $\beta(mf_1)$ is the phase shift produced by the system at the same frequency.

Example 3-1

Determine the frequency spectrum of the periodic pulse train shown in Fig. 3-2.

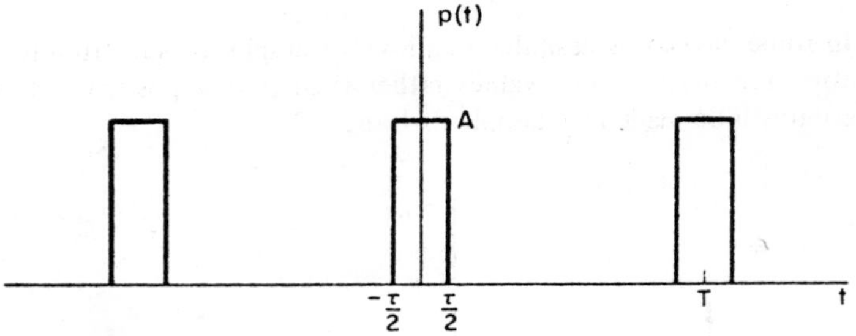

Figure 3-2 Periodic pulse train of Ex. 3-1.

Solution

Application of (3-5) to the given function yields the following sequence of steps:

$$
\begin{aligned}
c_m &= \frac{1}{T}\int_{-\tau/2}^{\tau/2} A\epsilon^{-jm\omega_1 t}\,dt \\
&= \frac{A}{-jm\omega_1 T}\,\epsilon^{-jm\omega_1 t}\Big]_{-\tau/2}^{\tau/2} \\
&= \frac{A}{jm\omega_1 T}\left[\epsilon^{jm\omega_1\tau/2} - \epsilon^{-jm\omega_1\tau/2}\right] \\
&= \frac{2A}{m\omega_1 T}\sin\frac{m\omega_1\tau}{2} = \frac{A\tau}{T}\,\frac{\sin m\omega_1\tau/2}{m\omega_1\tau/2}
\end{aligned}
\tag{3-11}
$$

Finally, this result can be expressed as

$$c_m = Ad \frac{\sin m\pi d}{m\pi d} \tag{3-12}$$

where the quantity d is called the *duty cycle* and is defined as $d = \tau/T$.

For this example, the values of c_m are all real. To avoid phase discontinuities of ± 180°, we will interpret the amplitude spectral components to be both positive and negative, yielding $\phi_m = 0$. Hence, the amplitude spectrum is equivalent to c_m, and a sketch of this function for the particular value $d = 0.2$ is shown in Fig. 3-3.

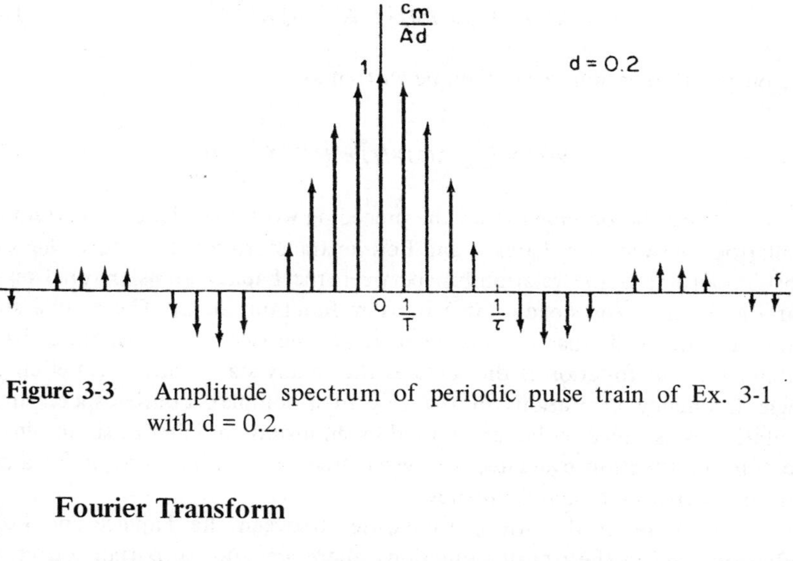

Figure 3-3 Amplitude spectrum of periodic pulse train of Ex. 3-1 with d = 0.2.

3-2 Fourier Transform

In the last section, we saw that the spectrum of a periodic signal could be represented in terms of a Fourier series. Assume now that it is desired to define the spectrum of a *non-periodic* signal. For this purpose, the class of signals under consideration will be limited to those containing finite energy. We may think of the nonperiodic signal as arising from a periodic signal in which the period is allowed to increase without limit. Following this logic, it can be deduced that the difference f_1 between successive components decreases as the period increases. In the limit, the difference between successive components approaches zero, and the curve becomes a continuous function of frequency. In this case, the Fourier integral transform pair is defined as

$$x(t) = \int_{-\infty}^{\infty} X(f)\epsilon^{j\omega t}\, df \tag{3-13}$$

$$X(f) = \int_{-\infty}^{\infty} x(t)\epsilon^{-j\omega t} dt \tag{3-14}$$

where $X(f)$ is defined as the Fourier transform of $x(t)$.

A significant point to observe for the *non-periodic* signal is that its spectrum is *continuous*, consisting of components at all frequencies over the range for which it is non-zero.

Assume now that a non-periodic signal excites a CTLTI stable system with transfer function $G(s)$. As in the case of a single frequency or for a particular component of a discrete spectrum, the response due to a given frequency in the continuous spectrum can be determined by weighting the input with the transfer function. In this case, the Fourier transform of the output $Y(f)$ is obtained by weighting the spectrum of the input $X(f)$ by the Fourier transfer function $G(j\omega)$.

$$Y(f) = G(j\omega)X(f) = A(f)X(f)\epsilon^{j\beta(f)} \tag{3-15}$$

The output time response can then be written as

$$y(t) = \int_{-\infty}^{\infty} A(f)X(f)\,\epsilon^{j[\omega t+\beta(f)]}\, df \tag{3-16}$$

It can be observed from the preceding work that there are certain close similarities between the Laplace and Fourier transform relationships. One of the most important is the relationship between the Laplace transfer function $G(s)$ and the Fourier (or steady-state) transfer function $G(j\omega)$. The simple substitution $s = j\omega$ is all that is required to relate the two functions. Note that the Fourier transfer function is the same as the steady-state transfer function for a single frequency excitation. In the case of a complex Fourier spectrum, the excitation is assumed to be represented by an infinite number of sinuosoids, but the transfer function evaluated at a given frequency is the same as for a single sinusoid of that particular frequency.

In spite of the strong similarities between the Laplace and Fourier definitions and in the transfer functions, there are some important differences, particularly in regard to the transforms of various waveforms. Some of these differences arise from existence conditions and from the fact that the most widely employed form of the Laplace transform is defined only with respect to positive time (one-sided Laplace transform), while the Fourier transform is defined for both negative and positive time.

As in the case of a discrete spectrum, the Fourier transform is a complex function and may be expressed as

$$X(f) = |X(f)|\,\epsilon^{j\phi(f)} \tag{3-17}$$

where $|X(f)|$ is the *amplitude* or *magnitude spectrum* and $\phi(f)$ is the *phase spectrum*. As in the case of non-periodic functions, the amplitude spectrum may be allowed to assume negative values in some cases. Some of the most common Fourier transform operation pairs are given in Table 3-1.

$x(t)$	$X(f) = F[x(t)]$	
$ax_1(t) + bx_2(t)$	$aX_1(f) + bX_2(f)$	(FO-1)
$\frac{d^n x(t)}{dt^n}$	$(j\omega)^n X(f)$	(FO-2)
$\int_{-\infty}^{t} x(\tau)d\tau$	$\frac{X(f)}{j\omega}$	(FO-3)
$x(t-a)$	$\epsilon^{-j\omega a} X(f)$	(FO-4)
$\epsilon^{j2\pi f_o t} x(t)$	$X(f-f_o)$	(FO-5)
$x(at)$	$\frac{1}{a} X(\frac{f}{a})$	(FO-6)
$\int_{-\infty}^{\infty} x_1(\tau)x_2(t-\tau)d\tau$	$X_1(f)\, X_2(f)$	(FO-7)
$x_1(t)\, x_2(t)$	$\int_{-\infty}^{\infty} X_1(\bar{f})\, X_2(f-\bar{f})d\bar{f}$	(FO-8)

Table 3-1 Some common Fourier transform operation pairs.

Example 3-2

Determine the Fourier transform of the non-periodic pulse *p(t)* shown in Fig. 3-4.

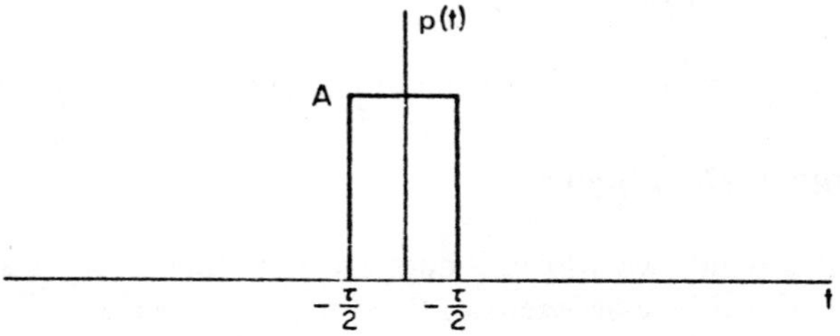

Figure 3-4 Non-periodic pulse of Ex. 3-2.

Solution

Using the basic definition given by (3-14), the sequence of steps follows:

$$P(f) = \int_{-\tau/2}^{\tau/2} A\epsilon^{-j\omega t}\, dt$$

$$= \frac{A}{-j\omega}\, \epsilon^{-j\omega t}\Big]_{-\tau/2}^{\tau/2} \qquad (3\text{-}18)$$

$$= \frac{A}{j\omega}\, [\epsilon^{j\omega\tau/2} - \epsilon^{-j\omega\tau/2}]$$

$$= \frac{2A}{\omega} \sin \frac{\omega\tau}{2}$$

This result can be expressed as

$$P(f) = A\tau \frac{\sin \pi f\tau}{\pi f\tau} \qquad (3\text{-}19)$$

As in the case of Ex. 3-1, by choosing the amplitude spectrum to be both positive and negative, the phase spectrum in this case is simply $\phi(f) = 0$. The form of $P(f)$ is shown in Fig. 3-5.

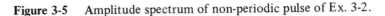

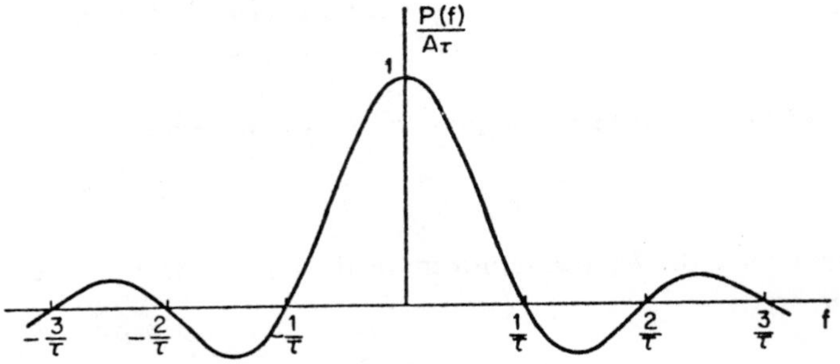

Figure 3-5 Amplitude spectrum of non-periodic pulse of Ex. 3-2.

3-3 Sampled-Data Signals

At this point, we will introduce an important class of signals whose properties serve as a link between continuous-time signals and discrete-time or digital signals. A *sampled-data signal* can be considered as arising from sampling a continuous-time signal at periodic intervals of time T as illustrated in Fig. 3-6. The *sampling rate* or *sampling frequency* is $f_s = 1/T$.

Initially, we will assume that each sample has a width τ, so that the resulting signal consists of a series of relatively narrow pulses whose amplitudes are modulated by the original continuous-time signal. This particular form of a sampled-data signal is designated in communications systems as a pulse amplitude modulated (PAM) signal.

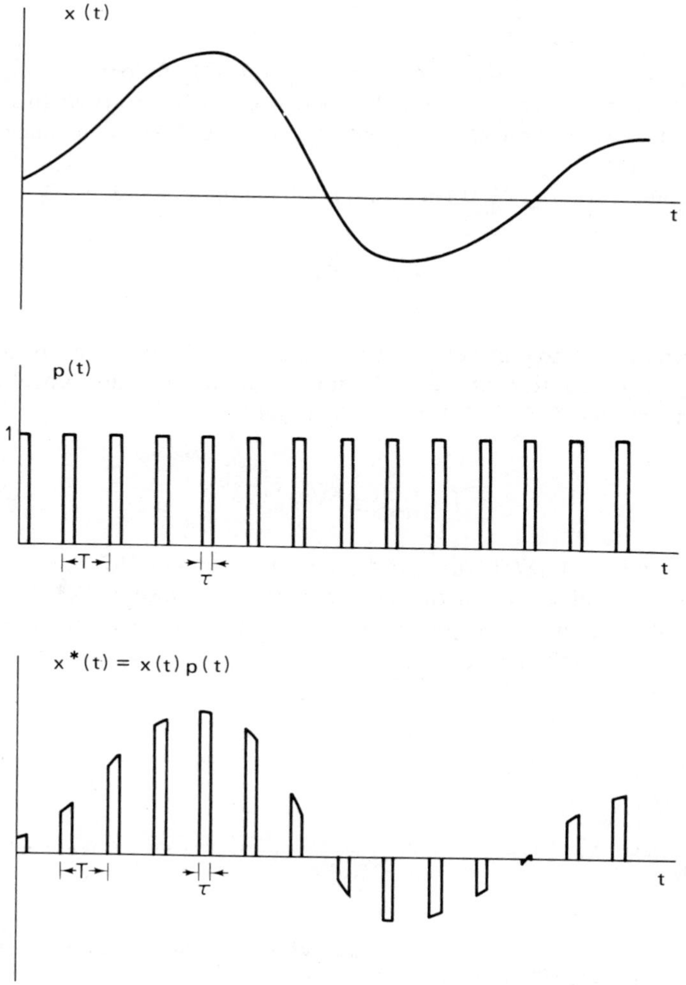

Figure 3-6 Development of sampled-data signal using non-zero width pulse sampling.

Let $x^*(t)$ represent the sampled-data signal, and let $x(t)$ represent the original continuous-time signal. We may consider $x^*(t)$ as the product of $x(t)$ and a hypothetical pulse train $p(t)$ as illustrated in Fig. 3-6. Thus,

$$x^*(t) = x(t)p(t) \tag{3-20}$$

An important property of the sampled-data signal is its spectrum $X^*(f)$. This can be derived by first expressing $p(t)$ in the Fourier series form

$$p(t) = \sum_{-\infty}^{\infty} c_m \epsilon^{jm\omega_s t} \tag{3-21}$$

where $\omega_s = 2\pi f_s = 2\pi/T$. The coefficients c_m in (3-21) follow a ($\sin m\pi d/m\pi d$) frequency variation. (See Ex. 3-1.) However, it is not necessary at this point to actually introduce the values for c_m into (3-21) as long as we understand their general behavior.

Substitution of (3-21) in (3-20) results in the expression

$$x^*(t) = \sum_{-\infty}^{\infty} c_m x(t)\epsilon^{jm\omega_s t} \tag{3-22}$$

The spectrum may now be determined by taking the Fourier transforms of both sides of (3-22). Each term of the series on the right may be transformed with the help of operation (FO-5) of Table 2-1. The result is

$$X^*(f) = \sum_{-\infty}^{\infty} c_m X(f - mf_s) \tag{3-23}$$

Typical sketches of $|X(f)|$ and $|X^*(f)|$ are shown in Fig. 3-7. Due to lack of space, only a small section of the negative frequency range of $|X^*(f)|$ is shown, but since it is an even function of frequency, its behavior in the negative frequency range is readily understood.

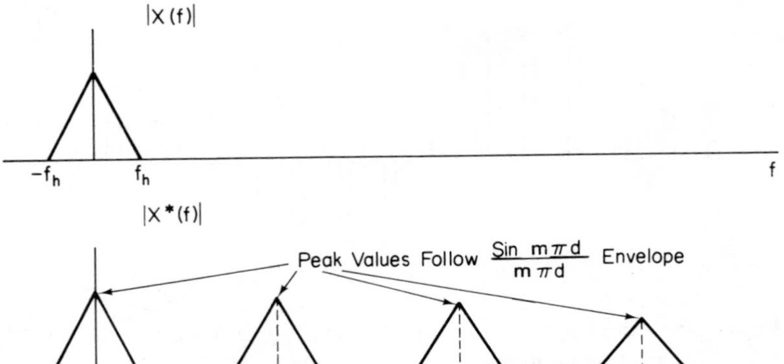

Figure 3-7 Spectrum of sampled-data signal using non-zero width pulse sampling.

It can be observed that the spectrum of a sampled-data signal consists of the original spectrum plus an infinite number of translated versions of the original spectrum. These various translated functions are shifted in frequency by amounts equal to the sampling frequency and its harmonics. The magnitudes are multiplied by the c_m coefficients so that they diminish with frequency. However, for a very short duty cycle ($\tau \ll T$), the components drop off very slowly, so the spectrum would be extremely wide in this case.

Assume that the spectrum of $x(t)$ is band-limited to $0 \leqslant f \leqslant f_h$ in the positive frequency sense as illustrated in Fig. 3-7, where f_h is the highest possible frequency. In order to be able to eventually recover the original signal from the sampled-data form, it is necessary that none of the shifted spectral components overlap each other. If portions of any of the shifted functions overlap, certain frequencies appear to be different from their actual values, and it becomes impossible to separate or recover these particular components. This process of spectral overlap is called *aliasing*, and it can occur if either of the following conditions exist: (a) The signal is not band-limited to a finite range. (b) The sampling rate is too low.

Theoretically, if the signal is not band-limited, there is no way of avoiding the aliasing problem with the basic sampling scheme employed. However, the spectra of most real-life signals are such that they may be assumed to be band-limited. Furthermore, a common practice employed in many sampled-data systems is to filter the continuous-time signal before sampling to ensure that it does meet the band-limited criterion closely enough for all practical purposes.

Let us now turn to the concept of the sampling rate. In order to avoid aliasing in Fig. 3-7, it is necessary that $f_s - f_h \geqslant f_h$. This leads to the important inequality:

$$f_s \geqslant 2f_h \tag{3-24}$$

Equation (3-24) is a statement of *Shannon's Sampling Theorem*, which states that a signal must be sampled at a rate at least as high as twice the highest frequency in the spectrum. In practice, the sampling rate must be chosen to be somewhat greater than $2f_h$ to ensure recovery with practical hardware limitations.

If no aliasing occurs, the original signal can be recovered by passing the sampled-data signal through a low-pass filter having a cutoff frequency somewhere between f_h and $f_s - f_h$. It is impossible to build filters having an infinite sharpness of cutoff, so that a *guard band* between f_h and $f_s - f_h$ is desired. This illustrates the need for a sampling rate somewhat greater than the theoretical minimum.

A convenient definition that is useful in sampling analysis is the *folding frequency* f_0. It is given by

$$f_0 = \frac{f_s}{2} = \frac{1}{2T} \tag{3-25}$$

The folding frequency is simply the highest frequency that can be processed by a given discrete-time system with sampling rate f_s. Any frequency greater than f_0

will be "folded" and cannot be recovered. In addition, it will obscure data within the correct frequency range; so it is important to clearly limit the frequency content of a signal before sampling.

A word about terminology should be mentioned here. The highest frequency f_h in the signal is called the *Nyquist frequency*, and the minimum sampling rate $2f_h$ at which the signal could theoretically be recovered is called the *Nyquist rate*.

A point of ambiguity is that the frequency $f_0 = f_s/2$ is also referred to as the Nyquist frequency in some references. To avoid confusion in terminology, we will use the term *folding frequency* in reference to $f_0 = f_s/2$, as suggested in reference 1 of Chapt. 1 and as previously discussed in this chapter.

3-4 Ideal Impulse Sampling

The sampled-data signal of the last section was derived on the assumption that each of the samples had a non-zero width τ. We now wish to consider the limiting case that results when the width τ is assumed to approach zero. In this case, the samples will be represented as a sequence of impulse functions.

While the analog samples of any real sampled-data signal derived directly from a continuous-time signal could never reach the extreme limit of zero width, the limiting concept serves two important functions: (a) If the widths of the actual pulse samples are quite small compared with the various time constants of the system under consideration, the impulse function assumption is a good approximation, and it leads to simplified analysis. (b) When a signal is sampled, converted from analog to digital form, and subsequently processed with digital circuitry, it may be considered simply as a number occurring at a specific instant of time. A very convenient way of modeling a digital signal of this form is through the impulse sampling representation. This second concept is the most important one for our purposes, as it will be utilized extensively in the analysis of digital signals throughout the text.

The form of the ideal impulse sampled-data signal is illustrated in Fig. 3-8. As in the previous section, $x^*(t)$ will be used to represent the sampled-data signal, and $x(t)$ will represent the original continuous-time signal. The pulse function is designated as $p_\delta(t)$, and it is assumed to be a train of impulse functions of the form

$$p_\delta(t) = \sum_{-\infty}^{\infty} \delta(t - nT) \tag{3-26}$$

The sampled-data signal $x^*(t)$ can be expressed as

$$x^*(t) = x(t)p_\delta(t) = x(t)\sum_{-\infty}^{\infty} \delta(t - nT) \tag{3-27}$$

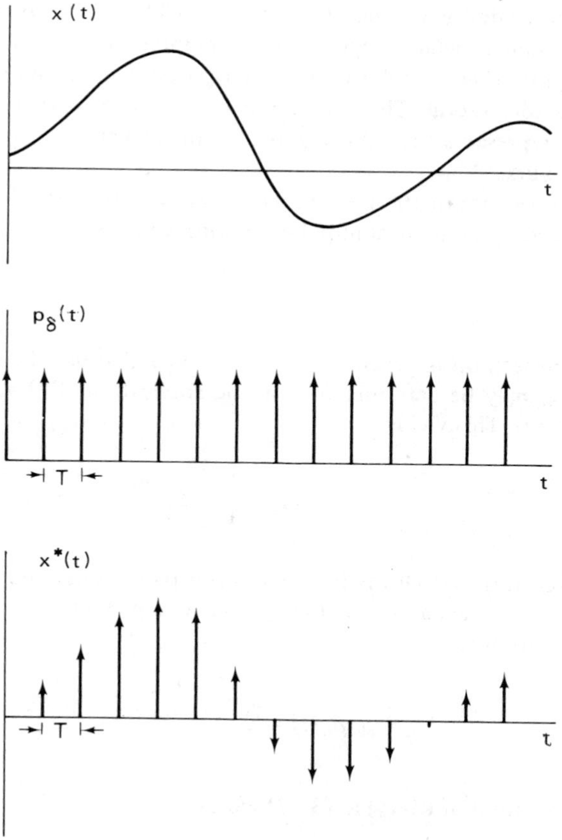

Figure 3-8 Development of sampled-data signal using ideal impulse sampling.

The only values of $x(t)$ having significance in (3-27) are those at $t = n\mathrm{T}$. Hence, an alternate form for the sampled-data signal is

$$x^*(t) = \sum_{-\infty}^{\infty} x(n\mathrm{T})\delta(t - n\mathrm{T}) \tag{3-28}$$

Both the forms of (3-27) and (3-28) will be used in subsequent work. The first expression is useful in deriving spectral relationships due to the product form given. The second form provides the interpretation that the sampled-data signal is composed of a series of equally-spaced impulses whose weights represent the values of the original signal at sampling instants.

In making these interpretations, the reader is urged to accept the use of the impulse function without too much concern about some of the common "mysteries" associated with this function in CTLTI systems. It turns out that a sequence of numbers which appears in a computer can be conveniently represented as weights of an impulse train for purposes of mathematical analysis, so the concept is very useful. The main point to remember is that the weight of a given impulse represents the value (or digital number) at the instant of time that the impulse occurs.

The spectrum of the ideal impulse train can be derived by utilizing the integration property of an ideal impulse function which states

$$\int_{-\infty}^{\infty} \delta(t-a)dt = 1 \tag{3-29}$$

Since the impulse train is periodic, it may be expanded in a Fourier series. The coefficients c_m may be determined from the application of (3-5) to (3-26) with the help of (3-29). This yields

$$c_m = \frac{1}{T} \tag{3-30}$$

This result indicates that all of the spectral components have equal weights, and there is no convergence at all for the spectral components! The function $p_\delta(t)$ may then be written as

$$p_\delta(t) = \sum_{-\infty}^{\infty} \frac{1}{T} \epsilon^{jm\omega_s t} \tag{3-31}$$

Substitution of (3-31) in (3-27) yields

$$x^*(t) = \frac{1}{T} \sum_{-\infty}^{\infty} x(t)\epsilon^{jm\omega_s t} \tag{3-32}$$

The Fourier transform may now be applied to both sides of (3-32), and transform operation (FO-5) can be applied to each of the terms on the right. The result is

$$X^*(f) = \frac{1}{T} \sum_{-\infty}^{\infty} X(f-mf_s) \tag{3-33}$$

The form of the spectrum of the ideal impulse sampled-data signal is shown in Fig. 3-9. The general form is similar to that of the sampled-data signal derived from the non-zero sampling process shown in Fig. 3-7, and the basic sampling requirements developed in the last section apply here. Comparison of Figs. 3-7 and 3-9 and equations (3-23) and (3-33) indicates that the major difference is the behavior of the levels of the spectral components. The spectral

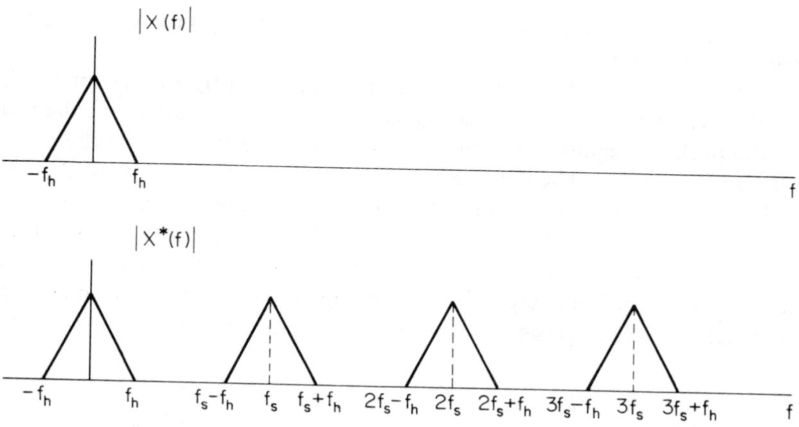

Figure 3-9 Spectrum of sampled-data signal using ideal impulse sampling.

components derived with non-zero pulse widths gradually diminish with frequency and follow a sin $m\pi d/m\pi d$ envelope. However, the spectral components derived from ideal impulse sampling are all of equal magnitude, and they do not diminish with frequency.

An important deduction from this discussion is that the spectrum of an impulse sampled-data signal is a periodic function of frequency. The period in the frequency domain is equal to the sampling frequency f_s. The sampling process in the time domain leads to a periodic function in the frequency domain. This concept will continually appear in many forms throughout the text, so it is important that it be understood at this point.

As an additional relationship for use in the next chapter, assume now that the signal $x(t)$ is defined only in the positive time region $0 \leqslant t \leqslant \infty$. With this assumption, the one-sided Laplace transform may be applied to (3-28). The result is readily obtained as

$$X^*(s) = \sum_{n=0}^{\infty} x(nT)\epsilon^{-nTs} \tag{3-34}$$

3-5 Holding Circuit

It was mentioned in Sec. 3-3 that a continuous-time signal could be recovered from its sampled-data form by passing the sampled-data signal through a low-pass filter having a cutoff somewhere between f_h and $f_s - f_h$. This process of reconstruction can be aided by the use of a *holding circuit*, which actually performs a portion of the filtering required, thus permitting the use of a less complex filter for the final smoothing. Although a number of holding circuits of varying complexity have been devised, we will restrict the consideration here to the *zero-order* holding circuit.

The zero-order holding circuit is best explained by first assuming that we are dealing with real samples having sufficiently small widths that the variation in the peak is insignificant during the interval τ. Hence, a given pulse may be assumed as rectangular. The holding circuit simply accepts the value of the pulse at the beginning of a sampling interval and holds it to the beginning of the next interval, at which time it changes to the new value. This process is illustrated in Fig. 3-10. The resulting function is, of course, not normally the same as the original signal before sampling, but it is now in the form of a continuous-time function, and it will be easier to perform subsequent processing on it in this form.

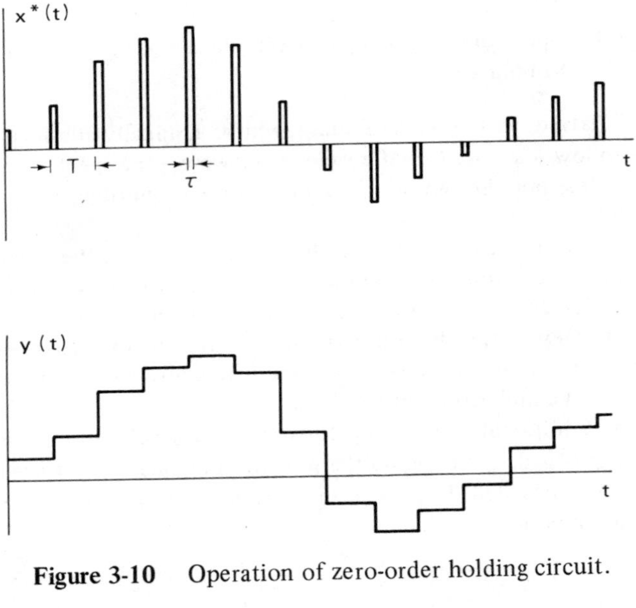

Figure 3-10 Operation of zero-order holding circuit.

One way in which the zero-order holding circuit can be implemented is shown in Fig. 3-11. The delay block represents an ideal analog delay line having a delay of T seconds. The delayed signal is subtracted from the direct signal, and the net difference is integrated over the sampling interval to yield the output.

The sequence of events for a sampled-data signal begins with the appearance of a very short pulse at the beginning of an interval. Since the delayed signal will not initially appear at the input of the difference circuit, the integrator reaches a value proportional to the area of the pulse in a time τ. This value is held until the delayed signal reaches the inverted input after T seconds. By superposition, the effect of the delayed and inverted pulse is to cancel out the

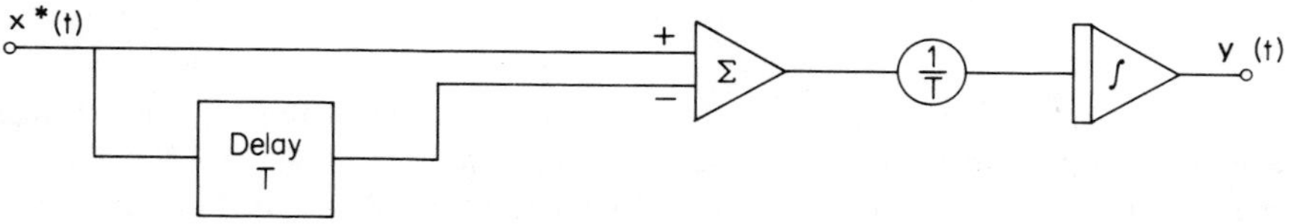

Figure 3-11 Possible implementation of zero-order holding circuit.

output of the integrator previously established. Hence, the next output value of the integrator will be a function of the next input pulse only.

A continuous transfer function may be derived for the zero-order holding circuit. This is best achieved by assuming now that a given input pulse may be approximated by an impulse. For convenience, assume that the given impulse occurs at $t = 0$. The output $y(t)$ produced by this impulse is illustrated in Fig. 3-12. It can be expressed as

$$y(t) = \frac{1}{T}\,[u(t) - u(t - T)] \tag{3-35}$$

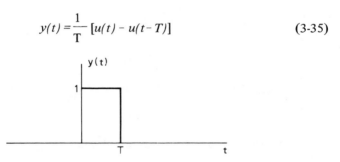

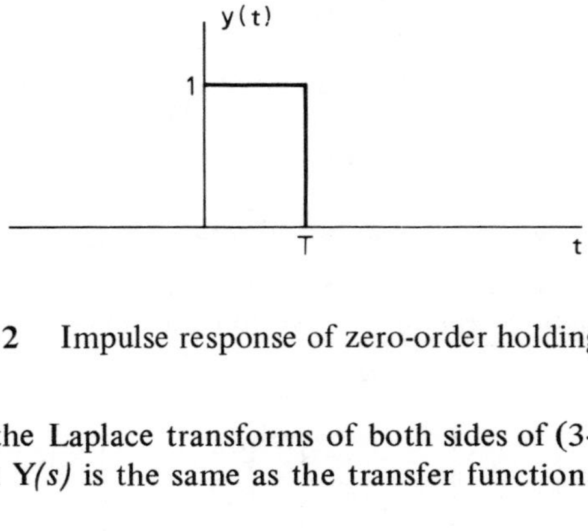

Figure 3-12 Impulse response of zero-order holding circuit.

We may now take the Laplace transforms of both sides of (3-35). Furthermore, since $X(s) = 1$, then $Y(s)$ is the same as the transfer function $G(s)$, and we have

$$G(s) = \frac{1}{sT}\,(1 - \epsilon^{-sT}) \tag{3-36}$$

The steady-state frequency response $G(j\omega)$ is obtained by setting $s = j\omega$ in (3-36). We will leave as an exercise for the reader to show (Prob. 3-18) that the amplitude response $A(f)$ and the phase response $\beta(f)$ of this circuit may be expressed as

$$A(f) = \frac{\sin \pi f T}{\pi f T} \tag{3-37}$$

and

$$\beta(f) = -\pi f T \tag{3-38}$$

(As in the case of some previous functions, we are permitting $A(f)$ to assume negative values here.) The amplitude response is shown in Fig. 3-13. We see that the circuit does function as a type of low-pass filter, although it is not particularly outstanding in this capacity. Normally, additional filtering of the signal will be required to effectively remove components of the sampled-data signal about the sampling frequency and its harmonics, but the presence of the holding circuits eases the requirements.

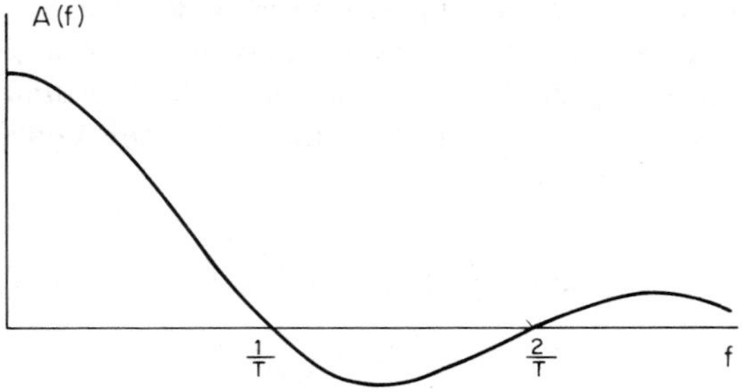

Figure 3-13 Amplitude response of zero-order holding circuit

PROBLEMS

3-1 Verify Equations (3-6), (3-7), and (3-8).

3-2 Determine the frequency spectrum of the function of Fig. P3-2. Express in the form of an amplitude spectrum and a phase spectrum.

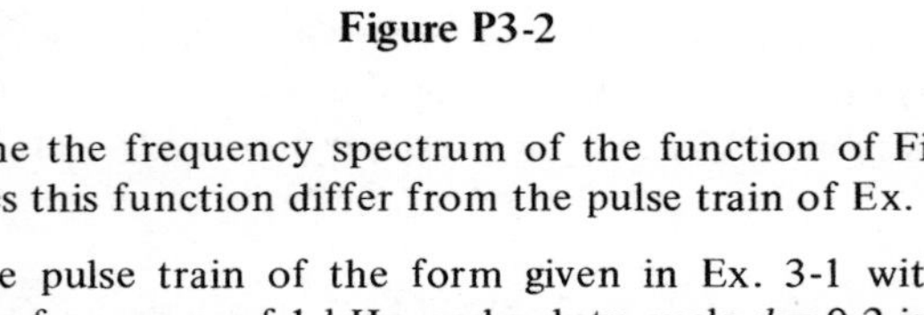

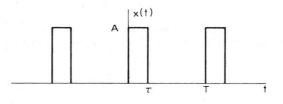

Figure P3-2

3-3 Determine the frequency spectrum of the function of Fig. P3-3. (Hint: How does this function differ from the pulse train of Ex. 3-1?)

3-4 A voltage pulse train of the form given in Ex. 3-1 with A = 10 V, a repetition frequency of 1 kHz, and a duty cycle $d = 0.2$ is used to excite the first-order low-pass filter shown in Fig. P3-4. (a) Determine an expression for the output frequency spectrum c_{m2}. Express in the form of an amplitude spectrum and a phase spectrum. (b) Determine an

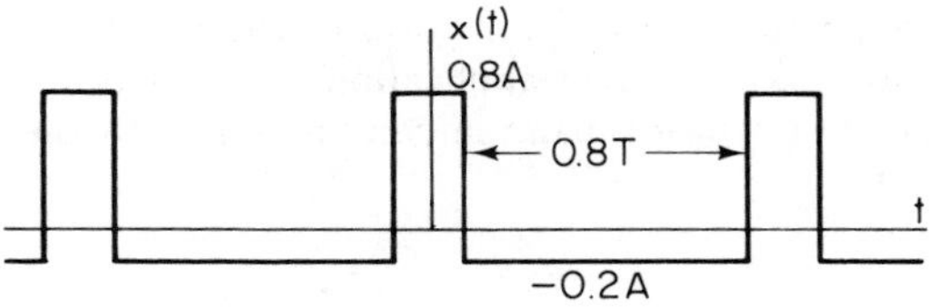

Figure P3-3

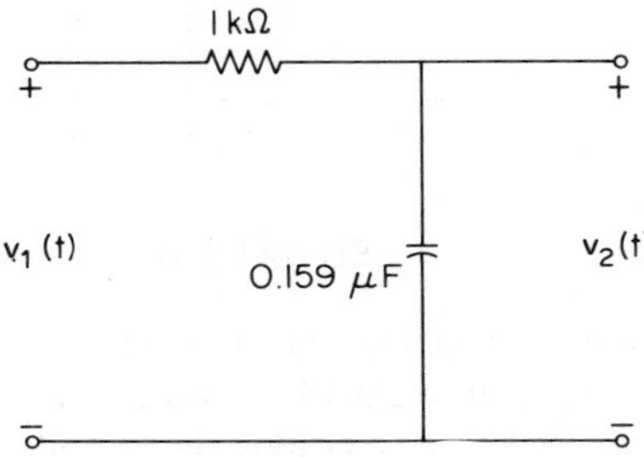

Figure P3-4

expression for the output steady-state time signal $v_2(t)$ in terms of the spectral components.

3-5 Prove the following two statements for a periodic signal $x(t)$ and its spectrum c_m:

(a) If $x(t)$ is *even*, c_m is *real*.

(b) If $x(t)$ is *odd*, c_m is *imaginary*.

3-6 A pulse train of the form given in Ex. 3-1 has a fixed pulse repetition rate of 1 kHz, but the pulse width τ can be varied. Sketch the amplitude spectrum for each of the following values of τ, and label the frequencies of all spectral components in each case: (a) $\tau = 0.5$ *ms*, (b) $\tau = 0.2$ *ms*, (c) $\tau = 0.05$ *ms*.

3-7 A pulse train of the form given in Ex. 3-1 has a fixed pulse width of $\tau =$ 1 μs, but the period T can be varied. Sketch the amplitude spectrum for each of the following values of T, and label the frequencies of all spectral components in each case:

(a) T = 4 μs, (b) T = 10 μs, (c) T = 40 μs.

3-8 Consider a pulse train of the form given in Ex. 3-1 with duty cycle d. Consider the case where $1/d = T/\tau$ is an integer N. Show that the spectral components are zero at the set of frequencies nNf_1, where n is any integer except zero, and f_1 is the fundamental frequency.

3-9 Derive the following Fourier transform operation pairs: (a) (FO-2), (b) (FO-3), (c) (FO-4), (d) (FO-5), (e) (FO-6)

3-10 Determine the Fourier transform of the function shown in Fig. P3-10 two ways: (a) by direct application of the definition, and (b) by use of one of the operation pairs in conjunction with the results developed in the text.

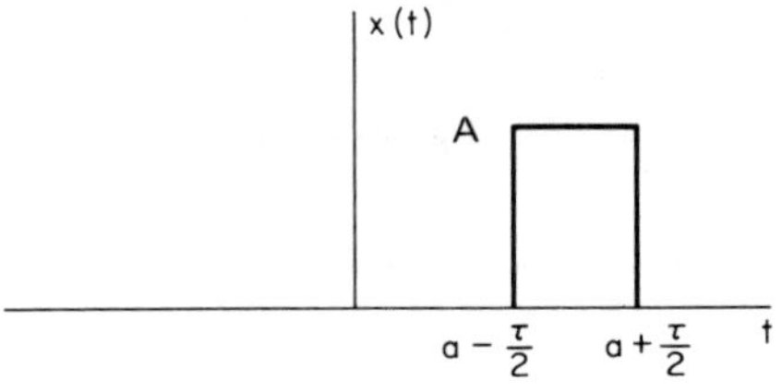

Figure P3-10

3-11 The function shown in Fig. P3-11 represents the amplitude response of an ideal frequency domain filter (which is not realizable). Assuming a phase response of zero, determine the impulse response *g(t)* of the ideal filter by taking the inverse Fourier transform.

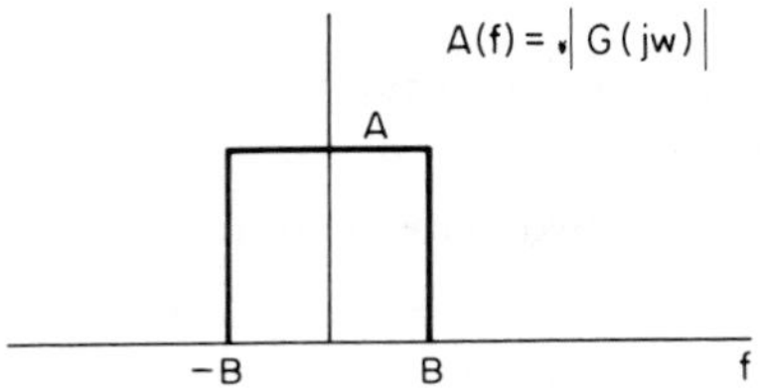

Figure P3-11

3-12 Prove the following two statements for a signal $x(t)$ and its Fourier transform $X(f)$.

(a) If $x(t)$ is *even*, $X(f)$ is *real*.

(b) If $x(t)$ is *odd*, $X(f)$ is *imaginary*.

3-13 Sketch the amplitude spectrum of a single pulse with a width $\tau = 1\ \mu s$.

3-14 A signal having a spectrum ranging from near dc to 10 kHz is to be sampled and converted to discrete form. What is the theoretical minimum number of samples per second that must be taken to ensure recovery?

3-15 A certain continuous-time signal is 2 minutes long. The spectrum of the signal ranges from near dc to 100 Hz. It is to be sampled and converted to digital form for computer processing. (a) What is the theoretical minimum number of samples that must be taken? (b) Assume that each sample is represented as a 12 bit binary number. What is the minimum core storage in bits required to handle this signal?

3-16 A certain continuous-time signal contains a dc component and the following three additional frequencies: 1 kHz, 2 kHz, 3 kHz. The signal is sampled at a rate of 10 kHz by a narrow pulse train. Draw the spectrum of the sampled signal showing all components between dc and 45 kHz.

3-17 Assume that the signal of Prob. 3-16 is sampled at a rate of 5 kHz. By drawing a spectral diagram, show that it would be impossible to recover the original signal by simple filtering.

3-18 Show that the amplitude and phase response functions of the zero-order holding circuit are given by equations (3-37) and (3-38) respectively.

REFERENCES

1. A. Bruce Carlson, *Communications Systems*. New York: McGraw-Hill, 1968.

2. G. R. Cooper and C. D. McGillem, *Methods of Signal and Systems Analysis*. New York: Holt, Rinehart, and Winston, 1967.

3. F. F. Kuo, *Network Analysis and Synthesis*, 2nd Ed. New York: Wiley, 1966.

4. Athanasios Papoulis, *The Fourier Integral and its Applications*. New York: McGraw-Hill, 1962.

5. Mischa Schwartz, *Information Transmission, Modulation, and Noise*, 2nd Ed. New York: McGraw-Hill, 1970.

6. M. E. Van Valkenburg, *Network Analysis*, 2nd Ed. Englewood Cliffs, N. J.: Prentice-Hall, 1964.

CHAPTER FOUR

DISCRETE-TIME SYSTEM ANALYSIS

4-0 Introduction

The starting point for developing the concept of a digital signal processor such as a digital filter is the theory of the discrete-time system. Much of this theory was originally developed in conjunction with sampled-data control systems, but it is equally applicable to digital filters. In this chapter the techniques for discrete-time system analysis will be developed and discussed. This will include both z-transform procedures and related numerical concepts. It should be understood that a *discrete-time* signal may represent either a purely *digital* signal as would be employed in a computer, or a *sampled-data* signal which occurs in certain hybrid systems. However, the underlying theory is essentially the same, so we will emphasize the broader discrete-time concepts in this chapter in order to obtain more generality. Of course, the major application considered in this book will be in digital systems designed or programmed for signal processing or simulation.

Some of the developments given in this chapter utilize the concepts of contour integration and residue theory. However, it is expected that many readers may not be familiar with these techniques. Such readers will usually be able to omit these developments without any great loss of continuity. Actually, while the analytical methods of complex integration are very powerful in developing some of the material given in this chapter, the end results are presented in simpler forms in most cases. Interested readers may refer to various textbooks on applied mathematics, which usually have treatments of complex integration and residue theory.

4-1 Discrete-Time Signals

In the preceding chapter, the concept of a sampled-data signal was established. This was achieved by expressing the sampled signal as the product of a reference continuous-time or analog signal and a pulse train consisting of narrow rectangular pulses. If the pulses are assumed to become very narrow, the pulse train can be conveniently represented mathematically as an impulse train.

To enhance the process of steady-state Fourier analysis, the sampled-data signals in the last chapter were permitted to extend over both the negative and positive time regions. On the other hand, the developments of this chapter are best achieved by assuming that the signal exists only for positive time. Thus, we will begin by representing any sampled-data signal of interest in the form

$$x^*(t) = \sum_{n=0}^{\infty} x(n\mathrm{T})\delta(t - n\mathrm{T}) \tag{4-1}$$

The Laplace transform of (4-1) is given by

$$\mathrm{X}^*(s) = \sum_{n=0}^{\infty} x(n\mathrm{T})\epsilon^{-n\mathrm{T}s} \tag{4-2}$$

The interpretation of (4-1), along with its Laplace transform in (4-2), is a very important one, and we will return to it frequently in developing various discrete-time system results. In fact, this result serves somewhat as a link in relating some of the purely continuous-time system results to those of discrete-time systems.

Consider now the case of a general discrete-time signal which is defined only at integer multiples of a basic interval T. This signal differs from the sampled-data signal $x^*(t)$ only in the sense that it may not necessarily have arisen from sampling a continuous-time signal. Instead, it may have arisen from some purely discrete or digital process. Nevertheless, we can still interpret the signal in the form of (4-1) whenever desirable.

Except where it is desirable to use the sampled-data interpretation, the most straight-forward notation for a discrete-time signal is simply $x(n)$, where n is an integer defined over some range $n_1 \leqslant n \leqslant n_2$. The integer n defines the particular location in the sequence corresponding to a given sample. If the discrete-time signal is derived from sampling a continuous-time signal $x_1(t)$, the signals are related by

$$\begin{aligned} x(n) &= x_1(n\mathrm{T}) \text{ for } n \text{ an integer} \\ &= 0 \text{ otherwise} \end{aligned} \tag{4-3}$$

In effect, (4-3) states that the discrete-time signal is equal to the continuous-time signal at sample points and is zero elsewhere.

4-2 Z-Transform

The Z-transform is an operational function which may be applied to discrete-time systems in the same manner as the Laplace transform is applied to continuous-time systems. We will develop this concept through the use of the *one-sided* z-transform, which is most conveniently related to the concepts of continuous-time systems as discussed earlier in the book. The z-transform of a discrete-time signal $x(n)$ is denoted by $X(z)$. The symbolic forms for the z-transform and inverse z-transform are given by

$$X(z) = \mathfrak{Z}[x(n)] \tag{4-4}$$

and

$$x(n) = \mathfrak{Z}^{-1}[X(z)] \tag{4-5}$$

The actual definition of the one-sided z-transform is

$$X(z) = \sum_{n=0}^{\infty} x(n) z^{-n} \tag{4-6}$$

The function $X(z)$ is a series which converges outside the circle $|z| > R$, where R is called the radius of absolute convergence.

A comparison of (4-2) and (4-6), with recognition of the fact that T does not appear in (4-6), yields some useful relationships between the s-plane and the z-plane. We note that

$$X(z) = [X^*(s)]_{z=\epsilon^{sT}} \tag{4-7}$$

The s and z variables are related by

$$z = \epsilon^{sT} \tag{4-8}$$

and

$$s = \frac{1}{T} \ln z \tag{4-9}$$

It is of interest to note the effect of the transformation of (4-8) and (4-9) as shown in Fig. 4-1. The left-hand half of the s-plane maps to the interior of the unit circle in the z-plane, and the right-hand half of the s-plane maps to the exterior of the unit circle in the z-plane. The $j\omega$ axis in the s-plane maps to the boundary of the unit circle in the z-plane. The transformation from z to s is a multivalued transformation as can be seen from (4-9), with recognition of the properties of the complex logarithm. In fact, there are an infinite number of values in the s-plane corresponding to a given point in the z-plane. This

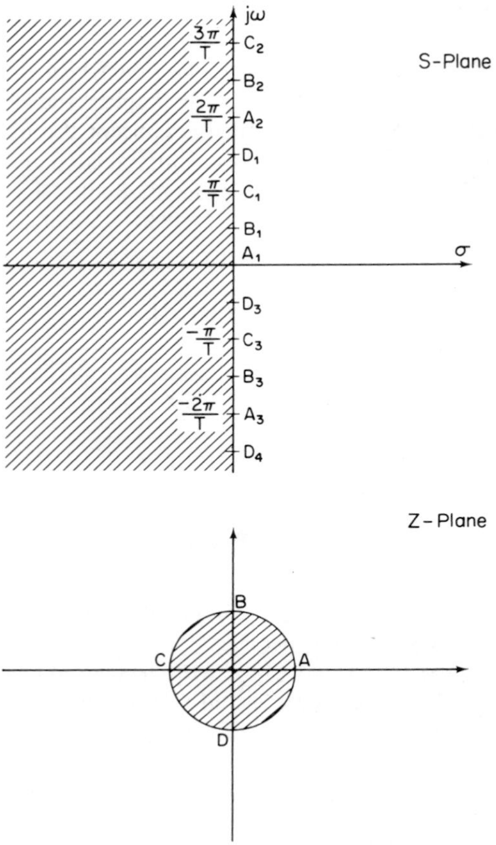

Figure 4-1 Complex mapping relationship between s-plane and z-plane.

property is closely related to the concept of the spectrum of a sampled signal as was developed in the previous chapter.

The boundaries of major interest in this transformation are the $j\omega$ axis in the s-plane and the unit circle in the z-plane. This situation results from letting $s = j\omega$, which is equivalent to

$$z = \epsilon^{j\omega T} \tag{4-10}$$

As the cyclic frequency f varies over the range $-1/2T \leqslant f \leqslant 1/2T$, the argument of (4-10) varies from $-\pi$ to π. This is equivalent to a complete rotation around the unit circle in the z-plane. As the frequency increases beyond $1/2T$, the locus in the z-plane continues to rotate around the same path again, with a complete rotation for each increase of $\omega T = 2\pi$. Once again, the concept of the sampling theorem is evident. In later work, we will be particularly interested in the sinusoidal steady-state behavior of discrete-time systems, and the expression of (4-10) will serve as a major step in observing this behavior. This is essentially the same procedure as letting $s = j\omega$ in a continuous-time system.

We will now consider the process of actually calculating the z-transform of a given discrete signal. In general, this may be accomplished by either (a) use of the definition as given by (4-6) or (b) by application of a contour integral to the Laplace transform of a corresponding continuous-time signal (if such can be found).

Application of the basic definition of (4-6) results in a series in which the value of a particular sample in the sequence is readily observed by the weight of the corresponding z coefficient. For a finite length signal, the basic power series may be the most ideal form in which to express the transform, particularly if the series is fairly short in duration. On the other hand, for either long or infinite series, it is often desirable, if possible, to represent the transform as a closed-form expression. This is rarely possible with a "real-life" random signal. However, in the same spirit that continuous-time systems are continually analyzed with simple inputs such as the impulse, step, sinusoid, etc., so it is with discrete-time systems. The response of a discrete-time system to such standard waveforms serves to define clear impressions and boundaries of what the response due to any waveform would be like, and thus it is very useful to give these signals great attention.

To apply the contour integral method, we have to refer the discrete-time signal $x(n)$ back to a particular continuous-time signal $x(t)$ from which the sampled signal $x^*(t)$ could be derived. Let $X^*(s)$ represent the Laplace transform of $x^*(t)$. It can be shown that $X^*(s)$ can be derived from the Laplace transform of the unsampled signal $x(t)$ by means of the contour integral

$$X^*(s) = \frac{1}{2\pi j} \int_C \frac{X(p)dp}{1 - \epsilon^{-sT} \epsilon^{pT}} \tag{4-11}$$

where C is a contour enclosing all singularities of $X(s)$ in the s-plane and p is a dummy variable.

The z-transform of $x(n)$ is then obtained by application of (4-7) to (4-11). This results in

$$X(z) = \frac{1}{2\pi j} \int_C \frac{X(p)dp}{1 - z^{-1} \epsilon^{pT}} \tag{4-12}$$

By means of Cauchy's Residue Theorem, (4-12) can be expressed as

$$X(z) = \sum_m \text{Res} \left[\frac{X(p)}{1 - z^{-1} \epsilon^{pT}} \right]_{p=p_m} \tag{4-13}$$

where p_m represents the set of poles of $X(p)$ and Res [ ] represents the residue of the argument at a particular pole. The residues are summed over all the poles of $X(p)$. This result allows one to determine the z-transform of a discrete-time signal from the Laplace transform of the continuous-time signal which can be thought of as the "generator" for the signal.

$x(n)$	$X(z)$	$X(s)$	
$\delta(n) = \begin{cases} 1 & n=0 \\ 0 & \text{otherwise} \end{cases}$	1	1	(ZT-1)
1 or $u(n)$	$\dfrac{z}{z-1}$	$\dfrac{1}{s}$	(ZT-2)
nT	$\dfrac{Tz}{(z-1)^2}$	$\dfrac{1}{s^2}$	(ZT-3)
ϵ^{-naT}	$\dfrac{z}{z-\epsilon^{-aT}}$	$\dfrac{1}{s+a}$	(ZT-4)
a^n	$\dfrac{z}{z-a}$	$\dfrac{1}{s-\frac{\ln a}{T}}$	(ZT-5)
$\sin naT$	$\dfrac{z \sin aT}{z^2 - 2z \cos aT + 1}$	$\dfrac{a}{s^2+a^2}$	(ZT-6)
$\cos naT$	$\dfrac{z^2 - z \cos aT}{z^2 - 2z \cos aT + 1}$	$\dfrac{s}{s^2+a^2}$	(ZT-7)

Table 4-1   Z-transform function pairs.

A summary of some of the most common function pairs is given in Table 4-1, and a summary of certain operations is given in Table 4-2. As a point of convenience, the corresponding Laplace transforms of the unsampled functions are given in the last column of Table 4-1. These are not intended as comprehensive tables, but they provide adequate information to deal with most of the standard waveforms of interest in digital signal processing. The examples that follow and the problems at the end of the chapter illustrate the derivation of some of these entries.

Example 4-1

Derive the z-transform of the discrete unit step function $u(n)$ in two ways: (a) application of the definition and (b) use of the contour integral method.

x(n)	X(z) = 3 [x(n)]	
$ax_1(n) + bx_2(n)$	$aX_1(z) + bX_2(z)$	(ZO-1)
[1] $x(n-m)$	$z^{-m}X(z)$	(ZO-2)
$\epsilon^{-n\alpha T}x(n)$	$X(\epsilon^{\alpha T}z)$	(ZO-3)
$a^{-n}x(n)$	$X(az)$	(ZO-4)
$n^{\ell}x(n)$	$(-z\frac{d}{dz})^{\ell}X(z)$	(ZO-5)
$x(o)$	$\lim_{z \to \infty} X(z)$	(ZO-6)
$x(\infty)$	[2] $\lim_{z\to 1} \frac{z-1}{z} X(z)$	(ZO-7)
$x(n)h(n)$	$\frac{1}{2\pi j}\int_c \frac{X(\bar{z})H(z/\bar{z})d\bar{z}}{z}$	(ZO-8)
$\sum_{m=0}^{n} x(m)h(n-m)$	$X(z)H(z)$	(ZO-9)

Table 4-2 Z-transform operation pairs.

[1] It is assumed that x(n-m) = 0 for n<m. Otherwise, initial condition terms are required.

[2] This theorem is valid only if all the poles of $\frac{z-1}{z}$ X(z) lie *inside* the unit circle.

Solution

(a) The discrete unit step function *u(n)* is defined by

$$u(n) = 1 \text{ for } n \geqslant 0$$
$$= 0 \text{ for } n < 0 \tag{4-14}$$

Utilization of the definition of the *z*-transform yields

$$X(z) = \sum_0^{\infty} x(n)z^{-n} = \sum_0^{\infty} (1)z^{-n} \tag{4-15}$$

The infinite summation given by (4-15) can be expressed in closed form for $|z| > 1$ as

$$X(z) = \frac{1}{1 - z^{-1}} = \frac{z}{z - 1} \tag{4-16}$$

(b) We may consider that the discrete-time signal has been derived from the reference continuous-time signal $x(t) = u(t)$, whose Laplace transform is $X(s) = 1/s$. Thus, there is only one pole of $X(s)$, and this is located at $s = 0$. By use of (4-13), $X(z)$ can be expressed as

$$\begin{aligned} X(z) &= \text{Res}\left[\frac{1}{p(1 - z^{-1}\epsilon^{pT})}\right]_{p=0} \\ &= \frac{1}{1 - z^{-1}} = \frac{z}{z-1} \end{aligned} \tag{4-17}$$

Example 4-2

Derive operation pair (ZO-2).

Solution

Considering that $x(n-m) = 0$ for $n<m$, application of the definition of the z-transform yields

$$\mathcal{Z}\,[x(n-m)] = \sum_{n=m}^{\infty} x(n-m)z^{-n} \tag{4-18}$$

Let $n-m = k$. Substitution of this quantity yields

$$\begin{aligned} \mathcal{Z}\,[x(n-m)] &= \sum_{k=0}^{\infty} x(k)z^{-k}z^{-m} \\ &= z^{-m}\sum_{k=0}^{\infty} x(k)z^{-k} = z^{-m}X(z) \end{aligned} \tag{4-19}$$

4-3 Transfer Function

Let us now consider a discrete-time, linear, time-invariant (DTLTI) system consisting of a single input $x(n)$ and a single output $y(n)$. Such a system can be described by a linear difference equation with constant coefficients of the form

$$\begin{aligned} &y(n) + b_1y(n-1) + b_2y(n-2) + \cdots + b_ky(n-k) = \\ &a_0x(n) + a_1x(n-1) + a_2x(n-2) + \cdots + a_kx(n-k) \end{aligned} \tag{4-20}$$

This equation describes an ordinary difference equation of order k with constant coefficients. For convenience in notation, the difference order k has been chosen to be the same on both sides of (4-20). In the event they are different, one need only specify that certain coefficients are zero. It should be observed that this equation has certain features similar to the differential equation input-output relationship of a continuous-time system as described in Chapt. 2.

If (4-20) is solved for $y(n)$, the result is

$$y(n) = \sum_{i=0}^{k} a_i x(n-i) - \sum_{i=1}^{k} b_i y(n-i) \tag{4-21}$$

A very interesting feature of (4-21) is that it can be completely solved by the basic arithmetic operations of multiplication, addition, and subtraction. All that is required to start a solution is to specify the input function $x(n)$ and the first k values of the output $y(n)$. The algorithm of (4-21) is then applied step by step. As each successive value of $y(n)$ is calculated, the integer n is advanced one step, and a computation of the next value is made. The solution of a difference equation is seen to be considerably simpler in concept than that of the corresponding differential equation.

Let us now consider a *relaxed* system, i.e., one with no initial values stored in the system. If we take the z-transforms of both sides of (4-20) and employ operation (ZO-2) of Table 4-2, we obtain after factoring

$$\begin{aligned}(1 + b_1 z^{-1} + b_2 z^{-2} + \cdots + b_k z^{-k})\, Y(z) &= \\ (a_0 + a_1 z^{-1} + a_2 z^{-2} + \cdots + a_k z^{-k})\, X(z)&\end{aligned} \tag{4-22}$$

Solving for $Y(z)$ we obtain

$$Y(z) = \frac{(a_0 + a_1 z^{-1} + a_2 z^{-2} + \cdots + a_k z^{-k})}{(1 + b_1 z^{-1} + b_2 z^{-2} + \cdots + b_k z^{-k})}\, X(z) \tag{4-23}$$

We now may define the *transfer function* $H(z)$ of the discrete-time system as

$$H(z) = \frac{N(z)}{D(z)} = \frac{a_0 + a_1 z^{-1} + a_2 z^{-2} + \cdots + a_k z^{-k}}{1 + b_1 z^{-1} + b_2 z^{-2} + \cdots + b_k z^{-k}} \tag{4-24}$$

where $N(z)$ is the numerator polynomial and $D(z)$ is the denominator polynomial.

The expression of (4-24) is arranged in *negative* powers of z, which is usually the most natural form in which the function occurs. On the other hand, it is frequently desirable to express $H(z)$ in *positive* powers of z, particularly when we wish to factor the polynomials or to perform a partial fraction expansion. This is done by multiplying numerator and denominator by z^k, and the result is

$$H(z) = \frac{a_0 z^k + a_1 z^{k-1} + a_2 z^{k-2} + \cdots + a_k}{z^k + b_1 z^{k-1} + b_2 z^{k-2} + \cdots + b_k} \tag{4-25}$$

Using the transfer function concept, the input-output relationship becomes

$$Y(z) = H(z)X(z) \tag{4-26}$$

Thus, a discrete-time system can be represented by the same type of transfer function relationship as for a continuous-time system. In this case, however, the transfer function and the transformed variables are functions of the discrete variable z. To distinguish this transfer function from that of a continuous-time system, we will refer to $H(z)$ simply as a *discrete transfer function*.

In the same fashion as for a continuous transfer function, we may determine poles and zeros for the discrete transfer function and represent them, for this case, in the z-plane. Various geometrical techniques have been developed for analyzing system performance in terms of relative pole and zero locations. Let $z_1, z_2, \cdots z_k$ represent the k zeros, and let $p_1, p_2, \cdots p_k$ represent the k poles. The transfer function may then be expressed in positive powers of z as

$$H(z) = \frac{a_0(z - z_1)(z - z_2) \cdots (z - z_k)}{(z - p_1)(z - p_2) \cdots (z - p_k)} \tag{4-27}$$

If desired, this result may also be expressed in negative powers of z as

$$H(z) = \frac{a_0(1 - z_1 z^{-1})(1 - z_2 z^{-1}) \cdots (1 - z_k z^{-1})}{(1 - p_1 z^{-1})(1 - p_2 z^{-1}) \cdots (1 - p_k z^{-1})} \tag{4-28}$$

As in the case of a continuous-time system, we may define the *impulse response* by assuming that the input is simply $x(n) = \delta(n)$. In the case of a continuous-time system, the impulse response is often somewhat difficult to implement physically. However, for a discrete-time system, the "impulse function" is simply a number (usually unity) applied at a single sampling instant, which is readily implemented in an actual system. Since $\mathfrak{Z}[\delta(n)] = 1$, the impulse response $h(n)$ is seen to be

$$h(n) = \mathfrak{Z}^{-1}[H(z)] \tag{4-29}$$

In general, when a discrete-time system is excited by an arbitrary input $x(n)$, the transform $X(z)$ is found and multiplied by $H(z)$ to obtain the output transform $Y(z)$. The discrete-time output signal is then determined by inverting $Y(z)$ to give $y(n)$. Of course, it may actually be faster to program the original difference equation directly on a digital computer or programmable calculator and obtain a solution point by point. However, the major advantage of the z-transform approach is the powerful conceptual and operational basis that it provides in studying discrete-time system behavior. For that reason, the next section will be devoted to various procedures for inverting z-transforms.

4-4 Inverse Z-Transform

The next problem to be considered is that of finding the discrete-time signal $y(n)$ corresponding to a given transform $Y(z)$, which is the process of inverse transformation. In general, the inverse z-transform may be determined by at least three separate procedures: (a) partial fraction expansion and use of transform pair tables, (b) inversion integral method, and (c) power series expansion.

Partial Fraction Expansion. The method most widely used in routine problems is probably the partial fraction expansion technique. This approach is very similar to the one employed with Laplace transforms in continuous-time system analysis. One must be careful to make sure that all the terms in the expansion fit forms that may be easily recognized from a combination of the table of pairs and the table of operations. As in the case of all partial fraction expansion methods, there are "tricks" that one acquires with experience. In the end, the expansion can always be recombined as a check on its validity, if there is any doubt.

Assume that we are given a z-transform $Y(z)$ for which we wish to determine the inverse $y(n)$. Any transform of interest in most digital signal processing systems can usually be described by a rational function of z. Since the transfer function $H(z)$ is also a rational function, as can be deduced from (4-24) and (4-25), the resultant $Y(z)$ is also a rational function of z and will have the same general form as the transfer function, except that it will normally have more poles and zeros due to the excitation $X(z)$. We will assume that $Y(z)$ can be represented in positive powers of z as

$$Y(z) = \frac{c_0 z^{\ell} + c_1 z^{\ell-1} + \cdots + c_{\ell}}{z^{\ell} + d_1 z^{\ell-1} + \cdots + d_{\ell}} \tag{4-30}$$

Assume now that the poles of $Y(z)$ are known. The function may then be expressed in the form

$$Y(z) = \frac{c_0 z^{\ell} + c_1 z^{\ell-1} + \cdots + c_{\ell}}{\prod_{m=1}^{\ell} (z - p_m)} \tag{4-31}$$

The form of the partial fraction expansion and the subsequent inverse transform will depend on the nature of the given poles. The simplest, and by far the most common, case is where all the poles are of simple order; i.e., there are no repeated roots in the denominator polynomial. The partial fraction expansion method may be adapted to multiple-order poles, but due to the additional labor involved, we will defer this case to one of the later methods. In general, poles may be either real or complex. In the case of complex poles, a pole will always be accompanied by its complex conjugate in the case where all the polynomial coefficients are real.

Probably the most straightforward procedure for the case where all the poles are of simple order is to first divide both sides of (4-31) by z and then expand $Y(z)/z$ in a partial fraction expansion. Such an expansion will usually be of the form

$$\frac{Y(z)}{z} = \frac{A_1}{z - p_1} + \frac{A_2}{z - p_2} + \cdots + \frac{A_\ell}{z - p_\ell} \tag{4-32}$$

A given coefficient A_m may be determined by multiplying both sides of (4-32) by $z-p_m$ and setting $z = p_m$. This results in zero for all the resulting terms on the right except the A_m term, in which the multiplicative factor has been cancelled by the denominator. The result is then

$$A_m = (z - p_m) \left.\frac{Y(z)}{z}\right]_{z=p_m} \tag{4-33}$$

This expression is valid only for poles of simple-order.

If the coefficients of both the numerator and denominator polynomials of $Y(z)$ are real, then it can be shown that complex poles of $Y(z)$ always occur in conjugate pairs. Furthermore, in this case the corresponding coefficients are also complex conjugates. (See Prob. 4-15.) This means that such a pair can be manipulated into the product of an exponential function and a sinusoidal function. To illustrate this process, assume that a given first-order complex pole $p_r = |p_r| \angle\theta_r$ and its conjugate $\tilde{p}_r = |p_r| \angle{-\theta_r}$ are present. Assume that the corresponding coefficients are $A_r = |A_r|\angle\phi_r$ and $\tilde{A}_r = |A_r| \angle{-\phi_r}$. The reader is invited to show (Prob. 4-16) that this combination can be expressed as

$$A_r(p_r)^n + \tilde{A}_r(\tilde{p}_r)^n = 2|A_r|(|p_r|)^n \cos(n\theta_r + \phi_r) \tag{4-34}$$

Example 4-3

By partial fraction expansion, obtain the inverse z-transform of

$$Y(z) = \frac{1}{(1 - z^{-1})(1 - 0.5z^{-1})} \tag{4-35}$$

Solution

As a first step, we eliminate the negative powers of z by multiplying numerator and denominator by z^2.

$$Y(z) = \frac{z^2}{(z-1)(z-0.5)} \tag{4-36}$$

We now form $Y(z)/z$ and express it in partial fraction form as

$$\frac{Y(z)}{z} = \frac{z}{(z-1)(z-0.5)} = \frac{A_1}{z-1} + \frac{A_2}{z-0.5} \tag{4-37}$$

Application of (4-33) yields $A_1 = 2$ and $A_2 = -1$. Multiplication of both sides of (4-37) by z and inversion yields

$$y(n) = 2 - (0.5)^n \tag{4-38}$$

Several values are tabulated as follows:

n	0	1	2	3	4	5	6	∞
$y(n)$	1	1.5	1.75	1.875	1.9375	1.96875	1.984375	2

Example 4-4

The difference equation describing the input-output relationship of a certain initially relaxed DTLTI system is given by

$$y(n) - y(n-1) + 0.5\,y(n-2) = x(n) + x(n-1) \tag{4-39}$$

Find (a) the transfer function $H(z)$, (b) the impulse response $h(n)$, and (c) the output response when a unit step function is applied at $n = 0$.

Solution

(a) Taking the z-transform of both sides of (4-39) and arranging in the form of (4-24) yields

$$H(z) = \frac{1 + z^{-1}}{1 - z^{-1} + 0.5z^{-2}} \tag{4-40}$$

The transfer function can be arranged in positive powers of z by multiplying numerator and denominator by z^2. This yields

$$H(z) = \frac{z(z+1)}{z^2 - z + 0.5} \tag{4-41}$$

The zeros are $z_1 = 0$ and $z_2 = -1$, and the poles are $p_1, p_2 = 0.5 \pm j0.5 = 0.707107 \angle{\pm 45°}$. The factored form of $H(z)$ is then

$$H(z) = \frac{z(z+1)}{(z - 0.5 - j0.5)(z - 0.5 + j0.5)} \tag{4-42}$$

(b) To obtain the impulse response, we expand $H(z)$ in a partial fraction expansion according to the procedure previously discussed. The result is

$$H(z) = \frac{Az}{z - 0.5 - j0.5} + \frac{\tilde{A}z}{z - 0.5 + j0.5} \tag{4-43}$$

where $A = 1.581139 \angle{-71.5651°}$ and $\tilde{A} = 1.581139 \angle{71.5651°}$. Inversion and use of (4-34) yield

$$h(n) = 3.162278(0.707107)^n \cos(45n° - 71.5651°) \tag{4-44}$$

where the argument of the cosine function is expressed in degrees for convenience. An alternate approach would be to force the given transform into the approximate forms of pairs (ZT-6) and (ZT-7) with modification by use of operation (ZO-4). However, this approach is probably more cumbersome.

(c) In order to solve for the response due to a step excitation, we multiply the transfer function by the transform of the step function in accordance with (4-26). The result is

$$Y(z) = \frac{z^2(z+1)}{(z-1)(z^2 - z + 0.5)} \tag{4-45}$$

Expansion yields

$$Y(z) = \frac{A_1 z}{z - 1} + \frac{A_2 z}{z - 0.5 - j0.5} + \frac{\tilde{A}_2 z}{z - 0.5 + j0.5} \tag{4-46}$$

where $A_1 = 4$, $A_2 = 1.581139 \angle{-161.5651°}$, and $\tilde{A}_2 = 1.581139 \angle{161.5651°}$. Inversion and subsequent simplification result in

$$y(n) = 4 + 3.162278(0.707107)^n \cos(45n° - 161.5651°) \tag{4-47}$$

Inversion Integral. A powerful analytical method for determining the inverse z-transform is the inversion integral method. The function $Y(z)$ can be considered as a Laurent series in the complex z-plane. A given coefficient in such a series may be determined by an integral relationship. It can be shown that application of this concept to $Y(z)$ yields for the inverse transform

$$y(n) = \frac{1}{2\pi j} \oint_C Y(z) z^{n-1} dz \tag{4-48}$$

where C is a contour chosen to include all singularities of the integrand. By Cauchy's Residue Theorem, this integral can be reduced to

$$y(n) = \sum_m \text{Res}[Y(z)z^{n-1}]_{z=p_m} \tag{4-49}$$

where p_m represents a pole of $Y(z)z^{n-1}$ and Res [ ] represents the residue at $z = p_m$.

So far, we have restricted the consideration in this text to the one-sided z-transform as defined by (4-6). This implies that $y(n) = 0$ for $n < 0$; thus, we are not normally interested in (4-49) for negative n. Assume that $Y(z)$ has a zero of order r at the origin, i.e., a numerator factor z^r, where $r > 0$. In this case, the product of z^r times z^{n-1} in (4-49) results in a net factor z^{r+n-1}. If $r \geqslant 1$, then $r + n - 1 \geqslant 0$ for $n \geqslant 0$, and there is no pole at $z = 0$ in the total integrand. On the other hand, if $r \leqslant 0$, there will be a pole at $z = 0$ for one or more non-negative values of n. A separate inversion of (4-49) will be required at one or more values of n for this case. This concept will be illustrated in Ex. 4-6.

Example 4-5

Invert the transform of Ex. 4-3 by means of the inversion integral and residue procedure.

Solution

The function is

$$Y(z) = \frac{z^2}{(z - 1)(z - 0.5)} \tag{4-50}$$

From (4-49), this can be expressed as

$$y(n) = \sum_m \text{Res}\left[\frac{z^{n+1}}{(z - 1)(z - 0.5)}\right]_{z=p_m} \tag{4-51}$$

The degree of z in the numerator of (4-51) is positive for $n \geqslant 0$, so there is no pole at $z = 0$ for this range of n. The poles are at $z = 1$ and $z = 0.5$. The residues are calculated as follows:

$$\operatorname{Res}\left[\frac{z^{n+1}}{(z-1)(z-0.5)}\right]_{z=1} = \left[\frac{z^{n+1}}{z-0.5}\right]_{z=1} = 2 \tag{4-52}$$

$$\operatorname{Res}\left[\frac{z^{n+1}}{(z-1)(z-0.5)}\right]_{z=0.5} = \left[\frac{z^{n+1}}{z-1}\right]_{z=0.5} = -(0.5)^n \tag{4-53}$$

Addition of (4-52) and (4-53) yields the solution previously obtained, which was given by (4-38).

Example 4-6

Determine the inverse transform of

$$Y(z) = \frac{1 + 2z^{-1} + z^{-3}}{(1 - z^{-1})(1 - 0.5z^{-1})} \tag{4-54}$$

Note that the maximum negative power of z in the numerator is larger than for the denominator. Multiplication of numerator and denominator by z^3 results in

$$Y(z) = \frac{z^3 + 2z^2 + 1}{z(z-1)(z-0.5)} \tag{4-55}$$

According to (4-49), we may determine the inverse transform from

$$y(n) = \sum_m \operatorname{Res}\left[\frac{(z^3 + 2z^2 + 1)z^{n-2}}{(z-1)(z-0.5)}\right]_{z=p_m} \tag{4-56}$$

We must examine z^{n-2} to see if there are any values of n for which there is a pole at the origin. Indeed, for $n = 0$ there is a second-order pole at $z = 0$, and for $n = 1$ there is a simple pole at $z = 0$. However for $n \geqslant 2$, the only poles are $z = 1$ and $z = 0.5$. Let us first determine the inverse transform pertinent to this latter range. We have

$$\begin{aligned} y(n) &= \operatorname{Res}[\quad]_{z=1} + \operatorname{Res}[\quad]_{z=0.5} \\ &= 8 - 13(0.5)^n \text{ for } n \geqslant 2 \end{aligned} \tag{4-57}$$

The values of $y(0)$ and $y(1)$ can be determined from the expressions

$$y(0) = \sum_m \text{Res}\left[\frac{z^3 + 2z^2 + 1}{z^2(z-1)(z-0.5)}\right]_{z=p_m}$$
$$= \text{Res}\,[\quad]_{z=0} + \text{Res}\,[\quad]_{z=1} + \text{Res}\,[\quad]_{z=0.5} \tag{4-58}$$

$$y(1) = \sum_m \text{Res}\left[\frac{z^3 + 2z^2 + 1}{z(z-1)(z-0.5)}\right]_{z=p_m}$$
$$= \text{Res}\,[\quad]_{z=0} + \text{Res}\,[\quad]_{z=1} + \text{Res}\,[\quad]_{z=0.5} \tag{4-59}$$

The reader is invited to demonstrate that the sum of the last two residues in each of (4-58) and (4-59) is the same as would be obtained by taking (4-57) and evaluating it for $n = 0$ and $n = 1$ respectively. Thus, instead of performing a complete evaluation of all the residues for $n = 0$ and $n = 1$, it is necessary only to determine the additional residues at $z = 0$ in each case. For (4-58), we have

$$\text{Res}\left[\frac{z^3 + 2z^2 + 1}{z^2(z-1)(z-0.5)}\right]_{z=0} = 6 \tag{4-60}$$

For (4-59), we have

$$\text{Res}\left[\frac{z^3 + 2z^2 + 1}{z(z-1)(z-0.5)}\right]_{z=0} = 2 \tag{4-61}$$

This gives

$$y(0) = 6 + 8 - 13 = 1 \tag{4-62}$$

$$y(1) = 2 + 8 - 13(0.5) = 3.5 \tag{4-63}$$

For $n \geqslant 2$, the expression of (4-57) is applicable. An alternate way to write $y(n)$ for $n \geqslant 0$ in one expression is the equation

$$y(n) = 6\delta(n) + 2\delta(n-1) + 8 - 13(0.5)^n \tag{4-64}$$

A few values are tabulated in the following table:

n	0	1	2	3	4	5	6	∞
$y(n)$	1	3.5	4.75	6.375	7.1875	7.59375	7.796875	8

Power-Series Expansion. The last method that we will consider for inverting z-transforms is the power-series method. This method is particularly useful when the inverse transform has no simple closed-form solution or when it is desired to represent the signal as a sequence of numbers defined at sample points. The key to this approach is the basic definition of the z-transform as given by (4-6). A given transform is manipulated to yield a power series of the appropriate form. The values of the signal at sample points are then read directly from the coefficients of the terms in the power series. The pertinent power series may be obtained by dividing the numerator polynomial by the denominator polynomial, both arranged in descending powers of z.

Example 4-7

Determine several points in the inverse z-transform of the function given in Ex. 4-6 by the power series method.

Solution

We first arrange as a ratio of polynomials.

$$Y(z) = \frac{z^3 + 2z^2 + 1}{z^3 - 1.5z^2 + 0.5z} \tag{4-65}$$

The power series is obtained by a division process as follows:

$$\begin{array}{r|l}
 & 1 + 3.5z^{-1} + 4.75z^{-2} + 6.375z^{-3} + \cdots \\
\hline
z^3 - 1.5z^2 + 0.5z & z^3 + 2z^2 \qquad + 1 \\
 & \underline{z^3 - 1.5z^2 + 0.5z} \\
 & \quad 3.5z^2 - 0.5z + 1 \\
 & \quad \underline{3.5z^2 - 5.25z + 1.75} \\
 & \qquad 4.75z - 0.75 \\
 & \qquad \underline{4.75z - 7.125 + 2.375z^{-1}} \\
 & \qquad\qquad 6.375 - 2.375z^{-1}
\end{array}$$

The first few terms of the series may then be written as

$$Y(z) = 1 + 3.5z^{-1} + 4.75z^{-2} + 6.375z^{-3} + \cdots \tag{4-66}$$

By inspection we see that $y(0) = 1$, $y(1) = 3.5$, $y(2) = 4.75$, and $y(3) = 6.375$. These results are in agreement with Ex. 4-6.

Example 4-8

Determine the inverse transform of

$$Y(z) = 1 + 5z^{-1} - 3z^{-2} + 2z^{-4} \qquad (4\text{-}67)$$

Solution

This transform is already in the form of a power series. Note that this corresponds to a signal of finite length having only a few specified points. By inspection, we note that $y(0) = 1, y(1) = 5, y(2) = -3, y(3) = 0$, and $y(4) = 2$. All other values of $y(n)$ are zero.

4-5 Response Forms and Stability

We will now investigate the different forms associated with the response terms of DTLTI systems. It will be seen that this development closely parallels the corresponding situation for a CTLTI system as given in Chapt. 2.

It has previously been shown that the transfer function of a DTLTI system can be expressed in the form

$$H(z) = \frac{a_0(z - z_1)(z - z_2) \cdots (z - z_k)}{(z - p_1)(z - p_2) \cdots (z - p_k)} = \frac{a_0(1 - z^{-1}z_1)(1 - z^{-1}z_2)\cdots}{(1 - z^{-1}p_1)(1 - z^{-1}p_2)\cdots} \qquad (4\text{-}68)$$

When the system is excited by an arbitrary signal $x(n)$, the transform of the output signal $y(n)$ is obtained by multiplying $H(z)$ by $X(z)$. The poles contained in $Y(z)$ may result from two sources: (a) poles due to the transfer function $H(z)$ and (b) poles due to the input $X(z)$.

The *natural response* is defined as that portion of the response due to the poles of $H(z)$. The *forced response* is defined as that portion of the response due to the poles of $X(z)$. If the natural response vanishes after a sufficiently long time, it is called a *transient response*. In this case only the forced response remains, and it is called a steady-state response. In order for this latter condition to exist, the system must be *stable*.

As in the case of a continuous-time system, a discrete-time system is said to be stable if every finite input produces a finite output. The stability concept may be readily expressed by conditions relating to the impulse response $h(n)$. These conditions are:

(a) *Stable system.* A DTLTI system is stable if $h(n)$ vanishes after a sufficiently long time.

(b) *Unstable system.* A DTLTI system is unstable if $h(n)$ grows without bound after a sufficiently long time.

(c) *Marginally stable system.* A DTLTI system is marginally stable if $h(n)$ approaches a constant non-zero value or a bounded oscillation after a sufficiently long time.

Stability may be determined directly from the transfer function if the poles are given. A complex pole of the form $p_m = |p_m| \angle \phi m$ can be thought of as producing one or more time response terms of the form

$$y_m(n) = An^r p_m{}^n \tag{4-69}$$

It can be shown that the only condition required for $y_m(n)$ to eventually vanish is that $|p_m| < 1$. Likewise, if $|p_m| > 1$, then $y_m(n)$ will grow without bound. If $|p_m| = 1$ and $r = 0$ (corresponding to a first-order pole), $y_m(n)$ will be either a constant ($p_m = 1$) or a constant amplitude oscillation. However, if $|p_m| = 1$ and $r > 0$ (corresponding to a multiple-order pole), $y_m(n)$ will grow without bound.

A summary of the preceding points and a few other deductions follow:

(a) Poles of a discrete transfer function inside the unit circle represent stable terms regardless of their order.

(b) Poles of a discrete transfer function outside the unit circle represent unstable terms regardless of their order.

(c) First-order poles on the unit circle represent marginally stable terms, but multiple-order poles on the unit circle represent unstable terms.

(d) A discrete system is only as stable as its least stable part. Thus, all poles of a perfectly stable system must lie *inside* the unit circle.

(e) In general, zeros are permitted to lie anywhere in the z-plane.

Example 4-9

A system is described by the difference equation

$$y(n) + 0.1y(n-1) - 0.2y(n-2) = x(n) + x(n-1) \tag{4-70}$$

(a) Determine the transfer function $H(z)$ and discuss its stability.

(b) Determine the impulse response $h(n)$.

(c) Determine the response due to a unit step function excitation if the system is initially relaxed.

Solution

(a) Taking the z-transforms of both sides of (4-70) and solving for $H(z)$, we obtain

$$H(z) = \frac{Y(z)}{X(z)} = \frac{1 + z^{-1}}{1 + 0.1z^{-1} - 0.2z^{-2}} \tag{4-71}$$

The poles and zeros are best obtained by momentarily arranging numerator and denominator polynomials in positive powers of z.

$$H(z) = \frac{z^2 + z}{z^2 + 0.1z - 0.2} = \frac{z(z+1)}{(z-0.4)(z+0.5)} \tag{4-72}$$

The poles are located at $+0.4$ and -0.5, which are inside the unit circle. Thus, the system is stable.

(b) The impulse response may be obtained by expanding $H(z)$ in a partial fraction expansion according to the procedure of the preceding section. This yields

$$H(z) = \frac{1.555556z}{z - 0.4} - \frac{0.555556z}{z + 0.5} \tag{4-73}$$

Inversion of (4-73) yields

$$h(n) = 1.555556(0.4)^n - 0.555556(-0.5)^n \tag{4-74}$$

It can be readily seen that the impulse response $h(n)$ vanishes after a sufficiently long time as expected, since this is a stable transfer function.

(c) To obtain the response due to $x(n) = 1$, we multiply $X(z)$ by $H(z)$ and obtain

$$Y(z) = \frac{z^2(z+1)}{(z-1)(z-0.4)(z+0.5)} \tag{4-75}$$

Partial fraction expansion yields

$$Y(z) = \frac{2.222222z}{z-1} - \frac{1.037037z}{z-0.4} - \frac{0.185185z}{z+0.5} \tag{4-76}$$

The inverse transform is

$$y(n) = 2.222222 - 1.037037(0.4)^n - 0.185185(-0.5)^n \tag{4-77}$$

4-6 Discrete-Time Convolution

An alternate approach for relating the input and output of a discrete-time system is through the convolution concept. We will choose to develop this concept through a rather intuitive approach, which provides some insight into the process itself. Assume that a given DTLTI system has an impulse response $h(n)$. This means that an impulse (unit sample) occurring at $n = 0$ will produce a response $h(n)$. A delayed impulse $\delta(n-m)$ occurring at $n = m$ will produce a delayed response $h(n-m)$. The discrete-time input signal can be thought of as an impulse train in which each successive impulse has a weight equal to that particular sample value. The forms for the various impulses and the responses they produce can be outlined as follows:

$$\begin{aligned}
x(0)\delta(n) &\longrightarrow x(0)h(n)\\
x(1)\delta(n-1) &\longrightarrow x(1)h(n-1)\\
x(2)\delta(n-2) &\longrightarrow x(2)h(n-2)\\
&\vdots\\
x(m)\delta(n-m) &\longrightarrow x(m)h(n-m)
\end{aligned} \tag{4-78}$$

In general, the response at any arbitrary value of n is obtained by summing all the components that have occurred up to that point, i.e.,

$$y(n) = \sum_{m=0}^{n} x(m)h(n-m) \tag{4-79}$$

The convolution operation can be shown to be commutative, which means that (4-79) can be expressed as

$$y(n) = \sum_{m=0}^{n} h(m)x(n-m) \tag{4-80}$$

From earlier work in this chapter, it is known that

$$Y(z) = H(z)X(z) \tag{4-81}$$

Performing the z-transformation on both sides of (4-79) and comparing with (4-81), operation (ZO-9) of Table 4-2 is readily obtained. In some discrete-time system developments, it is desirable to replace the upper limit on the summations of (4-79) and (4-80) with ∞. This change in notation does not affect the value of the summation for a causal system since $h(n-m) = 0$ for $n < m$.

The convolution approach represents an alternate technique for analyzing a discrete system or for signal processing as compared with the direct difference equation approach. With the convolution approach, the values of $h(n)$ may be stored in the system memory. As the samples of the input signal enter the system, the operation of (4-79) or (4-80) is performed to yield successive output samples.

The direct convolution approach to signal processing, as discussed in this section, is used primarily when the impulse response is relatively short in duration. Otherwise, the number of operations required to compute each new value of $y(n)$ will become excessive. On the other hand, fast Fourier transfer methods can be used to achieve high-speed convolution for relatively long impulse responses. This approach will be discussed in Chapts. 9 and 10.

PROBLEMS

4-1 Derive transform pair ZT-4 two ways: (a) by application of the basic z-transform definition, and (b) by use of the contour integral method.

4-2 Derive transform pair ZT-3 three ways: (a) by application of the basic z-transform definition, (b) by use of the contour integral method, and (c) from transform pair ZT-2 and the use of an appropriate operation pair.

4-3 Derive transform pairs ZT-6 and ZT-7 from ZT-4 with the help of Euler's equation.

4-4 Derive operation pairs ZO-3 and ZO-4.

4-5 Derive $x(n)$ from $X(z)$ for transform pairs ZT-4 and ZT-5 two ways: (a) by use of the inversion integral, and (b) from a power series expansion.

4-6 Determine the inverse transform of

$$X(z) = z^{-1} + 6z^{-4} - 2z^{-7}$$

4-7 By the simplest procedure, determine the first three values of the inverse transform of

$$X(z) = \frac{3z^3 + 2z^2 + 2z + 5}{z^3 + 4z^2 + 3z + 2}$$

4-8 Determine the inverse transform of the function listed below two ways: (a) by partial fraction expansion, and (b) by use of the inversion integral.

$$X(z) = \frac{10}{(1 - 0.5z^{-1})(1 - 0.25z^{-1})}$$

4-9 Determine the inverse transform of the function listed below two ways: (a) by partial fraction expansion, and (b) by use of the inversion integral.

$$X(z) = \frac{10z^2}{(z - 1)(z + 1)}$$

4-10 Determine the inverse transform of

$$X(z) = \frac{1 + z^{-3}}{(1 - 0.5z^{-1})(1 - 0.25z^{-1})}$$

4-11 Determine if each of the following transfer functions is stable, unstable, or marginally stable. In each case, write the difference equation algorithm relating $x(n)$ and $y(n)$.

(a) $\dfrac{z+2}{8z^2 - 2z - 3}$ (b) $\dfrac{8(1 - z^{-1} + z^{-2})}{2 + 5z^{-1} + 2z^{-2}}$

(c) $\dfrac{2z^2 - 4}{2z^2 + z - 1}$ (d) $\dfrac{1 + z^{-1}}{1 - z^{-1} + z^{-2}}$

4-12 A system is described by the difference equation

$$y(n) + y(n-1) = x(n) \qquad y(n) = 0 \text{ for } n < 0$$

(a) Determine the transfer function and discuss the stability of the system.

(b) Determine the impulse response $h(n)$ and show that it behaves according to the conclusion of (a).

(c) Determine the response when $x(n) = 10$ for $n \geqslant 0$. Assume that the system is initially relaxed.

4-13 (a) Determine the transfer function of the zero-order integrator described by the algorithm

$$y(n) = y(n-1) + Tx(n-1)$$

(b) Assuming that the system is initially relaxed, determine the response due to the exponential input

$$x(n) = \epsilon^{-n\alpha T}$$

and compare with the exact integral of the continuous-time exponential

$$x(t) = \epsilon^{-\alpha t}$$

4-14 (a) Determine the transfer function of the first-order trapezoidal integrator

$$y(n) = \frac{T}{2}\,[x(n) + x(n-1)] + y(n-1)$$

(b) Assuming that the system is initially relaxed, determine the response due to the exponential input of Prob. 4-13, and compare with the exact integral of the continuous-time exponential.

4-15 Assume that all the polynomial coefficients in a rational function $H(z)$ are restricted to be real. Show then that the numerator coefficients at conjugate poles in a partial fraction expansion are also conjugates of each other.

4-16 Show that the result of equation (4-34) is correct.

4-17 Because of the emphasis on the transfer function concept in this chapter, we have assumed initially relaxed systems for most of our work. The form of (ZO-2) as given in Table 4-2 was appropriate in this case. Assume now that $x(n-m) \neq 0$ for $n < m$. Continuing to use the one-sided z-transform, show that

$$\mathfrak{Z}\left[x(n-m)\right] = z^{-m}X(z) + \sum_{i=1}^{m} x(-i)z^{i-m}$$

4-18 Using the result of Prob. 4-17, solve the difference equation below subject to the initial conditions given.

$$y(n) + 0.1y(n-1) - 0.02y(n-2) = 10$$

$$y(-1) = 4, y(-2) = 6$$

REFERENCES

1. H. Freeman, *Discrete-Time Systems*. New York: Wiley, 1965.
2. E. I. Jury, *Sampled-Data Control Systems*. New York: Wiley, 1958.
3. E. I. Jury, *Theory and Application of the Z-Transform Method*. New York: Wiley, 1964.
4. B. C. Kuo, *Analysis and Synthesis of Sampled-Data Control Systems*. Englewood Cliffs, N.J.: Prentice-Hall, 1963.
5. D. P. Lendorff, *Theory of Sampled-Data Control Systems*. New York: Wiley, 1964.
6. J. D. Markel, "Z-transform applications using digital computers", Electro-Technology, pp. 21-36, Dec. 1968.
7. A. J. Monroe, *Digital Processes for Sampled Data Systems*, New York: Wiley, 1962.
8. J. R. Ragazzini and G. F. Franklin, *Sampled-Data Control Systems*. New York: McGraw-Hill, 1958.
9. R. Saucedo and E. E. Schiring, *Introduction to Continuous and Digital Control Systems*. New York: Macmillan, 1968.
10. J. T. Tou, *Digital and Sampled-Data Control Systems*. New York: McGraw-Hill, 1959.

CHAPTER FIVE

REALIZATION AND FREQUENCY RESPONSE OF DISCRETE-TIME SYSTEMS

5-0 Introduction

The basic concepts of discrete-time systems were introduced in the last chapter. Emphasis was directed toward the use of z-transform methods for analyzing difference equations that arise in discrete-time systems, and the transfer function concept was developed in some detail.

In this chapter, continued emphasis will be made on the development and application of transfer function concepts. The first aspect that will be considered is that of system realization from the transfer function or difference equation. The realization of a discrete-time system consists of determining the physical layout of a combination of arithmetic and storage operations that would produce the given transfer function or difference equation. The end result might eventually be a software realization such as a computer program, or it might be a hardware realization involving digital circuitry.

The second primary area of emphasis in this chapter is that of the steady-state frequency response of discrete-time systems. As in the case of continuous-time systems, the concept of the frequency response serves a very important role in both the analysis and design of discrete-time systems. Various properties of the steady-state frequency response will be developed in detail.

5-1 Discrete-Time System Operations

The first problem considered in this chapter is the realization of a discrete-time system from a knowledge of the transfer function (or from the difference equation). For the moment, we will not be concerned with where the transfer function is obtained, but rather we wish to investigate the manner in which the system can be designed. In later chapters, such transfer functions will be obtained through the process of digital filter design.

The realization problem will be considered first because its treatment relates very nicely to the basic theory of the discrete-time system as considered in the previous chapter. On the other hand, the approximation problem will require more development through the next several chapters before a complete solution can be discussed.

The realization of a discrete-time system may involve either *hardware* or *software* (or both in some cases). In the hardware approach, it is desirable to actually design and construct a discrete-time system using digital circuitry. The ultimate goal in this case might be a special purpose processor (e.g. for radar or sonar signals) that would more or less be committed to a specific purpose.

In the software approach, the end product might be a computer program for a general purpose computer or minicomputer. In some cases, a special purpose processor with programmable characteristics might be used. When the design represents software, the computer might be programmed to process some real-life signal, or the program might represent the simulation of another physical system whose characteristics are to be studied.

Regardless of the ultimate goal, the form achieved will be that of a *realization diagram* providing the layout of the signal processing functions required. The realization diagram can then be used for either a hardware or a software design.

In this text, we will consider the basic operations outlined in Fig. 5-1 for developing realizations. The operations will now be discussed individually.

The *unit delay* operation shown in (a) represents the process of delaying or storing a particular sample by T seconds, at which time it appears at the output. Since all operations in a uniformly-sampled system occur at integer multiples of the basic sample time T, we refer to a delay of T as a "unit delay". The output of the unit delay block can be expressed as

$$y(n) = x(n-1) \tag{5-1}$$

The *adder/subtractor* operation shown in (b) represents the arithmetic process of combining the two signals $x(n)$ and $y(n)$ by either addition or subtraction in the form

$$w(n) = x(n) \pm y(n) \tag{5-2}$$

In many realization diagrams, more than two signals will be combined in the same unit. In such cases, the signs adjacent to the various input branches may be used to identify whether a given value is added or subtracted. If the signs are omitted, it will be understood that all of the signals are *added* algebraically in the adder itself.

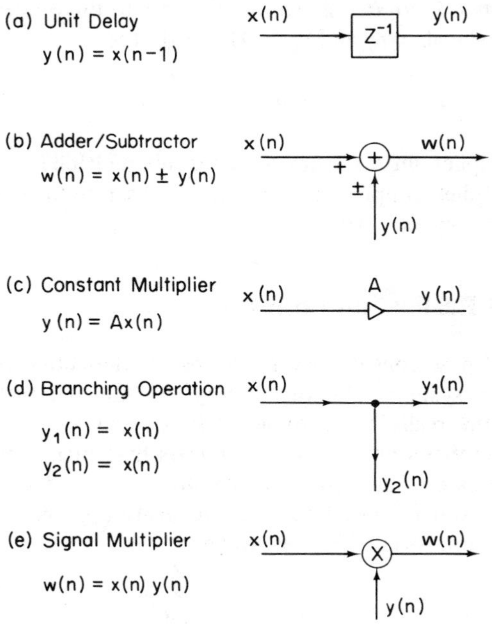

Figure 5-1 Basic operations in discrete-time system realizations.

The *constant multiplier* shown in (c) represents the arithmetic process of multiplying the signal $x(n)$ by a constant according to the equation

$$y(n) = Ax(n) \tag{5-3}$$

The constant A may be rigidly fixed in the system, or it may be programmable. However, if the system is considered to be time-invariant, it will usually be constant for definite intervals of time.

The *branching operation* shown in (d) simply refers to the process of simultaneously connecting a signal to two or more points in the system. If $y_1(n)$ and $y_2(n)$ represent the two points for which $x(n)$ is to appear, we have

$$\begin{aligned} y_1(n) &= x(n) \\ y_2(n) &= x(n) \end{aligned} \tag{5-4}$$

The primary limitation on branching in hardware design is the fact that for each additional branch, more power must be supplied by the previous stage. Consequently, there will be some maximum number of branches that could be driven by a specific digital circuit, depending on the type of circuitry and the nature of the input circuitry that follows.

The *signal multiplier* shown in (e) refers to the process of multiplication of two dynamic signals $x(n)$ and $y(n)$. The output is

$$w(n) = x(n)\,y(n) \tag{5-5}$$

The signal multiplier differs from the constant multiplier in the sense that the signal unit multiplies samples of two separate discrete-time signals whose values may both continually vary with time.

5-2 Direct Realization Forms

We will now consider several forms for the actual realization diagrams of discrete-time systems. In the theory of continuous-time systems, the complexity of the realization problem has necessitated the development of a large body of synthesis procedures. It appears that such a massive effort is not necessary in the case of discrete-time systems. In fact, a few basic forms seem to be adequate as a starting point for most realization problems. We will consider the transfer function form of interest to be

$$H(z) = \frac{N(z)}{D(z)} = \frac{\sum_{i=0}^{k} a_i z^{-i}}{1 + \sum_{i=1}^{k} b_i z^{-i}} \tag{5-6}$$

The first approach will be designated as the *direct form 1* method. The difference equation corresponding to (5-6) is given by

$$y(n) = \sum_{i=0}^{k} a_i x(n-i) - \sum_{i=1}^{k} b_i y(n-i) \tag{5-7}$$

The realization diagram of Fig. 5-2 represents a direct implementation of this equation. Notice that the delay operations on the left provide successively shifted values of $x(n)$, while those on the right provide the comparable values of $y(n)$. One disadvantage of the *direct form 1* method is that it may require up to $2k$ delay elements or operations for a kth order system.

The second approach will be designated as the *direct form 2* method. This method is best understood by manipulating $H(z)$ in a different form. We start with

$$Y(z) = H(z)X(z) = \frac{N(z)X(z)}{D(z)} \tag{5-8}$$

We will define a new variable $W(z)$ by the equation

$$W(z) = \frac{X(z)}{D(z)} \tag{5-9}$$

It follows from (5-8) and (5-9) that

$$Y(z) = N(z)W(z) \tag{5-10}$$

The inverse transforms of (5-9) and (5-10) can be expressed as

$$w(n) = x(n) - \sum_{i=1}^{k} b_i w(n-i) \tag{5-11}$$

and

$$y(n) = \sum_{i=0}^{k} a_i w(n-i) \tag{5-12}$$

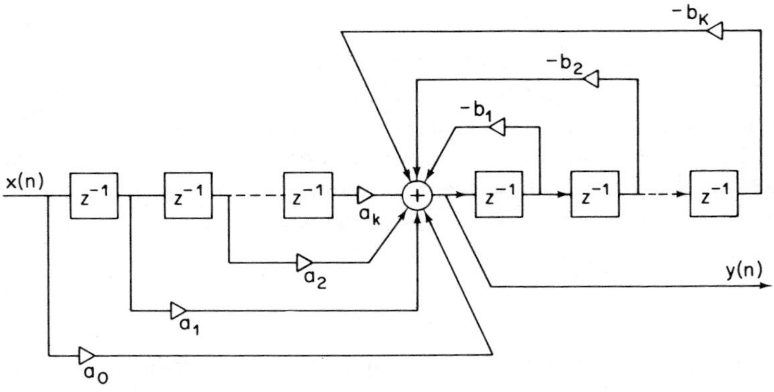

Figure 5-2 Layout of the direct form 1 realization.

The layout of the direct form 2 realization is shown in Fig. 5-3. The variable $w(n)$ represents the output of the first adder on the left. Moving to the right, the output of the first delay element represents $w(n-1)$; the output of the second element represents $w(n-2)$, etc. The relationships of (5-9) and (5-11) are best seen by momentarily disconnecting all the forward a_i paths. The various values of $w(n-i)$ are then multiplied by the b_i coefficients and added to form $w(n)$ according to (5-11). Connection of the forward paths does not change this relationship since these paths merely sense the values at the output of the successive delay elements, multiply these values by the appropriate constants, and sum them at the output to yield $y(n)$. The sum of all the forward paths can be seen to satisfy the conditions of (5-10) and (5-12). Notice that the *direct*

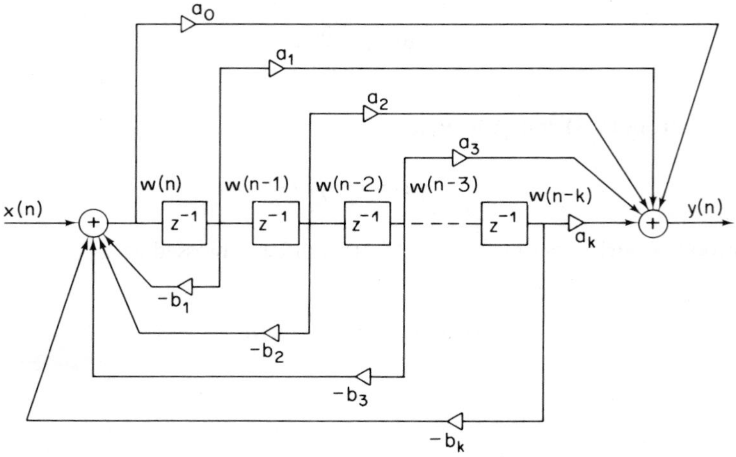

Figure 5-3 Layout of the direct form 2 realization.

form 2 method requires only k delay elements or operations for a kth order system.

The terms "direct form 1" and "direct form 2" have been used in accordance with the suggestions in reference 1 of Chapt. 1. In much of the literature, the direct form 1 realization is called simply the *direct form*, and the direct form 2 realization is called the *canonic form*. However, it has been pointed out that both of these forms (and some others) can be considered to be canonic forms, so we will use the terms previously discussed.

Example 5-1

Develop realization diagrams for the system described by the transfer function below in two forms: (a) direct form 1, and (b) direct form 2.

$$H(z) = \frac{3 + 3.6z^{-1} + 0.6z^{-2}}{1 + 0.1z^{-1} - 0.2z^{-2}} \tag{5-13}$$

Solution

(a) For the direct form 1, we will convert (5-13) to the difference equation form and solve for $y(n)$.

$$y(n) = 3x(n) + 3.6x(n-1) + 0.6x(n-2) - 0.1y(n-1) + 0.2y(n-2) \tag{5-14}$$

The realization is readily implemented by the procedure of the last section and is shown in Fig. 5-4a.

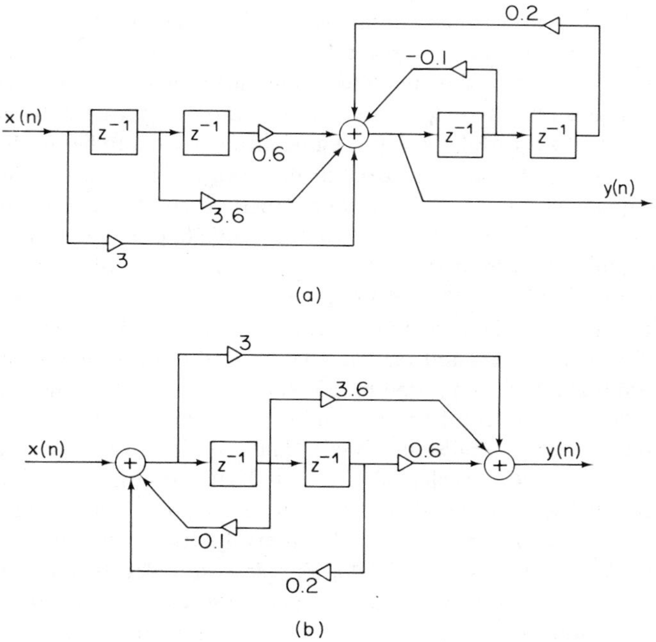

Figure 5-4 Realizations for system of Ex. 5-1.

(b) For the direct form 2, we can solve for $W(z)$ and $Y(z)$ as indicated by (5-9) and (5-10) and invert them as indicated by (5-11) and (5-12). The quantities $w(n)$ and $y(n)$ are then given by

$$w(n) = x(n) - 0.1w(n-1) + 0.2w(n-2) \tag{5-15}$$

and

$$y(n) = 3w(n) + 3.6\, w(n-1) + 0.6w(n-2) \tag{5-16}$$

This realization is shown in Fig. 5-4b. If desired, one can always go directly to the standard form in a "mechanical" fashion, but the preceding development provides some insight into the process.

5-3 Parameter Quantization Effects

Before proceeding with the development of realization schemes, we will pause for a brief look at the effects of parameter quantization in discrete-time system design. The problem arises because of the practical necessity to limit the number of bits representing various signal samples and coefficients. This subject has been introduced at this point because the realization procedures to be discussed in the next section are used to minimize certain of these effects.

In general, there are three major sources of parameter quantization error: (a) quantization of the input signal into a finite number of discrete levels, (b) accumulation of roundoff errors in the arithmetic operations in the system, and (c) quantization of the transfer function coefficients a_i and b_i when represented by a finite number of bits. A complete analysis of these various effects requires the use of statistical methods, and it is not within the intended scope of this book. In this section, we will present some of the qualitative aspects of these problems as they relate to the practical realization of discrete transfer functions. Interested readers seeking quantitative details may refer to a series of journal articles reprinted in reference 2 at the end of this chapter.

The first source of error is due to the quantization of the input signal into a finite number of discrete levels. This problem was briefly discussed in Chapt. 1, and it was explained there that the resulting uncertainty in the amplitude can be considered as an additive source of noise, which is called *quantization noise*. Let q represent the interval between successive levels in the quantizer. Assume that a given analog sample is rounded to the nearest level in each case. The quantization noise is usually considered as white noise, with a uniform probability density function over the range from $-q/2$ to $q/2$. In this case, it can be shown that the variance of the noise is $\sigma^2 = q^2/12$.

The second source of error is due to the accumulation of roundoff errors in the arithmetic processes of a discrete-time system. Roundoff errors occur when the sum or product of two numbers for a particular arithmetic operation exceeds the number of bits available, and it is necessary to represent the result with fewer bits. There are some unusual effects caused by roundoff that may appear. One is a *deadband* effect in which the steady-state output due to a constant input or initial condition may reach a single output value, which is fixed for a certain limited range of the input. Another related effect is the possible presence of small oscillations about the correct output signal.

The third source of error is due to the representation of the coefficients a_i and b_i of the transfer function by a finite number of bits. It has been shown that this problem becomes more severe for either of the following two conditions: (a) The sampling rate increases relative to the frequency range of the transfer function being realized. (b) The order of the difference equation increases.

In many cases, the first condition is inherently fixed as a portion of the design process, and it cannot be changed. For the second condition, it has been shown that if a higher order difference equation is represented in terms of two or more lower-order equations rather than as a single higher-order equation, the effects can be reduced drastically. This leads to the conclusion that the direct forms of realization discussed in the last section should be carefully examined for coefficient accuracies when they are used for higher-order systems.

5-4 Cascade and Parallel Realization Forms

The direct forms of realization discussed earlier in the chapter are more sensitive to coefficient quantization errors as the order of the transfer function increases, as was mentioned in the last section. This may not necessarily present a problem for software realizations of moderate orders on general purpose computers where high precision is available. In addition, realizations having no feedback, i.e., all values of $b_i = 0$, may not be particularly sensitive even for relatively large orders. However, the problem can become serious in many realizations, particularly those involving special purpose hardware designs with limited coefficient accuracies.

The two methods discussed in this section are actually decomposition procedures which permit complex transfer functions to be realized in terms of several simpler functions. In this manner, a system may be made to be less sensitive to coefficient inaccuracies.

The *cascade canonic form* (or *series form*) is obtained by decomposing $H(z)$ into the *product* of several simpler transfer functions as given by

$$\begin{aligned} H(z) &= a_0 H_1(z) H_2(z) \cdots H_\ell(z) \\ &= a_0 \prod_{i=1}^{\ell} H_i(z) \end{aligned} \tag{5-17}$$

In most cases, the individual transfer functions are chosen to be either *first-order* or *second-order* sections. A first-order section will have the form

$$H_i(z) = \frac{1 + a_{i1} z^{-1}}{1 + b_{i1} z^{-1}} \tag{5-18}$$

A second-order section will have the form

$$H_i(z) = \frac{1 + a_{i1} z^{-1} + a_{i2} z^{-2}}{1 + b_{i1} z^{-1} + b_{i2} z^{-2}} \tag{5-19}$$

Note that if it is desired to place any a_{io} coefficients in any of the individual sections, the overall gain constant in (5-17) would not be a_0.

The general layout of a cascade realization is shown in Fig. 5-5. The individual sections may be realized by either of the direct methods. The typical forms for these sections are illustrated in Fig. 5-6 using the direct form 2 realization in each case.

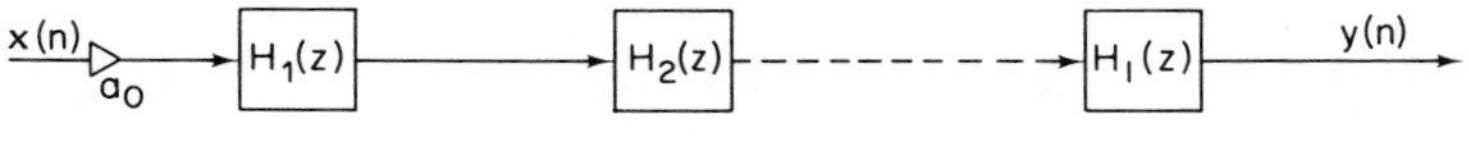

Figure 5-5 Form of a cascade or series realization.

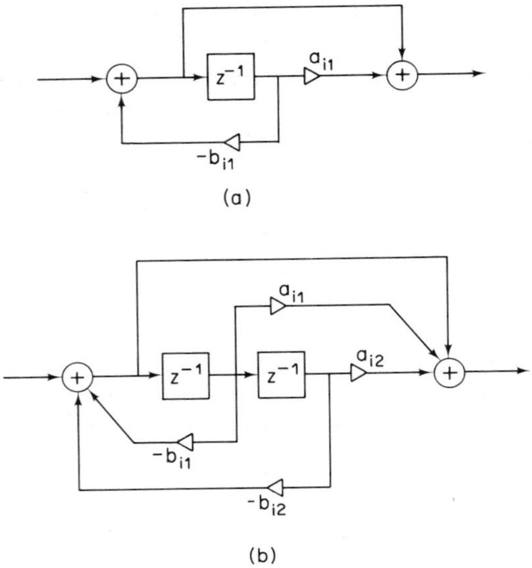

Figure 5-6 Typical forms for sections used in cascade realization.

The *parallel canonic form* is obtained by decomposing $H(z)$ into the sum of several simpler transfer functions (first or second-order) and a constant as expressed by

$$\begin{aligned} H(z) &= A + H_1(z) + H_2(z) + \cdots + H_r(z) \\ &= A + \sum_{i=1}^{r} H_i(z) \end{aligned} \tag{5-20}$$

Because of the presence of the constant term in (5-20), a first-order section can be chosen in the simple form

$$H_i(z) = \frac{a_{i0}}{1 + b_{i1}z^{-1}} \tag{5-21}$$

A second-order section can be chosen in the form

$$H_i(z) = \frac{a_{io} + a_{i1}z^{-1}}{1 + b_{i1}z^{-1} + b_{i2}z^{-2}} \tag{5-22}$$

The general layout of a parallel realization is shown in Fig. 5-7. Once again, the individual sections may be realized by either of the direct methods. The typical forms for these sections are illustrated in Fig. 5-8 using the direct form 2 realization in each case.

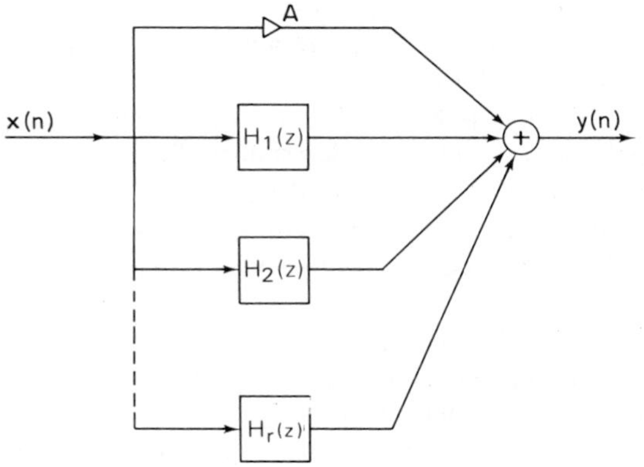

Figure 5-7 Form of a parallel realization.

Both the cascade and the parallel forms require that the transfer function be mathematically decomposed for realization. If the poles and zeros of the overall transfer function are known, the sections of a cascade realization can be obtained by grouping complex conjugate pairs of poles and complex conjugate pairs of zeros to produce second-order sections, and by grouping real poles and real zeros to produce either first or second-order sections. Of course, a pair of real zeros may be grouped with a pair of complex conjugate poles, or vice versa.

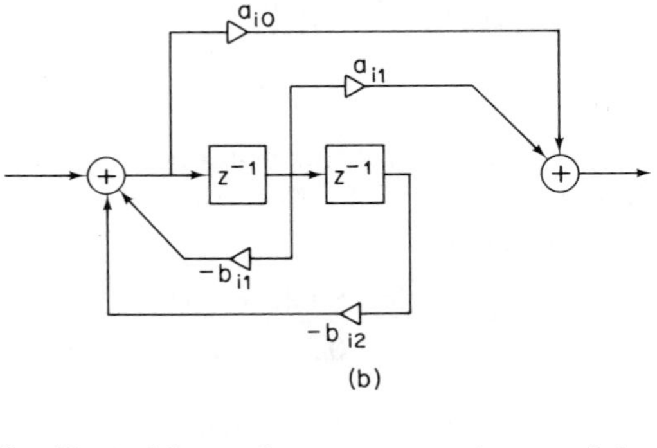

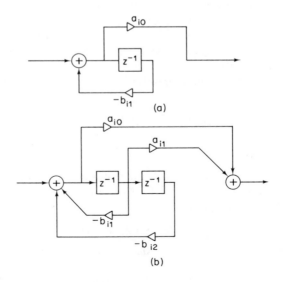

Figure 5-8 Typical forms for sections used in parallel realization.

The same procedure discussed for the cascade realization applies to the parallel realization as far as the *poles* are concerned. The various denominator polynomials may be determined by grouping pairs of complex conjugate poles, grouping pairs of real poles, or by use of a single real pole. However, the numerator polynomials cannot be determined directly from the zeros. Instead, it is necessary to first carry out a partial fraction expansion in terms of individual poles or in terms of a combination of first-order and second-order denominator polynomials. These procedures are best illustrated by the examples that follow this section.

In general, there are no simple guidelines that can be given regarding the groupings for the decomposition. This may be quite arbitrary in many cases, and a comprehensive design effort might warrant the investigation of several possible designs. Various tradeoffs such as the number of arithmetic operations, the range of coefficients, and the availability of components could be studied for each alternative.

Example 5-2

For the sake of illustration, develop both (a) cascade and (b) parallel realization schemes for the system of Ex. 5-1.

Solution

(a) It should be pointed out that decomposition is done here only for the sake of illustration as the system is a second-order function, and it would not normally require a cascade or a parallel type of realization. In fact, it would not be possible to decompose it into functions with real coefficients if either the poles or the zeros were complex. However, the poles and zeros are all real in this case, as we will see shortly.

As a first step in decomposition, we will express (5-13) in positive powers of z as

$$H(z) = \frac{3z^2 + 3.6z + 0.6}{z^2 + 0.1z - 0.2} \tag{5-23}$$

Factorization of the numerator and denominator polynomials yields zeros at -1 and -0.2 and poles at -0.5 and 0.4. (Note that the system is stable.) The function may then be expressed as

$$H(z) = \frac{3(z+1)(z+0.2)}{(z+0.5)(z-0.4)} \tag{5-24}$$

As an arbitrary grouping, the first polynomial factor in the numerator will be grouped with the first factor in the denominator, and a similar grouping will be used for the second factors. The gain constant will be maintained as a separate constant factor, as suggested in (5-17). After conversion back to negative powers of z, the separate functions may be expressed as

$$H_1(z) = \frac{1 + z^{-1}}{1 + 0.5z^{-1}} \tag{5-25}$$

$$H_2(z) = \frac{1 + 0.2z^{-1}}{1 - 0.4z^{-1}} \tag{5-26}$$

The realization is shown in Fig. 5-9a.

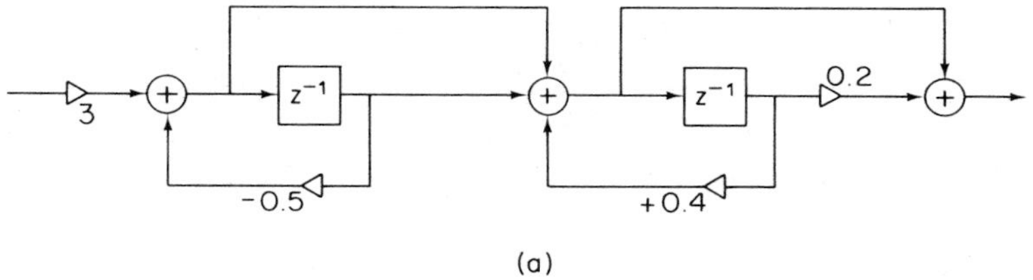

Figure 5-9a Realizations for system of Ex. 5-2.

(b) The parallel development is best achieved by first expanding $H(z)/z$ in a partial fraction expansion. We have

$$\frac{H(z)}{z} = \frac{3(z+1)(z+0.2)}{z(z+0.5)(z-0.4)} = \frac{A_1}{z} + \frac{A_2}{z+0.5} + \frac{A_3}{z-0.4} \tag{5-27}$$

The coefficients are determined to be $A_1 = -3$, $A_2 = -1$, and $A_3 = 7$. After multiplication by z and conversion back to negative powers of z, the various quantities may be expressed as

$$A = -3 \tag{5-28}$$

$$H_1(z) = \frac{-1}{1 + 0.5z^{-1}} \tag{5-29}$$

$$H_2(z) = \frac{7}{1 - 0.4z^{-1}} \tag{5-30}$$

The realization is shown in Fig. 5-9b.

Example 5-3

The partially factored form of a certain transfer function is given by

$$H(z) = \frac{2(z - 1)(z^2 + 1.4142136z + 1)}{(z + 0.5)(z^2 - 0.9z + 0.81)} \tag{5-31}$$

Develop a cascade realization of the function using a first-order section and a second-order section.

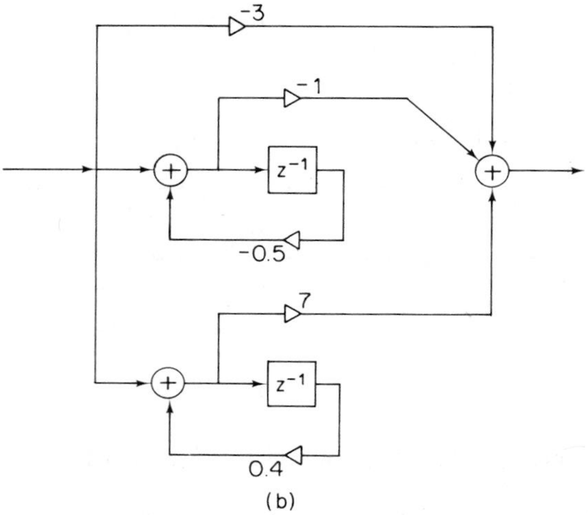

Figure 5-9b Realizations for system of Ex. 5-2.

Solution

As a check to determine various possible grouping combinations, the roots of the two quadratics will be determined. Factorization of the numerator quadratic reveals that two zeros are located at $z = 1 \angle \pm 135°$. A similar procedure applied to the denominator quadratic indicates that two poles are located at $z = 0.9 \angle \pm 60°$.

As long as we are restricted to real coefficients, this means that the decomposition must contain a second-order section representing the two second-order polynomials and a first-order section representing the two first-order polynomials. Arranging in negative powers of z and allowing for $a_0 = 2$, we have

$$H_1(z) = \frac{1 - z^{-1}}{1 + 0.5z^{-1}} \tag{5-32}$$

and

$$H_2(z) = \frac{1 + 1.4142136z^{-1} + z^{-2}}{1 - 0.9z^{-1} + 0.81z^{-2}} \tag{5-33}$$

The realization is shown in Fig. 5-10.

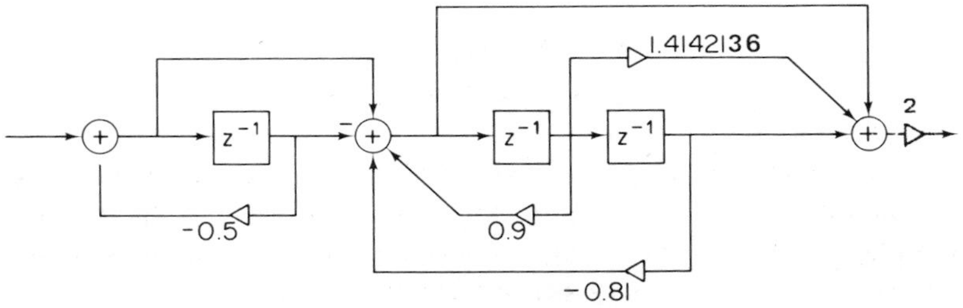

Figure 5-10 Realization for system of Ex. 5-3.

Example 5-4

Develop a parallel realization for the system of Ex. 5-3.

Solution

The development is best achieved by expanding $H(z)/z$ in a partial fraction expansion. In some cases, it appears that less labor is involved by expanding $H(z)/z$ in a complete partial fraction breakdown involving all poles separately and then recombining certain of the pole pairs (especially complex conjugate pairs) into second-order functions. In other cases, it may be simpler to retain portions of the expansion having complex conjugate poles in their second-order polynomial forms. No general guidelines may be given on this point since it depends, to some extent, on individual preferences.

We will follow the approach here of maintaining the two complex poles in the form of a second-degree polynomial in the expansion, which reads

$$\frac{H(z)}{z} = \frac{2(z-1)(z^2+1.4142136z+1)}{z(z+0.5)(z^2-0.9z+0.81)}$$
$$= \frac{A_1}{z} + \frac{A_2}{z+0.5} \quad \frac{A_3 z + A_4}{z^2 - 0.9z + 0.81} \tag{5-34}$$

The constants A_1 and A_2 can be determined by the usual partial fraction procedure for first-order poles, but A_3 and A_4 must be determined in a different fashion. One way this can be achieved is to simply choose some non-singular values of z and substitute on both sides of (5-34) to yield a series of simultaneous linear equations.

Following the preceding steps, we first determine that $A_1 = -4.9382716$ and $A_2 = 2.1571915$. Placing these two values in (5-34), we next seek some simple values of z to substitute in the equation. The values $z = 1$ and z

= -1 seem suitable. After some simplification, substitution of these values results in the following simultaneous equations:

$$\begin{aligned} A_3 + A_4 &= 3.1851310 \\ -A_3 + A_4 &= -6.3770293 \end{aligned} \tag{5-35}$$

Solution of (5-35) yields $A_3 = 4.7810802$ and $A_4 = -1.5959492$. After substituting these values in (5-34), the proper form of the expansion is obtained by multiplying both sides by z and rearranging in negative powers. Note that A in (5-20) corresponds to A_1 in (5-34). The parallel functions are

$$A = -4.9382716 \tag{5-36}$$

$$H_1(z) = \frac{2.1571915}{1 + 0.5z^{-1}} \tag{5-37}$$

$$H_2(z) = \frac{4.7810802 - 1.5959492z^{-1}}{1 - 0.9z^{-1} + 0.81z^{-2}} \tag{5-38}$$

The system realization is shown in Fig. 5-11.

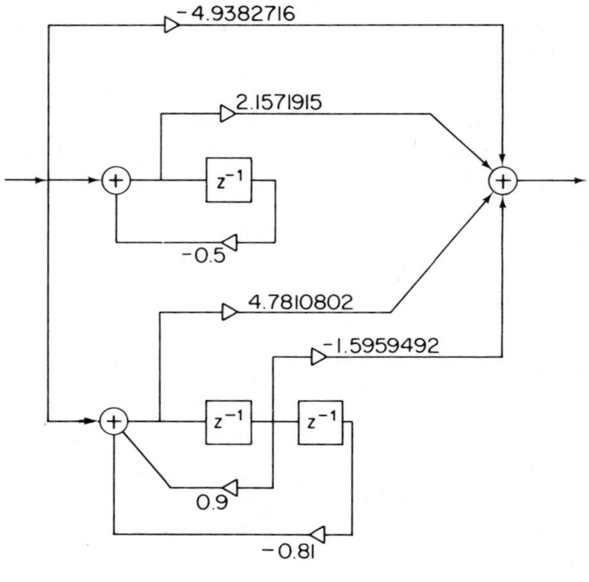

Figure 5-11 Realization for system of Ex. 5-4.

5-5 Steady-State Frequency Response Concepts

As in the case of continuous-time systems, the most important special case of interest for discrete-time systems is probably the steady-state response due to a sinusoidal input. In this case, the input sinusoid is a sequence of samples representing points on the sinusoidal curve.

In order for the steady-state response to have meaning, it is necessary that the system be perfectly stable; i.e., all poles must lie inside the unit circle. In this case, the steady-state output will be a sampled sinusoid of the same frequency as the input sinusoid. Thus, it is necessary to determine only the magnitude and phase of the output.

Assume that the input is of the form

$$x(n) = X\epsilon^{j(n\omega T + \phi_x)} \tag{5-39}$$

where ω is the radian frequency, f is the cyclic frequency, and $\omega = 2\pi f$. We may specify either the real or the imaginary part depending on whether we desire a cosine or a sine input. Letting $y(n)$ represent the *steady-state* response in this case, it will be of the form

$$y(n) = Y\epsilon^{j(n\omega T + \phi_y)} \tag{5-40}$$

We need only determine Y and ϕ_y to complete the solution.

Taking the z-transform of (5-39) and multiplying by the discrete transfer function $H(z)$, the output transform is given by

$$Y(z) = \frac{zX\epsilon^{j\phi_x}}{z - \epsilon^{j\omega T}} H(z) \tag{5-41}$$

Inversion of the steady-state portion only of (5-41) yields

$$y(n) = H(\epsilon^{j\omega T})\, X\epsilon^{j(n\omega T + \phi_x)} \tag{5-42}$$

Substitution of (5-40) in (5-42) and cancellation of the exponential factors yield

$$Y\epsilon^{j\phi_y} = H(\epsilon^{j\omega T})\, X\epsilon^{j\phi_x} \tag{5-43}$$

The input and output variables may now be expressed as phasors.

$$\overline{X} = X\epsilon^{j\phi_x} \triangleq X\underline{/\phi_x} \tag{5-44}$$

$$\overline{Y} = Y\epsilon^{j\phi_y} \triangleq Y\underline{/\phi_y} \tag{5-45}$$

We then have

$$\overline{Y} = H(\epsilon^{j\omega T})\,\overline{X} \tag{5-46}$$

or

$$\frac{\overline{Y}}{\overline{X}} = H(\epsilon^{j\omega T}) \tag{5-47}$$

The quantity $H(\epsilon^{j\omega T})$ represents the *steady-state* or *Fourier transfer function* for a discrete-time system. While a single frequency has been assumed in the preceding development, the result can now be generalized by considering ω as a variable. The function obtained describes the *frequency response* of the system, and this can be expressed in complex form as

$$H(\epsilon^{j\omega T}) = A_0(f)\, \epsilon^{j\beta_0(f)} = A_0(f)\underline{/\beta_0(f)} \tag{5-48}$$

The function $A_0(f)$ is called the *amplitude* or *magnitude response* and $\beta_0(f)$ is called the *phase response*. (The subscripts are used at this point because the forms of these functions will be modified later in the section.) Normally, $A_0(f)$ is simply the magnitude of the complex function $H(\epsilon^{j\omega T})$, but there are a few situations in which the amplitude response is permitted to assume negative values. Both the amplitude and phase are real functions of frequency.

The steady-state transfer function for the discrete-time system is simply the z-domain transfer function evaluated for $z = \epsilon^{j\omega T}$. Moreover, since $\epsilon^{j\omega T}$ is a periodic function with period $\omega T = 2\pi$, then $H(\epsilon^{j\omega T})$ is also periodic. The conventional forms for complex number representations lead to the conditions that $A_0(f)$ is an *even* function of frequency, and $\beta_0(f)$ is an *odd* function of frequency. These properties result in the constraint that the behavior of $H(\epsilon^{j\omega T})$ in the range of $\pi < \omega T < 2\pi$ is uniquely related to the behavior in the range $0 < \omega T < \pi$. Thus, the maximum unambiguous positive value for ωT is π. This corresponds to the *folding* frequency f_0 since $2\pi f_0 T = \pi$ or

$$f_0 = \frac{1}{2T} = \frac{f_s}{2} \tag{5-49}$$

Because of the importance of the folding frequency f_0 in establishing the frequency limits in a discrete-time system, this author has found it extremely convenient to normalize all frequencies with respect to the folding frequency in practical problem solutions. We will define a *normalized frequency variable* ν as

$$\nu = \frac{f}{f_0} = 2Tf \tag{5-50}$$

where f is any particular frequency of interest.

The quantity ωT can be expressed in terms of the normalized frequency as

$$\omega T = \pi \frac{f}{f_0} = \pi\nu \tag{5-51}$$

Similarly, the quantity $H(\epsilon^{j\omega T})$ can be expressed in either of the forms

$$H(\epsilon^{j\omega T}) = H(\epsilon^{j\pi(f/f_o)}) = H(\epsilon^{j\pi\nu}) \tag{5-52}$$

The notation expressed in (5-51) and (5-52) will be used freely in subsequent work, and these different forms will be interchanged when desirable.

As ωT varies over the range $0 \leqslant \omega T \leqslant 2\pi$, the normalized frequency varies over the range $0 \leqslant \nu \leqslant 2$, so the period on the normalized scale is 2 units. As previously explained, the frequency response is unique over only half this range. Thus, the highest normalized frequency at which the response is unambiguous is $\nu = 1$, and this value corresponds to the folding frequency.

The amplitude and phase functions can now be expressed in terms of ν. The functions will be denoted as $A(\nu)$ and $\beta(\nu)$, and they are defined as

$$\begin{aligned} A(\nu) &= A_0(f) \\ \beta(\nu) &= \beta_0(f) \end{aligned} \tag{5-53}$$

Thus, the form of the steady-state transfer function that will be used in most subsequent work is

$$H(\epsilon^{j\pi\nu}) = A(\nu)\underline{/\beta(\nu)} \tag{5-54}$$

The general form of a representative amplitude response expressed in terms of ν is shown in Fig. 5-12. (Most of the negative frequency range is not shown.) In many of the problems in the text, we will display the frequency response only in the range $0 \leqslant \nu \leqslant 1$, since this is the range of practical interest.

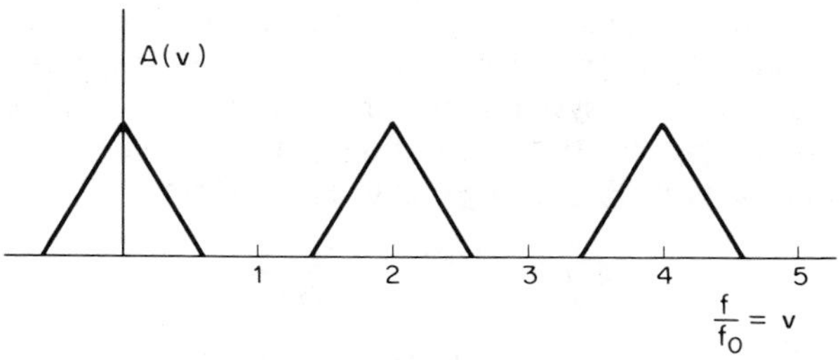

Figure 5-12 General form for amplitude response of discrete-time system.

A discrete-time sinusoidal signal may also be expressed in terms of its normalized frequency. Consider a function of the form

$$x(n) = A \sin(n\omega_1 T + \theta) \tag{5-55}$$

Let $f_1 = \omega_1/2\pi$ represent the cyclic frequency of the sinusoid, and let $\nu_1 = f_1/f_0$. We will leave as an exercise for the reader (Prob. 5-6) to show that $x(n)$ can be expressed as

$$x(n) = A \sin(n\pi\nu_1 + \theta) \tag{5-56}$$

As in continuous-time systems, it is often desirable to express the amplitude response in terms of a *decibel* (dB) level relative to some reference value. Let A_r represent any arbitrary reference level. The decibel amplitude response $A_{db}(\nu)$ can be defined as

$$A_{db}(\nu) = 20 \operatorname{Log}_{10} \frac{A(\nu)}{A_r} \tag{5-57}$$

In most of our work, the reference level used will be $A_r = 1$. Thus, relative to a reference level of unity, the decibel response is

$$A_{db}(\nu) = 20 \operatorname{Log}_{10} A(\nu) = 10 \operatorname{Log}_{10} A^2(\nu) \tag{5-58}$$

The form of the decibel response in (5-58) is expressed in the sense of a *gain*. This means that if $A(\nu) > 1$, the decibel level is positive, but if $A(\nu) < 1$, the decibel level is negative. In some cases, particularly for filter functions having $A(\nu) \ll 1$ over a wide range of frequencies, it may be more convenient to express the amplitude response as a positive *attenuation* or *loss*. Using a reference value of unity again, the decibel attenuation or loss function $\alpha_{db}(\nu)$ can be defined as

$$\alpha_{db}(\nu) = 20 \operatorname{Log}_{10} \frac{1}{A(\nu)} = -20 \operatorname{Log}_{10} A(\nu) = -A_{db}(\nu) \tag{5-59}$$

In the case of the attenuation function, a positive decibel value indicates that the output is lower than the input; i.e., some attenuation has taken place.

Some additional definitions pertaining to the steady-state frequency response of discrete-time systems are the *phase delay* and *group delay*. Momentarily returning to the phase function $\beta_0(f)$ given in (5-48), the definitions of phase delay $T_p(f)$ and group delay $T_g(f)$ are

$$T_p(f) = \frac{-d\beta_0(f)}{\omega} = \frac{-\beta_0(f)}{2\pi f} \tag{5-60}$$

$$T_g(f) = \frac{-d\beta_0(f)}{d\omega} \quad \frac{-1}{2\pi} \frac{d\beta_0(f)}{df} \tag{5-61}$$

We may now define the *normalized phase delay* $\gamma_p(\nu)$ and the *normalized group delay* $\gamma_g(\nu)$ as

$$\gamma_p(\nu) = \frac{-\beta(\nu)}{\nu} \tag{5-62}$$

$$\gamma_g(\nu) = \frac{-d\beta(\nu)}{d\nu} \tag{5-63}$$

(Different types of symbols are used here because these functions are dimensionless.) The definitions given by (5-62) and (5-63) are those that would be used directly in dealing with a frequency response function expressed in terms of the normalized frequency ν. However, while the actual levels of the amplitude and phase functions are not affected by the scaling change involved with using the normalized frequency, the phase and group delay functions are affected. We will leave as an exercise for the reader to show (Prob. 5-7) that the actual phase and group delay functions are related to the normalized functions by

$$T_p(f) = \frac{\gamma_p(\nu)}{2\pi f_0} = \frac{T}{\pi}\gamma_p(\nu) \tag{5-64}$$

and

$$T_g(f) = \frac{\gamma_g(\nu)}{2\pi f_0} = \frac{T}{\pi}\gamma_g(\nu) \tag{5-65}$$

where f_0 is the folding frequency, T is the sampling interval, and $\nu = f/f_0$.

Definitions for the phase and group delay functions for continuous-time systems were given in Chapt. 2, and a discussion of the practical significance of these quantities will be given in Chapt. 6. The discussion there applies equally well to the corresponding functions for a discrete-time system, so we will postpone further consideration of these concepts until then.

Example 5-5

(a) Determine the frequency response (amplitude and phase) for the system described by the difference equation

$$y(n) = 0.5y(n-1) + x(n) + x(n-1) \tag{5-66}$$

(b) For a sampling frequency of 1 kHz, determine the *steady-state* output for an input sine wave with an amplitude of 10 and a frequency of 100 Hz.

Solution

(a) The transfer function is readily determined from (5-66) as

$$H(z) = \frac{Y(z)}{X(z)} = \frac{1 + z^{-1}}{1 - 0.5z^{-1}} \tag{5-67}$$

The folding frequency is $f_0 = 1000/2 = 500$ Hz. For convenience, the normalized frequency variable will be used. For any actual frequency f, the normalized frequency ν is

$$\nu = \frac{f}{500} \tag{5-68}$$

The steady-state transfer function is obtained by substitution of $\epsilon^{j\pi\nu}$ into (5-67). This yields

$$H(\epsilon^{j\pi\nu}) = \frac{1 + \epsilon^{-j\pi\nu}}{1 - 0.5\epsilon^{-j\pi\nu}} \tag{5-69}$$

This expression must be converted into the form of a magnitude and a phase. This could always be done by expanding the numerator and denominator into their real and imaginary parts and applying the basic rules of complex number manipulations. In some cases, a clever rearrangement of numerator and denominator polynomials may lead to groupings in which trigonometric functions may be identified. However, this latter approach seems to develop with experience, so we will postpone it until some later examples. Expressing numerator and denominator polynomials of (5-69) in real and imaginary parts we have

$$H(\epsilon^{j\pi\nu}) = \frac{1 + \cos \pi\nu - j\sin \pi\nu}{1 - 0.5 \cos \pi\nu + j0.5 \sin \pi\nu} \tag{5-70}$$

For convenience, the amplitude response will be expressed in squared form. From (5-70), we have

$$A^2(\nu) = \frac{(1 + \cos \pi\nu)^2 + (-\sin \pi\nu)^2}{(1 - 0.5 \cos \pi\nu)^2 + (0.5 \sin \pi\nu)^2} \tag{5-71}$$

and

$$\beta(\nu) = \tan^{-1}\left[\frac{-\sin \pi\nu}{1 + \cos \pi\nu}\right] - \tan^{-1}\left[\frac{0.5 \sin \pi\nu}{1 - 0.5 \cos \pi\nu}\right] \tag{5-72}$$

If desired, these results can be simplified by the use of standard trigonometric identities. We will leave as exercise for the interested reader (Prob. 5-8) to show that (5-71) and (5-72) can be expressed as

$$A^2(\nu) = \frac{2 + 2\cos \pi\nu}{1.25 - \cos \pi\nu} \tag{5-73}$$

and

$$\beta(\nu) = -\tan^{-1}\left(3\tan \frac{\pi\nu}{2}\right) \tag{5-74}$$

(b) The normalized frequency of the input signal is $\nu_1 = 100/500 = 0.2$. The amplitude and phase evaluated at this frequency are obtained from (5-73) and (5-74) as

$$\begin{aligned} A(0.2) &= 2.864345 \\ \beta(0.2) &= -44.26770^\circ \\ &= -0.77261712 \text{ rad} \end{aligned} \tag{5-75}$$

The phase angle of the input sine wave will be assumed to be zero, so that the signal can be expressed as

$$\begin{aligned} x(n) &= 10 \sin 36n^\circ \qquad &\text{(angle in degrees)} \\ &= 10 \sin (0.2\pi n) \qquad &\text{(angle in radians)} \end{aligned} \tag{5-76}$$

The output *steady-state* signal is

$$\begin{aligned} y(n) &= 28.64345 \sin (36n^\circ - 44.26770^\circ) \\ &\qquad \text{(angle in degrees)} \\ &= 28.64345 \sin (0.2\pi n - 0.77261712) \\ &\qquad \text{(angle in radians)} \end{aligned} \tag{5-77}$$

For the sake of illustration, the arguments of the functions in (5-76) and (5-77) have been expressed both in terms of *radians* and *degrees*. Either form can be used as long as *all* terms are expressed in the same units *and* it is understood what units are involved.

Example 5-6

Determine general expressions for the amplitude and phase of the system of Example 4-9.

Solution

The transfer function is

$$H(z) = \frac{1 + z^{-1}}{1 + 0.1z^{-1} - 0.2z^{-2}} \tag{5-78}$$

The steady-state transfer function is

$$H(\epsilon^{j\pi\nu}) = \frac{1 + \epsilon^{-j\pi\nu}}{1 + 0.1\epsilon^{-j\pi\nu} - 0.2\epsilon^{-2j\pi\nu}} \tag{5-79}$$

$$= \frac{1 + \cos \pi\nu - j\sin \pi\nu}{(1 + 0.1 \cos \pi\nu - 0.2 \cos 2\pi\nu) + j(-0.1 \sin \pi\nu + 0.2 \sin 2\pi\nu)}$$

$$= \frac{A_1 + jA_2}{B_1 + jB_2}$$

where A_1 and A_2 are the real and imaginary parts of the numerator and B_1 and B_2 are the real and imaginary parts of the denominator. In terms of these quantities, the amplitude and phase are

$$A(\nu) = \sqrt{\frac{A_1^{\ 2} + A_2^{\ 2}}{B_1^{\ 2} + B_2^{\ 2}}} \tag{5-80}$$

and

$$\beta(\nu) = \tan^{-1} \frac{A_2}{A_1} - \tan^{-1} \frac{B_2}{B_1} \tag{5-81}$$

If the appropriate quantities are substituted in (5-80) and (5-81), the resulting expressions could eventually be reduced to simpler forms by the use of various trigonometric identities. However, since we are not interested in any final numerical results, we will leave the answer in the form developed.

The results of this problem illustrate that as the order of a transfer function increases, the form of the complex steady-state function $H(\epsilon^{j\pi\nu})$ becomes increasingly more difficult to express quickly and simply in the form of amplitude and phase functions. Furthermore, it is quite difficult to obtain much insight regarding the nature of the frequency response from the forms of these functions. On the other hand, a computer program may be readily written to evaluate the amplitude and phase functions for discrete transfer functions on a point-by-point basis. Since the only significant frequency range of interest is $0 \leqslant \nu \leqslant 1$, the frequency may be stepped through this range in as many points as desired in a loop, and the amplitude and phase can be calculated at each point.

Example 5-7

A programmable calculator is used to perform a smoothing or averaging process on a set of random measurements $x(n)$. As each measured value is received, the calculator computes a simple average of the four values consisting of the present measurement and the preceding three measurements. Calculate the frequency response corresponding to this operation.

Solution

Letting $y(n)$ represent the output of the calculator, the averaging algorithm can be expressed as

$$y(n) = \tfrac{1}{4}[x(n) + x(n-1) + x(n-2) + x(n-3)] \tag{5-82}$$

The transfer function corresponding to (5-82) is

$$H(z) = \frac{1 + z^{-1} + z^{-2} + z^{-3}}{4} \tag{5-83}$$

The steady-state transfer function is

$$H(\epsilon^{j\pi\nu}) = \frac{1 + \epsilon^{-j\pi\nu} + \epsilon^{-j2\pi\nu} + \epsilon^{-j3\pi\nu}}{4} \tag{5-84}$$

The series in (5-84) is a finite geometric series and can be expressed as

$$H(\epsilon^{j\pi\nu}) = \frac{1 - \epsilon^{-j4\pi\nu}}{4(1 - \epsilon^{-j\pi\nu})} \tag{5-85}$$

After several manipulations in (5-85), the following form results:

$$H(\epsilon^{j\pi\nu}) = \frac{(\epsilon^{j2\pi\nu} - \epsilon^{-j2\pi\nu})}{4(\epsilon^{j(\pi/2)\nu} - \epsilon^{-j(\pi/2)\nu})}\, \epsilon^{-j(3\pi/2)\nu} \tag{5-86}$$

This result can finally be expressed as

$$H(\epsilon^{j\pi\nu}) = \frac{\sin 2\pi\nu}{4\sin(\pi/2)\nu} \angle -\frac{3\pi\nu}{2} \tag{5-87}$$

The amplitude and phase functions are

$$A(\nu) = \frac{\sin 2\pi\nu}{4\sin(\pi\nu/2)} \tag{5-88}$$

$$\beta(\nu) = \frac{-3\pi}{2}\nu \tag{5-89}$$

The phase response is seen to be a linear function of frequency, and the delay can be computed as $T_g = T_p = 1.5T$. The form of the amplitude response given in (5-88), which was obtained by various manipulations used to express the result in the simplest trigonometric form, actually assumes negative values over certain ranges of ν(e.g. $0.5 < \nu < 1$).

The form of the function $|A(\nu)|$ over the range $0 \leqslant \nu \leqslant 1$ is shown in Fig. 5-13. Some insight into the averaging process can be deduced from this curve. Note that the overall response decreases as the frequency increases, indicating that the algorithm is functioning somewhat as a low-pass filter. This seems logical, since the averaging process is used to reduce random fluctuations that occur in the different values of measured data. Such fluctuations can be considered as "higher frequencies" so that they are suppressed by this process. On the other hand, it is assumed that the true value being sought by the measurements does not fluctuate as much over a longer period of time, and that it falls in the lower portion of the frequency range.

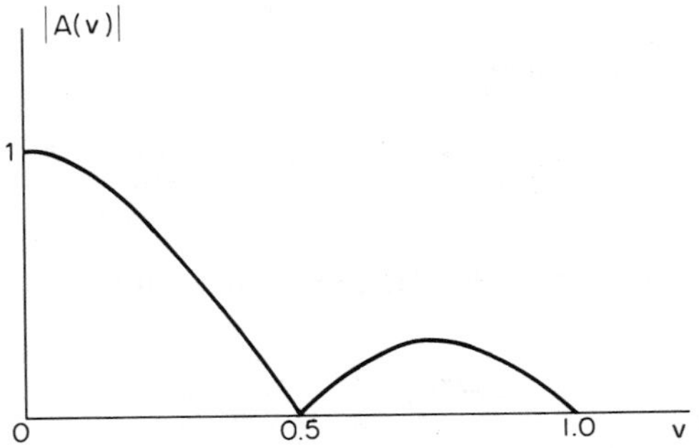

Figure 5-13 Amplitude response for averaging algorithm of Ex. 5-7.

5-6 Properties of the Amplitude Response

In this section, some useful properties of the amplitude response of a discrete-time system will be developed. These properties provide some insight into the general form of an amplitude response with reference to both the analysis and design of discrete-time systems.

The square of the magnitude of a complex number can be expressed as the product of the number and its complex conjugate. Using ~ to represent the complex conjugate, we can write

$$A^2(\nu) = |H(\epsilon^{j\pi\nu})|^2 = H(\epsilon^{j\pi\nu})\,\widetilde{H}(\epsilon^{j\pi\nu}) \tag{5-90}$$

where $H(z)$ is assumed to be stable. Although there are some special transfer functions in which the numerator and denominator coefficients a_i and b_i are permitted to be complex, we will restrict the consideration here to the case where all coefficients of $H(z)$ are real. In this case, the reader may wish to verify (Prob. 5-9) that

$$\widetilde{H}(\epsilon^{j\pi\nu}) = H(\epsilon^{-j\pi\nu}) \tag{5-91}$$

Substituting (5-91) in (5-90) yields

$$A^2(\nu) = H(\epsilon^{j\pi\nu})\,H(\epsilon^{-j\pi\nu}) \tag{5-92}$$

Since $H(\epsilon^{j\pi\nu})$ can be considered as $H(z)$ evaluated for $z = \epsilon^{j\pi\nu}$, (5-92) can be expressed in the form

$$A^2(\nu) = H(z)H(z^{-1})]_{z=\epsilon^{j\pi\nu}} \tag{5-93}$$

The function $H(z)H(z^{-1})$ has an interesting pole-zero pattern in the z-plane. For a given pole or zero of $H(z)$ at $z = z_i$, there will be a pole or zero of $H(z^{-1})$ at $z = 1/z_i$. Thus, the poles and zeros of $H(z)H(z^{-1})$ occur in pairs having an inverse relationship with respect to the unit circle. Since $H(z)$ is presently assumed to have only real coefficients, all complex poles and zeros of $H(z)$ occur in conjugate pairs. Thus complex poles and zeros of $H(z)H(z^{-1})$ will occur in symmetrical groups of four, and real poles and zeros will occur in groups of two. It can be shown (Prob. 5-10) that zeros on the unit circle occur in even multiplicity. We will assume that there are no poles of $H(z)$ on the unit circle since we are considering a stable system. Hence, there can be no poles of $H(z)H(z^{-1})$ on the unit circle.

The nature of this symmetry is illustrated for a typical case in Fig. 5-14. The integer *2* above the two unit circle zeros identifies them as second-order zeros.

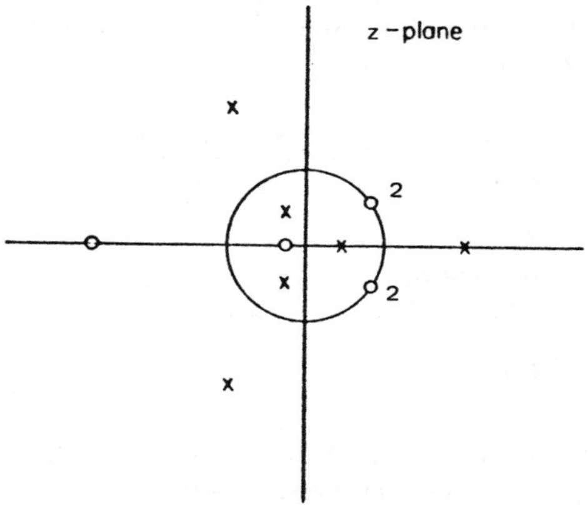

Figure 5-14 Typical pole-zero pattern for $H(z)H(z^{-1})$ illustrating symmetry involved.

The numerator and denominator polynomials resulting from the multiplication of $H(z)$ by $H(-z)$ display an interesting type of symmetry. Let $p(z)$ represent either a numerator or denominator polynomial. Expressed in positive powers of z, the degree of $p(z)$ will always be even, and the polynomial can be expressed as

$$\begin{aligned} p(z) = \; & c_k z^{2k} + c_{k-1} z^{2k-1} + \cdots + c_1 z^{k+1} + c_0 z^k \\ & + c_1 z^{k-1} + c_2 z^{k-2} + \cdots + c_{k-1} z + c_k \end{aligned} \tag{5-94}$$

where k is the degree of the original polynomial from which $p(z)$ is derived. Although the degree of $p(z)$ is $2k$, there are only $k + 1$ unique coefficients. The coefficients at the same distance on either side of c_0 are equal, and a symmetrical pattern thus exists about c_0. This type of polynomial is called a *mirror-image polynomial.*

The next step that we will perform is to multiply both sides of (5-94) by z^{-k} and rearrange the terms in symmetrical groups. This operation yields

$$\begin{aligned} z^{-k}p(z) &= c_0 + c_1(z + z^{-1}) + c_2(z^2 + z^{-2}) \\ &\quad + \cdots + c_k(z^k + z^{-k}) \end{aligned} \tag{5-95}$$

Letting $z = \epsilon^{j\pi\nu}$, we have

$$\begin{aligned} \epsilon^{-jk\pi\nu}p(\epsilon^{j\pi\nu}) &= c_0 + c_1(\epsilon^{j\pi\nu} + \epsilon^{-j\pi\nu}) + c_2(\epsilon^{j2\pi\nu} + \epsilon^{-j2\pi\nu}) \\ &\quad + \cdots + c_k(\epsilon^{jk\pi\nu} + \epsilon^{-jk\pi\nu}) \\ &= c_0 + 2c_1 \cos\pi\nu + 2c_2 \cos 2\pi\nu + \cdots + 2c_k \cos k\pi\nu \end{aligned} \tag{5-96}$$

We will assume that the degrees of the numerator and denominator polynomials of $H(z)$ are the same. Multiplication of $H(z)$ by $H(z^{-1})$ yields the following form for $A^2(\nu)$:

$$\begin{aligned} A^2(\nu) &= \frac{c_0 + c_1 \cos\pi\nu + \cdots + c_k \cos k\pi\nu}{d_0 + d_1 \cos\pi\nu + \cdots + d_k \cos k\pi\nu} \\ &= \frac{\sum_{i=0}^{k} c_i \cos i\pi\nu}{\sum_{i=0}^{k} d_i \cos i\pi\nu} \end{aligned} \tag{5-97}$$

The result of (5-97) provides some interesting insights into the amplitude response of a DTLTI system. From an analysis viewpoint, the amplitude response can always be expressed in this form if desired. Of course, trigonometric functions occur in a variety of different forms, so (5-97) is not the *only* way, or even necessarily the best way, in which to express a given amplitude response, but it is always a form that could be used when needed. From a synthesis viewpoint, this form could be used to produce a required amplitude response by determining the coefficients c_i and d_i in (5-97) properly. More will be said about this problem in later chapters.

Example 5-8

Using the procedure of this section, calculate the amplitude-squared response corresponding to the discrete transfer function

$$H(z) = \frac{z^2 + 1}{z^2 - 0.9z + 0.81} \tag{5-98}$$

Solution

As a first step, we form the product

$$\begin{aligned} H(z)H(z^{-1}) &= \left[\frac{z^2 + 1}{z^2 - 0.9z + 0.81}\right]\left[\frac{z^{-2} + 1}{z^{-2} - 0.9z^{-1} + 0.81}\right] \\ &= \frac{(z^2 + 1)(z^2 + 1)}{(z^2 - 0.9z + 0.81)(0.81z^2 - 0.9z + 1)} \\ &= \frac{z^4 + 2z^2 + 1}{0.81z^4 - 1.629z^3 + 2.4661z^2 - 1.629z + 0.81} \end{aligned} \tag{5-99}$$

It can be observed at this point that both the numerator and denominator polynomials of $H(z)H(z^{-1})$ are mirror-image polynomials as expected. If desired, the poles and zeros may be determined. The poles and zeros are

$$\begin{aligned} p_1 &= 0.45 + j0.779423 = 0.9\angle 60^\circ \\ p_2 &= 0.45 - j0.779423 = 0.9\angle -60^\circ \\ p_3 &= 0.555556 + j0.962250 = 1.111111\angle 60^\circ \\ p_4 &= 0.555556 - j0.962250 = 1.111111\angle -60^\circ \end{aligned} \tag{5-100}$$

$$\begin{aligned} z_1, z_2 &= j = 1\angle 90^\circ \text{ (2nd order)} \\ z_3, z_4 &= -j = 1\angle -90^\circ \text{ (2nd order)} \end{aligned} \tag{5-101}$$

Note that p_4 is the reciprocal of p_1, p_3 is the reciprocal of p_2, and z_3 and z_4 are the reciprocals of z_1 and z_2. Observe that the zeros on the unit circle occur in even multiplicity as expected.

The amplitude response is determined by multiplying numerator and denominator of (5-99) by z^{-2} and letting $z = \epsilon^{j\pi\nu}$. This yields

$$\begin{aligned} A^2(\nu) &= \frac{2 + \epsilon^{j2\pi\nu} + \epsilon^{-j2\pi\nu}}{2.4661 - 1.629(\epsilon^{j\pi\nu} + \epsilon^{-j\pi\nu}) + 0.81(\epsilon^{j\pi\nu} + \epsilon^{-j2\pi\nu})} \\ &= \frac{2 + 2\cos 2\pi\nu}{2.4661 - 3.258\cos \pi\nu + 1.62\cos 2\pi\nu} \end{aligned} \tag{5-102}$$

PROBLEMS

5-1 Draw a realization diagram for the system of Ex. 5-3 as a single direct from 1 section.

5-2 Draw a realization diagram for the system of Ex. 5-3 as a single direct form 2 section.

5-3 The partially factored form of a certain transfer function is given by

$$H(z) = \frac{4(1 - z^{-1})(1 - z^{-1} + z^{-2})}{(1 - 0.5z^{-1})(1 - 1.272792z^{-1} + 0.81z^{-2})}$$

Develop a cascade realization of the function using a first-order section and a second-order section.

5-4 Develop a parallel realization for the system of Prob. 5-3.

5-5 (a) Write a pair of difference equations relating $g(n)$ to $x(n)$ and $y(n)$ to $g(n)$ for the system of Fig. P5-5. (b) Obtain the transfer function $H(z) = Y(z)/X(z)$.

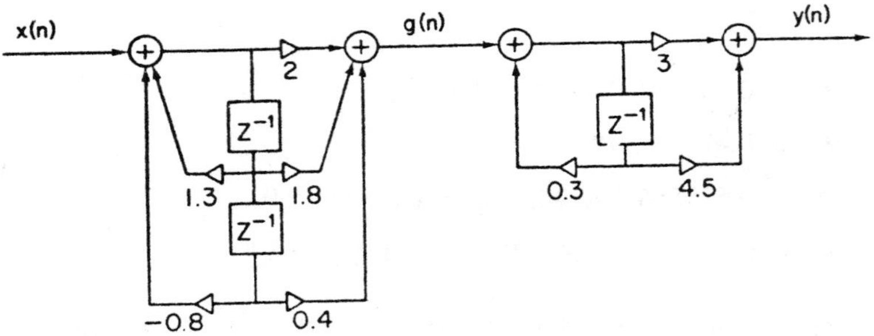

Figure P5-5

5-6 Show that equation (5-55) can be expressed in the form of equation (5-56).

5-7 Verify equations (5-64) and (5-65).

5-8 Show that the functions given in (5-71) and (5-72) can be expressed in the forms of (5-73) and (5-74).

5-9 Verify equation (5-91).

5-10 Show that the zeros of $H(z)H(z^{-1})$ on the unit circle occur in even multiplicity.

5-11 Determine the frequency response (amplitude and phase) for the system of Prob. 4-12.

5-12 Determine the frequency response (amplitude and phase) of the zero-order integrator of Prob. 4-13.

5-13 Determine the frequency response (amplitude and phase) of the first-order trapezoidal integrator of Prob. 4-14.

5-14 Determine the frequency response (amplitude and phase) of the simple averaging algorithm given by

$$y(n) = \frac{1}{2}[x(n) + x(n-1)]$$

5-15 Obtain the amplitude response of the function in Ex. 5-5 by the procedure of Sec. 5-6.

5-16 Obtain the amplitude response of the function in Ex. 5-6 by the procedure of Sec. 5-6.

5-17 Assume that the averaging algorithm in Ex. 5-7 is to be generalized to take the average of N measurements, which are to be the present and past N-1 values.

(a) Show that the amplitude and phase functions are

$$A(\nu) = \frac{\sin(N\pi\nu/2)}{N\sin(\pi\nu/2)}$$

$$\beta(\nu) = -(N-1)\pi\nu/2$$

(b) Sketch the general shape of $A(\nu)$ for some reasonably large value of N and compare with the case of N = 4 as given in Fig. 5-13.

REFERENCES

Most of the references listed at the end of Chapt. 4 are applicable to this chapter. The following additional references are given:

1. B. Gold and C. M. Rader, *Digital Processing of Signals*. New York: McGraw-Hill, 1969.

2. L. R. Rabiner and C. M. Rader, Eds. *Digital Signal Processing*. New York: IEEE Press, 1972.

CHAPTER SIX

PROPERTIES OF ANALOG FILTERS

6-0 Introduction

The purpose of this chapter is to present some of the more important general properties of continuous-time, linear, time-invariant filter characteristics. Because of widespread usage, the term *analog* will be freely used in reference to these characteristics. Although our ultimate goal is that of digital processing, analog filter functions are used extensively as prototype models for developing digital filters. Consequently, it is necessary to consider some of the more basic analog filter properties.

Primary emphasis in the chapter is directed toward functions that approximate the behavior of an ideal frequency-domain filter in terms of amplitude and/or phase. Several filter approximations will be discussed, and filter functions of the low-pass, band-pass, band-rejection, and high-pass varieties will be considered. Some useful design data, including tables of transfer function coefficients and curves for predicting the amplitude response of certain filters, will be presented.

6-1 Ideal Frequency-Domain Filter Models

Before considering any realistic filter characteristics, the properties of the ideal frequency-domain filter will be discussed. While such a filter is not realizable, the concept serves as a very useful reference model for comparing actual filter designs.

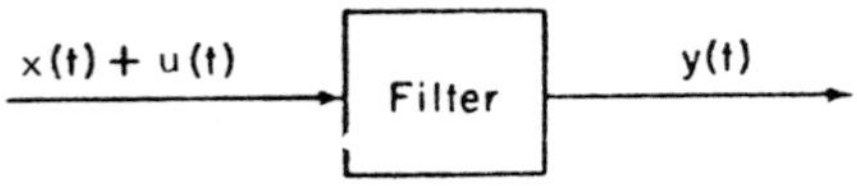

Figure 6-1 Block diagram of filter.

Consider the block diagram of a filter as illustrated in Fig. 6-1. Assume that the input can be expressed as $x(t)+u(t)$, where $x(t)$ represents a desired signal at the input and $u(t)$ represents an undesired signal (or composite of signals). The purpose of the filter is to eliminate $u(t)$ while preserving $x(t)$ as close to its original form as possible. The process of filtering requires a certain amount of delay and possible changes in the signal level, so the best we can hope for is that the output signal will be a delayed version of the original desired signal with a possible difference in amplitude, but with the correct shape preserved. Thus, the output of a distortionless filter can be expressed as

$$y(t) = Kx(t-\tau) \tag{6-1}$$

where K represents a level change and τ is the delay. This concept is illustrated in Fig. 6-2.

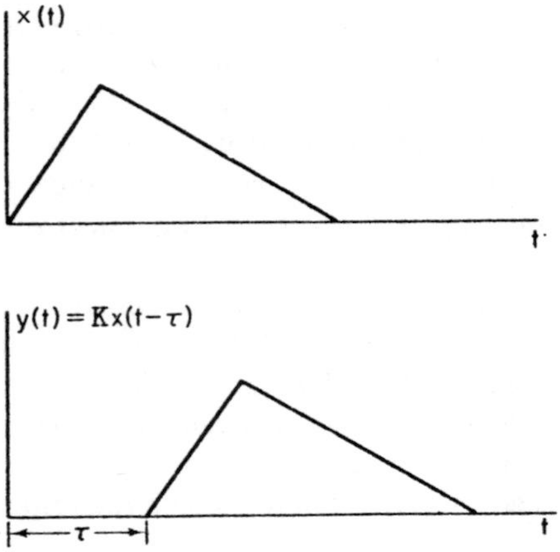

Figure 6-2 Input and output of distortionless filter.

The frequency domain interpretation of the ideal filter can be seen by taking the Fourier transforms of both sides of (6-1). This operation yields

$$Y(f) = K\epsilon^{-j\omega\tau} X(f) \tag{6-2}$$

Solving for the steady-state transfer function $G(j\omega)$, we obtain

$$G(j\omega) = K\epsilon^{-j\omega\tau} = K \underline{/-\omega\tau} \tag{6-3}$$

The amplitude response $A(f)$ and the phase response $\beta(f)$ are determined as

$$A(f) = K \tag{6-4}$$

$$\beta(f) = -\omega\tau \tag{6-5}$$

From these results, it can be seen that the amplitude response of the ideal filter should be constant and the phase response should be a linear function of frequency. However, these conditions apply only with respect to the frequency range of the desired signal $x(t)$. If the amplitude response were constant everywhere, the undesired signal would not be removed at all! To utilize the most basic form of frequency-domain filtering, it must be assumed that the spectrum of the undesired signal occupies a different frequency range than that of the desired signal, and the amplitude response must approximate zero in the frequency range of the undesired signal. The conclusion is that a distortionless frequency-domain filter should have constant amplitude response and linear phase response over the frequency band representing the spectrum of the desired signal. Outside this band, the amplitude response should drop toward zero as rapidly as possible, and the phase response in this range is usually unimportant. The frequency range in which a signal is transmitted through the filter is called the *passband*, and the frequency range in which a signal is rejected is called the *stopband*.

It can be shown that the attainment of both ideal constant amplitude and ideal linear phase is physically impossible in a practical filter. Furthermore, as the amplitude approximation is improved, the phase response often becomes poorer, and vice versa. However, it is possible to provide approximations that approach the ideal conditions sufficiently close to satisfy most applications, particularly if a relatively complex filter is permitted.

Practical filters are characterized by a *transition band* between the passband and the stopband. The exact locations of the boundaries of these different bands are somewhat arbitrary. The forms of the amplitude and phase characteristics of a filter having nearly ideal characteristics in the passband, but with a non-zero transition band, are illustrated in Fig. 6-3. The phase shift is often best represented as a negative quantity, so $-\beta(f)$ is shown for convenience.

In certain applications, the time delay of a signal passing through a filter is of more significance than the phase shift. It can be recalled that two definitions of delay functions were given in Chapt. 2. These were the *phase delay* T_p and the *group (or envelope) delay* T_g; the definitions are repeated here for convenience.

$$T_p(f) = \frac{-\beta(f)}{\omega} \tag{6-6}$$

$$T_g(f) = \frac{-d\beta(f)}{d\omega} \tag{6-7}$$

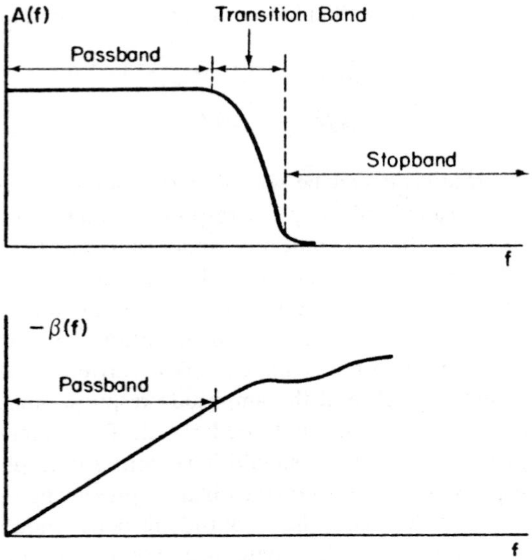

Figure 6-3 Amplitude and phase characteristics of a filter with ideal passband response.

The graphical significance of these definitions is illustrated in Fig. 6-4. It can be seen that the phase delay at a given frequency represents the slope of the secant line from dc to the particular frequency and is a sort of overall average delay parameter. The group delay at a given frequency represents the slope of the tangent line at the particular frequency and represents a local or narrow-range delay parameter.

Consider now the case of a filter with a constant-amplitude response and a linear-phase response as described by (6-4) and (6-5). It is readily seen that

$$T_p(f) = T_g(f) = \tau \tag{6-8}$$

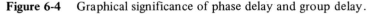

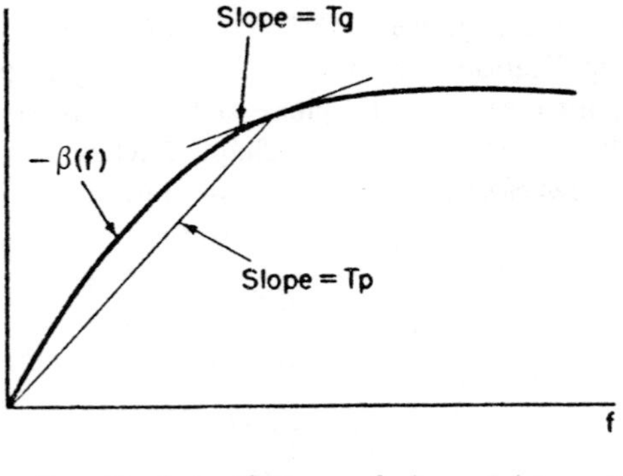

Figure 6-4 Graphical significance of phase delay and group delay.

For the ideal filter, the phase and group delays are identical and represent the exact delay of the signal, which has not been distorted in this case. In the general case where the amplitude response is not constant in the passband and the phase response is not linear, it is more difficult to precisely define the exact delay since a signal will undergo some distortion in passing through the filter. In fact, any attempt to define the exact delay will result in some variation of delay as different types of signals are applied to the filter. Nevertheless, the preceding definitions are quite useful in describing the approximate delay characteristics of a filter.

The phase delay parameter is often used to estimate the delay of a low-pass type signal, such as a basic pulse waveform, when it is passed through a low-pass filter. The phase delay is computed over the frequency range representing the major portion of the input signal spectrum. If the phase response does not deviate too far from linearity over the range involved, this value may represent a reasonable approximation to the actual delay of the waveform involved.

A case of significance involving both phase delay and group delay is that of a narrow-band modulated signal. It can be shown (Prob. 6-16) that when a narrow-band modulated signal is passed through a filter, the carrier is delayed by a time equal to the phase delay, while the envelope (or intelligence) is delayed by a time approximately equal to the group delay. Since the intelligence represents the desired information contained in such signals, strong emphasis on good group delay characteristics is often made in filters designed for processing modulated waveforms.

Returning to the ideal frequency-domain filter concept, it is convenient to consider several models representing the amplitude responses for various classes of filters as illustrated in Fig. 6-5. The four models shown are the *low-pass*, *high-pass,* *band-pass*, and *band-rejection* ideal frequency-domain amplitude functions. The corresponding ideal phase functions should be linear over the passband in each case. It should be emphasized again that these *exact* ideal functions are not physically realizable, but they may be approximated sufficiently close to meet engineering requirements.

So far, we have studied the ideal filter concept only from the frequency-domain point of view. An alternate, and often equally important, point of view is the time domain or transient behavior of the filter. From that standpoint, the ideal filter considered here exhibits significant ringing and overshoot. This property is caused by the finite discontinuity in the assumed ideal block amplitude characteristic. The form of the step-response of the ideal low-pass filter (with some assumed delay) is illustrated in Fig. 6-6. (See Prob. 6-18.) The actual transient response of a real filter results from a combination of both the amplitude and phase characteristics. As long as the phase response does not deviate too far from linearity, the transient response of a real filter will be superior to that of the ideal filter. Thus, while the ideal frequency-domain filter represents a goal which we constantly seek, it is not necessarily the best result we could achieve, particularly from the transient point of view.

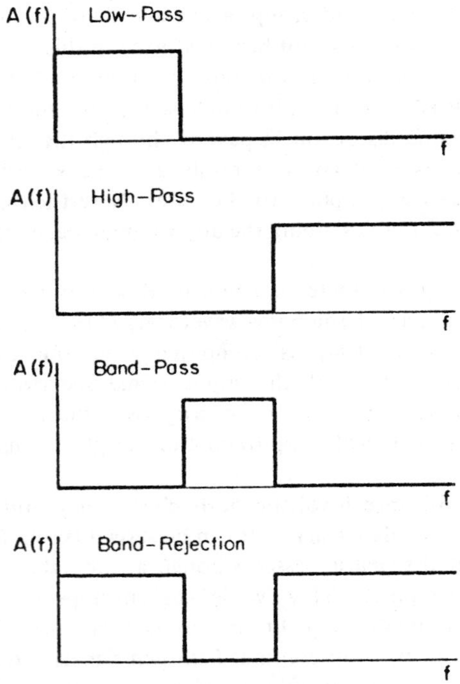

Figure 6-5 Ideal frequency-domain amplitude response models.

6-2 General Approaches

The treatment in this chapter will be devoted to a discussion of filters designed from CTLTI lumped system functions. The basic time-domain and frequency-domain properties of such systems were developed in Chapt. 2. The desired filter functions are obtained by determining an appropriate transfer

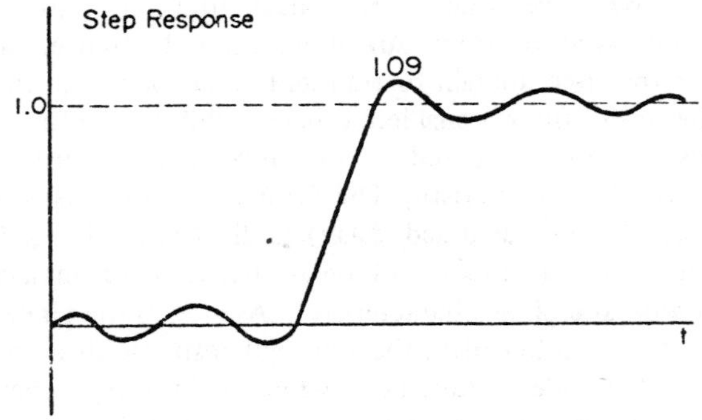

Figure 6-6 Step response of ideal frequency-domain low-pass filter.

function $G(s)$ whose frequency or time response meets the desired specifications. In actual analog filter design applications, it is necessary to realize the filter function in the form of a physical network. However, the principal purpose here is to consider only the approximation problem for analog filters, so we will devote primary attention to the problem of relating the prescribed amplitude and/or phase characteristics to the transfer function. Certain of the digital filter design procedures that will be developed in later chapters center around the concept of forcing the digital filter frequency response to closely approximate a reference analog response over a reasonable frequency range.

In general, it is necessary to convert a given set of design specifications into the form of a realizable transfer function. Fortunately, a number of very useful approximating functions and their associated realizations have been derived and tabulated. This permits the designer to use tables for many standard filter requirements.

The most common approach for representing a filter function, and the one in which we will concentrate primary emphasis, is to specify the amplitude response $A(f)$. It was shown in Chapt. 2 that the amplitude-squared function $A^2(f)$ can be expressed in the form

$$A^2(f) = G(s)G(-s)\big]_{s=j\omega} \tag{6-9}$$

Since $G(s)$ is a rational function and (6-9) is equivalent to multiplying a complex function by its conjugate, $A^2(f)$ can be expressed as a nonnegative rational function of ω^2 having the general form

$$A^2(f) = \frac{K(c_k\omega^{2k} + c_{k-1}\omega^{2k-2} + \cdots + c_0)}{(d_k\omega^{2k} + d_{k-1}\omega^{2k-2} + \cdots + d_0)} \tag{6-10}$$

Assume now that (6-10) is specified in a given application. How do we determine the $G(s)$ that corresponds to the given $A^2(f)$? In effect, this means that we have to go "backwards" to find a function $G(s)$ that when multiplied by $G(-s)$ and evaluated for $s = j\omega$ yields the given function. The key to this question is related to the s-plane interpretation of (6-9). Assume that a given critical frequency (either pole or zero) of $G(s)$ is located at $s = s_0$. The corresponding critical frequency of $G(-s)$ is located at $s = -s_0$. In the case of a critical frequency of $G(s)$ on the negative real axis, the corresponding critical frequency of $G(-s)$ is located on the positive real axis. In the case of a complex pair of critical frequencies of $G(s)$ located at $-a \pm jb$, the corresponding critical frequencies of $G(-s)$ are located at $a \mp jb$. Note that purely imaginary critical frequencies result in *double-order* roots. The behavior of these critical frequencies in the s-plane is displayed in Fig. 6-7. The resulting symmetrical pattern is said to have *quadrantal symmetry*. The exponent above the $j\omega$-axis zeros identifies them as second-order roots.

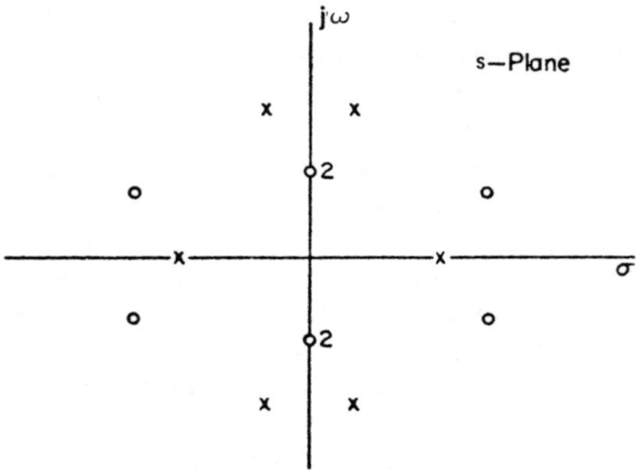

Figure 6-7 Pole-zero plot of G(s)G(−s) illustrating quadrantal symmetry.

From the s-plane plot, it is possible to associate the various critical frequencies with $G(s)$ and $G(-s)$. Any practical filter of interest will be stable. Consequently, its poles must lie in the left-hand half-plane. The poles in the left-hand half-plane may then be associated with $G(s)$, and those in the right-hand half-plane may be associated with $G(-s)$.

The association of the zeros is not always unique unless the transfer function is a *minimum-phase* type. For the minimum-phase type, all left-hand half-plane zeros are associated with $G(s)$ in the same manner as poles. For non-minimum phase systems, various other combinations involving both left and right-hand half-plane zeros of $G(s)$ and $G(-s)$ may be possible. In any event, the amplitude response is unaffected, but the phase will depend on the choice of zeros. Since non-minimum phase functions are used primarily in special filter applications involving phase or delay control, one is usually aware of those applications in which right-hand half-plane zeros are to be used.

The procedure for determining $G(s)$ from $A^2(f)$ may now be stated. From (6-9) it follows that

$$G(s)\,G(-s) = A^2(f)\big]_{\omega^2=-s^2} \qquad \text{(6-11)}$$

By substituting $\omega^2 = -s^2$, we obtain an s-plane function which has been shown to have quadrantal symmetry. The various poles and zeros are then determined by factoring the numerator and denominator polynomials of (6-11). Assuming that the transfer function is to be a minimum-phase form, the poles and zeros in the left-hand half-plane are assigned to $G(s)$. Any $j\omega$-axis zeros and poles must occur in even multiplicity, so that half of each conjugate set is assigned to $G(s)$. The gain constant is determined by comparing either the low-frequency or the high-frequency behavior of $A(f)$ with $G(s)$, depending on which pair is easier to use. The transfer function is determined by forming the numerator and denominator polynomials from the various zeros and poles and multiplying by the gain constant.

The heart of the approximation problem consists of determining the various constants in (6-10) so that the resulting amplitude function meets the desired specifications. In general, this is a difficult task, and there is usually no single unique solution. Because of simplicity, it is often convenient to use the *low-pass* filter as a basis for developing approximating functions. There are transformations available that permit one to "map" a low-pass form into either a band-pass, band-rejection, or high-pass form, and some of these transformations will be explored later in the chapter.

The simplest type of low-pass amplitude-squared function is one in which all zeros of $G(s)$ are located at $s = \infty$. In this case, (6-10) reduces to the form

$$A^2(f) = \frac{d_0}{d_0 + d_1\omega^2 + d_2\omega^4 + \cdots + d_k\omega^{2k}} \tag{6-12}$$

where the dc gain has been adjusted to unity. The low-pass functions that will be considered in more depth in this chapter are of this form.

At high frequencies, (6-12) reduces to

$$A^2(f) \approx \frac{d_0/d_k}{\omega^{2k}} \tag{6-13}$$

It can be readily shown that this corresponds to a $6k$ dB/octave (or a $20k$ dB/decade) attenuation rate. Of course, the response in the passband may have a variety of forms, and the actual level of the response in the stopband will depend on d_0 and d_k. Nevertheless, it is interesting to note that the high-frequency attenuation rate of any low-pass filter of order k, having all transmission zeros at infinity, will eventually become asymptotic to a curve with a slope of $-6k$ dB/octave (or $-20k$ dB/decade).

An additional point of significance before considering specific approximations is the concept of frequency normalization or scaling. The development of specific approximating functions or models is often enhanced by choosing a simple value such as $\omega = 1$ rad/s as a reference cutoff or center frequency. The final results may then be scaled to any particular desired frequency range. Most available design tables and charts have been developed using this normalized approach, and we will use it extensively in later sections.

Example 6-1

Determine the transfer function corresponding to the amplitude-squared function

$$A^2(f) = \frac{25(4 - \omega^2)^2}{(9 + \omega^2)(16 + \omega^2)} \tag{6-14}$$

Solution

The function satisfies the requirements for an amplitude-squared function since it is a rational non-negative function of ω^2, and the zeros on the $j\omega$-axis are of even multiplicity. We first replace ω^2 by $-s^2$ according to (6-11) and obtain

$$G(s)G(-s) = \frac{25(4 + s^2)^2}{(9 - s^2)(16 - s^2)} \tag{6-15}$$

The zeros of (6-15) are located at $s = \pm j2$ (second-order). The poles are located at $s = \pm 3$ and at ± 4. Selecting the left-hand half-plane poles, one pair of the imaginary-axis zeros, and a gain constant such as to make $G(0) = A(0)$, the required transfer function is

$$G(s) = \frac{5(s^2 + 4)}{(s + 3)(s + 4)} = \frac{5s^2 + 20}{s^2 + 7s + 12} \tag{6-16}$$

6-3 Butterworth Approximation

The first function that will be considered is the *Butterworth* or *maximally-flat* amplitude approximation. The Butterworth low-pass amplitude-squared function is defined by

$$A^2(f) = \frac{1}{1 + (\omega/\omega_c)^{2k}} = \frac{1}{1 + (f/f_c)^{2k}} \tag{6-17}$$

where k represents the order of the corresponding transfer function. The cyclic frequency f_c (or radian frequency $\omega_c = 2\pi f_c$) is defined as the "cutoff" frequency in (6-17). At this frequency, the amplitude response is $1/\sqrt{2}$ times the dc gain, and this corresponds to an attenuation of 3.01 dB. In most applications, this value is rounded off to 3 dB, and this assumption will be made in subsequent filter calculations. In many developments, it is convenient to normalize the frequency scale by selecting $\omega_c = 1$ rad/s in (6-17). The general form of a typical Butterworth amplitude response on a linear scale is illustrated in Fig. 6-8.

The Butterworth amplitude response can be shown to be optimum at dc in the maximally-flat sense. This means that the difference between the ideal amplitude response and the approximation and as many lower-order derivatives as possible are equated to zero at $\omega = 0$. (See Probs. 6-19 and 6-21). The Butterworth response is a monotonically decreasing function of frequency in the positive frequency range. As the order k increases, the response becomes

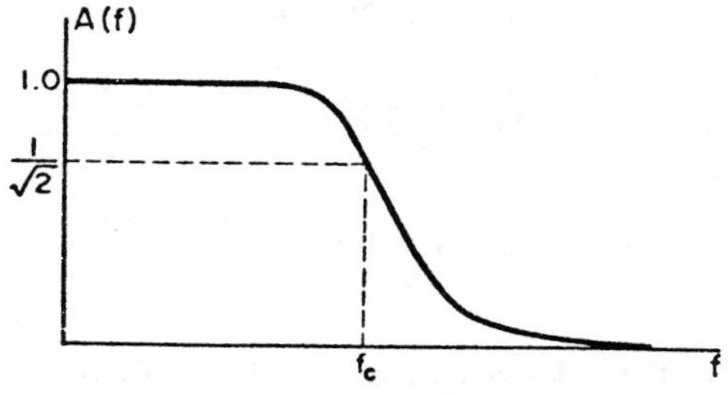

Figure 6-8 Form of the amplitude response of a Butterworth filter.

"flatter" in the passband, and the attenuation is greater in the stopband. Above cutoff, the Butterworth amplitude response of order k approaches a high-frequency asymptote having a slope of $-6k$ dB/octave.

Example 6-2

Derive the transfer function for the third-order Butterworth low-pass filter with $\omega_c = 1$ rad/s.

Solution

The amplitude-squared function is

$$A^2(f) = \frac{1}{1 + \omega^6} \tag{6-18}$$

Setting $\omega^2 = -s^2$, we have

$$G(s)G(-s) = \frac{1}{1 - s^6} \tag{6-19}$$

The poles of (6-19) are determined as follows:

$$\begin{aligned} s_1 &= 1 \angle 0^\circ &&= 1 \\ s_2 &= 1 \angle 60^\circ &&= \frac{1}{2} + j\frac{\sqrt{3}}{2} \\ s_3 &= 1 \angle 120^\circ &&= -\frac{1}{2} + j\frac{\sqrt{3}}{2} \end{aligned} \tag{6-20}$$

$$s_4 = 1 \angle 180^\circ = -1$$

$$s_5 = 1 \angle -120^\circ = -\frac{1}{2} - j\frac{\sqrt{3}}{2}$$

$$s_6 = 1 \angle -60^\circ = \frac{1}{2} - j\frac{\sqrt{3}}{2}$$

Notice that all of the poles lie on a circle. This is one of the characteristics of the Butterworth function. The transfer function is formed from the left-hand half-plane poles (s_3, s_4, and s_5) and is

$$G(s) = \frac{1}{s^3 + 2s^2 + 2s + 1} \tag{6-21}$$

6-4 Chebyshev Approximation

The next function that will be considered is the *Chebyshev* or *equiripple* amplitude approximation. This approximation is derived from the Chebyshev polynomials $C_k(x)$, which are a set of orthogonal functions possessing certain interesting properties. Some of the basic properties are: (a) The polynomials have equiripple amplitude characteristics over the range $-1 \leqslant x \leqslant 1$ with ripple oscillating between -1 and $+1$. (b) $C_k(x)$ increases more rapidly for $x > 1$ than any other polynomial of order k bounded by the limits stated in (a).

There are numerous other properties and variations of the Chebyshev polynomials which have been tabulated (ref. 7), but our purposes can be met by considering only a few. These polynomials can be derived from either of the equations

$$C_k(x) = \cos(k \cos^{-1} x) \tag{6-22}$$

or

$$C_k(x) = \cosh(k \cosh^{-1} x) \tag{6-23}$$

The form of (6-22) is most useful in the range $|x| < 1$, and (6-23) is most useful in the range $|x| > 1$. While neither (6-22) nor (6-23) appears to be a polynomial, it can be shown that these expressions can be expanded in polynomial form. The Chebyshev polynomials of orders one through six are listed in Table 6-1. The forms for the polynomials of orders two through five are illustrated in Fig. 6-9. The behavior for negative x is readily obtained by noted that $C_k(x)$ is even for k even, and it is odd for k odd.

K	$C_K(X)$
1	X
2	$2X^2-1$
3	$4X^3-3X$
4	$8X^4-8X^2+1$
5	$16X^5-20X^3+5X$
6	$32X^6-48X^4+18X^2-1$

Table 6-1 Several of the Chebyshev polynomials.

The basic Chebyshev amplitude response is defined by

$$A^2(f) = \frac{\alpha}{1+\epsilon^2 C_k{}^2(\omega/\omega_c)} = \frac{\alpha}{1+\epsilon^2 C_k{}^2(f/f_c)} \tag{6-24}$$

where k represents both the order of the Chebyshev polynomial and the order of the corresponding transfer function. The quantity ϵ^2 is a parameter chosen to provide the proper passband ripple, and α is a constant chosen to determine the proper dc gain level. The cyclic frequency f_c (or radian frequency ω_c) is defined as the "cutoff frequency", and its significance will be discussed shortly. The form of the Chebyshev amplitude response for k odd ($k = 3$ and 2 dB ripple) is illustrated in Fig. 6-10, and the form for k even ($k = 4$ and 2 dB ripple) is illustrated in Fig. 6-11.

Several properties of the Chebyshev amplitude response should be carefully noted. The passband is defined as the range over which the ripple is constrained to oscillate between constant bounds, i.e., the range from dc to f_c. The frequency f_c is the "cutoff frequency", and it is the highest frequency at which the response is governed by the passband ripple bound. Above f_c, the response moves into the transition band. The passband dB ripple (r) is defined by

$$r = 10 \operatorname{Log}_{10} \frac{A^2{}_{max}}{A^2{}_{min}} = 20 \operatorname{Log}_{10} \frac{A_{max}}{A_{min}} \tag{6-25}$$

where A_{max} is the maximum value of $A(f)$ and A_{min} is the minimum value of $A(f)$ within the passband.

The quantity ϵ^2 may be related to the passband ripple by utilizing (6-24) and (6-25). The maximum and minimum values of $A^2(f)$ are $A^2{}_{max} = \alpha$ and $A^2{}_{min} = \alpha/(1+\epsilon^2)$. The dB ripple is then given by

$$r = 10 \operatorname{Log}_{10} (1+\epsilon^2) \tag{6-26}$$

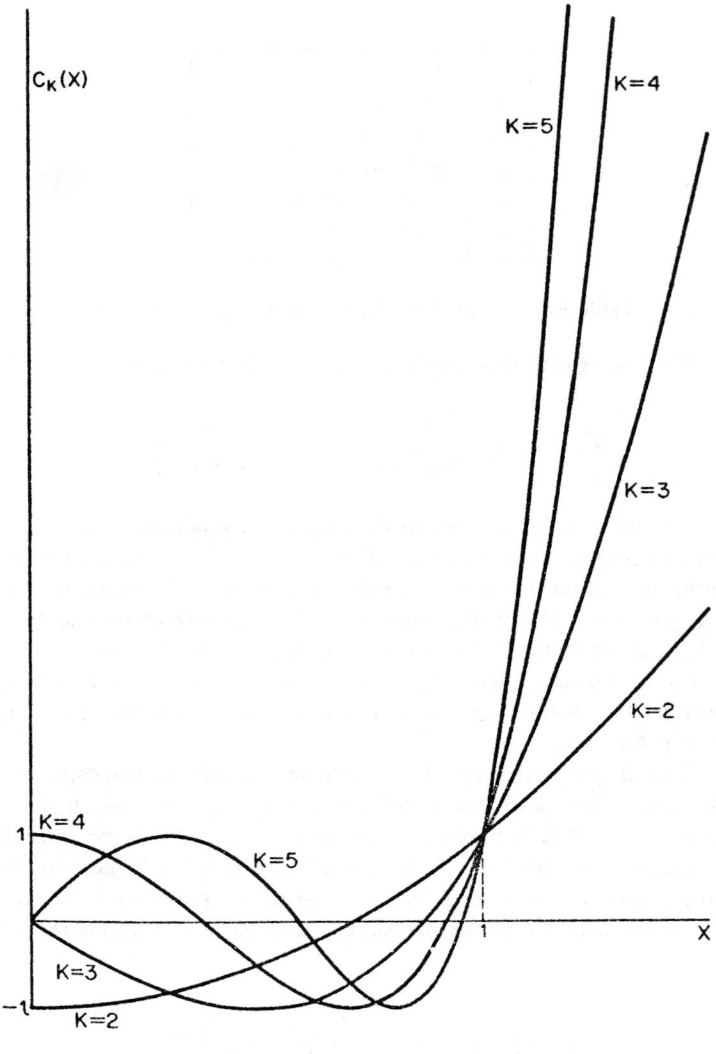

Figure 6-9 Forms for several of the Chebyshev polynomials.

or

$$\epsilon^2 = 10^{(r/10)} - 1 \tag{6-27}$$

The stopband attenuation at a given frequency will increase as the passband ripple is allowed to increase for a given number of poles. Thus, a Chebyshev design always represents a tradeoff between the allowable passband ripple and the desired attenuation in the stopband.

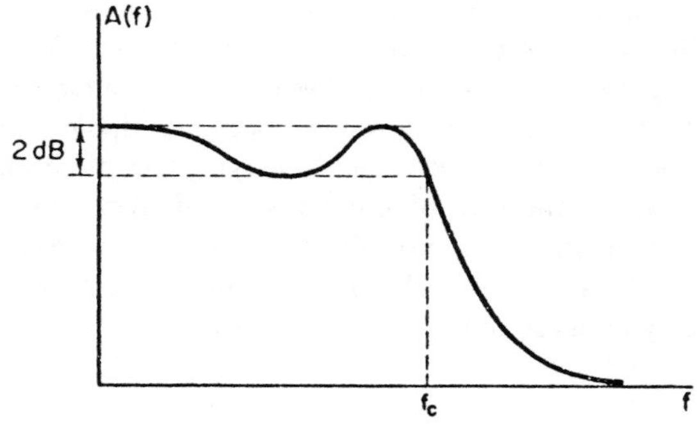

Figure 6-10 Chebyshev amplitude response for k=3 and 2 dB passband ripple.

The total number of maxima and minima in the passband is equal to the order k. For k odd, there is a maximum at $f = 0$, and if it is desired that the dc gain be unity, the numerator constant in (6-24) should be selected as $\alpha = 1$ in this case. On the other hand, for k even there is a minimum at $f = 0$, and the choice of α depends on additional considerations. If it is still desired that the dc gain be unity, it is left as an exercise for the reader (Prob. 6-7) to show that the gain constant should be selected to be $\alpha = 1 + \epsilon^2$. In this case, the gain at the maxima will be greater than unity. In some passive synthesis procedures, this condition poses certain constraints on the realization forms, but this fact is of no major consequence for our purposes.

In some cases, it is desirable that the maximum gain be adjusted to unity. This is accomplished by setting $\alpha = 1$ in (6-24). The gain at dc will now be less than unity for k even. This approach was used in determining the relative response curves given in Sec. 6-10, so it is important to recognize this fact when comparing the Chebyshev response curves in that section.

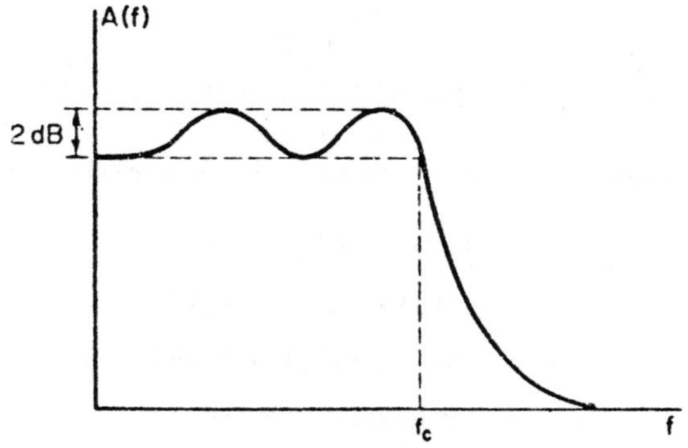

Figure 6-11 Chebyshev amplitude response for k=4 and 2 dB passband ripple.

The manner in which the cutoff frequency is defined for a Chebyshev filter is compatible with the Butterworth filter only for a 3 dB pass-band ripple. The Chebyshev definition is convenient because many filter specifications are stated in terms of a maximum allowable passband ripple over a particular frequency range, so the highest frequency satisfying this constraint is usually of primary interest. As in the case of the Butterworth function, the Chebyshev amplitude response of order k approaches a high-frequency asymptote having a slope of $-6k$ dB/octave. Also, the radian cutoff frequency ω_c is often normalized to unity in developing Chebyshev designs.

Example 6-3

Derive the transfer function for the second-order Chebyshev transfer function with 1 dB passband ripple, a normalized cutoff frequency $\omega_c = 1$ rad/s, and unity dc gain.

Solution

The required value of ϵ^2 is determined from (6-27) as

$$\epsilon^2 = 10^{0.1} - 1 = 0.25892541 \tag{6-28}$$

$C_2(x)$ is then obtained from Table 6-1 and substituted in (6-24) to yield

$$A^2(f) = \frac{1.2589254}{1.0357016\omega^4 - 1.0357016\omega^2 + 1.2589254} \tag{6-29}$$

where the numerator constant has been chosen to make the dc gain unity. Setting $\omega^2 = -s^2$, we have

$$G(s)G(-s) = \frac{1.2589254}{1.0357016s^4 + 1.0357016s^2 + 1.2589254} \tag{6-30}$$

The poles are determined from the roots of the denominator polynomial to be

$$\begin{aligned} s_1 &= 1.0500049\angle 58.484569^\circ \\ s_2 &= 1.0500049\angle 121.51543^\circ \\ s_3 &= 1.0500049\angle -121.51543^\circ \\ s_4 &= 1.0500049\angle -58.484569^\circ \end{aligned} \tag{6-31}$$

It can be shown that the poles of a Chebyshev polynomial lie on an ellipse. The transfer function is formed from the left-hand half-plane roots (s_2 and s_3), and the gain constant is again set to give unity gain at dc. The result is

$$G(s) = \frac{1.1025103}{s^2 + 1.0977343s + 1.1025103} \tag{6-32}$$

6-5 Survey of Other Approximations

In this section, a general survey of several other important analog filter frequency response approximations will be made. The actual details of these and other approximations are developed in the various texts on network synthesis listed in the references.

The Butterworth and Chebyshev functions were both obtained from approximations involving only the amplitude response, and no attention was paid to the phase response in either case. We will now consider the *maximally flat time-delay* (MFTD) approximation. The major characteristic of this function is that the group delay is made to be maximally-flat in the vicinity of dc.

The amplitude characteristic that results from the MFTD approximation has a low-pass shape with a monotonically decreasing behavior as the frequency is increased. However, the passband response is not as flat as for the Butterworth function, and the stopband attenuation is not as great at a given frequency as for either the Butterworth or the Chebyshev function of the same order. As the order k increases, the amplitude response of the MFTD approximation approaches the form of a Gaussian probability density function.

This author has seen variations of this filter referred to by each of the following names: Bessel filter, Gaussian filter, Thomson filter, Storch filter. The first name results from the fact that Bessel polynomials are used in the development of the approximation, and the second name refers to the property mentioned in the last paragraph. The last two names are those of investigators who made contributions to the development of the approximation.

The MFTD filter is used where excellent phase shift (or time delay) characteristics are required, but where the amplitude response need not display a rapid attenuation increase just above cutoff. As in the case of both the Butterworth and Chebyshev functions, the high-frequency attenuation rate of the MFTD filter will eventually approach $6k$ dB/octave, but the total attenuation will not be as great. The general form of the amplitude response is illustrated in Fig. 6-12.

The three filter functions considered thus far have all the zeros of transmission at infinity. Of these three types, the Chebyshev is normally considered to have the "best" amplitude response (more attenuation in the stopband for a given passband ripple bound) and the "poorest" phase response (most nonlinear). At the opposite extreme, the MFTD filter has the "best" phase response and the "poorest" amplitude response. The Butterworth filter represents a reasonable compromise between amplitude and phase. No doubt this is one of the reasons for its widespread popularity.

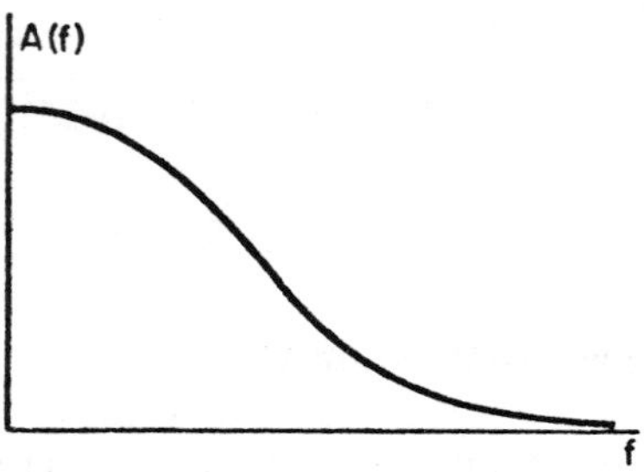

Figure 6-12 Form of the amplitude response for the maximally-flat time-delay filter.

Filter functions having all of the zeros of transmission at infinity have the limitation that infinite attenuation cannot be achieved at any finite frequency. In some cases, it may be desirable to provide a very large attenuation in the lower portion of the stopband. This can be accomplished by permitting the transfer function to contain one or more pairs of purely imaginary zeros. The attenuation in the neighborhood of such a zero can be made to increase very rapidly, thus providing the possibility of extremely sharp cutoff characteristics if the zeros are located properly.

The first function of this type that will be considered is the *inverted Chebyshev approximation*. (This function is sometimes called a Chebyshev type II response in contrast to the standard form, which could be called a Chebyshev type I response.) The amplitude-squared response for this approximation can be expressed in the form

$$A^2(f) = \frac{\epsilon^2 C_k{}^2(\omega_s/\omega)}{1 + \epsilon^2 C_k{}^2(\omega_s/\omega)} \tag{6-33}$$

The development of some of the properties of this function will be left as exercises for the reader (Probs. 6-22 through 6-26). It can be shown that this amplitude response has a maximally-flat characteristic at low frequencies (Prob. 6-22), but it has an equiripple nature in the stopband.

The form of the Chebyshev inverted amplitude response for k odd (k = 5 in this case) is illustrated in Fig. 6-13, and the form for k even (k = 4 in this case) is illustrated in Fig. 6-14. The cyclic frequency f_s (or radian frequency ω_s) defines the *beginning of the stopband* in this case. For $f > f_s$, the amplitude response oscillates between 0 and $\epsilon^2/(1 + \epsilon^2)$, meaning that the decibel attenuation oscillates between infinity and some finite large value, depending on the value of ϵ^2. For frequencies well above the highest infinite attenuation frequency, the amplitude response eventually becomes asymptotic to a curve with slope −6 dB/octave for k odd and to a constant finite level of attenuation for k even. (See Probs. 6-24 and 6-25.)

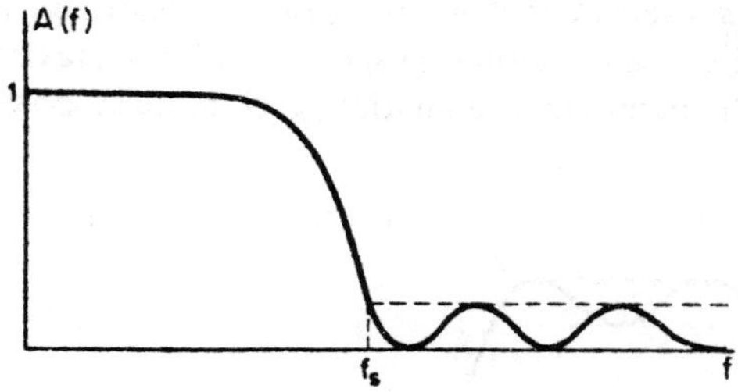

Figure 6-13 Form of the inverted Chebyshev amplitude response with k=5.

The last filter type that we will mention is the *Cauer or elliptic function* filter, which is characterized by equiripple response in both the passband and in the stopband. The general form of the low-pass amplitude-squared function is given by

$$A^2(f) = \frac{1}{1 + R_k^{\,2}(f)} \tag{6-34}$$

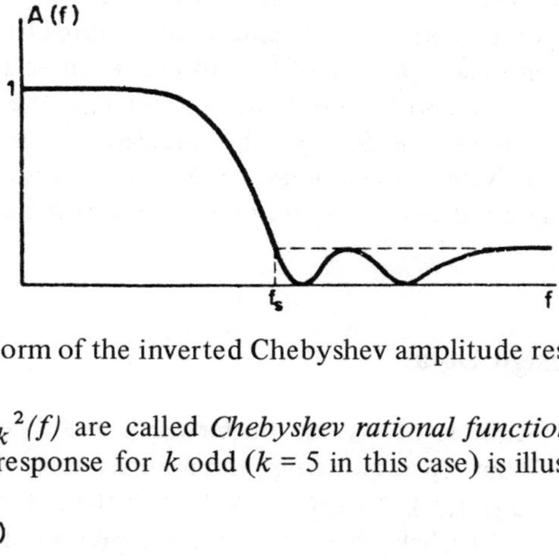

Figure 6-14 Form of the inverted Chebyshev amplitude response with k=4.

The functions $R_k^{\,2}(f)$ are called *Chebyshev rational functions*. The form of an elliptic function response for *k* odd (*k* = 5 in this case) is illustrated in Fig. 6-15,

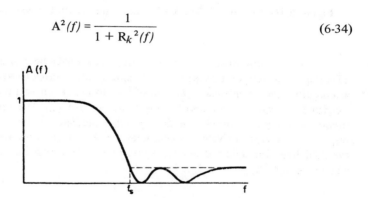

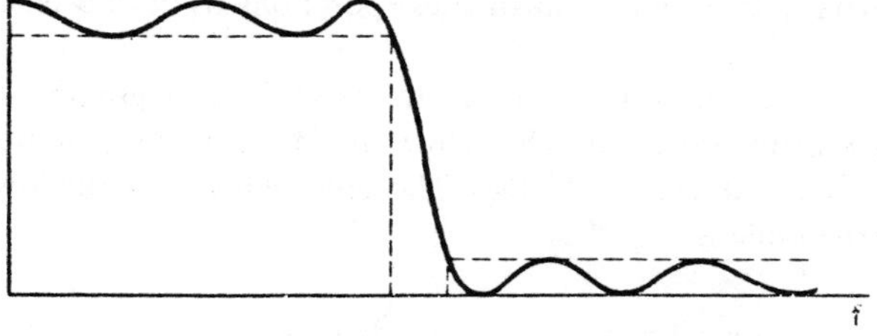

Figure 6-15 Form of the elliptic function amplitude response with k=5.

and the form for k even ($k = 4$ in this case) is illustrated in Fig. 6-16. With elliptic function filters, it is possible to specify both the maximum ripple level in the passband and the minimum attenuation level in the stopband.

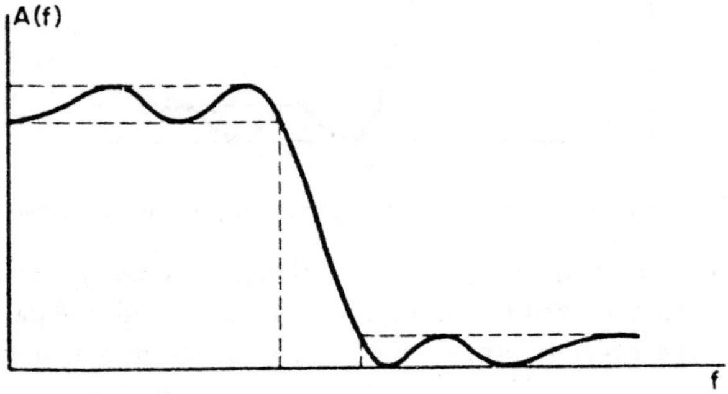

Figure 6-16 Form of the elliptic function amplitude response with k=4.

Filter functions with zeros on the $j\omega$-axis have been shown to offer the advantages of sharper transition bands and greater control over the minimum attenuation level in the lower portion of the stopband. These advantages must be weighted against certain disadvantages which are: (a) The resulting transfer functions are more complex with a possible increase in the sensitivity of the response to parameter value inaccuracies. (b) For a given number of poles, the eventual high-frequency attenuation rate will be less than that of filters having all zeros at infinity.

6-6 Filter Design Data

The pole locations of various Butterworth and Chebyshev filters and the coefficients of the corresponding polynomials have been derived and tabulated by Weinberg (ref. 9). An abbreviated set of the polynomial coefficients for the Butterworth and Chebyshev functions are presented here. In addition, and for convenience in developing certain types of digital filter designs later in the book, partially factored forms of these polynomials have been calculated and tabulated.

The polynomials are given in the basic form required for constructing the low-pass transfer function. The radian cutoff frequencies in both (6-17) and (6-24) are normalized to $\omega_c = 1$ rad/s. The general form for the low-pass transfer functions in the table is

$$G(s) = \frac{A_0}{B_0 + B_1 s + B_2 s^2 + \cdots + B_k s^k} \tag{6-35}$$

The denominator coefficients of (6-35) are tabulated in Table 6-2 for the Butterworth function and Chebyshev functions for four possible values of

Coefficients of Low–Pass Filter Denominator Polynomials.
(Note: Coefficients are Defined in Accordance with Equation 6–35.)

Order	B_0	B_1	B_2	B_3	B_4	B_5
			BUTTERWORTH			
1	1	1				
2	1	1.4142136	1			
3	1	2	2	1		
4	1	2.6131259	3.4142136	2.6131259	1	
5	1	3.2360680	5.2360680	5.2360680	3.2360680	1
		CHEBYSHEV 0.5 DB RIPPLE (ϵ^2 = 0.1220184)				
1	2.8627752	1				
2	1.5162026	1.4256245	1			
3	0.7156938	1.5348954	1.2529130	1		
4	0.3790506	1.0254553	1.7168662	1.1973856	1	
5	0.1789234	0.7525181	1.3095747	1.9373675	1.1724909	1
		CHEBYSHEV 1 DB RIPPLE (ϵ^2 = 0.2589254)				
1	1.9652267	1				
2	1.1025103	1.0977343	1			
3	0.4913067	1.2384092	0.9883412	1		
4	0.2756276	0.7426194	1.4539248	0.9528114	1	
5	0.1228267	0.5805342	0.9743961	1.6888160	0.9368201	1
		CHEBYSHEV 2 DB RIPPLE (ϵ^2 = 0.5848932)				
1	1.3075603	1				
2	0.6367681	0.8038164	1			
3	0.3268901	1.0221903	0.7378216	1		
4	0.2057651	0.5167981	1.2564819	0.7162150	1	
5	0.0817225	0.4593491	0.6934770	1.4995433	0.7064606	1
		CHEBYSHEV 3 DB RIPPLE (ϵ^2 = 0.9952623)				
1	1.0023773	1				
2	0.7079478	0.6448996	1			
3	0.2505943	0.9283480	0.5972404	1		
4	0.1769869	0.4047679	1.1691176	0.5815799	1	
5	0.0626391	0.4079421	0.5488626	1.4149847	0.5744296	1

(These results were Obtained from L.A. Weinberg, Network Analysis and Synthesis, McGraw–Hill, 1962, with permission of the author.)

Table 6-2 Coefficients of low-pass filter denominator polynomials. (Note: Coefficients are defined in accordance with equation 6-35.)

passband ripple (0.5 dB, 1 dB, 2 dB, and 3 dB). The orders of the filters used are from $k = 1$ through $k = 5$. More extensive data are available in Weinberg (ref. 9). If unity gain at dc is desired, the numerator constant is selected as $A_0 = B_0$.

Partially factored forms of the denominator polynomials of (6-35) are tabulated in Table 6-3. Letting $D(s)$ represent any one of the polynomials, the form of the transfer function is given by

$$G(s) = \frac{A_0}{D(s)} \tag{6-36}$$

The choice for A_0 follows the same logic discussed in the preceding paragraph.

In using the tables, it is important to remember that these functions are normalized with respect to a *radian frequency* of $\omega_c = 1$ rad/s, whereas most specifications are given in terms of *cyclic frequency*. As obvious as this may seem, a very common source of error in using such tables is the failure to convert properly between radian and cyclic frequencies in scaling to the required frequency range.

Order			
		BUTTERWORTH	
1	$(1 + s)$		
2		$(1 + 1.4142136s + s^2)$	
3	$(1 + s)$	$(1 + s + s^2)$	
4		$(1 + 0.7653668s + s^2)$	$(1 + 1.8477590s + s^2)$
5	$(1 + s)$	$(1 + 0.6180340s + s^2)$	$(1 + 1.6180340s + s^2)$
		CHEBYSHEV 0.5 DB RIPPLE	
1	$(2.8627752 + s)$		
2		$(1.5162026 + 1.4256244s + s^2)$	
3	$(0.6264565 + s)$	$(1.1424477 + 0.6264564s + s^2)$	
4		$(1.0635187 + 0.3507062s + s^2)$	$(0.3564119 + 0.8466796s + s^2)$
5	$(0.3623196 + s)$	$(1.0357841 + 0.2239258s + s^2)$	$(0.4767669 + 0.5862454s + s^2)$
		CHEBYSHEV, 1.0 DB RIPPLE	
1	$(1.9652267 + s)$		
2		$(1.1025104 + 1.0977344s + s^2)$	
3	$(0.4941706 + s)$	$(0.9942046 + 0.4941706s + s^2)$	
4		$(0.9865049 + 0.2790720s + s^2)$	$(0.2793981 + 0.6737394s + s^2)$
5	$(0.2894933 + s)$	$(0.9883149 + 0.1789168s + s^2)$	$(0.4292978 + 0.4684100s + s^2)$
		CHEBYSHEV 2.0 DB RIPPLE	
1	$(1.3075603 + s)$		
2		$(0.6367681 + 0.8038164s + s^2)$	
3	$(0.3689108 + s)$	$(0.8860951 + 0.3689108s + s^2)$	
4		$(0.9286753 + 0.2097744s + s^2)$	$(0.2215684 + 0.5064404s + s^2)$
5	$(0.218308s + s)$	$(0.9521670 + 0.1349220s + s^2)$	$(0.3931500 + 0.3532302s + s^2)$
		CHEBYSHEV 3.0 DB RIPPLE	
1	$(1.0023773 + s)$		
2		$(0.7079478 + 0.6448996s + s^2)$	
3	$(0.2986202 + s)$	$(0.8391740 + 0.2986202s + s^2)$	
4		$(0.9030867 + 0.1703408s + s^2)$	$(0.1959800 + 0.4112390s + s^2)$
5	$(0.1775085 + s)$	$(0.9360176 + 0.1097062s + s^2)$	$(0.3770008 + 0.2872148s + s^2)$

(These results are based on data obtained from L. A. Weinberg, <u>Network Analysis and Synthesis</u>, McGraw-Hill, 1962, with permission of the author.)

Table 6-3 Partially factored forms for low-pass filter denominator polynomials (Refer to equation 6-36.)

The process of scaling the filter functions obtained from the table to the required frequency range consists of a linear scale change on the frequency axis. All frequencies are scaled in direct proportion. For example, if the scale change is such that the normalized cutoff of 1 rad/s is scaled to a cyclic frequency of 10 kHz, the original normalized response at 3 rad/s corresponds to the final scaled response at 30 kHz.

Let ω_{rn} represent some reference radian frequency in the normalized response, and assume that the desired corresponding reference radian frequency in the scaled response is to be ω_r. Note that ω_r may or may not be the cutoff frequency of the normalized response, as the scaling can center around any particular frequency desired. Let $G(s)$ represent the normalized transfer function, and let $G_1(s)$ represent the final transfer function after scaling. The scaled transfer function is obtained by replacing s by $\omega_{rn}s/\omega_r$ in all terms of the original transfer function. Hence,

$$G_1(s) = G\left(\frac{\omega_{rn}s}{\omega_r}\right) \tag{6-37}$$

If desired, the subscript in $G_1(s)$ could now be dropped as long as it is understood that this function has been scaled to the correct frequency range.

Example 6-4

Determine the transfer function for a third-order low-pass Butterworth filter with a cutoff frequency of 1 kHz.

Solution

The normalized transfer function $G(s)$ is obtained from Table 6-2 and is

$$G(s) = \frac{1}{s^3 + 2s^2 + 2s + 1} \tag{6-38}$$

In this case, the reference frequency of the scaled function is the cutoff frequency, and it is $\omega_r = 2\pi f_r = 2\pi \times 10^3$ rad/s. The normalized reference frequency is, of course, $\omega_{rn} = 1$ rad/s. The final transfer function $G_1(s)$ is

$$G_1(s) = G\left(\frac{s}{2\pi \times 10^3}\right) \tag{6-39}$$

Application of (6-39) to (6-38) yields after some manipulation

$$G_1(s) = \frac{2.4805021 \times 10^{11}}{s^3 + 1.2566371 \times 10^4 s^2 + 7.8956835 \times 10^7 s + 2.4805021 \times 10^{11}} \tag{6-40}$$

6-7 Low-Pass to Band-Pass Transformation

A very popular procedure for designing band-pass filters involves the use of a low-pass to band-pass geometric transformation. Using this approach, a low-pass prototype transfer function is first derived, and by means of the transformation is converted to a band-pass function.

In developing the transformation and others that follow in this chapter, it will be necessary to use more than one Laplace complex variable, which has previously been denoted by s. We will reserve s and ω(or f) for the *final* Laplace and steady-state frequency variables of the desired function, whether it be low-pass, band-pass, band-rejection, or anything else. This means that when we start with a low-pass function and wish to convert it to another form, we will introduce one or more dummy variables in the process. This could be confusing to the reader where we start with data tabulated in the last section in terms of s and use a different variable than s in the initial formulation. Likewise, some reference frequency that was previously expressed in terms of ω will be expressed in terms of a new reference frequency variable.

The following notation will be employed in this section:

p = *low-pass* prototype Laplace variable
s = *band-pass* final Laplace variable
λ = steady-state radian frequency corresponding to p ($p = j\lambda$)
ω = steady-state radian frequency corresponding to s ($s = j\omega$)
$G_{\ell p}(p)$ = low-pass prototype transfer function
$G_{bp}(s)$ = band-pass final transfer function
λ_r = a particular low-pass prototype reference radian frequency (often the cutoff frequency λ_c)
f_r = $\lambda_r/2\pi$ = cyclic frequency corresponding to λ_r
ω_1 = lower radian frequency in band-pass function corresponding to $-\lambda_r$ in prototype
ω_3 = upper radian frequency in band-pass function corresponding to $+\lambda_r$ in prototype
ω_2 = geometric center radian frequency in band-pass function
f_1, f_2, f_3 = cyclic frequencies in band-pass function corresponding to ω_1, ω_2, and ω_3

The low-pass to band-pass transformation reads

$$p = \frac{s^2 + \omega_2{}^2}{s} \tag{6-41}$$

The steady-state nature of this transformation can be seen by letting $s = j\omega$ in (6-41). The resulting function for λ is everywhere purely imaginary, meaning that the imaginary axis of the s-plane maps to the imaginary axis of the p-plane. Setting $p = j\lambda$ and cancelling j's, a relationship is obtained between the two frequency variables.

$$\lambda = \frac{\omega^2 - \omega_2{}^2}{\omega} \tag{6-42}$$

$\omega = \omega_2 \Rightarrow \lambda = 0$
imaginary axis of p maps to itself in s

In terms of cyclic frequencies, (6-42) becomes

$$\frac{\lambda}{2\pi} = \frac{f^2 - f_2{}^2}{f} \tag{6-43}$$

The relationship of (6-42) is shown in Fig. 6-17 for positive ω. The low-pass frequency $\lambda = 0$ (dc) is mapped to $\omega = \omega_2$, $\lambda = +\lambda_r$ is mapped to $\omega = \omega_3$, and $\lambda = -\lambda_r$ is mapped to $\omega = \omega_1$. (The reader should not be disturbed by the apparent negative frequency, since this is primarily a "quirk" of the mathematical development. Actually, the amplitude response is usually considered as an even function of frequency extending over both positive and negative frequencies.)

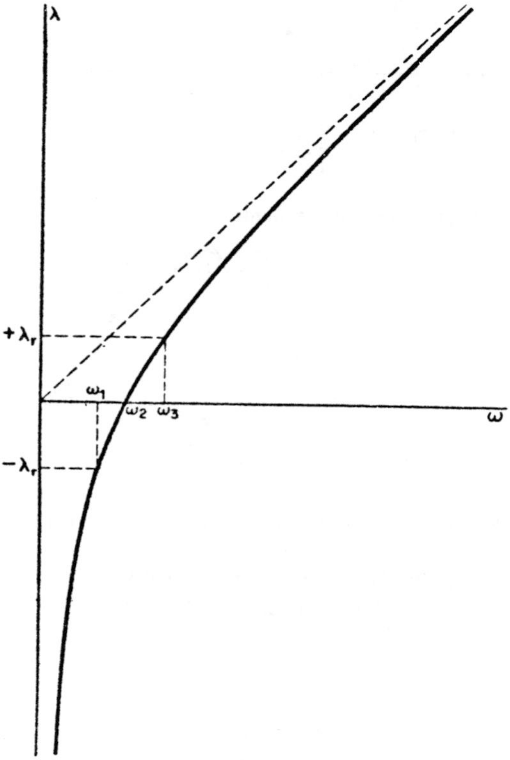

Figure 6-17 Steady-state frequency relationship for low-pass to band-pass transformation.

The effect of this transformation is that the original low-pass prototype amplitude response from dc to any reference frequency f_r is shifted to the range from f_2 to f_3. Since the amplitude response is even, this same response (from dc to $-f_r$) is also translated to the range from f_2 to f_1 in a reverse sense. If the translation were perfectly linear over the range from f_1 to f_3, the resulting band-pass response would display arithmetic symmetry, and the amplitude segments on either side of f_2 would be mirror images of each other. However, this is not the case since the transformation curve is not linear. In fact, the frequency interval from f_2 to f_3 is greater than the interval from f_1 to f_2. An illustration of the general form of the resulting band-pass function compared with the prototype low-pass function is shown in Fig. 6-18.

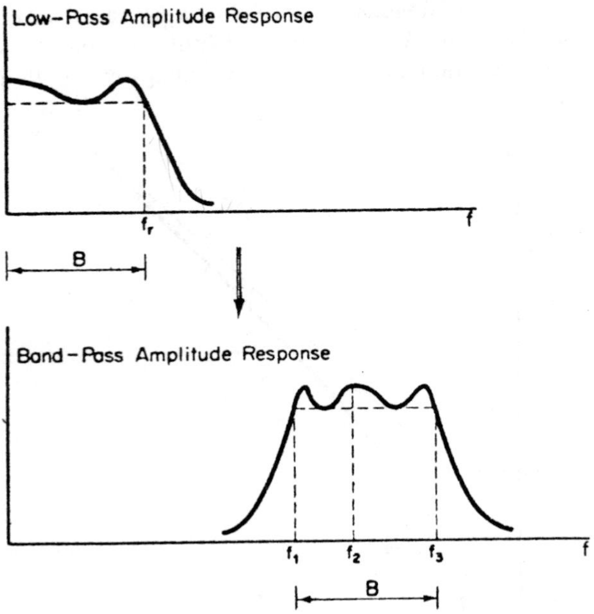

Figure 6-18 Effect of the low-pass to band-pass transformation.

Some interesting quantitative relationships governing transformation parameters can be deduced by relating f_r to f_3 and $-f_r$ to f_1. From (6-43), we have

$$f_r = \frac{f_3{}^2 - f_2{}^2}{f_3} \tag{6-44}$$

and

$$-f_r = \frac{f_1{}^2 - f_2{}^2}{f_1} \tag{6-45}$$

Alternate addition and subtraction of (6-44) and (6-45) and some simplification result in two important relationships

$$f_2 = \sqrt{f_1 f_3} \tag{6-46}$$

and

$$B = f_3 - f_1 = f_r \tag{6-47}$$

where the quantity B is defined as the *bandwidth* of interest in the bandpass filter. The first relationship implies that the band-pass response derived by this procedure will have *geometric symmetry* about the center frequency. Since f_1 and f_3 represent any arbitrary frequencies corresponding to a given reference low-pass frequency, this property of geometric symmetry holds with respect to any corresponding matched pair of frequencies on either side of the center frequency. The second relationship implies that any particular bandwidth of interest in the band-pass filter will be identical to the corresponding bandwidth of the low-pass filter, as long as this bandwidth is measured between the frequencies f_3 and f_1 at which the amplitude response corresponds to the low-pass response at f_r.

Practical utilization of the low-pass to band-pass transformation for determining a band-pass transfer function $G_{bp}(s)$ can be achieved as follows:

(a) Determine a low-pass transfer function $G_{\ell p}(p)$ in which the reference bandwidth f_r is equal to the desired band-pass bandwidth $B = f_3 - f_1$. This will usually require frequency scaling of the low-pass function if normalized design tables are used.

(b) Obtain the band-pass transfer function $G_{bp}(s)$ by substitution of the transformation of (6-41).

$$G_{bp}(s) = G_{\ell p}(p)]_{p = (s^2 + \omega_2{}^2)/s} \tag{6-48}$$

In general, if the low-pass prototype transfer function is of order k, the band-pass transfer function will be of order $2k$, and it will contain $2k$ finite poles. If all the k transmission zeros of the low-pass function are located at infinity, the band-pass function will also have k zeros at infinity, and, in addition, will have k zeros at the origin. At very low frequencies, the response is asymptotic to a curve with slope $+6k$ db/octave, and at very high frequencies, the response is asymptotic to a curve with slope $-6k$ dB/octave.

Example 6-5

Determine the transfer function of a band-pass filter having the following characteristics: (a) 4 poles, (b) Butterworth response, (c) geometric center frequency = 1 kHz, (d) 3 dB bandwidth = 200 Hz.

Solution

Since the band-pass function is to have 4 poles, the low-pass prototype function should have 2 poles. The low-pass normalized Butterworth function of order 2 is given by

$$G_{\ell p}(p) = \frac{1}{p^2 + 1.4142136p + 1} \tag{6-49}$$

The first step required is to change the frequency scale of (6-49) so that the cutoff frequency is equal to the desired bandwidth of the band-pass function, namely 200 Hz. This is achieved by replacing p in (6-49) by $p/(2\pi \times 200)$. The resulting function $G_{1\ell p}(p)$ is

$$G_{1\ell p}(p) = \frac{1.5791367\text{x}10^6}{p^2 + 1.7771532\text{x}10^3 p + 1.5791367\text{x}10^6} \tag{6-50}$$

The radian center frequency is $\omega_2 = 2\,\pi \times 10^3$, and the transformation is

$$p = \frac{s^2 + 3.9478418\text{x}10^7}{s} \tag{6-51}$$

Substitution of (6-51) in (6-50) yields the band-pass transfer function $G_{bp}(s)$.

$$G_{bp}(s) = \frac{1.5791367\text{x}10^6 s^2}{s^4 + 1.7771532\text{x}10^3 s^3 + 8.0535973\text{x}10^7 s^2 + 7.0159197\text{x}10^{10} s + 1.5585455\text{x}10^{15}} \tag{6-52}$$

6-8 Low-Pass to Band-Rejection Transformation

By simple inversion and a slight modification of a constant in the transformation of the last section, a new form can be obtained which permits the transformation from a low-pass function to a band-rejection function. The notation of the last section will be used again except for the following modifications:

(a) The Laplace variable s now represents the band-rejection function variable.

(b) The frequencies ω_1, ω_2, ω_3 now represent frequencies associated with the band of rejection.

(c) The lower radian frequency ω_1 now corresponds to $+\lambda_r$ in the prototype, and the upper radian frequency ω_3 now corresponds to $-\lambda_r$ in the prototype.

(d) The quantity $B = f_2 - f_1$ now represents the width of any rejection band of interest.

The actual transformation reads

$$p = \frac{\omega_2^2 s}{s^2 + \omega_2^2} \tag{6-53}$$

Letting $s = j\omega$ and $p = j\lambda$, it can be readily seen that the imaginary axis of the s-plane maps to the imaginary axis of the p-plane. Cancelling j's, we obtain the relationship between the frequency variables.

$$\lambda = \frac{\omega_2^2 \omega}{\omega_2^2 - \omega^2} \tag{6-54}$$

In terms of cyclic frequencies, (6-54) becomes

$$\frac{\lambda}{2\pi} = \frac{f_2^2 f}{f_2^2 - f^2} \tag{6-55}$$

The relationship of (6-54) is shown in Fig. 6-19 for positive ω. The low-pass frequency $\lambda = 0$ is mapped to $\omega = 0$ and $\omega = \infty$, and $\lambda = \pm\infty$ is mapped to $\omega = \omega_2$. The response at $\lambda = +\lambda_r$ maps to $\omega = \omega_1$, and the response at $\lambda = -\lambda_r$ maps to $\omega = \omega_3$.

The effect of the transformation is that the original low-pass prototype amplitude response from dc to any reference frequency f_r becomes the new response *outside* of the interval from f_1 to f_3. However, the response of the low-pass function above f_r (usually the low-pass stopband) becomes the new response in the interval from f_1 to f_3. An illustration of the general form of the resulting band-rejection function compared with the prototype low-pass function is shown in Fig. 6-20.

The reader is invited to derive (Prob. 6-17) the following two relationships:

$$f_2 = \sqrt{f_1 f_3} \tag{6-56}$$

$$B = f_3 - f_1 = \frac{f_2^2}{f_r} = \frac{f_1 f_3}{f_r} \tag{6-57}$$

The first relationship is identical with the corresponding relationship for the band-pass case. However, note that the second relationship implies that the width of any rejection band of interest B is *inversely proportional* to the reference bandwidth f_r of the low-pass prototype.

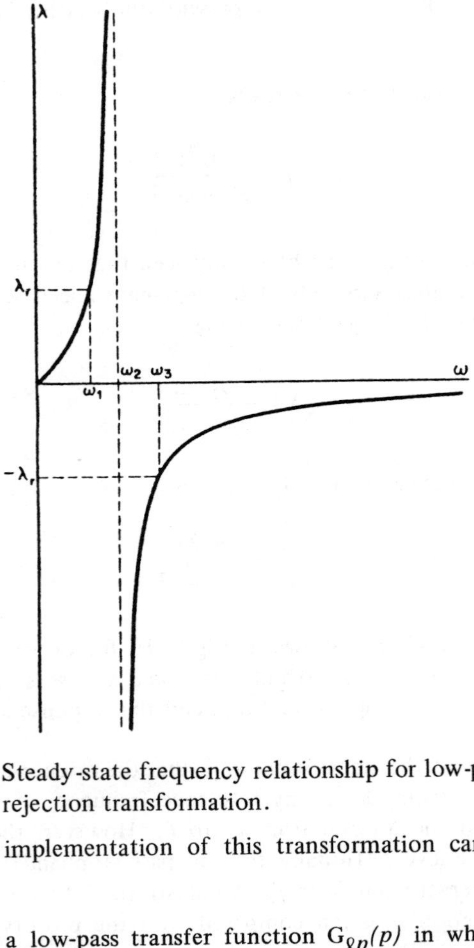

Figure 6-19 Steady-state frequency relationship for low-pass to band-rejection transformation.

Practical implementation of this transformation can be achieved as follows:

(a) Determine a low-pass transfer function $G_{\ell p}(p)$ in which the reference bandwidth f_r is inversely proportional to the desired width B of the rejection band according to (6-57). This will usually require frequency scaling of the low-pass function if normalized design tables are used.

(b) Obtain the band-rejection transfer function $G_{br}(s)$ by substitution of the transformation of (6-53).

$$G_{br}(s) = G_{\ell p}(p)\Big]_{p\,=\,\omega_2{}^2 s/(s^2 + \omega_2{}^2)} \tag{6-58}$$

In general, if the low-pass prototype transfer function is of order k, the band-rejection transfer function will be of order $2k$, and it will contain $2k$ poles. If all the zeros of the low-pass function are located at infinity, the band-rejection function will have $2k$ zeros on the $j\omega$-axis, corresponding to k purely imaginary pairs all located at $\pm j\omega_2$.

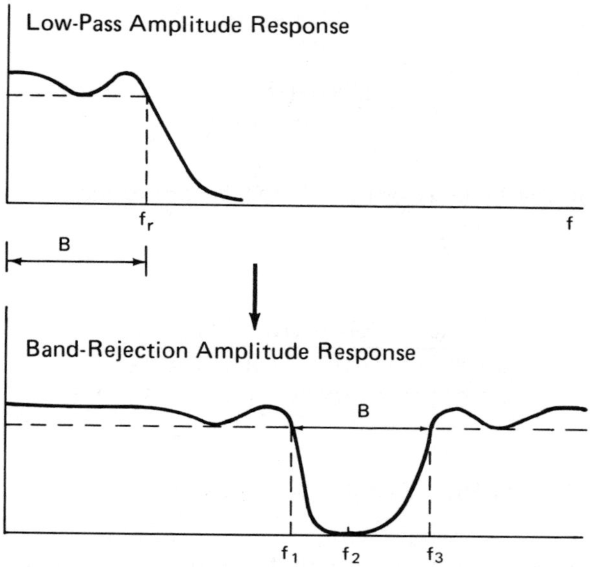

Figure 6-20 Effect of the low-pass to band-rejection transformation.

Example 6-6

Determine the transfer function of a band-rejection filter having the following characteristics: (a) 4 poles, (b) Butterworth response, (c) geometric center of rejection band = 1 kHz, (d) width of 3 dB rejection band = 200 Hz.

Solution

The low-pass prototype is a second-order Butterworth response which was given in (6-49) of Ex. 6-5. The reference frequency required in the low-pass prototype can be determined from (6-57) and is

$$f_r = \frac{(10^3)^2}{200} = 5 \times 10^3 \text{ Hz} \tag{6-59}$$

The low-pass prototype must then be scaled so that its 3 dB cutoff frequency is 5×10^3 Hz. This is achieved by replacing p by $p/(2\pi \times 5000)$, and the resulting function $G_{1\ell p}(p)$ is

$$G_{1\ell p}(p) = \frac{9.8696044 \times 10^8}{p^2 + 4.4428829 \times 10^4 p + 9.8696044 \times 10^8} \tag{6-60}$$

The transformation is

$$p = \frac{3.9478418 \times 10^7 s}{s^2 + 3.9478418 \times 10^7} \tag{6-61}$$

Substitution of (6-61) in (6-60) yields the band-rejection transfer function $G_{br}(s)$.

$$G_{br}(s) = \frac{(s^2 + 3.9478418 \times 10^7)^2}{s^4 + 1.7771532 \times 10^3 s^3 + 8.0535973 \times 10^7 s^2 + 7.0159196 \times 10^{10} s + 1.5585455 \times 10^{15}} \tag{6-62}$$

6-9 Low-Pass to High-Pass Transformation

In this section, a transformation for mapping a low-pass function to a high-pass function will be discussed. The following notation will be employed:

p = *low-pass* prototype Laplace variable
s = *high-pass* final Laplace variable
λ = steady-state radian frequency corresponding to $p (p = j\lambda)$
ω = steady-state radian frequency corresponding to $s (s = j\omega)$
$G_{\ell p}(p)$ = low-pass prototype transfer function
$G_{hp}(s)$ = high-pass transfer function
λ_r = a particular low-pass prototype reference radian frequency (often the cutoff frequency λ_c)
ω_r = radian frequency in high-pass function corresponding to λ_r in prototype.

The transformation reads

$$p = \frac{\lambda_r \omega_r}{s} \tag{6-63}$$

Letting $s = j\omega$, it can be seen that the imaginary axis of the s-plane maps to the imaginary axis of the p-plane. Letting $p = j\lambda$ and cancelling j's, a relationship can be obtained between the two frequency variables. It turns out that the negative imaginary axis of the s-plane corresponds to the positive imaginary axis of the p-plane and vice-versa. The relationship can be expressed as

$$\frac{\lambda}{\lambda_r} = \frac{-\omega_r}{\omega} \tag{6-64}$$

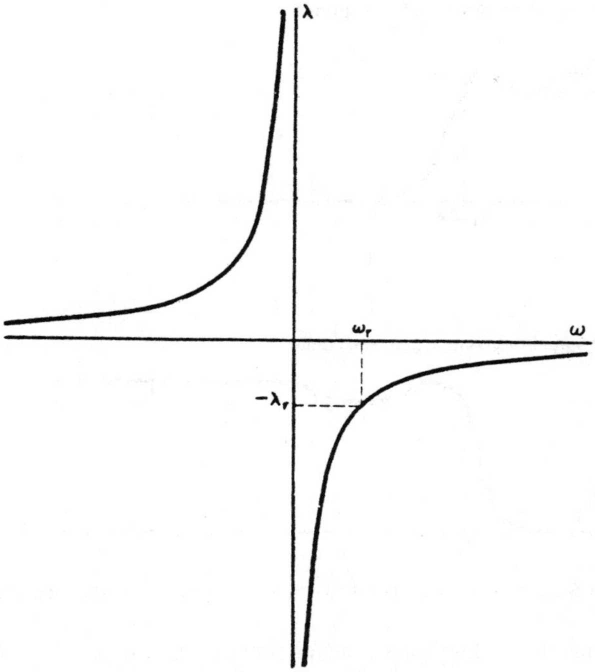

Figure 6-21 Steady-state frequency relationship for low-pass to high-pass transformation.

The form of (6-64) is shown in Fig. 6-21.

The low-pass frequency $\lambda = 0$ is mapped to $\omega = \infty$, and $\lambda = \infty$ is mapped to $\omega = 0$. The low-pass frequency $\lambda = -\lambda_r$ is mapped to $\omega = \omega_r$. The effect of this transformation is that the original low-pass prototype amplitude response from dc to any reference frequence λ_r is shifted to the high-pass range from ω_r to ∞ in a reverse sense. In many cases, the low-pass prototype is initially scaled in frequency so that $\lambda_r = \omega_r$. In this case, the low-pass passband width is equal to the high-pass stopband width. An illustration of the general form of the resulting high-pass function compared with the prototype low-pass function is shown in Fig. 6-22.

Practical implementation of the transformation for obtaining a high-pass transfer function can be achieved as follows:

(a) Determine a low-pass transfer function $G_{\ell p}(p)$, and specify the low-pass reference radian frequency λ_r at which the response is to correspond to the high-pass reference radian frequency ω_r.

(b) Obtain the high-pass transfer function $G_{hp}(s)$ by substituting the transformation of (6-63).

$$G_{hp}(s) = G_{\ell p}(p)\big]_{p = (\lambda_r \omega_r / s)} \tag{6-65}$$

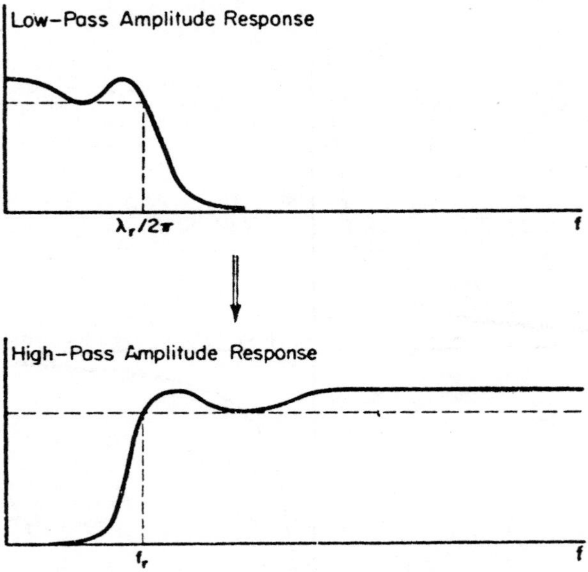

Figure 6-22 Effect of the low-pass to high-pass transformation.

In general, the high-pass transfer function will be of the same order as the low-pass prototype function. If all the zeros of transmission of the low-pass functions are located at $s = \infty$, then all the zeros of the high-pass function will be located at the origin. At very low frequencies, the slope of the amplitude response will then approach $6k$ dB/octave.

Example 6-7

Determine the transfer function of a high-pass transfer function having the following requirements: (a) 3 poles, (b) Butterworth response, (c) 3 dB lower cutoff frequency = 100 Hz.

Solution

The low-pass third-order Butterworth prototype response is given by

$$G_{\ell p}(p) = \frac{1}{p^3 + 2p^2 + 2p + 1} \tag{6-66}$$

The low-pass cutoff frequency $\lambda_r = 1$ rad/s must correspond to $\omega_r = 2\pi \times 100$ rad/s in the high-pass response. From (6-63), the transformation is

$$p = \frac{200\pi}{s} \tag{6-67}$$

Substitution of (6-67) in (6-66) yields the high-pass function

$$G_{hp}(s) = \frac{s^3}{s^3 + 1.2566371 \times 10^3 s^2 + 7.8956835 \times 10^5 s + 2.4805021 \times 10^8} \qquad (6\text{-}68)$$

6-10 Filter Response Curves

This section will be devoted to a presentation of the stopband amplitude responses of some of the filter types previously discussed. The filter functions considered are as follows: Butterworth, 0.5 dB Chebyshev, 1 dB Chebyshev, 2 dB Chebyshev, and 3 dB Chebyshev. These functions are shown in Figures 6-23 through 6-27 respectively. For each particular characteristic, curves

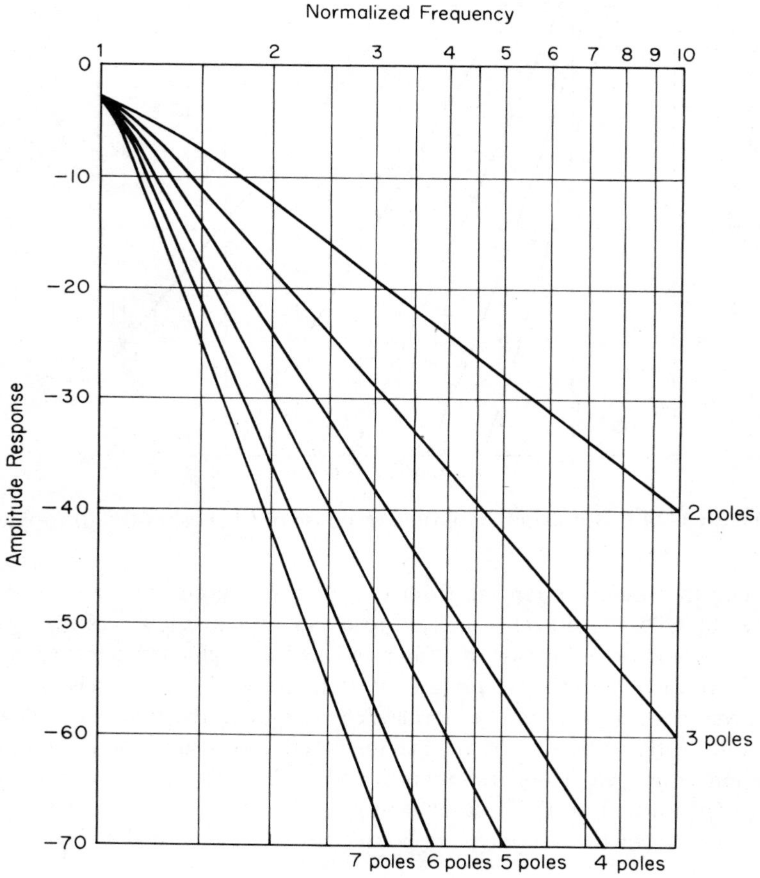

Figure 6-23 Stopband amplitude response of Butterworth filters.

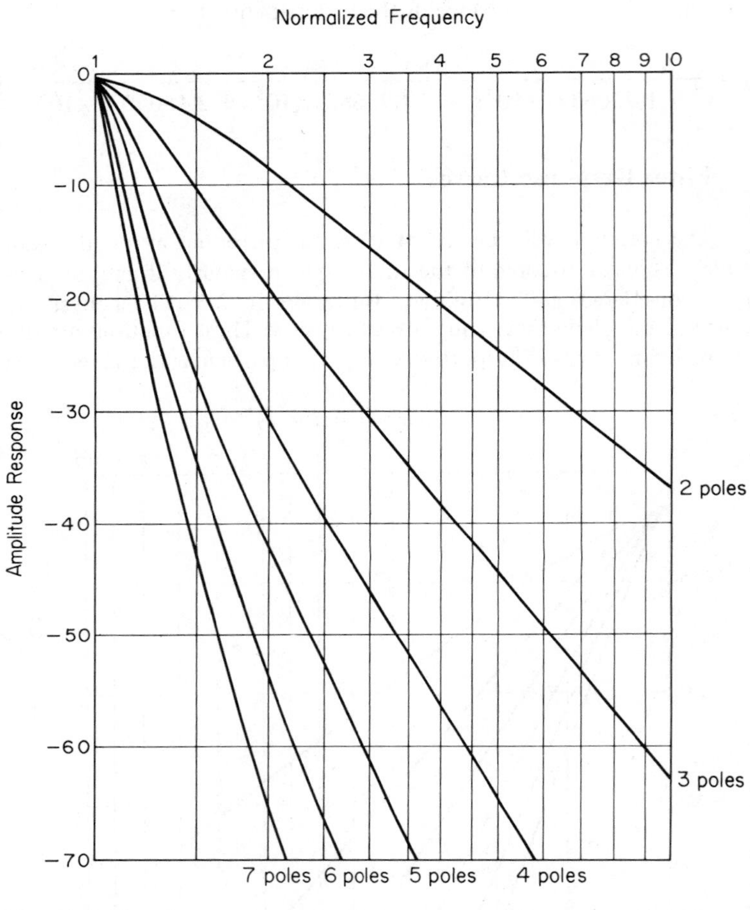

Figure 6-24 Stopband amplitude response of Chebyshev 0.5 dB ripple filters.

providing the responses ranging from two poles to seven poles are given. The number of poles (or order) is referred to either an actual low-pass filter or the low-pass prototype in the case of a filter designed through a transformation.

In each case, the reference "cutoff frequency" is the abscissa at which the curves begin (unity on the normalized scale), and the response is down at this point with reference to the maximum level according to the particular definition employed. Thus, Butterworth and 3 dB Chebyshev curves begin at a level 3 dB down from the maximum response, while the other curves begin at levels down from the maximum responses corresponding to the ripple in each case.

The abscissa "Normalized Frequency" (N.F.) has a different interpretation for different types of filters. In the discussion that follows, refer to Fig.

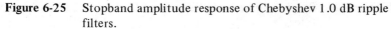

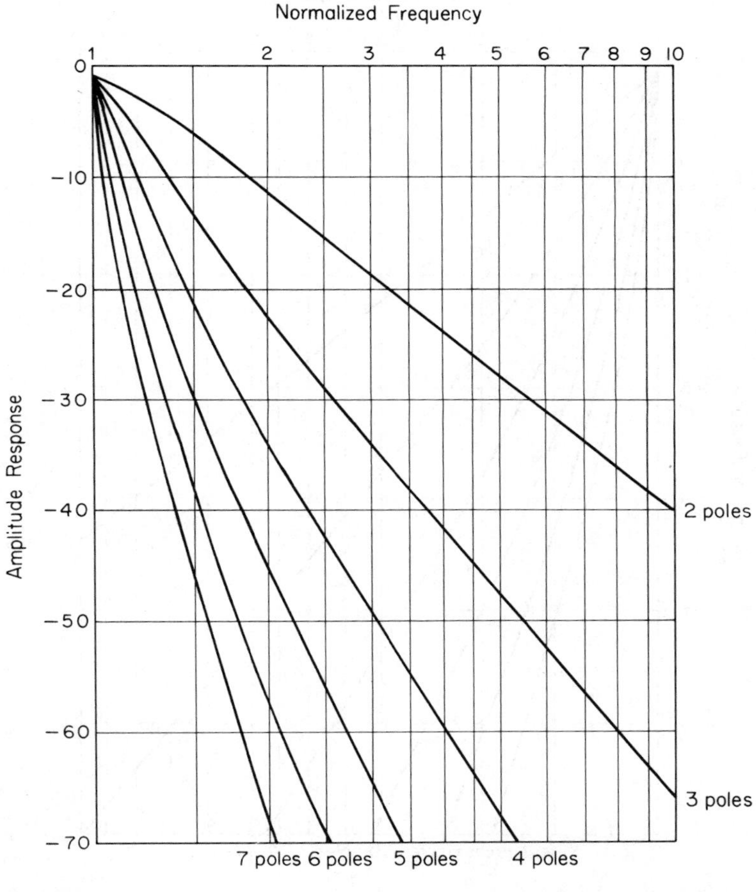

Figure 6-25 Stopband amplitude response of Chebyshev 1.0 dB ripple filters.

6-28. For each type of filter, let B represent the reference bandwidth as defined for that particular form.

Let B_x represent some other bandwidth at which the response is actually desired. The normalized frequency is then defined as follows:

(a) *Low-Pass* and *Band-Pass*

$$\text{N.F.} = \frac{B_x}{B} \tag{6-69}$$

(b) *High-Pass* and *Band-Rejection*

$$\text{N.F.} = \frac{B}{B_x} \tag{6-70}$$

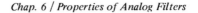

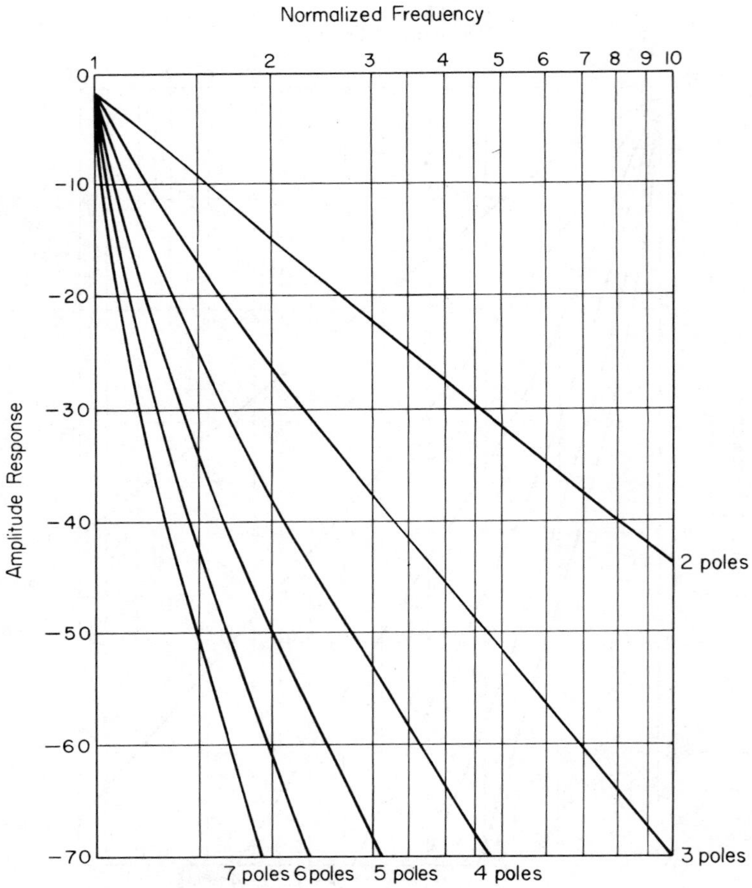

Figure 6-26 Stopband amplitude response of Chebyshev 2.0 dB ripple filters.

It should be emphasized again that the decibel responses of all the curves involved are scaled in reference to the *maximum* response in the passband. For all Butterworth functions and Chebyshev functions of odd order this poses no unusual interpretation, since the maximum values of these functions occur at dc. On the other hand, for Chebyshev functions of even order, the maximum occurs at other than dc. This means that for these particular functions, we are comparing the response shown with the maximum response in each case rather than the dc response. If the actual response of a given filter within this group has been designed to have unity response at dc, the actual level of the measured response would be greater than that shown in the curves by the amount of passband ripple.

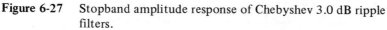

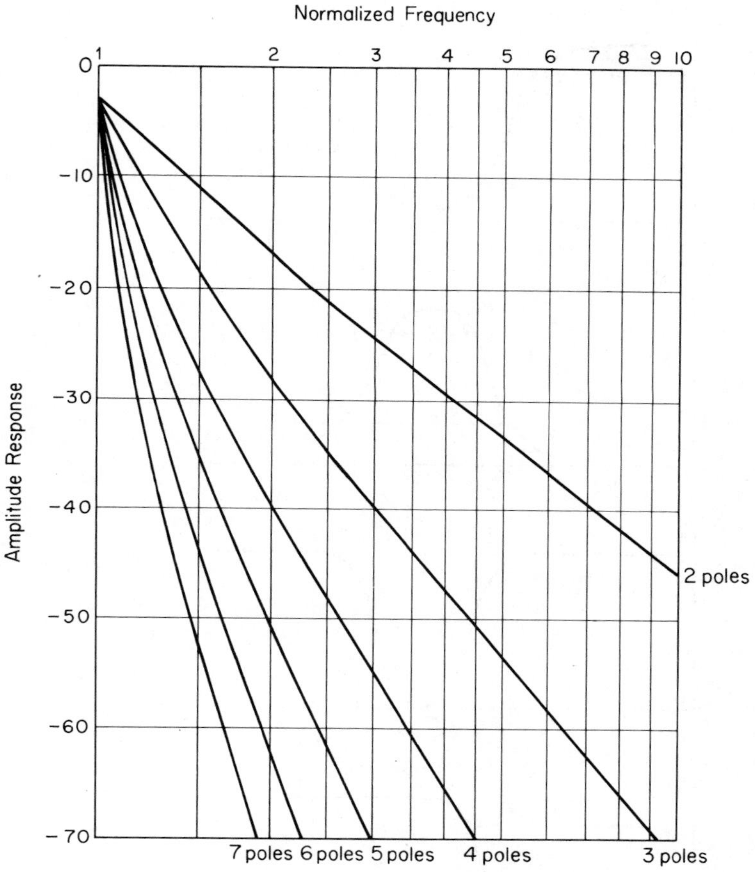

Figure 6-27 Stopband amplitude response of Chebyshev 3.0 dB ripple filters.

Example 6-8

A low-pass filter is needed to satisfy the following specifications:

(a) Amplitude response must not vary more than 3 dB from dc to 5 kHz.

(b) Attenuation $\geqslant$ 23 dB for $f \geqslant$ 10 kHz, as referred to maximum passband response.

Specify the minimum number of poles required in both a Butterworth and a Chebyshev filter that will satisfy the specifications.

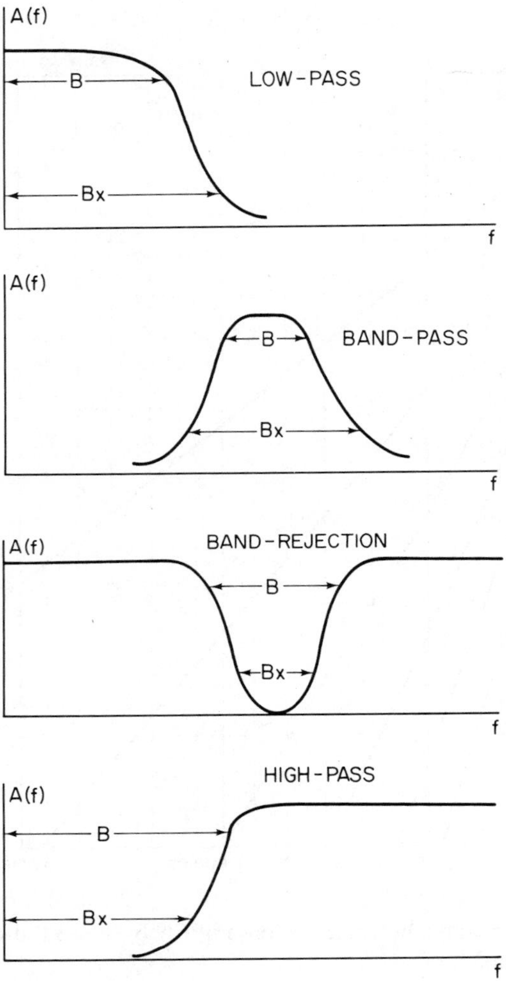

Figure 6-28 Illustration of bandwidth parameters for different types of filters.

Solution

While an analytical solution using the expressions for the pertinent amplitude functions could be done, the simplest procedure is to employ the curves. This approach is usually accurate enough for most applications. Since the definition of the Butterworth cutoff frequency is the 3 dB frequency, the normalized frequency at which the response must be at least 23 dB down is given by

$$\text{N.F.} = \frac{10\ \text{kHz}}{5\ \text{kHz}} = 2 \qquad (6\text{-}71)$$

Inspection of Fig. 6-23 shows that the lowest order Butterworth filter that meets the requirement is the 4-pole function. At this frequency, the attenuation is 24 dB, thus providing 1 dB more than required.

To satisfy the requirement with a Chebyshev filter, we will choose the 3 dB ripple filter. Referring to Fig. 6-27, it is seen that at N.F. = 2, the attenuation of a 3 pole Chebyshev is greater than 28 dB, thus providing more than 5 dB attenuation above the requirements.

In summary, the specifications could be met with either a fourth-order Butterworth filter or a third-order Chebyshev filter with 3 dB passband ripple. In each case, the stopband attenuation would be greater than actually required if the 3 dB frequency were set to exactly 10 kHz. Because the attenuation of the Chebyshev filter at 10 kHz is well in excess of that specified, it would be possible to use a 3-pole Chebyshev filter having less passband ripple and still satisfy the stopband attenuation requirements, if desired.

PROBLEMS

6-1 Determine the transfer function corresponding to the amplitude-squared function

$$A^2(f) = \frac{4}{6 + 5\omega^2 + \omega^4}$$

6-2 Determine the transfer function corresponding to the amplitude-squared function

$$A^2(f) = \frac{4(9-\omega^2)^2}{6 + 5\omega^2 + \omega^4}$$

6-3 Determine the transfer function corresponding to the amplitude-squared function

$$A^2(f) = \frac{1}{1 - \omega^2 + \omega^4}$$

6-4 Starting with the definition of the appropriate amplitude response, derive the transfer function of a fourth-order low-pass Butterworth filter with $\omega_c = 1$ rad/s.

6-5 Starting with the definition of the appropriate amplitude response, derive the transfer function of a second-order low-pass Chebyshev filter with $\omega_c = 1$ rad/s and 3 dB passband ripple.

6-6 Determine an expression for $A^2(f)$ in final rational function form for a third-order low-pass Chebyshev function with 1.5 dB passband ripple and $\omega_c = 1$ rad/s.

6-7 Consider the Chebyshev response of equation (6-24) with k even. (a) Show that for unity dc gain, the gain constant required is $\alpha = 1+\epsilon^2$. (b) Show that for the choice of α determined in (a), the amplitude response at maxima exceeds unity and is given by $A_{max} = \sqrt{1+\epsilon^2}$.

6-8 Using the tables in the text, determine the transfer function for a third-order Chebyshev low-pass filter with 3 dB passband ripple and a cutoff frequency of 5 kHz.

6-9 Using the tables in the text, determine the transfer function for a fourth-order Butterworth low-pass filter with a 3 dB cutoff frequency of 1 kHz.

6-10 Determine the transfer function for a band-pass filter with the following characteristics: (a) 4 poles, (b) Butterworth response, (c) geometric center frequency = 10 kHz, (d) 3 dB bandwidth = 1 kHz.

6-11 Determine the transfer function for a band-rejection filter with the following characteristics: (a) 4 poles, (b) Butterworth response, (c) geometric center of rejection band = 10 kHz, (d) 3 dB width of rejection band = 1 kHz.

6-12 Determine the transfer function for a fourth-order Butterworth high-pass filter with a 3 dB cutoff frequency of 1 kHz.

6-13 A low-pass filter is desired to satisfy the following requirements: (a) Response flat within 3 dB from dc to 5 kHz. (b) Attenuation $\geqslant$ 30 dB for $f \geqslant$ 10 kHz. Determine the minimum orders for both a Butterworth filter and a Chebyshev filter that will realize the specifications.

6-14 A low-pass filter is desired to satisfy the following requirements: (a) Response flat within 1 dB from dc to 10 kHz. (b) Attenuation $\geqslant$ 40 dB for $f \geqslant$ 25 kHz. Determine the minimum order of a filter that will realize the specifications, and specify the type.

6-15 A band-pass filter is desired to satisfy the following requirements: (a) Response flat within 3 dB over the range 100 kHz $\leqslant f \leqslant$ 105 kHz. (b) Attenuation at 3 times 3 dB bandwidth $\geqslant$ 38 dB. Determine the minimum order of the *band-pass* filter that will satisfy the requirements, and specify the type.

6-16 Consider an amplitude modulated signal of the form $x(t) = A(1 + m \cos \omega_m t) \cos\omega_c t$ where m is the modulation index, which is bounded by $0 \leqslant m \leqslant 1$, ω_m is the modulating frequency, and ω_c is the carrier frequency. Assume the signal passes through an analog filter having phase delay and group delay at ω_c given by $T_p(f_c)$ and $T_g(f_c)$. Show that the carrier of the output signal is delayed by $T_p(f_c)$, and the envelope is delayed approximately by $T_g(f_c)$. Assume that $\omega_c \gg \omega_m$ and that the phase is reasonably well-behaved in the vicinity of ω_c.

6-17 Derive equations (6-56) and (6-57).

6-18 The form of the step response of the ideal low-pass filter was illustrated in Fig. 6-6. Assuming that the impulse response has a delay of τ, determine an expression for the step response in two steps: (a) First, determine the impulse response $g(t)$. (b) Next, set up an expression for the step response involving integration of the result of (a). (Note: This integral requires numerical evaluation, so you are not asked to complete the problem.)

6-19 Assume that $x(f)$ represents some approximation to a desired frequency function $\overline{x}(f)$. Let $y(f) = \overline{x}(f) - x(f)$ represent the difference (or error) between the two functions. The quantity $x(f)$ will be defined as a *maximally-flat* approximation to $\overline{x}(f)$ of order m at $f = f_0$ if

$$y(f_0) = 0$$

$$\frac{d^i y(f_0)}{df^i} = 0 \text{ for } 1 \leqslant i \leqslant m$$

$$\neq 0 \text{ for } i = m + 1$$

(a) Show that this definition is equivalent to having the coefficients of all terms up to and including the term $(f-f_0)^m$ in the power series expansion about f_0 to vanish. (b) Show that if $x(f)$ is a maximally-flat approximation to $\overline{x}(f)$ of order m at $f = f_0$, then $1/x(f)$ is a maximally-flat approximation to $1/\overline{x}(f)$ of the same order and at the same point.

6-20 Assume that the amplitude-squared low-pass approximation to an ideal filter function is given by

$$A^2(f) = \frac{1 + c_1\omega^2 + c_2\omega^4 + \cdots + c_i\omega^{2i}}{1 + d_1\omega^2 + d_2\omega^4 + \cdots + d_k\omega^{2k}}$$

where $k > i$, and the ideal response in the passband is represented as

$$\overline{A^2(f)} = 1$$

Making use of the results of Prob. 6-19, show that the conditions for maximal flatness at $f = 0$ are

$$c_n = d_n \quad \text{for } 1 \leqslant n \leqslant i$$

$$d_n = 0 \quad \text{for } i < n < k$$

$$d_k \neq 0$$

(Note that the requirement $d_k \neq 0$ is necessary in order that the function represent a low-pass filter. Otherwise the response would degenerate to a constant of unity!)

6-21 Using the results of Prob. 6-19, show that the Butterworth function of equation (6-17) is a maximally-flat function of order $2k-1$ at $f = 0$.

6-22 Using the results of Prob. 6-19, show that the inverted Chebyshev function of equation (6-33) is a maximally-flat function of order $2k-1$ at $f = 0$.

6-23 Demonstrate that the inverted Chebyshev amplitude response can be derived from the normal Chebyshev amplitude response by application of the following two steps: (a) Subtract the normal Chebyshev response from unity. Sketch the result and show that it is a high-pass function with equiripple stopband behavior and a monotonically increasing passband behavior. (b) Utilize the low-pass to high-pass transformation of Sec. 6-9 to obtain the final response.

6-24 Show that the high-frequency amplitude response of the inverted Chebyshev filter becomes asymptotic to a curve with slope -6 dB/octave for k odd.

6-25 Show that when k is even, the high-frequency amplitude-squared function for the inverted Chebyshev filter becomes asymptotic to the constant value $\epsilon^2/(1+\epsilon^2)$.

6-26 Assume that the minimum stopband dB attenuation (expressed as a positive number) for an inverted Chebyshev filter is specified as R, in which the maximum amplitude response is used as the reference. Show that the required value of ϵ^2 is given by

$$\epsilon^2 = \frac{1}{10^{(R/10)} - 1}$$

REFERENCES

1. H. W. Bode, *Network Analysis and Feedback Amplifier Design.* Princeton, N. J.: Van Nostrand, 1945.

2. W. H. Chen, *Linear Network Design and Synthesis.* New York: McGraw-Hill, 1964.

3. E. A. Guillemin, *Synthesis of Passive Networks.* New York: Wiley, 1957.

4. D. S. Humphreys, *The Analysis, Design, and Synthesis of Electrical Filters.* Englewood Cliffs, N. J.: Prentice-Hall, 1970.

5. ITT Staff, *Reference Data for Radio Engineers*, 5th Ed. Indianapolis, Ind.: Howard W. Sams & Co., Inc.

6. F. F. Kuo, *Network Analysis and Synthesis*, 2nd Ed. New York: Wiley, 1966.

7. National Bureau of Standards, *Tables of Chebyshev Polynomials.* Washington: U.S. Government Printing Office, 1952.

8. M. E. Van Valkenburg, *Introduction to Modern Network Synthesis*. New York: Wiley, 1960.

9. L. Weinberg, *Network Analysis and Synthesis*. New York: McGraw-Hill, 1962.

CHAPTER SEVEN

INFINITE IMPULSE RESPONSE DIGITAL FILTER DESIGN

7-0 Introduction

The primary objective in this chapter is the development and application of some of the basic methods for designing digital filters of the infinite impulse response type. A digital filter may be defined as a computational process or algorithm which converts one sequence of numbers representing an input signal into another sequence of numbers representing an output signal, and in which the conversion changes the character of the signal in some prescribed fashion. In many applications, the processing operation may take the form of steady-state frequency domain filtering such as was discussed for analog systems in Chapt. 6. In other cases, a digital filter may perform functions such as differentiation, integration, or estimation.

A linear time-invariant digital filter is designed by determining the coefficients of the input-output algorithm by some approximation process. The major strategy in this chapter will be that of forcing the digital filter to behave very closely with some reference analog filter. This concept permits the use of well-developed analog approximating functions and design data for developing digital filters. The three general procedures developed in this chapter are the bilinear transformation method, the step-invariance method, and the impulse-invariance method. In addition, special forms of the bilinear transformation will be given for designing digital band-pass, band-rejection, and high-pass filters.

7-1 General Considerations

An important process in this chapter and in the next chapter is that of determining a discrete transfer function or difference equation which will achieve a prescribed signal filtering requirement. In Chapts. 4 and 5, various discrete-time system analysis methods were discussed in detail, but in all cases, the transfer function or difference equation was given. In this chapter, the situation is reversed in the sense that we are usually given a set of specific requirements, and we must determine a discrete-time system that will accomplish the chore.

Most of the concepts to be developed in this chapter and in Chapt. 8 apply to discrete-time systems in general as well as to sampled-data continuous-time systems. However, due to the widespread usage of the term, and in view of the principle area of interest intended for this book, we will use the term *digital filter* to refer to the end result of a given design procedure. The associated discrete transfer function will often be referred to as a *digital transfer function*. Thus, the general problem is that we are given a set of specific design requirements, and we must determine a digital filter to satisfy these requirements. The final digital filter may be in the form of a discrete or digital transfer function, a difference equation, or an impulse response.

The overall philosophy of digital filter design depends on the types of design criteria that could be used in actual applications. At the outset, it should be emphasized that most of the design concepts and criteria utilized in this book reflect the familiar frequency domain approach in terms of steady-state amplitude and/or phase behavior. This approach has long dominated the design procedures for most analog filters, and it is only natural that most of the newer digital filter design procedures should follow in the same strong tradition. On the other hand, the digital filter has made possible new approaches that were previously unattainable or, at best, quite difficult to implement with analog filters. Such concepts as time-variable, adaptive, and non-linear filters are possibilities with digital systems.

Since the frequency response concept plays the same powerful role in digital filter design as it does in analog design, it is only natural to classify many digital filters according to their frequency response characteristics. Digital filters designed on a frequency response basis can thus be classified as *low-pass*, *high-pass*, *band-pass*, and *band-rejection* types, as illustrated by the ideal models in Fig. 7-1. (Only the positive frequency ranges are shown.) It should be observed that such characteristics are actually periodic in nature, and the reference behavior is applied only with respect to the range from dc to the folding frequency f_0. As long as the sampling rate is sufficiently high, the filter behaves in the manner for which it is designed, but the overall periodic nature of the response is still a property that must be considered.

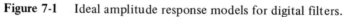

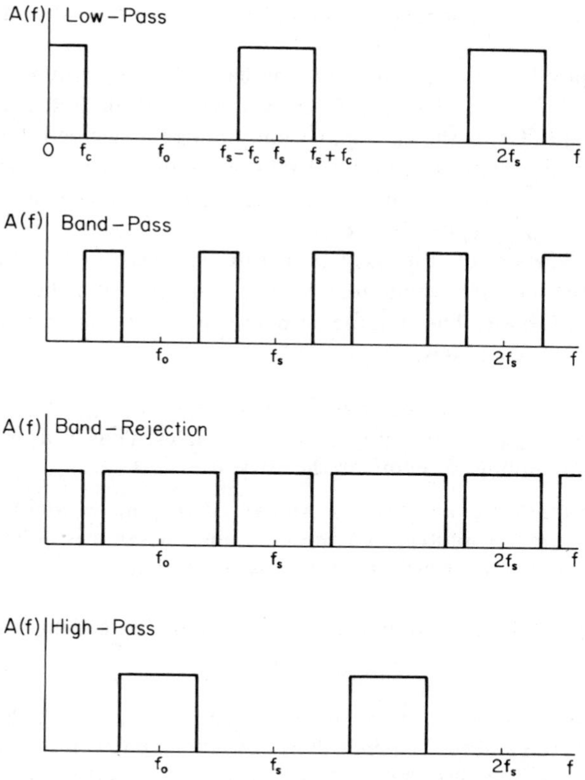

Figure 7-1 Ideal amplitude response models for digital filters.

It was shown in Chapt. 4 that the input-output difference equation for a DTLTI system can be expressed in the form

$$y(n) = \sum_{i=0}^{k} a_i x(n-i) - \sum_{i=1}^{k} b_i y(n-i) \tag{7-1}$$

In the z-domain, (7-1) can be represented by the discrete transfer function.

$$H(z) = \frac{N(z)}{D(z)} = \frac{\sum_{i=0}^{k} a_i z^{-i}}{1 + \sum_{i=1}^{k} b_i z^{-i}} \tag{7-2}$$

where $N(z)$ is the numerator polynomial and $D(z)$ is the denominator polynomial.

The problem in digital filter design is to determine the set of coefficients a_i and b_i so that the filter will have the desired behavior. This concept is very similar to the approximation problem in analog filter design, for which some of the various approximations were discussed in the preceding chapter. Fortunately, as we will see later, use may be made of these analog functions in developing digital filter designs.

Digital filters of the DTLTI nature are classified both from the standpoint of the *duration of the impulse response* and from the standpoint of the *type of realization*. The impulse response duration characteristics can be divided into two broad classes:

(a) *Infinite Impulse Response (IIR)*. An IIR filter is one in which the impulse response $h(n)$ has an infinite number of samples. Thus, $h(n)$ is non-zero at an infinite number of points in the range $n_1 \leqslant n \leqslant \infty$.

(b) *Finite Impulse Response (FIR)*. An FIR filter is one in which the impulse response $h(n)$ is limited to a finite number of samples defined over the range $n_1 \leqslant n \leqslant n_2$, where n_1 and n_2 are both finite.

The possible realization procedures can be divided into three broad classes:

(a) *Recursive Realization*. A recursive realization is one in which the present value of the output depends both on the input (present and/or past values) and previous values of the output. A recursive filter is usually recognized by the presence of both a_i and b_i terms in a realization of the form of (7-1).

(b) *Nonrecursive (or Direct Convolution) Realization*. A nonrecursive or direct convolution realization is one in which the present value of the output depends only on the present and past values of the input. This usually means that all values of $b_i = 0$ in a realization of the form of (7-1).

(c) *Fast Fourier Transform (FFT) Realization*. This type of realization is achieved by transforming the input signal with the FFT, filtering the spectrum as desired, and performing an inverse transformation. This procedure is more closely related to the material in Chapters 9 and 10, and discussion will be postponed until then.

In general, an *IIR filter* is usually more easily implemented by a *recursive realization*, and an *FIR filter* is usually more easily implemented by either a *nonrecursive realization* or an *FFT realization*. For that reason, there are strong associations in *usage* between the terms *IIR* and *recursive* and between the terms *FIR* and *nonrecursive*. In much of the earlier literature, the terms recursive and nonrecursive were employed to describe digital filters both from the standpoints of impulse response duration and realization, as suggested by these associations. However, it has been shown (ref. 2) that both FIR and IIR functions may be implemented by either recursive or nonrecursive techniques. This suggested the need for clarification from both the standpoints of impulse response duration and realization. Typical realizations of third-order recursive and nonrecursive filters are compared in Fig. 7-2.

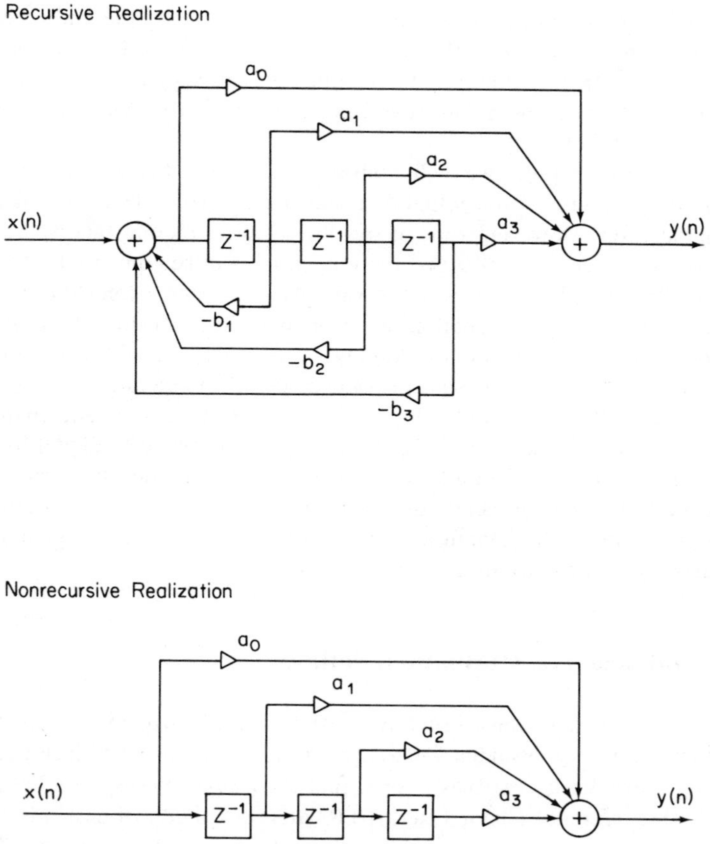

Figure 7-2 Typical recursive and nonrecursive realizations of digital filters.

This chapter will be devoted to the discussion of some of the most important methods for designing IIR filters. Many of these techniques utilize an analog transfer function as a prototype function, and by means of a suitable transformation, it is converted into a digital filter having similar characteristics. In most cases, a discrete transfer function of the form of (7-1) is obtained directly by such a process. In all cases within this chapter, the resulting impulse responses can be shown to have infinite duration.

7-2 Discussion of Notation

A short discussion concerning the notation employed in developing digital filter designs will be presented here so the reader will not feel that we are arbitrarily changing notation without reason. In some of the earlier chapters, where we were concerned with a given single transfer function, the variables s, ω, and f ($\omega = 2\pi f$), were used to denote, respectively, the complex Laplace variable, the steady-state radian frequency, and the steady-state cyclic frequency of the transfer function.

In this chapter, we will continue to reserve these same variables to describe the response of the actual final transfer function, which in this case will be a digital filter. However, some of these procedures require that we begin with an analog reference or prototype function, which will be converted into a digital function. We will always reserve the variables s, ω, and f (and the normalized frequency ν) for the final function, in order to avoid confusion; therefore, it will often be necessary to introduce dummy or reference variables for the analog filter prototype. This means that in some cases we will be taking analog transfer functions from the tables and data from the curves in Chapt. 6 and changing the variables to dummy variables so that they may be converted to digital form.

The important point to remember is that dummy variables are introduced whenever necessary in order that the final Laplace variable of the digital filter can be designated as s and the final steady-state frequency can be designated as ω or f without ambiguity.

7-3 Bilinear Transformation Method

The bilinear transformation method appears to be one of the best procedures currently available for designing many *IIR* filters with respect to the following two criteria: (a) It is desired that the frequency response be similar to that of some reference analog filter. (b) Relative simplicity of design is desirable. Because of its importance, we will explore this method in some depth before discussing other procedures.

The following notation will be employed in this section:

p = *analog* prototype Laplace variable
s = *digital* final Laplace variable
λ = steady-state radian frequency corresponding to $p (p = j\lambda)$
ω = steady-state radian frequency corresponding to $s (s = j\omega)$
f = cyclic frequency corresponding to $\omega (f = \omega/2\pi)$

ν = normalized frequency (with respect to folding frequency) $= f/f_0$
$G(p)$ = *analog* prototype transfer function
$H(z)$ = *discrete* or *digital* transfer function

Note that z is related to the final Laplace variable by the equation

$$z = \epsilon^{sT} \tag{7-3}$$

in accordance with the work of Chapt. 4.

The desired digital transfer function $H(z)$ is obtained by replacing p in $G(p)$ by an equation expressing p in terms of z. The bilinear transformation relating the prototype variable p to the discrete variable z is given by

$$p = \frac{C(1 - z^{-1})}{(1 + z^{-1})} \tag{7-4}$$

where C is a mapping constant to be discussed later. Substituting (7-3) in (7-4), we obtain the relationship between the prototype variable p and the final s variable.

$$p = \frac{C(1 - \epsilon^{-sT})}{(1 + \epsilon^{-sT})} = C \tanh \frac{sT}{2} \tag{7-5}$$

The relationships between the p, z, and s-planes are illustrated in Fig. 7-3. A careful study of the mapping geometry leads to the conclusion that some of the distortion between the z and s-planes is compensated for, in part, by the relationship between the z and p-planes. The overall result is that the p-plane and the s-plane have somewhat similar characteristics, at least over a portion of the s-plane.

These properties can be deduced by noting that the left-hand half of the p-plane corresponds to the left-hand half of the s-plane, and the imaginary axis of the p-plane corresponds to the imaginary axis of the s-plane. The primary difference is that the behavior in the p-plane over the infinite range $-\infty < \lambda < \infty$ maps to a principal value range in the s-plane of $-\pi < \omega T < \pi$. This means that the frequency response of the reference analog filter will be reproduced in the digital filter, but the frequency scale on which this response occurs will be compressed from an infinite interval in the analog filter to a finite interval in the digital filter. The value $\omega T = \pi$ corresponds to $f = 1/2T = f_0$, the folding frequency. Thus, the behavior of the analog prototype function over an infinite frequency range is mapped into the range from dc to f_0 in the digital filter. This corresponds to the range $0 \leqslant \nu \leqslant 1$ on the normalized frequency scale.

The relationship between the steady-state frequencies of the prototype response and the final design response can be seen more clearly by letting $p = j\lambda$

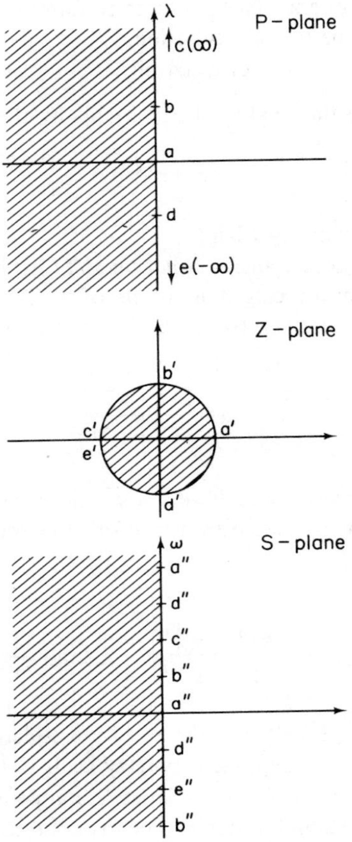

Figure 7-3 Relationships between the p, z, and s-planes.

and $s = j\omega$ in (7-5). Recognition of the fact that $\tanh jx = j \tan x$ and cancellation of the j's result in

$$\lambda = C \tan \frac{\omega T}{2} \tag{7-6}$$

In terms of the folding frequency f_0 and the normalized frequency ν, (7-6) can be expressed as

$$\lambda = C \tan \frac{\pi}{2} \frac{f}{f_0} = C \tan \frac{\pi}{2} \nu \tag{7-7}$$

The relationship of (7-7) is shown in Fig. 7-4 over a portion of the positive frequency range.

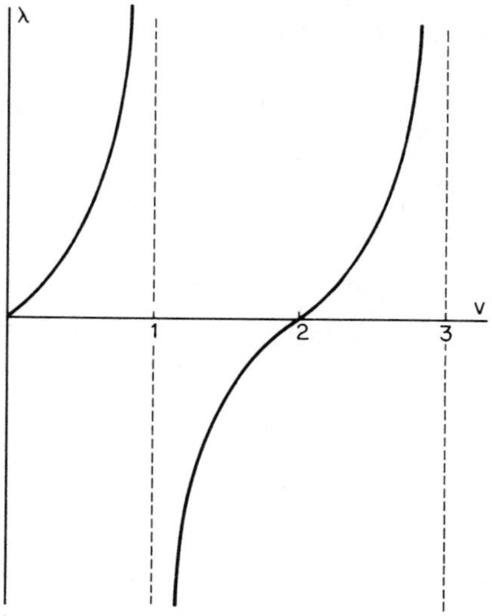

Figure 7-4 Relationship between frequency variables of the analog and digital functions.

The nature of the frequency mapping can now be observed. For relatively low frequencies compared to the folding frequency, i.e., $f/f_0 \ll 1$, there is an approximate linear relationship between the reference frequency scale and the actual frequency scale. This means that the relative behavior of the actual filter could correspond very closely to the behavior of the prototype filter in the low frequency range. However, as the frequency begins to approach the folding frequency, the actual frequency "quickly" covers the behavior of the prototype all the way to $\lambda = \infty$.

The forms for the amplitude characteristics of the analog prototype and the final digital function are compared for a typical case in Fig. 7-5. This particular example represents a low-pass function. Note that the digital response is low-pass only for frequencies less than the folding frequency. Thus, if the input signal contained a frequency component in the vicinity of $2f_0$ (or for that matter near any integer multiple of f_0), it would *not* be rejected by the filter since it would fall in one of the periodic passband regions produced by the nature of the sampling process. Such a component would be greater in frequency than f_0 and would be in violation of the sampling theorem. Since the sampling rate is inadequate, it would be impossible to distinguish this component at the output from a low frequency signal within the intended passband. This situation illustrates further the problem of aliasing, which results when the sampling rate is too low. As long as the sampling rate is known to be greater than twice the highest frequency of the signal, the passband regions above f_0 need cause no concern. Unless otherwise stated, we will assume adequate sampling in subsequent discussions, and this will normally mean that we need to display the response only over the range $0 \leqslant \nu \leqslant 1$.

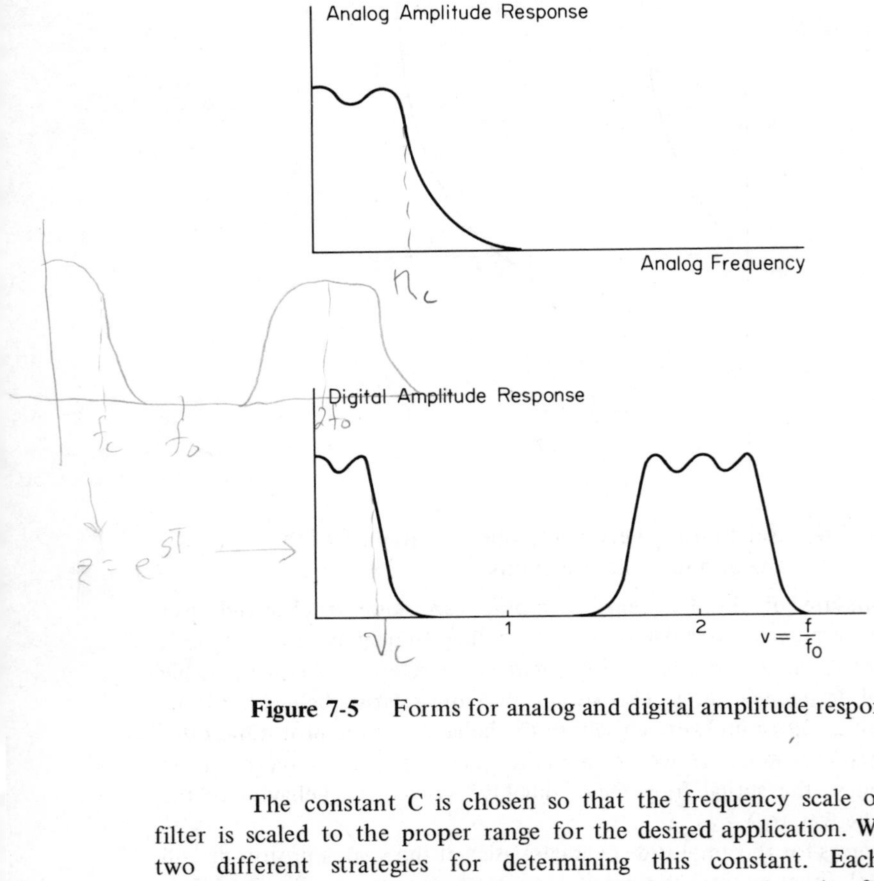

Figure 7-5 Forms for analog and digital amplitude response.

The constant C is chosen so that the frequency scale of the desired filter is scaled to the proper range for the desired application. We will discuss two different strategies for determining this constant. Each strategy is characterized by a somewhat different criterion, so that the final constants obtained may differ.

The first approach is that of achieving exact correspondence at *a particular frequency* in the behavior of the digital filter with respect to a particular frequency of the reference prototype analog filter. Quite often, for low and high-pass filters, this will be the cutoff frequency of the filters, and one is able to precisely control the location of this frequency using this approach. Let λ_r represent any particular reference analog frequency, and let ω_r represent the particular reference digital filter frequency at which the response is required to be the same. Let $\nu_r = f_r/f_0$. Substitution of these values into (7-6) or (7-7) and solution for C yield

$$C = \lambda_r \cot \frac{\omega_r T}{2} = \lambda_r \cot \frac{\pi}{2} \frac{f_r}{f_0} = \lambda_r \cot \frac{\pi}{2} \nu_r \tag{7-8}$$

Using this approach, it is neither necessary nor particularly desirable in most cases to scale the analog transfer function to the proper frequency range, as scaling is automatically accomplished in the process. The major advantage in this approach is that exact equality in the responses at a particular reference analog frequency and a particular desired digital frequency is quickly established.

The second approach results in reasonably good *low-frequency correspondence* between the prototype analog filter and the actual digital filter. It was observed in Fig. 7-4 that λ and ω have nearly a linear relationship for low frequencies. This is further illustrated by utilizing the approximation $\tan\theta \approx \theta$ for small θ in (7-6) and (7-7). The constant C can then be determined so that $\lambda \approx \omega$ in the range of approximation, and the reader is encouraged to show that

$$C = \frac{2}{T} = 2f_s = 4f_0 \tag{7-9}$$

Using this latter approach, we can say that the low-frequency behavior of the analog prototype filter is approximately the same as that of the digital filter, but no exact behavior at any particular frequency can be stipulated (except dc and f_0) without further calculation. It is necessary with this procedure that the analog filter be scaled to the proper frequency range prior to making the transformation so that the frequency scales will have the required correspondence.

If the reference frequency of the digital filter in the first procedure is quite small compared with the folding frequency, the resulting z-domain transfer functions employing either of the procedures will be approximately the same. (The constant C in the two cases would be approximately the same if the prototype transfer function is scaled to the proper frequency range in both cases before determining C. However, since it is not necessary to do this with the first procedure, the constants may be quite different.) If the reference frequency in the first procedure is not very small compared with the folding frequency, the resulting z-domain transfer functions employing the separate procedures may be quite different.

After the constant C is determined, the transfer function $H(z)$ is obtained by substituting p in terms of z in $G(p)$. Thus,

$$H(z) = G(p)\Big]_{p=\frac{C(1-z^{-1})}{1+z^{-1}}} \tag{7-10}$$

Observe that the number of poles (or order) of the digital filter will be the same as that of the reference analog filter.

The procedure of (7-10) is straightforward in concept, but the actual manipulations can become tedious. To assist in this step, some expressions relating the coefficients of the discrete transfer function to those of the analog transfer function have been worked out and tabulated. Assume that the transfer function of the reference analog function is given by

$$G(p) = \frac{A_0 + A_1 p + A_2 p^2 + \cdots + A_k p^k}{B_0 + B_1 p + B_2 p^2 + \cdots + B_k p^k} \tag{7-11}$$

The transfer function of the digital filter will be of the form

$$H(z) = \frac{a_0 + a_1 z^{-1} + a_2 z^{-2} + \cdots + a_k z^{-k}}{1 + b_1 z^{-1} + b_2 z^{-2} + \cdots + b_k z^{-k}} \tag{7-12}$$

Formulas for determining the coefficients of (7-12) in terms of the coefficients of (7-11) and the mapping constant C are tabulated for $k = 1$ through $k = 5$ in Tables 7-1 through 7-5. It should be understood that this data may be used only for filters designed with the form of the bilinear transformation used in this section and with the design process indicated by (7-10).

A	B_0+B_1C
a_0	$(A_0+A_1C)/A$
a_1	$(A_0-A_1C)/A$
b_1	$(B_0-B_1C)/A$

Table 7-1 Bilinear transformation digital filter coefficients in terms of analog filter coefficients (1st order).

A	$B_0+B_1C+B_2C^2$
a_0	$(A_0+A_1C+A_2C^2)/A$
a_1	$(2A_0-2A_2C^2)/A$
a_2	$(A_0-A_1C+A_2C^2)/A$
b_1	$(2B_0-2B_2C^2)/A$
b_2	$(B_0-B_1C+B_2C^2)/A$

Table 7-2 Bilinear transformation digital filter coefficients in terms of analog filter coefficients (2nd order).

A	$B_0+B_1C+B_2C^2+B_3C^3$
a_0	$(A_0+A_1C+A_2C^2+A_3C^3)/A$
a_1	$(3A_0+A_1C-A_2C^2-3A_3C^3)/A$
a_2	$(3A_0-A_1C-A_2C^2+3A_3C^3)/A$
a_3	$(A_0-A_1C+A_2C^2-A_3C^3)/A$
b_1	$(3B_0+B_1C-B_2C^2-3B_3C^3)/A$
b_2	$(3B_0-B_1C-B_2C^2+3B_3C^3)/A$
b_3	$(B_0-B_1C+B_2C^2-B_3C^3)/A$

Table 7-3 Bilinear transformation digital filter coefficients in terms of analog filter coefficients (3rd order).

A	$B_0+B_1C+B_2C^2+B_3C^3+B_4C^4$
a_0	$(A_0+A_1C+A_2C^2+A_3C^3+A_4C^4)/A$
a_1	$(4A_0+2A_1C-2A_3C^3-4A_4C^4)/A$
a_2	$(6A_0-2A_2C^2+6A_4C^4)/A$
a_3	$(4A_0-2A_1C+2A_3C^3-4A_4C^4)/A$
a_4	$(A_0-A_1C+A_2C^2-A_3C^3+A_4C^4)/A$
b_1	$(4B_0+2B_1C-2B_3C^3-4B_4C^4)/A$
b_2	$(6B_0-2B_2C^2+6B_4C^4)/A$
b_3	$(4B_0-2B_1C+2B_3C^3-4B_4C^4)/A$
b_4	$(B_0-B_1C+B_2C^2-B_3C^3+B_4C^4)/A$

Table 7-4 Bilinear transformation digital filter coefficients in terms of analog filter coefficients (4th order).

A	$B_0+B_1C+B_2C^2+B_3C^3+B_4C^4+B_5C^5$
a_0	$(A_0+A_1C+A_2C^2+A_3C^3+A_4C^4+A_5C^5)/A$
a_1	$(5A_0+3A_1C+A_2C^2-A_3C^3-3A_4C^4-5A_5C^5)/A$
a_2	$(10A_0+2A_1C-2A_2C^2-2A_3C^3+2A_4C^4+10A_5C^5)/A$
a_3	$(10A_0-2A_1C-2A_2C^2+2A_3C^3+2A_4C^4-10A_5C^5)/A$
a_4	$(5A_0-3A_1C+A_2C^2+A_3C^3-3A_4C^4+5A_5C^5)/A$
a_5	$(A_0-A_1C+A_2C^2-A_3C^3+A_4C^4-A_5C^5)/A$
b_1	$(5B_0+3B_1C+B_2C^2-B_3C^3-3B_4C^4-5B_5C^5)/A$
b_2	$(10B_0+2B_1C-2B_2C^2-2B_3C^3+2B_4C^4+10B_5C^5)/A$
b_3	$(10B_0-2B_1C-2B_2C^2+2B_3C^3+2B_4C^4-10B_5C^5)/A$
b_4	$(5B_0-3B_1C+B_2C^2+B_3C^3-3B_4C^4+5B_5C^5)/A$
b_5	$(B_0-B_1C+B_2C^2-B_3C^3+B_4C^4-B_5C^5)/A$

Table 7-5 Bilinear transformation digital filter coefficients in terms of analog filter coefficients (5th order).

Although this data could be extended to higher order functions, the resulting expressions tend to become unwieldly, and it is felt that data relating to such higher order functions would not be particularly useful. The reason is based on the practical tendency to realize higher order systems as cascade or parallel combinations of lower order functions.

In considering the problem of decomposing a digital filter into cascade and parallel sections, the bilinear transformation method has the interesting property that the decomposition may first be applied to the prototype function before the transformation is applied. Assume that the prototype function is represented in cascade form as

$$G(p) = G_1(p)G_2(p) \cdots G_\ell(p) \tag{7-13}$$

Then, the resulting discrete transfer function can be represented as

$$H(z) = H_1'(z)H_2'(z) \cdots H_\ell'(z) \tag{7-14}$$

where

$$H_i'(z) = G_i(p)]_{p=\frac{C(1-z^{-1})}{1+z^{-1}}} \tag{7-15}$$

Now assume that the prototype function is represented in parallel form as

$$G(p) = G_1(p) + G_2(p) + \cdots + G_r(p) \tag{7-16}$$

Then, $H(z)$ can be represented as

$$H(z) = H_1'(z) + H_2'(z) + \cdots + H_r'(z) \tag{7-17}$$

where a given $H_1'(z)$ is defined in the same form as in (7-15), but now with respect to the parallel functions.

The significance of the preceding results is that almost all of the decomposition can take place on the analog function, for which more tabulated information is usually available, and for which the manipulative steps of decomposition are usually easier. The bilinear transformation is then applied to each of the individual functions.

In actual practice, it may be desirable to modify the terms of (7-14) and (7-17) in different ways. In (7-14), it may be desirable to factor out the a_{oi} term from each function and lump them all together. The resulting decomposition will then be of the form

$$H(z) = a_0 H_1(z)H_2(z) \cdots H_\ell(z) \tag{7-18}$$

In (7-17), the various functions initially may have the same negative degree for both numerator and denominator polynomials. It may be desirable to extract constants from these different functions so that the resulting highest negative degree for each numerator is lower than the highest negative degree for the corresponding denominator. The resulting decomposition will then be of the form

$$H(z) = A + H_1(z) + H_2(z) + \cdots + H_r(z) \tag{7-19}$$

7-4 Bilinear Transformation Design Examples

This entire section will be devoted to the presentation and discussion of several design examples using the bilinear transformation procedure of the last section. Most of the calculations and the plots of the frequency response functions will be made in terms of the normalized frequency $\nu = f/f_0$. The reader should carefully observe the generality which this approach provides in each case. For example, suppose a given sampling frequency is 200 Hz and the cutoff frequency of a particular digital filter is 20 Hz. Since $f_0 = f_s/2 = 100$ Hz, the normalized cutoff frequency is $\nu_c = 20/100 = 0.2$. If the frequency response is plotted in terms of ν, the curve would apply to any digital filter of the same type (identical coefficients) as long as the same ratio of cutoff frequency to folding frequency holds. Thus, if the sampling frequency were changed to 1400 Hz, the value $\nu_c = 0.2$ now corresponds to 140 Hz, and the normalized curve still applies without change.

The bilinear transformation method may be used to design low-pass, high-pass, band-pass, and band-rejection filters. However, the basic form of the transformation as presented in the last section is easiest to apply directly to a low-pass function. Consequently, all the examples presented in this section will be restricted to functions having a low-pass nature. In later sections of the chapter, special forms of the bilinear transformation will be developed for simplifying the specification and design of band-pass, band-rejection, and high-pass filters.

Example 7-1

Design a low-pass digital filter derived from a second-order Butterworth analog filter with a 3 dB cutoff frequency of 50 Hz. The sampling rate of the system is 500 Hz.

Solution

The normalized analog transfer function of the Butterworth filter is obtained from Table 6-2. Using the dummy variable p, the function is

$$G(p) = \frac{1}{1 + 1.4142136p + p^2} \tag{7-20}$$

The frequency $\lambda_r = 1$ rad/s in the prototype must correspond to $f_r = 50$ Hz in the digital filter, so that the design should be based on exact correspondence at these frequencies. The folding frequency is $f_0 = 500/2 = 250$ Hz, and $\nu_r = 50/250 = 0.2$. The constant C is determined from (7-8) as

$$C = \cot\frac{\pi}{2}(0.2) = \cot\frac{\pi}{10} = 3.0776835 \tag{7-21}$$

The required transformation is

$$p = 3.0776835\,\frac{(1 - z^{-1})}{1 + z^{-1}} \tag{7-22}$$

Substitution of (7-22) into (7-20 or use of Table 7-2 yields

$$H(z) = \frac{0.0674553(1 + 2z^{-1} + z^{-2})}{1 - 1.14298z^{-1} + 0.412802z^{-2}} \tag{7-23}$$

The amplitude response of this digital filter expressed as a magnitude is shown as curve A in Fig. 7-11. The decibel form of the response is shown as curve A in Fig. 7-12. The other curves on each of the figures represent different approaches for the same function, and these will be discussed in later examples.

Example 7-2

The sampling rate in a certain digital processing system is 2000 Hz. It is desired to program a digital filter within the system to behave approximately like a simple first-order low-pass filter with a 3 dB frequency in the neighborhood of (but not necessarily equal to) 400 Hz. Rather, the major criterion is that the low-frequency response of the digital filter be close to that of the reference analog filter.

Solution

The requirements suggest the use of the bilinear transformation with the mapping constant selected to give good low-frequency correlation. The normalized low-pass analog transfer function with a cutoff frequency of 1 rad/s is

$$G_1(p) = \frac{1}{p + 1} \tag{7-24}$$

In this case, it is necessary to scale the analog filter to the proper frequency range before applying the transformation. This is achieved by replacing p by $p/(2\pi \times 400)$ as discussed in Chapt. 6. Letting $G_2(p)$ represent the resulting analog transfer function, we have

$$G_2(p) = G_1\left(\frac{p}{800\pi}\right) = \frac{800\pi}{p + 800\pi} \tag{7-25}$$

The bilinear transformation constant is obtained from (7-9) as

$$C = 2 \times 2000 = 4000 \tag{7-26}$$

The transformation is

$$p = 4000\,\frac{1 - z^{-1}}{1 + z^{-1}} \tag{7-27}$$

Substitution of (7-27) into (7-25) yields

$$H(z) = \frac{0.385870(1 + z^{-1})}{1 - 0.228261z^{-1}} \tag{7-28}$$

The reader is invited to verify by the use of (7-7) that the actual 3 dB frequency of the digital filter is about 357 Hz. An alternate approach to this problem would be to design for exact correspondence between the digital and analog filters at 400 Hz (Prob. 7-8). Since the cutoff frequency is 40% of the folding frequency, this latter approach would result in some difference between the analog and digital responses at very low frequencies.

Example 7-3

The transfer function of one unit within a particular analog control system is given by

$$G(p) = \frac{2}{(p + 1)(p + 2)} \tag{7-29}$$

The system is to be interfaced to a process control digital computer, and it is desired to replace many of the units within the system by software realizations. Determine the transfer function $H(z)$ of a possible replacement for the given analog unit. The sampling rate used in the system is 10 Hz.

Solution

Since the gain at dc is unity and since there are two zeros at $p = \infty$, it seems reasonable that an approximation emphasizing good correlation in the general low-frequency range would be suitable. Thus, the bilinear transformation method will be used, and the mapping constant will be selected according to (7-9). Note that the given transfer function is already scaled to the proper range, so the transformation is simply

$$p = \frac{20(1 - z^{-1})}{1 + z^{-1}} \tag{7-30}$$

Substitution of (7-30) in (7-29) yields

$$H(z) = \frac{0.0043290043(1 + z^{-1})^2}{1 - 1.7229437z^{-1} + 0.74025974z^{-2}} \tag{7-31}$$

In Ex. 7-1, the steady-state amplitude response of the digital filter was considered as the major function of interest. As an illustration of a different type of criterion in this case, we will compare the step response of (7-31) to that of the analog filter. These results are summarized in Table 7-6. The additional data represent different approaches for approximating the same function, and these will be discussed later.

n	Bilinear Transformation	Impulse Invariance	Analog Response and Step Invariance
0	0	0	0
4	0.1310	0.1295	0.1087
8	0.3273	0.3262	0.3032
12	0.5087	0.5075	0.4883
16	0.6526	0.6512	0.6370
20	0.7591	0.7575	0.7476
24	0.8349	0.8332	0.8268
28	0.8877	0.8860	0.8821
32	0.9240	0.9223	0.9201
36	0.9487	0.9470	0.9461
40	0.9655	0.9638	0.9637
44	0.9768	0.9751	0.9756
48	0.9844	0.9827	0.9836
52	0.9895	0.9878	0.9890
56	0.9929	0.9913	0.9926
60	0.9953	0.9936	0.9950
64	0.9968	0.9951	0.9966
68	0.9978	0.9962	0.9977
72	0.9985	0.9969	0.9985
76	0.9990	0.9973	0.9990
∞	1	1	1

Table 7-6 Step responses for filters of Examples 7-3, 7-7, and 7-9. (Note: Results are shown only at every fourth point up to n = 76.)

Example 7-4

Various specifications and parameters for a certain low-pass filter requirement are given as follows:

A. Bilinear transformation design with Butterworth type response.
B. Attenuation $\leqslant$ 3 dB for $0 \leqslant f \leqslant 25$ Hz
C. Attenuation $\geqslant$ 38 dB for $f \geqslant 50$ Hz
D. Sampling frequency = 200 Hz

(a) Determine a single transfer function $H(z)$ that will realize the requirements.

(b) Determine a cascade system of transfer functions, none of which exceeds second-order, that will realize the requirements.

Solution

(a) It is first necessary to determine the order of a transfer function that will meet the attenuation specifications. The folding frequency is $f_0 = 200/2 = 100$ Hz, and the normalized reference digital cutoff frequency is $\nu_r = 25/100 = 0.25$. The mapping constant will be chosen so that this frequency corresponds to $\lambda_r = 1$ rad/s in the analog prototype function. Hence,

$$C = \lambda_r \cot \frac{\pi}{2} \cdot \nu_r = \cot \frac{\pi}{8} = 2.4142136 \tag{7-32}$$

Let $\nu_a = 50/100 = 0.5$ represent the lowest frequency at which the stop-band attenuation requirement must be met. The corresponding analog reference frequency λ_a is determined from (7-7) as

$$\lambda_a = C \tan \frac{\pi}{2} \nu_a = 2.4142136 \tan \frac{\pi}{4} = 2.4142136 \tag{7-33}$$

Inspection of the curves of Fig. 6-23 reveals that at a normalized frequency of about 2.41, the attenuation of a 5-pole Butterworth filter is about 38 dB.

The analog prototype transfer function is obtained from Table 6-2 as

$$G(p) = \frac{1}{\begin{array}{l}(1 + 3.2360680p + 5.2360680p^2 \\ + 5.2360680p^3 + 3.2360680p^4 + p^5)\end{array}} \tag{7-34}$$

The required transformation is then

$$p = 2.4142132 \frac{(1 - z^{-1})}{1 + z^{-1}} \tag{7-35}$$

The formulas given in Table 7-5 may be used to simplify the transformation process. After considerable manipulation, the overall digital transfer function is

$$H(z) = \frac{3.279216\text{X}10^{-3}(1 + 5z^{-1} + 10z^{-2} + 10z^{-3} + 5z^{-4} + z^{-5})}{(1 - 2.4744163z^{-1} + 2.8110065z^{-2} - 1.7037724z^{-3} + 0.5444328z^{-4} - 0.07231569z^{-5})} \tag{7-36}$$

(b) A cascade decomposition may be obtained through the aid of Table 6-3 by first expressing $G(p)$ in analog cascade form. Let

$$G(p) = G_1(p)G_2(p)G_3(p) \tag{7-37}$$

where

$$G_1(p) = \frac{1}{1 + p} \tag{7-38}$$

$$G_2(p) = \frac{1}{1 + 0.6180340p + p^2} \tag{7-39}$$

$$G_3(p) = \frac{1}{1 + 1.618034p + p^2} \tag{7-40}$$

Assume that the digital transfer function is to be expressed as

$$H(z) = a_0 H_1(z)H_2(z)H_3(z) \tag{7-41}$$

The bilinear transformation may now be applied individually to each of the three analog functions. The constant a_0 is found by factoring out the respective a_{0i} constant for each function and forming the product. The results are

$$a_0 = 3.279216 \times 10^{-3} \tag{7-42}$$

$$H_1(z) = \frac{1 + z^{-1}}{1 - 0.4142136z^{-1}} \tag{7-43}$$

$$H_2(z) = \frac{1 + 2z^{-1} + z^{-2}}{1 - 1.1606108z^{-1} + 0.6413515z^{-2}} \tag{7-44}$$

$$H_3(z) = \frac{1 + 2z^{-1} + z^{-2}}{1 - 0.8995918z^{-1} + 0.2722149z^{-2}} \tag{7-45}$$

It can be verified that the product of the preceding four terms yields (7-36). Note how much simpler in form the three individual transfer functions of the cascade realization are than the overall system function. The cascade form here would probably be a much more desirable form for implementation than the direct form involving (7-36).

The amplitude response $A(\nu)$ is shown in Fig. 7-6, and $A_{db}(\nu)$ is shown in Fig. 7-7.

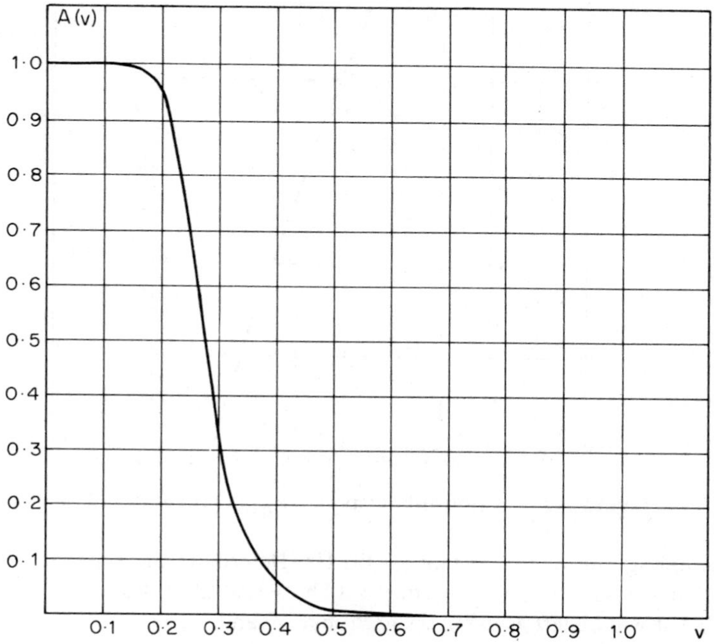

Figure 7-6 Amplitude response A(v) for Example 7-4.

Example 7-5

A low-pass digital IIR signal filter is desired to satisfy the following specifications:

A. Attenuation $\leqslant$ 1 dB for $0 \leqslant f \leqslant 5$ Hz
B. Attenuation $\geqslant$ 40 dB for $f \geqslant 10$ Hz

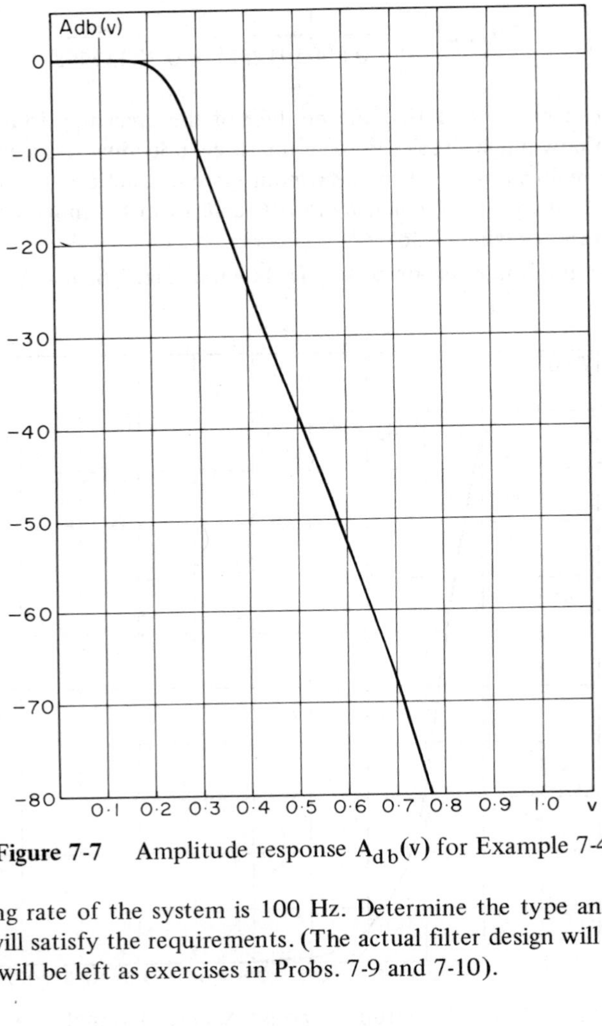

Figure 7-7 Amplitude response $A_{db}(v)$ for Example 7-4

The sampling rate of the system is 100 Hz. Determine the type and order of a filter that will satisfy the requirements. (The actual filter design will not be done here, but it will be left as exercises in Probs. 7-9 and 7-10).

Solution

The folding frequency is $f_0 = 100/2 = 50$ Hz. We will restrict our consideration to the types of filters for which design data have been given in the text. The form of the passband specifications suggests the use of a 1 dB Chebyshev filter, and the bilinear transformation method will be employed. The normalized reference frequency is $\nu_r = 5/50 = 0.1$ which will correspond to $\lambda_r = 1$ rad/s in the pertinent analog prototype filter of Chapt. 6. Let $\nu_a = 10/50 = 0.2$ represent the frequency at which the attenuation must be at least 40 dB, and let λ_a represent the corresponding analog prototype frequency.

The mapping constant is determined as

$$C = \cot \frac{\pi}{2}(0.1) = 6.3137515 \tag{7-46}$$

The frequency λ_a is determined from (7-7) as

$$\lambda_a = 6.3137515 \tan \frac{\pi}{2}(0.2) = 2.0514622 \tag{7-47}$$

From the curves of Fig. 6-25, it is seen that at a normalized frequency of about 2.05, the lowest order at which the attenuation exceeds 40 dB is a 5-pole filter. In fact, the attenuation at this frequency for a 5-pole filter actually exceeds 46 dB, so the requirement is met with some reserve.

Actually, the excess attenuation suggests the possibility that the passband ripple could be reduced, while still meeting the stopband requirement. Indeed, inspection of Fig. 6-24 reveals that a 0.5 dB ripple filter with 5 poles would have about 43 dB attenuation at $\nu_a = 0.2$. The choice between these alternatives would depend on whether it would be more important to reduce the passband ripple further or to provide additional stopband attenuation beyond the given requirements.

7-5 Numerical Interpretation of Bilinear Transformation

In this section, we will consider an alternate interpretation of the bilinear transformation as seen from a numerical analysis point of view. Consider a continuous signal *x(t)* from which a sampled signal *x(n)* is derived at multiples of $t = nT$. Suppose that it is desired to perform an approximate numerical integration on the sampled version of the signal. Of course, there are different approaches to this problem, with varying degrees of accuracy depending on the nature of the signal, the time interval, etc. However, assume that the trapezoidal algorithm is applied. This rather basic integration scheme assumes that the variation between successive points is linear as illustrated in Fig. 7-8. The

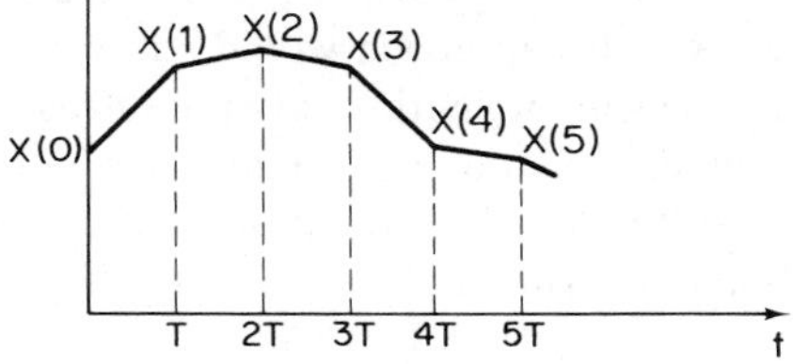

Figure 7-8 Integration using the trapezoidal algorithm.

resulting integration is achieved by summing the areas contained in a sequence of rectangles.

The trapezoidal algorithm may be expressed as

$$y(n) = y(n-1) + \frac{T}{2}[x(n) + x(n-1)] \tag{7-48}$$

Taking the z-transforms of both sides of (7-48) and solving for the transfer function, we obtain

$$H(z) = \frac{T}{2}\frac{(1+z^{-1})}{(1-z^{-1})} \tag{7-49}$$

Since integration in the time domain corresponds to division by the Laplace variable in the transform domain, we can establish a sort of equality between this operation and the z-domain operation representing an approximation to integration. To conform with previous notation concerning the reference analog domain, we will use p as the variable. Thus, in some approximate sense

$$\frac{1}{p} = \frac{T}{2}\frac{(1+z^{-1})}{(1-z^{-1})} \tag{7-50}$$

or

$$p = \frac{2}{T}\frac{(1-z^{-1})}{(1+z^{-1})} \tag{7-50a}$$

which was one form of the bilinear transformation as given earlier in the chapter.

Any analog transfer function can be represented as a complex combination of integrators and algebraic operations. If each of the integrators is replaced by the numerical operation implied by the trapezoidal algorithm, then a certain numerical approximation to the system will result. This is equivalent to replacing p in the transfer function by its equivalent z function as given by the bilinear transformation. Even if a constant other than 2/T is used (exact frequency correspondence), this approach would still be a trapezoidal approximation, but with a changed weighting of the areas. Thus, the bilinear transformation approach can be thought of as a discrete numerical approximation to a continuous system in which the process of integration is replaced by the trapezoidal algorithm approximation.

7-6 Impulse-Invariance Method

The next approach considered for designing IIR digital filters is the impulse-invariance method. The criterion for this approach is that the impulse response of the discrete-time system be the same as (or proportional to) the corresponding impulse response of the reference analog filter at sampling points. This idea is illustrated in Fig. 7-9.

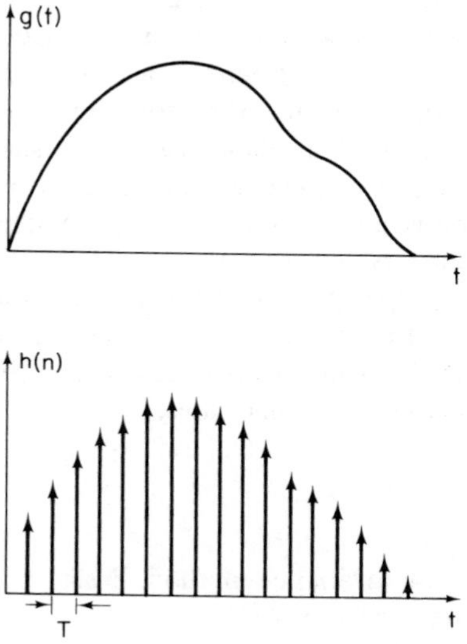

Figure 7-9 Illustration of the impulse-invariance concept.

Let $G(p)$ represent the reference analog transfer function, and let $H(z)$ represent the desired discrete transfer function. A discrete sample $x(n)$ of any given random input signal $x(t)$ should actually be represented by an impulse with the weight $Tx(n)$ in order to approximate the response of the corresponding analog system due to that segment of the signal. This can best be accomplished by leaving $x(n)$ as it is and multiplying the transfer function by T. The required transfer function can then be expressed as

$$H(z) = T\,\mathfrak{Z}\,[g(t)] = TG(z) \tag{7-51}$$

where $G(z)$ is the z-transform of the sampled representation of the continuous signal $g(t)$.

From the properties of a sampled signal as developed in Chapt. 3, the frequency response corresponding to (7-51) can be considered as the reference analog frequency response plus an infinite number of shifted versions of this response centered at integer multiples of the sampling frequency. This means that if the original analog filter displays only a moderate rolloff rate, the frequency aliasing error using this approach may be significant. On the other hand, if the original analog filter is sharply bandlimited, and if the sampling rate is sufficiently high, there will be little or no aliasing error, and the resulting frequency response may be very close to the reference analog response. Consequently, the impulse-invariance method should be seriously considered only for filter functions having sharp cutoff characteristics.

The actual design of impulse-invariance filters is usually more difficult from a computational point of view than for filters designed with the bilinear transformation. In the impulse-invariance case, it is necessary to determine the z-transform corresponding to an analog transfer function (or impulse response), which can be a laborious process for relatively complex functions. Since the z-transform of a product is *not* the product of the separate transforms, the cascade decomposition property discussed in conjunction with equations (7-13) through (7-15) and (7-18) may not be easily applied in this case. However, since the z-transform of a sum is a linear operation, it may be possible to develop a parallel decomposition directly in some cases.

Example 7-6

Using the impulse-invariance method, design a low-pass filter according to the requirements stated in Example 7-1.

Solution

The normalized analog transfer function will be expressed as

$$G_1(p) = \frac{1}{1 + 1.4142136p + p^2} \tag{7-52}$$

Before taking the z-transform, it is necessary to change the frequency scale of $G_1(p)$ so that its 3 dB cutoff frequency is 50 Hz. This can be achieved by replacing p in (7-52) by $p/(2\pi \times 50)$. The resulting transfer function is

$$G(p) = G_1\left(\frac{p}{100\pi}\right) = \frac{9.8696044 \times 10^4}{p^2 + 444.28829p + 9.8696044 \times 10^4} \tag{7-53}$$

The impulse response $g(t)$ is

$$g(t) = 444.28829\, \epsilon^{-222.14415t} \sin (222.14415t) \tag{7-54}$$

The z-transform corresponding to the sampled version of (7-54) can be found from the use of transform pair ZT-6 of Table 4-1 and operation pair ZO-3 of Table 4-2. First, we apply ZT-6 to the sinusoidal part of (7-54) to obtain

$$\mathfrak{Z}\,[\sin 222.14415t] = \frac{0.42981538z}{z^2 - 1.8058336z + 1} \tag{7-55}$$

$G(z)$ is then obtained by applying ZO-3 to (7-55). $H(z)$ is obtained by multiplying by T. After arrangement in negative powers of z, the result is

$$H(z) = \frac{0.2449203z^{-1}}{1 - 1.1580459z^{-1} + 0.41124070z^{-2}} \tag{7-56}$$

The amplitude response corresponding to (7-56) is shown as curve C in Figs. 7-11 and 7-12.

Example 7-7

Determine a possible digital filter for the system of Ex. 7-3 using the impulse-invariance method.

Solution

The impulse response $g(t)$ is determined from (7-29) as

$$g(t) = 2\epsilon^{-t} - 2\epsilon^{-2t} \tag{7-57}$$

The z-transform of the sampled version of (7-57) is

$$G(z) = \frac{2}{1 - \epsilon^{-0.1}z^{-1}} - \frac{2}{1 - \epsilon^{-0.2}z^{-1}} \tag{7-58}$$

The transfer function $H(z)$ is obtained by multiplying (7-58) by T. The result can be rearranged as

$$H(z) = \frac{0.017221333z^{-1}}{1 - 1.7235682z^{-1} + 0.74081822z^{-2}} \tag{7-59}$$

The step response of this transfer function is tabulated at a number of sample points in Table 7-6.

7-7 Step-Invariance Method

The step-invariance method results from the criteria that the step response of the digital filter must be the same as the corresponding step response of the reference analog filter at sampling times. Let $h_s(n)$ represent the digital step response, and let $g_s(t)$ represent the analog step response. This concept is illustrated in Fig. 7-10.

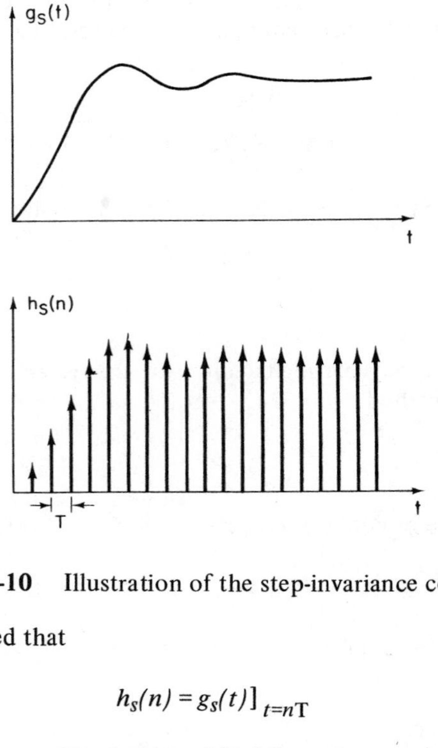

Figure 7-10 Illustration of the step-invariance concept.

It is required that

$$h_s(n) = g_s(t)]_{t=nT} \tag{7-60}$$

Taking the z-transforms of both sides of (7-60), we have

$$H_s(z) = G_s(z) \tag{7-61}$$

The digital step response $H_s(z)$ can be expressed in terms of the desired transfer function $H(z)$ as

$$H_s(z) = \frac{z}{z-1} H(z) \tag{7-62}$$

The z-transform of the analog transfer function can be expressed as

$$G_s(z) = \mathcal{Z}\left\{\mathcal{L}^{-1}\left[\frac{G(p)}{p}\right]\right\} \tag{7-63}$$

Note that the quantity in the inner brackets of (7-63) represents the Laplace transform of the step response, and its inverse represents the time domain form of the step response. After substituting (7-62) and (7-63) in (7-61), the transfer function is obtained as

$$H(z) = \frac{z-1}{z}\mathcal{Z}\left\{\mathcal{L}^{-1}\left[\frac{G(p)}{p}\right]\right\} \tag{7-64}$$

The development of one interesting interpretation of (7-64) is left as an exercise for the reader (Prob. 7-24), but a short discussion will be given here. Assume that an input signal $x(n)$ is applied to a zero-order holding circuit, which converts the discrete-time signal to a continuous-time signal consisting of a series of rectangles. If this signal is then applied to a continuous-time filter having a transfer function $G(p)$, the output signal at sample points will be equivalent to the discrete-time output of $H(z)$ in (7-64) when excited by $x(n)$. For this reason, the step-invariance function has also been referred to as a *zero-order hold filter*.

Filters designed with the step-invariance method are subject to some of the same possible aliasing difficulties as with impulse-invariance filters if the amplitude response is not sharply bandlimited. However, the presence of the $1/p$ factor in the inner brackets of (7-64) provides an additional 6 dB/octave high-frequency attenuation, so for a given filter function, the aliasing errors are usually smaller with the step-invariance method.

Example 7-8

Using the step-invariance method, design a low-pass filter according to the requirements of Example 7-1.

Solution

The analog transfer function was scaled to the proper frequency range in Example 7-6, and the result was given in (7-53). Multiplication by $1/p$ yields the Laplace transform of the step response. We must now determine the z-transform corresponding to the sampled version of the continuous-time step response. First, we will determine the analog step response. The result is

$$g_s(t) = 1 - \epsilon^{-222.14415t}(\sin 222.14415t + \cos 222.14415t) \tag{7-65}$$

The z-transform corresponding to (7-65) can be found from the use of transform pairs ZT-6 and ZT-7 of Table 4-1 and operation pair ZO-3 of Table 4-2. The result is

$$\begin{aligned} H_s(z) &= \frac{z}{z-1} - \frac{z^2 - 0.30339071z}{z^2 - 1.1580459z + 0.41124070} \\ &= \frac{0.14534481z^2 + 0.10784999z}{(z-1)(z^2 - 1.1580459z + 0.41124070)} \end{aligned} \tag{7-66}$$

The required transfer function $H(z)$ is now determined from (7-64). With final arrangement in negative powers of z, the result is

$$H(z) = \frac{0.14534481z^{-1} + 0.10784999z^{-2}}{1 - 1.1580459z^{-1} + 0.41124070z^{-2}} \tag{7-67}$$

The amplitude response corresponding to (7-67) is shown as curve B in Figs. 7-11 and 7-12.

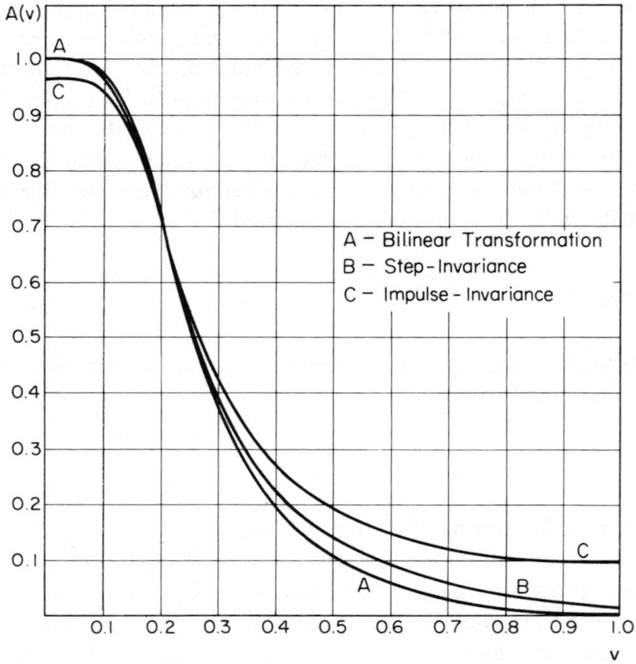

Figure 7-11 Amplitude response A(v) for Examples 7-1, 7-6, and 7-8.

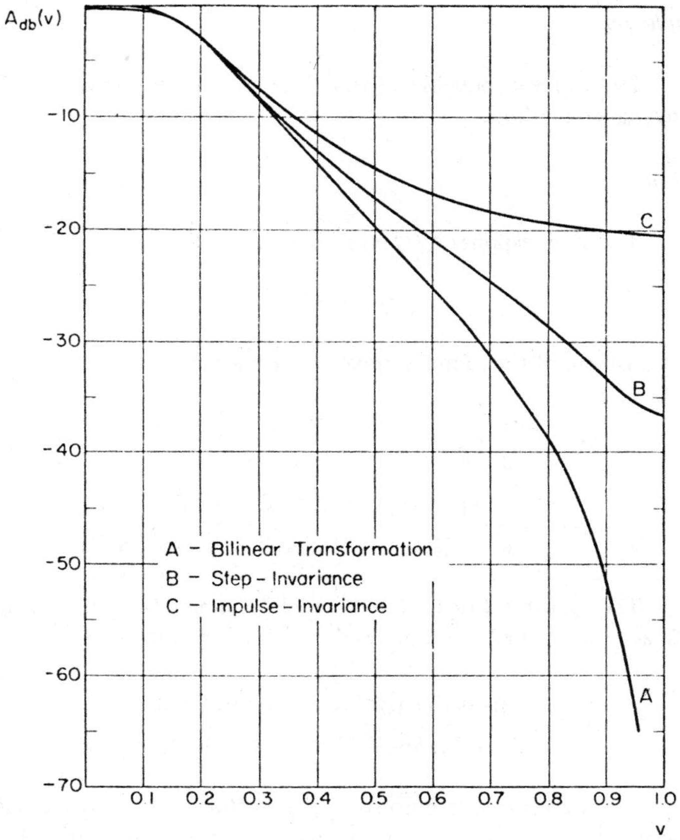

Figure 7-12 Amplitude response $A_{db}(v)$ for Examples 7-1, 7-6, and 7-8.

The reader can now compare the amplitude responses obtained using the three methods discussed in this chapter. In the passband, the three responses are all fairly close, with the exception that the gain of the impulse-invariance filter is slightly reduced. This problem is not serious since we could always adjust the overall gain level if desired. In the stopband, the bilinear transformation filter has the sharpest cutoff rate, and at the other extreme, the impulse-invariance filter exhibits relatively poor rolloff. In all fairness to the impulse-invariance filter, the analog filter in this problem was only a second-order function, so it was not sharply band-limited. Thus, both the impulse-invariance and the step-invariance filters display aliasing errors, although they are not as serious in the latter filter.

Example 7-9

Determine a possible digital filter for the system of Ex. 7-3 using the step-invariance method.

Solution

The step response $g_s(t)$ corresponding to (7-29) is

$$g_s(t) = 1 - 2\epsilon^{-t} + \epsilon^{-2t} \tag{7-68}$$

The z-transform of the sampled version of (7-68) is

$$\begin{aligned} G_s(z) &= \frac{z}{z-1} - \frac{2z}{z-\epsilon^{-0.1}} + \frac{z}{z-\epsilon^{-0.2}} \\ &= \frac{9.055917\text{X}10^{-3}z^2 + 8.194133\times10^{-3}z}{(z-1)(z^2 - 1.7235682z + 0.74081822)} \end{aligned} \tag{7-69}$$

The transfer function is then determined by multiplying (7-69) by $(z-1)/z$ according to (7-64). The result arranged in negative powers of z is

$$H(z) = \frac{9.055917\times10^{-3}(z^{-1} + 0.90483747z^{-2})}{1 - 1.7235682z^{-1} + 0.74081822z^{-2}} \tag{7-70}$$

The step response corresponding to this function is tabulated in Table 7-6 along with the other step responses previously considered. As expected in this case, the filter designed through the step-invariance method has identical values at sample points as the reference analog function. This does not imply that this filter is necessarily better than those filters designed with other methods, as the step response is only one of a number of possible criteria that could be employed. However, it might suggest that if the transient response due to step type inputs is to be a very important criterion, and if it is desired that the response correlate very closely with that of the reference analog filter, this particular realization might be the best one in this case.

7-8 Band-Pass Digital Filter Design

In this section, we will develop a procedure for designing a *band-pass digital* IIR filter directly from a *low-pass analog* prototype transfer function using a form of the bilinear transformation. This approach is based on a combination of the low-pass to band-pass analog transformation of Chapt. 6 and the bilinear transformation of this chapter.

Since there are two separate transformations involved, it is necessary to pay careful attention to notation in the development. The following quantities are defined:

p = *analog low-pass* reference Laplace variable
$\bar{s}$ = *analog band-pass* reference Laplace variable
s = *digital band-pass* final Laplace variable
λ = steady-state radian frequency corresponding to $p(p = j\lambda)$
$\bar{\omega}$ = steady-state radian frequency corresponding to $\bar{s}(\bar{s} = j\bar{\omega})$
$\bar{f}$ = $\bar{\omega}/2\pi$
ω = steady-state radian frequency corresponding to $s(s = j\omega)$
f = $\omega/2\pi$
λ_r = analog low-pass reference radian frequency (usually the cutoff frequency)
$\bar{\omega}_3, \bar{\omega}_1$ = analog band-pass radian frequencies corresponding to $\pm\ \lambda_r$ (usually the band-edge frequencies)
$\bar{\omega}_2$ = geometric center radian frequency of band-pass analog filter
ω_1 = lower radian frequency of digital band-pass filter corresponding to $-\lambda_r$ in analog low-pass filter and $\bar{\omega}_1$ in analog band-pass filter
ω_3 = upper radian frequency of digital band-pass filter corresponding to λ_r in analog low-pass filter and $\bar{\omega}_3$ in analog band-pass filter.
ω_2 = radian frequency of digital band-pass filter corresponding to $\bar{\omega}_2$ in analog band-pass filter. (The quantity ω_2 will be called the "center frequency" even though it is usually not at the exact center of the band.)
f_1, f_2, f_3 = $\omega_1/2\pi, \omega_2/2\pi, \omega_3/2\pi$
B = $f_3 - f_1$ = reference bandwidth of digital band-pass filter
ν_1, ν_2, ν_3 = normalized frequencies of digital filter relative to folding frequency = $f_1/f_0, f_2/f_0, f_3/f_0$
b = normalized reference bandwidth of digital band-pass filter relative to folding frequency = $(f_3 - f_1)/f_0 = \nu_3 - \nu_1$

Using the modified notation introduced in this section, the low-pass to band-pass transformation given by (6-41) can now be expressed as

$$p = \bar{s} + \frac{\bar{\omega}_2^{\,2}}{\bar{s}} \tag{7-71}$$

The bilinear transformation of (7-4) now becomes

$$\bar{s} = \frac{C(1 - z^{-1})}{1 + z^{-1}} \tag{7-72}$$

Substitution of (7-72) into (7-71) and some manipulation yield

$$p = \frac{C^2 + \overline{\omega}_2^{\,2}}{C} \; \frac{1 - 2[(C^2 - \overline{\omega}_2^{\,2})/(C^2 + \overline{\omega}_2^{\,2})]\, z^{-1} + z^{-2}}{1 - z^{-2}} \tag{7-73}$$

Before simplifying (7-73), several relationships will be developed. From the properties of the bilinear transformation developed in Sec. 7-3, the frequency scale $\overline{\omega}$ can be related to ω by the equation

$$\overline{\omega} = C \tan \frac{\omega T}{2} \tag{7-74}$$

Application of (7-74) to (6-46) and (6-47), with suitable modifications in notation, results in the relationships

$$\tan^2 \frac{\omega_2 T}{2} = \tan \frac{\omega_1 T}{2} \tan \frac{\omega_3 T}{2} \tag{7-75}$$

and

$$\tan \frac{\omega_3 T}{2} - \tan \frac{\omega_1 T}{2} = \frac{\lambda_r}{C} \tag{7-76}$$

The preceding relationships may be expressed in terms of normalized frequencies as

$$\tan^2 \frac{\pi}{2} \nu_2 = \tan \frac{\pi}{2} \nu_1 \tan \frac{\pi}{2} \nu_3 \tag{7-77}$$

and

$$\tan \frac{\pi}{2} \nu_3 - \tan \frac{\pi}{2} \nu_1 = \frac{\lambda_r}{C} \tag{7-78}$$

The constant C can now be chosen so that $\overline{\omega}_2$ in the analog band-pass filter maps to ω_2 in the digital band-pass filter. From (7-8), C is determined to be

$$C = \overline{\omega}_2 \cot \frac{\omega_2 T}{2} \tag{7-79}$$

Using the preceding several equations and standard trigonometric identities, the constants appearing in (7-73) may be manipulated to yield simpler forms in which the digital center frequency and/or band-edge frequencies appear explicitly. The actual steps in this process will be left as an exercise for the reader (Prob. 7-17). The final form of the transformation will be given as

$$p = D\left[\frac{1 - Ez^{-1} + z^{-2}}{1 - z^{-2}}\right] \quad \checkmark \tag{7-80}$$

The constants D and E can be expressed in terms of the bandwidth and center frequency as

$$D = \lambda_r \cot \frac{\pi B}{2f_0} = \lambda_r \cot\left(\frac{\pi}{2} b\right) \quad \checkmark \tag{7-81}$$

$$E = 2 \cos \omega_2 T = 2 \cos \pi \frac{f_2}{f_0} = 2 \cos \pi\nu_2 \quad \checkmark \tag{7-82}$$

Alternately, D and E can be expressed in terms of the band-edge frequencies as

$$D = \lambda_r \cot \frac{(\omega_3 - \omega_1)T}{2} = \lambda_r \cot \frac{\pi}{2}(\nu_3 - \nu_1) \quad \checkmark \tag{7-83}$$

$$E = \frac{2 \cos[(\omega_3 + \omega_1)T/2]}{\cos[(\omega_3 - \omega_1)T/2]} = \frac{2 \cos[(\pi/2)(\nu_3 + \nu_1)]}{\cos[(\pi/2)(\nu_3 - \nu_1)]} \quad \checkmark \tag{7-84}$$

In the design of a band-pass filter using this approach, it is necessary to specify either the center frequency and the bandwidth or the band-edge frequencies. If the former quantities are specified, (7-81) and (7-82) may be used to determine the constants D and E. If the latter quantities are specified, (7-83) and (7-84) may be used to determine the constants. After the transformation is determined, the digital band-pass transfer function $H(z)$ is determined from the analog low-pass transfer function $G(p)$ by the relationship

$$H(z) = G(p)]_{p=D\left[\frac{1-Ez^{-1}+z^{-2}}{1-z^{-2}}\right]} \tag{7-85}$$

Observe that the number of poles (or order) of the band-pass digital filter will be twice that of the low-pass analog filter.

The frequency scale of the digital band-pass filter will now be expressed in terms of the analog low-pass filter. Since the $j\lambda$ axis of the p-plane maps to the $j\bar{\omega}$ axis of the $\bar{s}$-plane, and the $j\bar{\omega}$ axis of the $\bar{s}$-plane maps to the $j\omega$ axis of the s-plane, it follows that the $j\lambda$ axis of the p-plane can be directly related to the $j\omega$

axis of the s-plane. Letting $z = \epsilon^{j\omega T}$ and $p = j\lambda$ in (7-80), it can be shown (Prob. 7-18) that the following relationship is obtained:

$$\frac{\lambda}{D} = \frac{\cos \omega_2 T - \cos \omega T}{\sin \omega T} \qquad (7\text{-}86)$$

$$= \frac{\cos \pi\nu_2 - \cos \pi\nu}{\sin \pi\nu}$$

The function of (7-86) can be used in conjunction with the filter response curves in Chapt. 6 for designing digital band-pass filters to satisfy particular filtering requirements. This concept will be illustrated in Examples 7-10 and 7-11.

Example 7-10

A certain digital signal processing system has a sampling rate of 2 kHz. A digital band-pass filter is desired for the system and the specifications are as follows:

(a) Range of passband is from 300 Hz to 400 Hz with attenuation permitted to be no greater than 3 dB at the two band-edge frequencies.

(b) Attenuation must be at least 18 dB at 200 Hz and 500 Hz.

(c) Butterworth type response is desired.

Solution

The folding frequency is $f_0 = f_s/2 = 1000$ Hz. The two frequencies 300 Hz and 400 Hz will be selected as the band-edge frequencies f_1 and f_3 respectively. For convenience, these quantities and all subsequent frequencies will be converted to normalized form. We have

$$\nu_1 = \frac{300}{1000} = 0.3$$

$$\nu_3 = \frac{400}{1000} = 0.4 \qquad (7\text{-}87)$$

$$b = \frac{400 - 300}{1000} = 0.1$$

The center frequency ν_2 is determined from (7-77).

$$\tan^2 \frac{\pi}{2} \nu_2 = \tan \frac{\pi}{2} \nu_1 \tan \frac{\pi}{2} \nu_3 \qquad (7\text{-}88)$$

$$\nu_2 = 0.34797502$$

The transformation constants D and E may now be determined from (7-83) and (7-84) with the assumption that $\lambda_r = 1$ rad/s.

$$D = \lambda_r \cot(0.05\pi) = 6.31375152 \qquad (7\text{-}89)$$

$$E = \frac{2\cos(0.35\pi)}{\cos(0.05\pi)} = 0.91929910 \qquad (7\text{-}90)$$

We must now determine the minimum order required to satisfy the specifications. The reference bandwidth $b = 0.1$ will be related to the normalized Butterworth function at $\lambda_r = 1$. In order to determine the number of poles required, we must first determine the reference analog frequencies corresponding to $\nu_a = 200/1000 = 0.2$ and $\nu_b = 500/1000 = 0.5$, which are the two frequencies specified in the stopband. Letting λ_a and λ_b represent the two analog frequencies, we can determine these values from the frequency transformation function of (7-86).

$$\frac{\lambda_a}{D} = \frac{\cos 0.34797502\pi - \cos 0.2\pi}{\sin 0.2\pi}$$

$$\lambda_a = -3.7527638 \qquad (7\text{-}91)$$

$$\frac{\lambda_b}{D} = \frac{\cos 0.34797502\pi - \cos 0.5\pi}{\sin 0.5\pi}$$

$$\lambda_b = 2.9021131 \qquad (7\text{-}92)$$

Since the amplitude response of the analog filter is even, the negative sign in (7-91) is ignored in using Fig. 6-23. Because λ_a and λ_b are different, the attenuation at ν_a and ν_b will be different. If the low-pass analog response at λ_b is chosen to satisfy the requirements, the response at λ_a will more than meet the specifications. Thus, we must require that the low-pass reference function be down at least 18 dB at a normalized frequency of about 2.9 in Fig. 6-23. It is seen that a 2-pole Butterworth analog low-pass function will accomplish the task. The response at a normalized frequency of 3.75 is down about 23 dB.

The required digital filter will be a 4-pole transfer function, and it can be obtained by the application of (7-85). After some manipulation, the result is

$$H(z) = \frac{0.020083366(1 - z^{-2})^2}{(1 - 1.63682036z^{-1} + 2.23760739z^{-2} - 1.30711515z^{-3} + 0.64135154z^{-4})} \tag{7-93}$$

The amplitude response $A_{db}(v)$ is shown in Fig. 7-13.

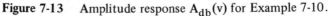

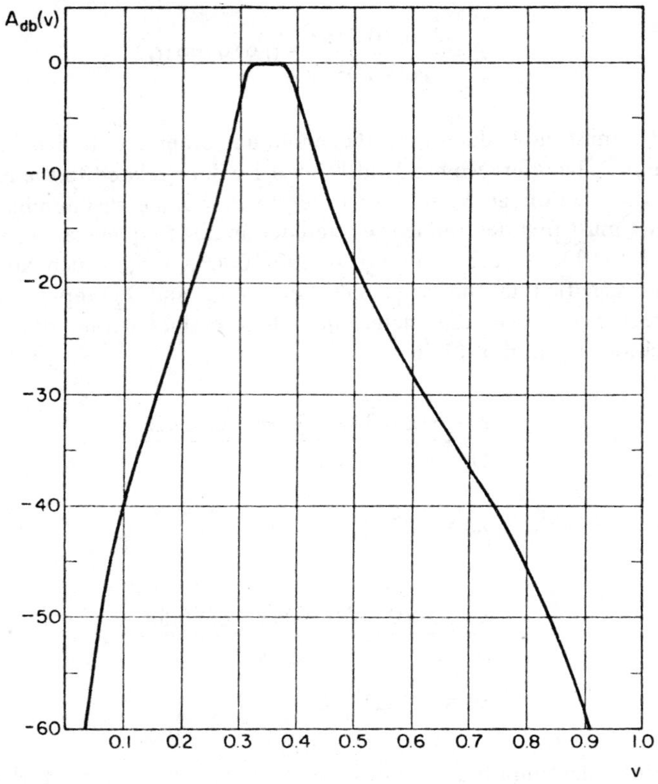

Figure 7-13 Amplitude response $A_{db}(v)$ for Example 7-10.

Example 7-11

Determine the type and the order of a digital band-pass filter having a sampling rate of 200 Hz that will satisfy the following requirements:

(a) Attenuation $\leqslant$ 1 dB for 19 Hz $\leqslant f \leqslant$ 21 Hz

(b) Attenuation $\geqslant$ 30 dB for $f \leqslant$ 18 Hz and $f \geqslant$ 20 Hz

Solution

The folding frequency is f_0 = 100 Hz. The band-edge frequencies are f_1 = 19 Hz and f_3 = 21 Hz. The normalized values are

$$\nu_1 = \frac{19}{100} = 0.19$$

$$\nu_3 = \frac{21}{100} = 0.21 \tag{7-94}$$

$$b = \frac{21 - 19}{100} = 0.02$$

The center frequency ν_2 is determined from

$$\tan^2 \frac{\pi}{2} \nu_2 = \tan \frac{\pi}{2} \nu_1 \tan \frac{\pi}{2} \nu_3$$

or (7-95)

$$\nu_2 = 0.19978361$$

The constant D is determined from (7-83) with the assumption that λ_r = 1 rad/s.

$$D = \cot \frac{\pi}{2}(0.02) = 31.820516 \tag{7-96}$$

The analog low-pass prototype frequencies corresponding to 18 Hz and 20 Hz may now be determined by means of the frequency transformation function of (7-86). Letting λ_a and λ_b represent these quantities, we have

$$\frac{\lambda_a}{D} = \frac{\cos(0.19978361\pi) - \cos(0.18\pi)}{\sin(0.18\pi)}$$

or (7-97)

$$\lambda_a = -2.0732504$$

$$\frac{\lambda_b}{D} = \frac{\cos(0.19978361\pi) - \cos(0.22\pi)}{\sin(0.22\pi)}$$

or (7-98)

$$\lambda_b = 1.9420640$$

We must ensure that the attenuation requirement is met at the lowest (in magnitude) analog low-pass frequency, which is λ_b. Choosing the 1 dB Chebyshev function of Fig. 6-25, we must determine the lowest order at which the response is down at least 30 dB at a normalized frequency of about 1.94. It is seen that a 4-pole function satisfies the requirement with over 2 dB to spare. At $\lambda_a = 2.07$, corresponding to the lower band-edge in the band-pass filter, the response is down over 35 dB. The final digital band-pass filter will thus have 8 poles.

7-9 Band-Rejection Digital Filter Design

In this section, the transformation developed in the last section will be modified to permit the design of a *band-rejection digital* IIR filter directly from a *low-pass analog* prototype transfer function. The notation introduced at the beginning of the last section will be used except for the following modifications:

(a) The variables $\bar{s}$ and s represent the Laplace variables for the analog and digital band-rejection functions.

(b) The frequencies ω_1, ω_2, and ω_3 now represent frequencies associated with the rejection band.

The details of this development follow a similar pattern to those of the last section, with the exception that here the analog low-pass to band-rejection transformation of (6-53) is combined with the bilinear transformation. The details will be left as exercises for the reader (Probs. 7-19 and 7-20), and the results will be summarized here.

The general form of the transformation is

$$p = \frac{D_1(1 - z^{-2})}{1 - E_1 z^{-1} + z^{-2}} \tag{7-99}$$

The constants D_1 and E_1 can be expressed in terms of the bandwidth and center frequency as

$$D_1 = \lambda_r \tan \frac{\pi}{2} \frac{B}{f_0} = \lambda_r \tan \frac{\pi}{2} b \tag{7-100}$$

$$E_1 = 2 \cos \omega_2 T = 2 \cos \frac{\pi f_2}{f_0} = 2 \cos \pi \nu_2 \tag{7-101}$$

Alternately, D_1 and E_1 can be expressed in terms of the band-edge frequencies as

$$D_1 = \lambda_r \tan \frac{(\omega_3 - \omega_1)T}{2} = \lambda_r \tan \frac{\pi}{2}(\nu_3 - \nu_1) \tag{7-102}$$

$$E_1 = \frac{2 \cos[(\omega_3 + \omega_1)T/2]}{\cos[(\omega_3 - \omega_1)T/2]} = \frac{2 \cos[(\pi/2)(\nu_3 + \nu_1)]}{\cos[(\pi/2)(\nu_3 - \nu_1)]} \tag{7-103}$$

It can be readily shown that ω_1, ω_2, and ω_3 may be related by

$$\tan^2 \frac{\omega_2 T}{2} = \tan \frac{\omega_1 T}{2} \tan \frac{\omega_3 T}{2} \tag{7-104}$$

or

$$\tan^2 \frac{\pi}{2} \nu_2 = \tan \frac{\pi}{2} \nu_1 \tan \frac{\pi}{2} \nu_3 \tag{7-105}$$

The frequency scale of the digital band-rejection filter is related to the frequency scale of the analog low-pass prototype by

$$\begin{aligned} \frac{\lambda}{D_1} &= \frac{\sin \omega T}{\cos \omega T - \cos \omega_2 T} \\ &= \frac{\sin \pi \nu}{\cos \pi \nu - \cos \pi \nu_2} \end{aligned} \tag{7-106}$$

The number of poles (or order) of the band-rejection digital filter will be twice that of the low-pass analog filter.

Example 7-12

A certain digital signal processing system operating at a sampling rate of 1 kHz is subjected to an undesirable interfering component at a frequency close to 100 Hz. A simple band-rejection algorithm is desired to eliminate the component. It appears that the following specifications will perform the task:

(a) 3 dB band-edge frequencies = 95 Hz and 105 Hz

(b) Two poles in final transfer function

Solution

Since the final transfer function is to contain two poles, the analog prototype filter is the simple one-pole function

$$G(p) = \frac{1}{1 + p} \tag{7-107}$$

in which the reference 3 dB frequency is $\lambda_r = 1$ rad/s. The folding frequency is $f_0 = 500$ Hz, and the various normalized frequencies are

$$\begin{aligned} \nu_1 &= \frac{95}{500} = 0.19 \\ \nu_3 &= \frac{105}{500} = 0.21 \\ b &= \frac{105 - 95}{500} = 0.02 \end{aligned} \tag{7-108}$$

The various constants required in the transformation are computed as follows:

$$D_1 = \tan\frac{\pi}{2}(0.02) = 0.031426266 \tag{7-109}$$

$$E_1 = \frac{2\cos((\pi/2)(0.4))}{\cos((\pi/2)(0.02))} = 1.61883279 \tag{7-110}$$

Substituting these constants in (7-99) and applying this transformation to (7-107), the transfer function is determined to be

$$H(z) = \frac{0.96953125(1 - 1.6188328z^{-1} + z^{-2})}{1 - 1.5695090z^{-1} + 0.9390625z^{-2}} \tag{7-111}$$

7-10 High-Pass Digital Filter Design

An inverted form of the bilinear transformation given in Sec. 7-3 may be used to design a *digital high-pass* filter directly from an *analog low-pass* prototype function. The same general conventions on notation established in Sec. 7-3 will be utilized here. The transformation is

$$p = \frac{C_1(1 + z^{-1})}{1 - z^{-1}} \tag{7-112}$$

The development of the results that follow will be left as exercises for the reader (Probs. 7-21 and 7-22).

The analog reference radian frequency λ is related to the digital frequency variables by

$$|\lambda| = C_1 \cot \frac{\omega T}{2} = C_1 \cot \frac{\pi}{2} \frac{f}{f_0} = C_1 \cot \frac{\pi}{2} \nu \tag{7-113}$$

The mapping constant C_1 can be determined from the stipulation that the low-pass amplitude response at λ_r be the same as the high-pass amplitude response at ω_r. Of course, in the low-pass case λ_r is at the upper end of the passband, but in the high-pass case ω_r is at the lower end of the passband. The constant is determined as

$$C_1 = \lambda_r \tan \frac{\omega_r T}{2} = \lambda_r \tan \frac{\pi}{2} \nu_r \tag{7-114}$$

The digital high-pass filter will have the same number of poles (or order) as the analog low-pass filter.

Example 7-13

Design a high-pass digital filter derived from a second-order Butterworth analog filter with a 3 dB cutoff frequency of 200 Hz. The sampling rate of the system is 500 Hz.

Solution

The low-pass analog prototype function is the same as was used in Ex. 7-1, so reference will be made to equation (7-20) for this function. The analog frequency $\lambda_r = 1$ rad/s must map to $f_r = 200$ Hz. The folding frequency is 250 Hz, so $\nu_r = 200/250 = 0.8$. The constant C_1 is determined as

$$C_1 = \tan \frac{\pi}{2}(0.8) = 3.0776835 \tag{7-115}$$

The transformation is

$$p = 3.0776835 \frac{(1 + z^{-1})}{(1 - z^{-1})} \tag{7-116}$$

Substitution of (7-116) into (7-20) yields

$$H(z) = \frac{0.0674553(1 - 2z^{-1} + z^{-2})}{1 + 1.14298z^{-1} + 0.412802z^{-2}} \tag{7-117}$$

Notice the similarity of this high-pass transfer function having a cutoff frequency of $\nu_c = 0.8$ with the low-pass transfer function of (7-23) having a cutoff frequency of $\nu_c = 0.2$. This similarity is more than coincidental, and the interested reader is referred to Prob. 7-23 for more details.

PROBLEMS

7-1 The sampling rate in a certain digital system is 100 Hz. It is desired to program a computer within the system to simulate the analog transfer function

$$G(s) = \frac{10}{s(s + 10)}$$

Good correspondence at low frequencies is a desirable criterion. Determine a single discrete transfer function using the bilinear transformation method.

7-2 Determine a discrete transfer function for the system of Prob. 7-1 using the impulse-invariance method.

7-3 Determine a discrete transfer function for the system of Prob. 7-1 using the step-invariance method.

7-4 Using the bilinear transformation method, design a low-pass digital filter derived from a second-order Chebyshev filter with 1 dB passband ripple.

The 1 dB "cutoff frequency" is 20 Hz, and the sampling rate of the system is 100 Hz.

7-5 Using the impulse-invariance method, design a filter to satisfy the requirements of Prob. 7-4.

7-6 Using the step-invariance method, design a filter to satsify the requirements of Prob. 7-4.

7-7 Using the bilinear transformation, design a third-order low-pass Butterworth digital filter with a 3 dB cutoff frequency at 10 Hz. The sampling rate of the system is 200 Hz.

7-8 Determine the digital transfer function for the system of Ex. 7-2 if the major criterion is that the amplitude response of the digital function be the same as the analog function at 400 Hz.

7-9 Determine a single transfer function utilizing the 1 dB Chebyshev function that will meet the requirements of Ex. 7-5.

7-10 Repeat Prob. 7-9 utilizing a cascade system of transfer functions, none of which exceeds second-order.

7-11 Determine the minimum order of a digital low-pass filter having a sampling rate of 2 kHz that will satisfy the following requirements:

(a) Bilinear transformation design based on a Chebyshev analog prototype function.

(b) Attenuation $\leqslant$ 2 dB for $0 \leqslant f \leqslant 250$ Hz

(c) Attenuation $\geqslant$ 70 dB for $f \geqslant 500$ Hz.

7-12 Determine the type and the minimum order of a digital band-pass filter having a sampling rate of 2 kHz that will satisfy the following requirements:

(a) Bilinear transformation design based on a Chebyshev analog prototype function.

(b) Attenuation $\leqslant$ 3 dB for 790 Hz $\leqslant f \leqslant$ 810 Hz

(c) Attenuation $\geqslant$ 16 dB for $f \leqslant$ 780 Hz and $f \geqslant$ 820 Hz.

7-13 Determine the minimum order of a high-pass filter having a sampling rate of 200 Hz that will satisfy the following requirements:

(a) Bilinear transformation design based on a Butterworth analog prototype function.

(b) Attenuation $\leqslant$ 3 dB for $f \geqslant 20$ Hz

(c) Attenuation $\geqslant$ 36 dB for $f \leqslant 5$ Hz

7-14 Determine a digital transfer function for a system satisfying the requirements of Prob. 7-12.

7-15 Determine the digital transfer function for a system satisfying the requirements of Prob. 7-13.

7-16 Design a band-rejection filter satisfying the following requirements:

(a) Two poles in final digital transfer function

(b) Sampling frequency = 2 kHz

(c) 3 dB band-edge frequencies of rejection band = 250 Hz and 300 Hz.

7-17 Verify the results of the analog low-pass to digital band-pass transformation given by equations (7-80) through (7-84). You can start with equation (7-73) and make use of any results developed up through equation (7-79) along with standard trigonometric identities.

7-18 Derive equation (7-86).

7-19 Using the bilinear transformation in conjunction with the analog low-pass to band-rejection transformation, derive the general form of the transformation given by equation (7-99) for designing band-rejection digital filters. Verify the results of equations (7-101) through (7-103). The development follows essentially the same pattern as for the band-pass case of Sec. 7-8.

7-20 Verify equation (7-106).

7-21 Derive equation (7-113).

7-22 Derive equation (7-114)

7-23 Consider a low-pass digital transfer function $H_{\ell p}(\overline{z})$, where $\overline{z}$ is momentarily used to denote the z-transform variable. Assume that the normalized cutoff frequency is $\overline{\nu}_c$. Consider the transformation

$$z = -\overline{z}$$

(a) Show that the resulting transfer function represents a *high-pass* digital filter having a cutoff frequency ν_c which is related to $\overline{\nu}_c$ by

$$\nu_c = 1 - \overline{\nu}_c$$

This means that a high-pass digital transfer function $H_{hp}(z)$ may be derived from a low-pass transfer function by means of the transformation

$$H_{hp}(z) = H_{\ell p}(-z)$$

(b) Use the results of (a) and the low-pass transfer function of Ex. 7-1 to determine the high-pass transfer function of Ex. 7-13.

7-24 Consider the system shown in Fig. P7-24. The input is a discrete-time signal, and it is converted to a continuous time signal by means of the

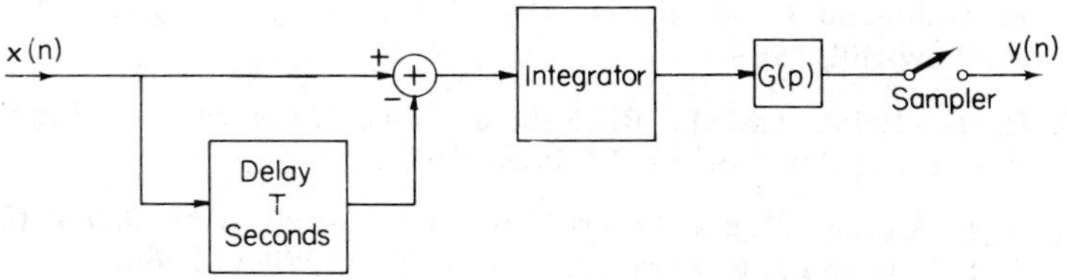

Figure P7-24.

zero-order holding circuit. This signal is then applied to a continuous-time filter having a transfer function $G(p)$, and the output is sampled. Show that the discrete transfer function $H(z)$ of this system is equivalent to the form derived in equation (7-64) using the step-invariance criteria.

Hint: $\mathfrak{Z}\left\{\mathcal{L}^{-1}\left[\epsilon^{-pT}F(p)\right]\right\} = z^{-1}F(z)$

7-25 Assume that it is desired to create a digital filter with *ramp-invariance*; i.e., the response due to a ramp input should be the same for the digital filter as for some prototype analog filter. Let $G(p)$ represent the prototype function and let $H(z)$ represent the desired discrete transfer function. Show that

$$H(z) = \frac{(z-1)^2}{Tz}\,\mathfrak{Z}\left\{\mathcal{L}^{-1}\left[\frac{G(p)}{p^2}\right]\right\}$$

7-26 Consider a digital band-pass filter designed with the procedure of Sec. 7-8 having a center frequency at half the folding frequency; i.e., $\nu_2 = 0.5$.

(a) Show that the amplitude response in this case has perfect arithmetic symmetry about the center frequency.

(b) Show that the transformation reduces to

$$p = D\left[\frac{1+z^{-2}}{1-z^{-2}}\right]$$

REFERENCES

1. A. T. Anderson, "Programmable digital filter performs multiple functions", *Electronics*, pp. 78-84, Oct. 26, 1970.
2. B. Gold and K. L. Jordan, Jr., "A note on digital filter synthesis", *Proc. IEEE*, vol. 55, pp. 1717-1718, Oct. 1968.

3. B. Gold and C. M. Rader, *Digital Processing of Signals*. New York: McGraw-Hill, 1969.

4. H. D. Helms and L. R. Rabiner, Eds., *Literature in Digital Signal Processing*. New York: IEEE Press, 1973.

5. J. F. Kaiser, "Digital Filters", in *System Analysis by Digital Computer*, F. F. Kuo and J. F. Kaiser, Eds., New York: Wiley, 1966.

6. L. R. Rabiner and C. M. Rader, Eds. *Digital Signal Processing*. New York: IEEE Press, 1972.

7. C. Rader and B. Gold, "Digital filter design techniques in the frequency domain", *Proc. IEEE*, vol. 55, pp. 149-171, Feb. 1967.

8. S. C. Silver, "The digital filter: potent processing tool", *Electronic Products*, pp. 32-37, March 1970.

9. W. D. Stanley, "Alignment of the digital filter frequency axis with the bilinear transformation", *Proc. IEEE*, vol. 60, pp. 341-342, March 1972.

10. J. V. Wait, "Digital Filters", in *Active Filters: Lumped, Distributed, Integrated, Digital, and Parametric*, L. P. Huelsman, Ed. New York: McGraw-Hill, 1970.

11. S. A. White and T. Mitsutomi, "The IC digital filter: a low-cost signal-processing tool", *Control Engineering*, pp. 58-68, June 1970.

CHAPTER EIGHT

FINITE IMPULSE RESPONSE DIGITAL FILTER DESIGN

8-0 Introduction

The primary objective in this chapter is the development of the basic properties of the finite impulse response (FIR) digital filter. FIR filters have both advantages and disadvantages as compared with infinite impulse response (IIR) filters considered in the last chapter, so it is important that these various properties be considered in determining the requirements for a particular application. Among the advantages of FIR filters are the possible achievement of ideal linear phase characteristics and less susceptibility of the actual implementation to parameter quantization effects. Among the disadvantages are possible long time delays, the necessity for higher-order functions to achieve prescribed filtering requirements, and the lack of simpler design procedures that would permit direct attainment of filter specifications.

It appears that FIR filters will experience increasing usage in the future, so it is expected that simpler design procedures will evolve. In this chapter, we will develop the fundamental properties of FIR filter functions, and some of the basic design concepts will be explored. Additional FIR filter design concepts will be discussed in Chapt. 10 in conjunction with the fast Fourier transform.

8-1 General Discussion

The basic differences between the IIR digital filter and the FIR digital filter were discussed at the beginning of Chapt. 7, and various approximation procedures for IIR filters were subsequently developed in that chapter. We will now direct our major efforts to the properties and design concepts of FIR filters.

An FIR filter is one in which the impulse response $h(n)$ is limited to a finite number of points. The impulse response can be expressed as

$$\begin{aligned} h(n) &= a_n \quad 0 \leqslant n \leqslant k \\ &= 0 \quad \text{elsewhere} \end{aligned} \tag{8-1}$$

In some cases, it is desirable to express $h(n)$ in the form

$$h(n) = \sum_{i=0}^{k} a_i \delta(n - i) \tag{8-2}$$

which is equivalent to (8-1). The transfer function corresponding to (8-1) or (8-2) can be expressed in the form

$$\begin{aligned} H(z) &= \sum_{m=0}^{k} a_m z^{-m} \\ &= a_0 + a_1 z^{-1} + a_2 z^{-2} + \cdots + a_k z^{-k} \end{aligned} \tag{8-3}$$

The integer k represents the *order* of the function.

Note that if no coefficients in (8-1) are missing, there will be $k + 1$ terms in the impulse response for a function of order k. The values of $h(n)$ at these points are readily determined from either of the forms (8-1), (8-2), or (8-3). We observe that $h(0) = a_0$, $h(1) = a_1$, $h(2) = a_2$, etc.

Many authors refer to the function of (8-3) as having only zeros and no poles. While this terminology is widely used in the literature, actually $H(z)$ has a pole of order k at $z = 0$. This is readily seen by multiplying numerator and denominator of (8-3) by z^k.

The difference equation relating the output to the input in (8-3) can be readily expressed as

$$y(n) = \sum_{i=0}^{k} a_i x(n - i) = \sum_{i=0}^{k} h(i) x(n - i) \tag{8-4}$$

Equation (8-4) describes a *nonrecursive* realization for the FIR transfer function. However, we also observe that since the difference equation involves only the input and the impulse response, it can be considered as a convolution summation between these two functions. This property was not encountered with IIR filters, since the input-output difference equation and convolution summation equation were quite different in form in that case. Thus, a nonrecursive realization of an FIR filter is equivalent to a direct convolution between the input and output from an implementation point of view.

As in the case of IIR filters, the basic design problem is to determine the constants in the transfer function (or impulse response) that will satisfy the given requirements. Since there are only numerator coefficients present in the transfer function of an FIR filter, the problem is somewhat more restricted now. The various transformations used in the preceding chapter cannot be used here since they usually yield IIR functions. Different procedures must be utilized for FIR filters, and it will be seen that the design process is usually more difficult in this case.

Some of the general properties of FIR filters are summarized as follows:

(a) Implementation is readily achieved by means of a nonrecursive or direct convolution type of realization. This type of implementation does not require feedback, so the direct form 1 and direct form 2 realizations are identical.

(b) Implementation is also possible by high-speed convolution using the Fast Fourier transform or by recursive techniques.

(c) Errors arising from quantization, roundoff, and coefficient inaccuracies are usually less critical in nonrecursive realizations of FIR filters than for IIR filters. This advantage is primarily due to the lack of feedback in FIR nonrecursive realizations.

(d) The transfer function of an FIR filter with a nonrecursive implementation has all of its poles at the origin and is always stable.

(e) FIR filters with ideal linear phase characteristics may be designed. This is seldom possible with IIR design procedures.

(f) A higher-order FIR filter is normally required to obtain the same sharpness of amplitude response control as compared with an IIR filter.

(g) The amount of time delay increases with the number of terms and can become quite large for a filter of relatively high order.

(h) In general, the overall approximation problem for FIR filters is somewhat more difficult than with the methods used for IIR filters. One of the primary problems is that the specification of such parameters as passband and stopband ripple bounds is more complicated for FIR filters. (The eventual compilation of a large number of actual designs may help to alleviate this problem.)

8-2 Fourier Series Method

In this section, we will consider the Fourier series method for approximating an FIR amplitude response. This approach is rather basic in the sense that all other methods for FIR filter response utilize much of the same underlying theory. The Fourier series method is relatively straightforward in concept, so it will be used as the primary basis for the efforts of this chapter. The major disadvantage is that one cannot easily specify in advance the exact levels for passband and stopband ripple levels, so it may be necessary to investigate several alternate designs to obtain a suitable function for a given filter requirement.

In actual practice, the Fourier series method is best used in conjunction with a "window function". To simplify the overall presentation, the basic concepts will be developed in this section without regard to such a function. In the next section, the theory of the window function will be discussed, and it will be related to the work of this section.

The key to the Fourier series method is the fact that the amplitude response $A(f)$ corresponding to a DTLTI impulse response $h(n)$ is a periodic function of *frequency* and as such can be expanded in a Fourier series in the *frequency-domain*. (Note that the most common application of Fourier series in signal analysis is that of expanding a periodic *time* function in a Fourier series in the *time* domain, so the senses of time and frequency are somewhat reversed in the present application.) The coefficients obtained from the Fourier series can then be related to the impulse response, and the desired coefficients of the FIR transfer function can then be obtained.

A significant advantage of FIR filter functions is the capability of obtaining linear phase (or constant time delay). In order to obtain constant time delay easily, it is necessary that the Fourier series have either cosine terms only or sine terms only, but not both at the same time.

Since the amplitude response is generally regarded as an even function of frequency, the concept of expanding it in a cosine series seems reasonable. On the other hand, the reader may be puzzled as to how a sine series, which normally arises in the expansion of an odd function, could be used to expand the amplitude response. The answer to this dilemma lies in the fact that we normally *interpret* the steady-state transfer function to have an *even amplitude* response and an *odd phase* response. In some applications it is desirable to interpret these quantities in an opposite sense, i.e., an *odd amplitude* response and an *even phase* response.

To illustrate this concept with a simple example, consider the steady-state transfer function of the analog differentiator, which is

$$G(j\omega) = j\omega \tag{8-5}$$

The usual manner for interpreting the amplitude and phase is

$$\begin{aligned} A(f) &= |\omega| \quad \text{for} \quad -\infty < \omega < \infty \\ \beta(f) &= -90^\circ \quad \text{for} \quad -\infty < \omega < 0 \\ &= +90^\circ \quad \text{for} \quad 0 < \omega < \infty \end{aligned} \tag{8-6}$$

This interpretation results in an even amplitude function and an odd phase function. On the other hand, we may write

$$\begin{aligned} A(f) &= \omega \quad \text{for} \quad -\infty < \omega < \infty \\ \beta(f) &= +90^\circ \quad \text{for} \quad -\infty < \omega < \infty \end{aligned} \tag{8-7}$$

This latter interpretation results in an odd amplitude function and an even phase function. Yet, the combination of the two functions in (8-6) produces the same overall transfer function as the combination in (8-7). As far as the present application is concerned, this would suggest that the usual interpretation of even amplitude and odd phase would be used in the case of a cosine series expansion, but the opposite interpretation could be made in case of a sine series expansion. The choice of which type of expansion to use in a given application will be discussed later.

Consider first the case of a *cosine series* representation. Let $A_d(f)$ denote some *desired* amplitude response. We will assume that this function is even and that it is periodic in f with a period f_s. (Note that $f_s = 1/T$ is the sampling frequency.) Let $A(f)$ represent the *approximation* to $A_d(f)$ that will result when the series is terminated after M terms. A representative case is illustrated in Fig. 8-1. The form of the finite series is

$$A(f) = \frac{\alpha_0}{2} + \sum_{m=1}^{M} \alpha_m \cos 2\pi m T f \tag{8-8}$$

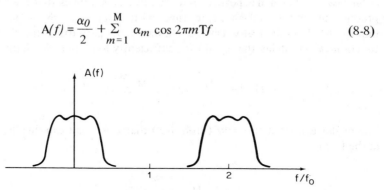

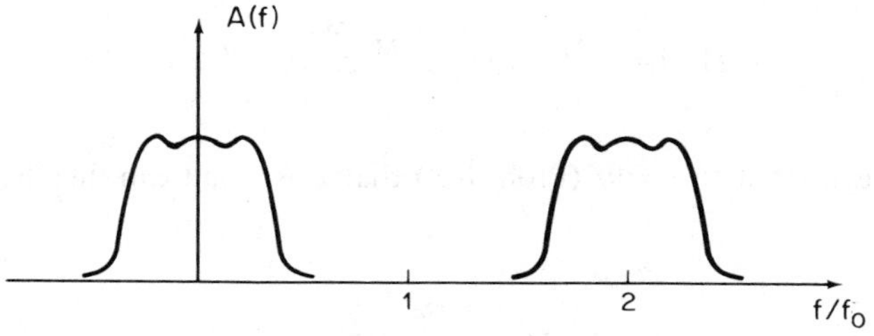

Figure 8-1 Fourier series approximation for even amplitude response.

From the basic properties of Fourier series (including the symmetry associated with an even function), the reader is invited to show (Prob. 8-1) that an expression for determining the coefficients is

$$\alpha_m = \frac{4}{f_s} \int_0^{f_s/2} A_d(f) \cos 2\pi m T f \, df \tag{8-9}$$

In exponential form, (8-8) can be expressed as

$$A(f) = \sum_{m=-M}^{M} c_m \epsilon^{j2\pi mTf} \tag{8-10}$$

where

$$c_m = c_{-m} = \frac{\alpha_m}{2} = \frac{2}{f_s} \int_0^{f_s/2} A_d(f) \cos 2\pi mTf\, df \tag{8-11}$$

Equation (8-10) can be considered as the evaluation of some unknown discrete transfer function on the unit circle in the z-plane. To perform such an evaluation, we normally let $z = \epsilon^{j\omega T} = \epsilon^{j2\pi Tf}$. In this case, we can reverse the process and replace $\epsilon^{j2\pi Tf}$ by z. Denoting this initial series by $H_1(z)$ and turning it around for later convenience, we have

$$H_1(z) = \sum_{m=M}^{-M} c_m z^m \tag{8-12}$$

The form of (8-12) represents an FIR transfer function, but it is *non-causal* in that it has positive powers of z. This implies that the filter would produce an output advanced in time with respect to the input, which is impossible. This difficulty can be alleviated by permitting the final transfer function $H(z)$ to delay the signal for a sufficiently long time. We define

$$H(z) = z^{-M} H_1(z) = z^{-M} \sum_{m=M}^{-M} c_m z^m \tag{8-13}$$

The reader is invited to verify (Prob. 8-3) that this result can then be expressed in the form

$$H(z) = \sum_{i=0}^{2M} a_i z^{-i} \tag{8-14}$$

where

$$a_i = c_{M-i} \tag{8-15}$$

The FIR transfer function of (8-14) is of order 2M, which implies that there will be 2M delays in a direct implementation. Letting τ represent the length of the impulse response, we have

$$\tau = 2MT \tag{8-16}$$

The amplitude response is completely unaffected by the time shift and is still $A(f)$. On the other hand, the additional time delay introduces a phase shift $\beta(f)$ for $H(z)$ which, in radians, is given by

$$\beta(f) = -MT\omega = -2\pi MTf \qquad (8\text{-}17)$$

Observe that the phase is a linear function of frequency representing a constant time delay of MT seconds. The delay increases linearly with the order of the filter.

Consider next the case of a *sine series* representation. In this case, it is necessary that the amplitude response $A_d(f)$ be an odd periodic function with a period f_s. Again, let $A(f)$ represent the approximation resulting from M terms. The form of the response in a typical case is illustrated in Fig. 8-2. The form of the finite series is

$$A(f) = \sum_{m=1}^{M} \beta_m \sin 2\pi mTf \qquad (8\text{-}18)$$

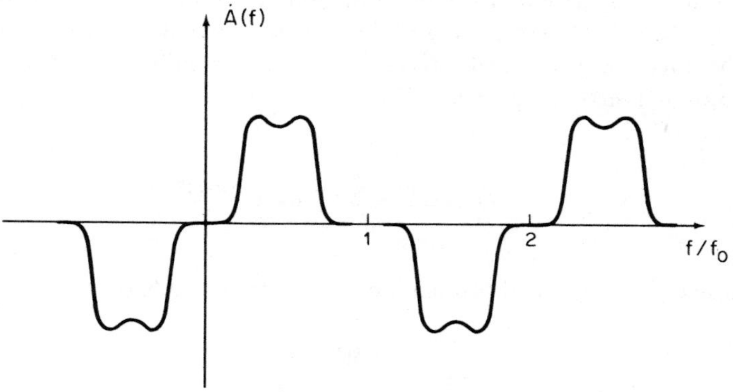

Figure 8-2 Fourier series approximation for odd amplitude response.

The reader is invited to show (Prob. 8-2) that the following expression can be obtained:

$$\beta_m = \frac{4}{f_s} \int_0^{f_s/2} A_d(f) \sin 2\pi mTf\, df \qquad (8\text{-}19)$$

In exponential form, (8-18) can be expressed as

$$A(f) = \sum_{m=-M}^{M} \frac{d_m}{j} \epsilon^{j2\pi mTf} \qquad (8\text{-}20)$$

where

$$d_m = \frac{\beta_m}{2} = \frac{2}{f_s} \int_0^{f_s/2} A_d(f) \sin 2\pi m T f \, df \tag{8-21}$$

and

$$d_{-m} = -d_m \tag{8-22}$$

Before we can convert (8-20) to a z-domain function, it is necessary to investigate the significance of the imaginary j factor in the denominator. This factor was not present for the cosine series, and there was no delay or phase shift at this stage of the development. Certainly, we want to eliminate any complex or imaginary factors before obtaining the final transfer function, since we have dealt only with real coefficients in that form.

The problem is rectified by the requirement that the phase must be even when the amplitude is assumed to be odd. Let $\beta_1(f)$ represent the phase corresponding to the initial transfer function. Thus, instead of $A(f)$, we actually need $A(f) \angle \beta_1(f)$ before changing to the z-plane function, and it is necessary that $\beta_1(f)$ be even. A phase shift $\beta_1(f) = \pi/2$, corresponding to a j factor in the numerator will serve the purpose. Thus,

$$A(f) \angle \beta_1(f) = \sum_{m=-M}^{M} d_m \epsilon^{j2\pi m T f} \tag{8-23}$$

Replacing $\epsilon^{j2\pi T f}$ by z and turning the series around, we have

$$H_1(z) = \sum_{m=M}^{-M} d_m z^m \tag{8-24}$$

As in the case of the cosine series, the initial result of (8-24) is a non-causal function. Again, we multiply by z^{-M} to obtain the required causal function. The reader is invited to verify (Prob. 8-4) that the result can be expressed as

$$H(z) = \sum_{i=0}^{2M} a_i z^{-i} \tag{8-25}$$

where

$$a_i = d_{M-i} \tag{8-26}$$

The resulting transfer function is of order 2M. Note that the middle term in (8-25) is missing in this case; i.e., $a_M = 0$. This property arises from the absence of a dc term in the sine series expansion.

As in the case of the cosine series, the amplitude response is unaffected by the delay and is simply $A(f)$. However, the resulting phase response $\beta(f)$ will be a combination of the phase associated with the non-causal function and the additional phase due to the added delay. The net result in radians is

$$\beta(f) = \frac{\pi}{2} - MT\omega = \frac{\pi}{2} - 2\pi MTf \tag{8-27}$$

The choice as to whether a given function should be expanded in cosine or sine terms usually depends on whether the phase shift should be an exact linear phase of the form of (8-17) or a constant 90° phase shift plus a linear phase term of the form of (8-27). If the desired response is a filter function whose passband exhibits a constant amplitude response, the cosine series is normally the form that would be used. The sine series is used primarily in special cases where the amplitude response is asymptotic at low frequencies to ω^k, with k odd. An example of this type is a digital differentiator. (The reader might wish to momentarily look ahead to Fig. 8-10 for an illustration of this function.)

Before leaving this section, we will present simplified alternate forms for obtaining the impulse response coefficients when the frequency response is expressed in terms of the normalized frequency $\nu = f/f_0$, where $f_0 = f_s/2$ is the folding frequency. Let $A_d(\nu)$ represent the desired amplitude response, and let $A(\nu)$ represent the approximation. With this approach, the period must always be selected as 2 units on the ν scale.

For the *cosine* series, expressions for $A(\nu)$ and c_m are

$$A(\nu) = \sum_{m=-M}^{M} c_m \epsilon^{jm\pi\nu} \tag{8-28}$$

$$c_m = \int_0^1 A_d(\nu) \cos m\pi\nu \, d\nu \tag{8-29}$$

For the *sine* series, expressions for $A(\nu)$ and d_m are

$$A(\nu) = \sum_{m=-M}^{M} \frac{d_m}{j} \epsilon^{jm\pi\nu} \tag{8-30}$$

$$d_m = \int_0^1 A_d(\nu) \sin m\pi\nu \, d\nu \tag{8-31}$$

The procedure for determining $H(z)$ is essentially the same as before. In this case, the non-causal form of the transfer function is obtained by substituting z

for $\epsilon^{j\pi\nu}$. From that point on, the process is the same as discussed earlier. The primary advantage of using the normalized form is that the results are independent of the actual values of frequencies involved, but are dependent only on the relative frequencies with respect to the folding or sampling frequency.

Example 8-1

A low-pass FIR digital filter is to be designed using the Fourier series approach. The desired amplitude response is

$$
\begin{aligned}
A_d(f) &= 1 \text{ for } 0 \leqslant f < 125 \text{ Hz} \\
&= 0 \text{ elsewhere in the range } 0 \leqslant f \leqslant f_0
\end{aligned}
$$

The sampling frequency is 1 kHz, and the impulse response is to be limited to 20 delays. Determine the transfer function using the techniques of this section.

Solution

The appropriate representation for the desired amplitude response is as an even function of frequency as shown in Fig. 8-3. The curve in (a) is shown in

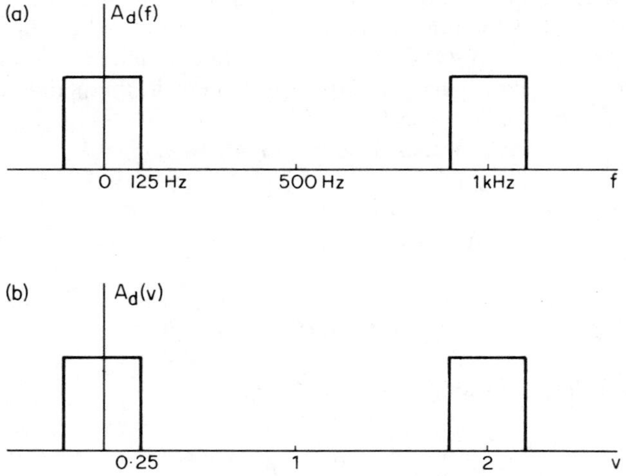

Figure 8-3 Desired amplitude response for Ex. 8-1.

terms of the actual frequency scale, while the curve in (b) corresponds to a normalized frequency scale. Note that the folding frequency is f_0 = 500 Hz. For convenience, the problem will be developed in terms of the normalized frequency. Thus, the desired response can be restated for expansion purposes as

$$A_d(\nu) = 1 \quad \text{for } -0.25 < \nu < 0.25$$
$$= 0 \text{ elsewhere in the range } -1 < \nu < 1$$

The coefficients c_m can be determined from (8-29). We have

$$c_m = \int_0^{0.25} (1) \cos m\pi\nu \, d\nu = \left. \frac{\sin m\pi\nu}{m\pi} \right]_0^{0.25} = \frac{\sin 0.25\, m\pi}{m\pi} \tag{8-32}$$

The requirement that the impulse response be limited to 20 delays implies that the order of the transfer function should be 20. There could be as many as 21 terms in the impulse response, since one component need not be delayed. The necessary coefficients may be obtained by evaluating (8-32) for m = 0 through m = 10. The various values are

$$\begin{array}{ll} c_0 = 0.25 & c_1 = 0.22507908 \\ c_2 = 0.15915494 & c_3 = 0.07502636 \\ c_4 = 0 & c_5 = -0.04501582 \\ c_6 = -0.05305165 & c_7 = -0.03215415 \\ c_8 = 0 & c_9 = 0.02500879 \\ c_{10} = 0.03183099 & \end{array} \tag{8-33}$$

The initial form of the transfer function is of the form of (8-12) with coefficients for negative i determined by $c_{-m} = c_m$. To make this function causal, we must multiply by z^{-10}. The final result can be expressed as

$$H(z) = \sum_{i=0}^{20} a_i z^{-i} \tag{8-34}$$

where $a_i = c_{10-i}$. This result will be discussed in more detail and extended in Ex. 8-2 at the end of Sect. 8-3. The final array of a_i coefficients in (8-34) may be observed in the column "Rectangular" in Table 8-1.

8-3 Window Functions

All of the window functions that will be considered share this property: they are even functions of time when centered at the origin. For that reason, it is desirable to momentarily return to the non-causal form of the filter impulse response to study the effects produced. After the impulse response has been

	Rectangular	Triangular	Hanning	Hamming	Kaiser ($\theta = 2\pi$)
a_0 a_{20}	0.03183099	0	0	0.00254648	0.00036542
a_1 a_{19}	0 02500879	0 00250088	0.00061201	0 00256375	0.00113712
a_2 a_{18}	0	0	0	0	0
a_3 a_{17}	-0.03215415	-0 00964624	-0 00662721	-0.00866936	-0.00637990
a_4 a_{16}	-0 05305165	-0.02122066	-0.01832889	-0.02110671	-0.01698822
a_5 a_{15}	-0.04501582	-0.02250791	-0.2250791	-0.02430854	-0.02092616
a_6 a_{14}	0	0	0	0	0
a_7 a_{13}	0.07502636	0.05251845	0.05956287	0 06079995	0.05758099
a_8 a_{12}	0. 15915494	0. 12732395	0. 14395700	0. 14517283	0 14168986
a_9 a_{11}	0. 22507908	0.2025717	0.21957100	0.22001165	0.21867619
a_{10}	0 25	0.25	0.25	0 25	0.25

Table 8-1 Digital filter coefficients for Exs. 8-1 and 8-2

appropriately modified, the required delay may be inserted to make the final result causal.

The results that follow will be developed in terms of the c_m coefficients of the cosine series. Should the series be a sine series, one need only replace the c_m coefficients by the d_m coefficients, and the results are equally valid.

Consider then the non-causal FIR transfer function

$$H_1(z) = \sum_{m=-M}^{M} c_m z^{-m} \tag{8-35}$$

The impulse response corresponding to (8-35) is

$$h_1(n) = \sum_{m=-M}^{M} c_m \delta(n - m) \tag{8-36}$$

The resulting impulse response is centered at the origin and is an even function of n in the case of the cosine series. (It would be an odd function of n for a sine series.)

If the coefficients of the FIR filter are determined from the procedure of the last section, a particular difficulty arises that has not yet been considered. The coefficients of the transfer function were obtained by terminating the Fourier series expansion of the desired frequency function with a finite number of terms. It will be recalled from the familiar Gibbs phenomenon that abrupt termination may result in poor convergence of the resulting series, particularly in the vicinity of discontinuities.

This problem is illustrated in Fig. 8-4. A hypothetical impulse response $h_d(n)$ with an infinite number of terms is shown in (a). For purposes of discussion, assume that this series will converge uniformly to represent the

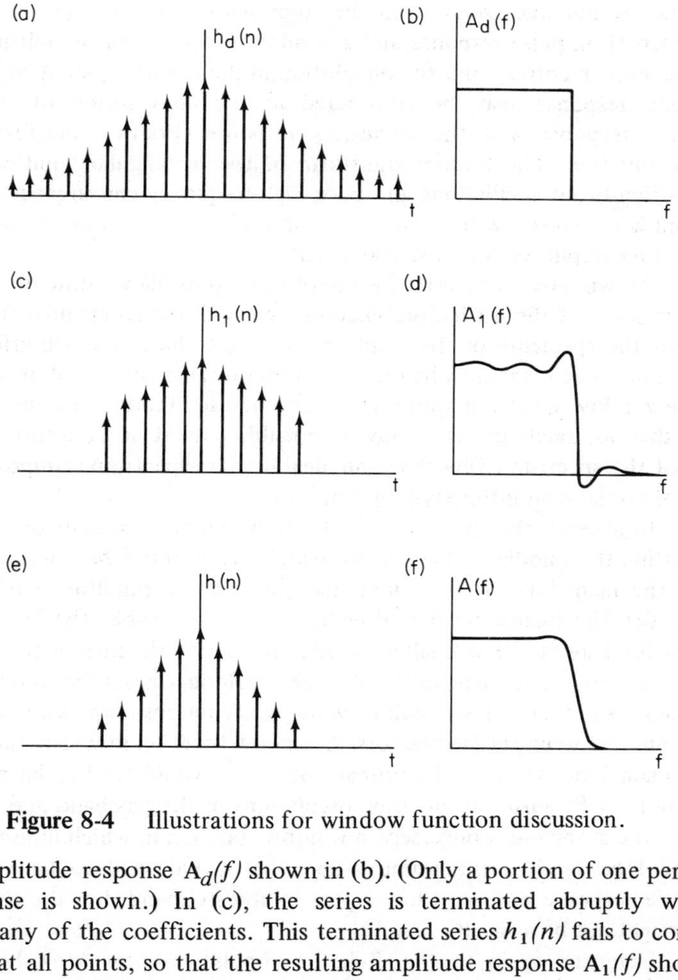

Figure 8-4 Illustrations for window function discussion.

desired amplitude response $A_d(f)$ shown in (b). (Only a portion of one period of the response is shown.) In (c), the series is terminated abruptly without modifying any of the coefficients. This terminated series $h_1(n)$ fails to converge uniformly at all points, so that the resulting amplitude response $A_1(f)$ shown in (d) suffers from oscillations and poor convergence.

The process of terminating the series after a finite number of terms can be thought of as multiplying the infinite-length impulse response by a finite-width *window function*. In a sense, the window function determines how much of the original impulse response that we can "see", so the term "window" is quite descriptive. In the case where the series is abruptly terminated without modification of any coefficients, we may consider the window function to be *rectangular*. The rectangular window function can be considered as the source of some of the convergence difficulties, as will be seen shortly.

Since it is necessary to terminate the series with a finite number of terms, the question arises whether there might be a better window function for this purpose. We can gain some insight into this concept by considering again that the terminated series can be represented as the product of the infinite-length impulse response and a window function. Since multiplication in the time-domain corresponds to convolution in the frequency-domain, the actual frequency response may be considered as the convolution of the desired frequency response and the frequency response (Fourier transform) of the window function. The Fourier transform of the rectangular window function exhibits significant oscillations and poor high-frequency convergence. When this spectrum is convolved with the desired amplitude response, poor convergence of the resulting amplitude response may result.

We will now investigate the use of other possible window functions that minimize some of the difficulties encountered with the rectangular function. In order for the spectrum of the window function to have minimal effect on the desired amplitude response when the two functions are convolved, it is necessary that the window spectrum approximate an impulse function in some sense. This means that as much of its energy as possible should be concentrated at the center of the spectrum. Obviously, an ideal impulse spectrum is impossible since this would require an infinitely-long window.

In general, the spectrum of a window function consists of a *main lobe* representing the middle of the spectrum and various *side lobes* located on either side of the main lobe. It is desired that the window function satisfy the two criteria: (a) The main lobe should be as narrow as possible. (b) The maximum side lobe level should be as small as possible relative to the main lobe.

It turns out that both of these criteria cannot be simultaneously optimized, so that most usable window functions represent a suitable compromise between the two factors. A window function in which minimization of the main lobe width is the primary objective would tend to have a sharper cutoff but might suffer from some oscillations in the passband and significant ripple in the stopband. Conversely, a window function in which minimization of the side lobe level is the primary objective would tend to have a smooth amplitude response and very low ripple in the stopband, but the sharpness of cutoff might not be as great.

Referring again to Fig. 8-4, the impulse response $h(n)$ shown in (e) represents the function obtained by multiplying the impulse response in (a) by a more desirable window function than the rectangular window. The modified response $A(f)$ shown in (f) is now smoother and has a lower ripple level in the stop band.

All window functions that will be considered are even functions of n when centered at the origin. Let w_m represent the various coefficients of a particular window function, and let c_m^1 represent the coefficients of the modified transfer function. The modification is simply

$$c_m' = w_m c_m \tag{8-37}$$

The modified non-causal transfer function $H_1'(z)$ is then

$$H_1'(z) = \sum_{m=-M}^{M} c'_m z^{-m} \tag{8-38}$$

The resulting function may be made causal by multiplying by z^{-M}, and the final result is

$$H(z) = \sum_{i=0}^{2M} a_i z^{-i} \tag{8-39}$$

where

$$a_i = c'_{M-i} \tag{8-40}$$

For a sine series, the various c_m terms in the preceding development should be replaced by d_m terms.

We will now discuss some of the window functions that either have been or could be used in designing FIR filters. It is appropriate to mention at this point that these same window functions may be used in spectral analysis in conjunction with the discrete Fourier transform, so that reference to them will be made again in Chapt. 10.

For convenience in development and presentation, all functions will be presented in continuous-time form as a function of the variable t. To apply these functions to a discrete-time function, the variable t should be replaced by $n\text{T}$, and the variable n can then assume values from 0 to M. All functions are even and are assumed to have a width τ, which is the desired width of the filter impulse response. Because of the even nature of these functions, the window coefficients in the range from -1 to $-\text{M}$ are readily obtained from those in the positive range.

In each case, we will let $w(t)$ denote the time-domain window function, and we let $W(f)$ represent its Fourier transform. Because of the number of curves involved and the application to spectral analysis in Chapt. 10, the window functions and their transforms are given in the Appendix. Figure numbers beginning with the letter A in the remainder of this section refer to curves in Appendix.

In studying the amplitude frequency response of window functions, it is desirable to employ a decibel scale. All of the amplitude response curves will be presented in terms of a decibel function $W_{db}(f)$. In each case, the decibel response is normalized with respect to the dc value W(0). The function $W_{db}(f)$ is then defined as

$$W_{db}(f) = 20 \log_{10} \frac{|W(f)|}{W(0)} \tag{8-41}$$

We will now consider some common window functions.

Rectangular Window. The rectangular window will be considered primarily as a basis for reference in studying other functions. The rectangular function is simply

$$w(t) = 1 \text{ for } |t| < \frac{\tau}{2} \qquad = 0 \text{ elsewhere} \tag{8-42}$$

The Fourier transform is

$$W(f) = \frac{\tau \sin \pi f \tau}{\pi f \tau} \tag{8-43}$$

The function $w(t)$ is one of the curves shown in Fig. A-1, and $W_{db}(f)$ is shown in Fig. A-2, both located in the Appendix.

Triangular Window. The triangular window function is defined as

$$w(t) = 1 - \frac{2|t|}{\tau} \quad |t| \leqslant \frac{\tau}{2} \qquad = 0 \text{ elsewhere} \tag{8-44}$$

We will leave as an exercise for the reader (Prob. 8-16) to show that the Fourier transform of (8-44) is

$$W(f) = \frac{\tau}{2}\left[\frac{\sin(\pi f \tau/2)}{(\pi f \tau/2)}\right]^2 \tag{8-45}$$

The function $w(t)$ is shown along with the rectangular window in Fig. A-1, and $W_{db}(f)$ is shown in Fig. A-3, both in the Appendix. The width of the main lobe of the triangular window function is about twice as wide as that of the rectangular window, but the side lobe level is much lower.

Hanning Window. The Hanning or cosine-squared window function is defined as

$$w(t) = \cos^2 \frac{\pi t}{\tau} = \frac{1}{2}\left(1 + \cos \frac{2\pi t}{\tau}\right) \text{ for } |t| \leqslant \frac{\tau}{2} \qquad = 0 \text{ elsewhere} \tag{8-46}$$

We will leave as an exercise for the reader (Prob. 8-17) to show that

$$W(f) = \frac{\tau}{2}\frac{\sin \pi f\tau}{\pi f\tau}\left[\frac{1}{1-(f\tau)^2}\right] \tag{8-47}$$

The function $w(t)$ is shown in Fig. A-4, and $W_{db}(f)$ is shown in Fig. A-5, in the Appendix.

Hamming Window. The Hamming window function is defined as

$$w(t) = 0.54 + 0.46 \cos \frac{2\pi t}{\tau} \quad \text{for} \quad |t| \leqslant \frac{\tau}{2} \tag{8-48}$$

$$= 0 \text{ elsewhere}$$

We will leave as an exercise for the reader (Prob. 8-18) to show that

$$W(f) = \frac{\tau \sin \pi f\tau}{\pi f\tau}\left[\frac{0.54 - 0.08(f\tau)^2}{1-(f\tau)^2}\right] \tag{8-49}$$

The function $w(t)$ is shown in Fig. A-6, and $W_{db}(f)$ is shown in Fig. A-7.

Kaiser Windows. A family of flexible window functions was developed by Kaiser (ref. 5). This family can be described by the equation

$$w(t) = \frac{I_0[\theta\sqrt{1-(2t/\tau)^2}\,]}{I_0(\theta)} \qquad \text{for} \quad |t| \leqslant \frac{\tau}{2} \tag{8-50}$$

where I_0 is the modified Bessel function of the first kind and order zero and θ is a parameter. By varying the parameter θ, the tradeoff between main lobe width and the side lobe level can be adjusted. Large values of θ correspond to wider main lobe widths and smaller side lobe levels. Several typical Kaiser functions are shown in Fig. A-8.

The Fourier transform corresponding to (8-50) can be expressed as

$$W(f) = \frac{\tau \sin[\sqrt{(\pi f\tau)^2 - \theta^2}\,]}{I_0(\theta)\sqrt{(\pi f\tau)^2 - \theta^2}} \tag{8-51}$$

When the expression under the radical in (8-51) is negative, the function can be expressed in terms of the hyperbolic sine function (Prob. 8-19). Curves of $W_{db}(f)$ corresponding to the three cases given in Fig. A-8 are shown in Figs. A-9, A-10, and A-11.

Other Window Functions. Other possible window functions include the *Blackman window* and the *Dolph-Chebyshev* window. The Blackman window consists of a constant and two cosine terms (See Prob. 8-20). The peak amplitude of the side lobe level of the Blackman window spectrum is more than 80 dB down from the main lobe level, but the main lobe has a width triple that of the rectangular window.

Helms (ref. 3) has applied the Dolph-Chebyshev window to the design of FIR filters. This function is optimum in the sense that the main-lobe width is as small as possible for a given side-lobe peak ripple level.

A classical work related to the development and selection of window functions is that of Blackman and Tukey (ref. 1). The properties of many of the window functions discussed here are discussed in considerable detail in that reference.

Example 8-2

Compare the various FIR digital filter designs for the response of Ex. 8-1 using each of the following window functions: (a) rectangular, (b) triangular, (c) Hanning, (d) Hamming, (e) Kaiser ($\theta = 2\pi$).

Solution

In each of the cases that follow, the coefficients representing the terms of the various transfer functions are listed in Table 8-1. The coefficients represent the product of the original unmodified transfer function (which corresponds to the coefficients of the rectangular window) and the window function for the particular case according to (8-37).

(a) *Rectangular Window.* This is the initial form obtained in Ex. 8-1, and it represents no modification in the original coefficients. The decibel amplitude response corresponding to this case is shown in Fig. 8-5. Note that while the response displays a reasonably sharp rate of cutoff, the sidelobe ripple level is rather high.

(b) *Triangular Window.* The coefficients of the triangular window are obtained in this case by setting $t = n\mathrm{T}$ and $\tau = 20\mathrm{T}$ in (8-44) with the result

$$w_m = 1 - \frac{|m|}{10} \quad \text{for } |m| \leqslant 10 \tag{8-52}$$

As previously discussed, the window coefficients are applied to the non-causal form of the transfer function centered at the origin. Of course, this is equivalent to considering the 10th coefficient in each column of Table 8-1 as the origin for this purpose.

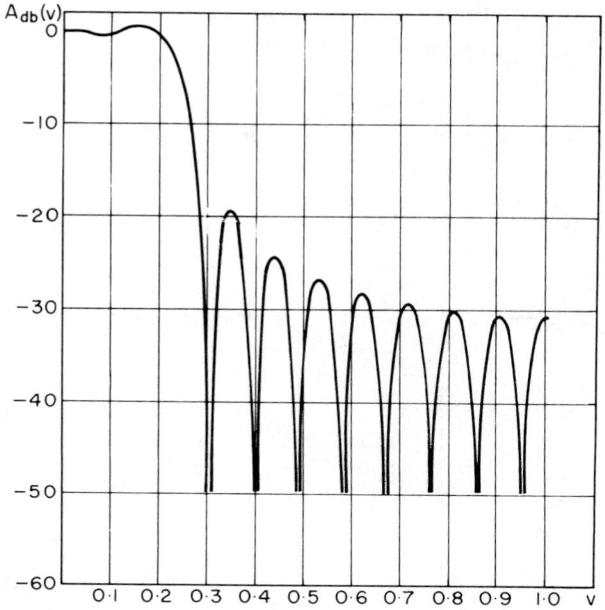

Figure 8-5 Amplitude response for Ex. 8-2 with rectangular window function.

The amplitude response is shown in Fig. 8-6. The sidelobe level has been reduced significantly, although the sharpness of cutoff is not as great.

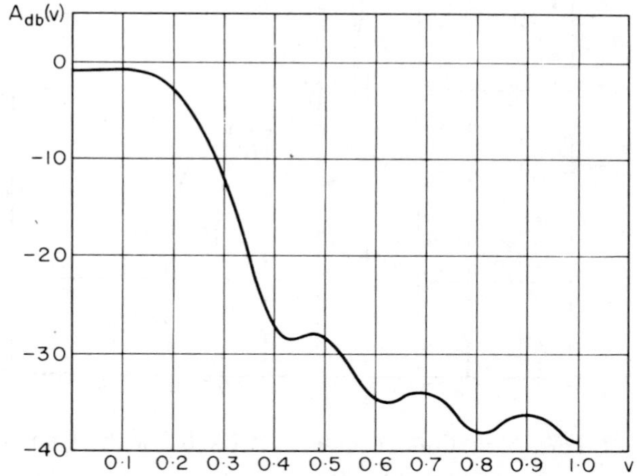

Figure 8-6 Amplitude response for Ex. 8-2 with triangular window function.

(c) *Hanning Window.* The coefficients of the Hanning window function are obtained from (8-46) and are given by

$$w_m = \frac{1}{2}\left(1 + \cos\frac{m\pi}{10}\right) \quad \text{for } |m| \leqslant 10 \tag{8-53}$$

The amplitude response is shown in Fig. 8-7.

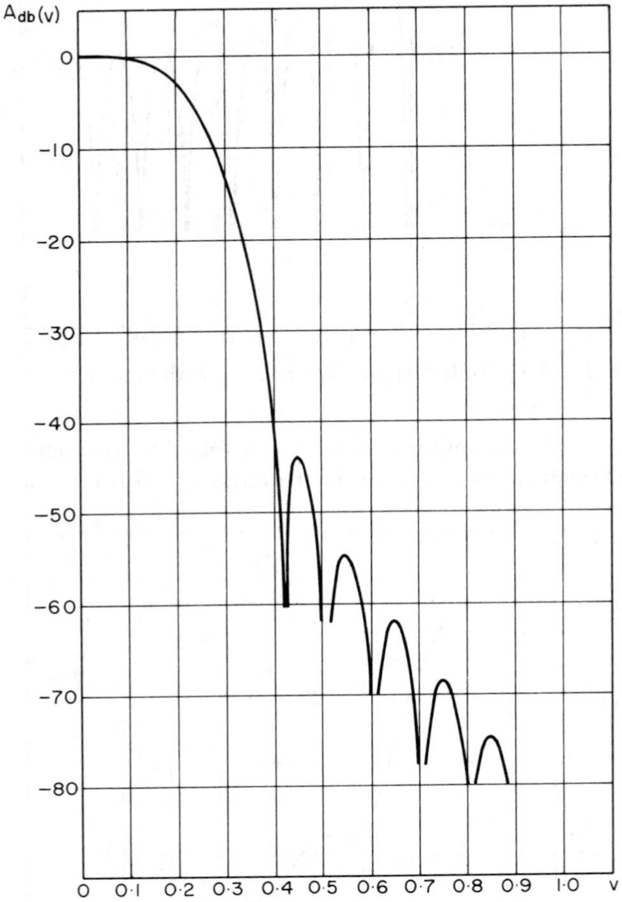

Figure 8-7 Amplitude response for Ex. 8-2 with Hanning window function

(d) *Hamming Window.* The coefficients of the Hamming window function are obtained from (8-48) and are given by

$$w_m = 0.54 + 0.46 \cos \frac{m\pi}{10} \quad \text{for } |m| \leq 10 \tag{8-54}$$

The amplitude response is shown in Fig. 8-8.

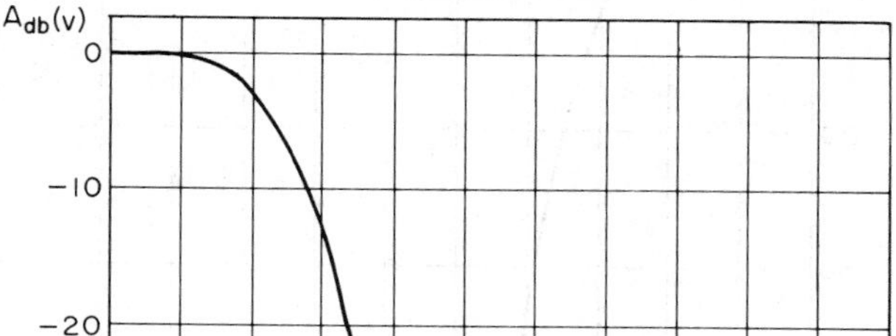

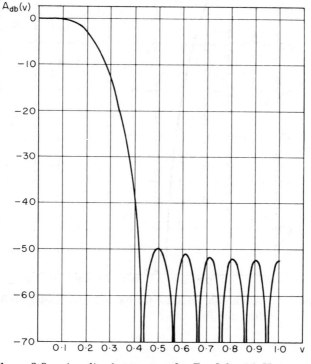

Figure 8-8 Amplitude response for Ex. 8-2 with Hamming window function.

(e) *Kaiser Window*. The coefficients of the Kaiser window function are obtained from (8-50) with $\theta = 2\pi$, and this results in

$$w_m = \frac{I_0\left[2\pi\sqrt{1-(m/10)^2}\,\right]}{I_0(2\pi)} \quad \text{for } |m| \leq 10 \tag{8-55}$$

The amplitude response is shown in Fig. 8-9.

Example 8-3

Design an FIR filter whose amplitude response approximates that of an ideal differentiator. The function is to be limited to a 12th order approximation, and the Hamming window function is to be used.

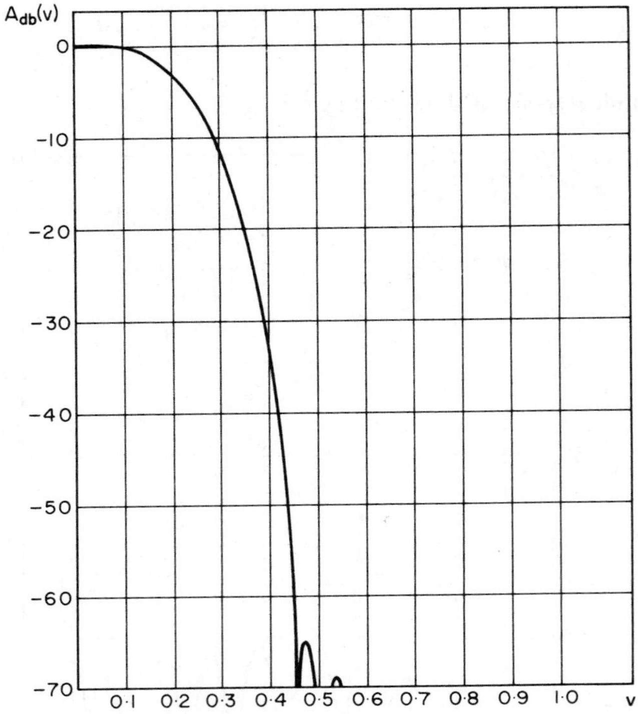

Figure 8-9 Amplitude response for Ex. 8-2 with Kaiser window function ($\theta = 2\pi$).

Solution

The amplitude response of an ideal analog differentiator is simply $A(f) = \omega$. The corresponding digital function must be periodic in nature. An odd function representation is the ideal choice in this case since an ideal differentiator should exhibit a constant 90° phase shift. The assumed form of the ideal amplitude response is shown in Fig. 8-10.

The frequency response expressed in terms of the actual frequency rather than the normalized form will be used in this case due to the presence of the first order variation with respect to the frequency. The desired response in one period can be written as

$$A_d(f) = \omega \quad \text{for} \; \frac{-f_s}{2} < f < \frac{f_s}{2} \tag{8-56}$$

The coefficients d_m are determined from (8-21) as

$$d_m = \frac{2}{f_s} \int_0^{f_s/2} \omega \sin 2\pi m\mathrm{T} f \, df$$

$$= \frac{4\pi}{f_s} \left[\frac{\sin 2\pi m\mathrm{T}f}{(2\pi m\mathrm{T})^2} - \frac{f \cos 2\pi m\mathrm{T}f}{2\pi m\mathrm{T}} \right]_0^{f_s/2} \tag{8-57}$$

$$= -\frac{\cos m\pi}{m\mathrm{T}} = \frac{(-1)^{m+1}}{m\mathrm{T}}$$

From the preceding result, it is seen that the sample time T must be specified before the final values can be obtained. For the purpose of this example, we will simply choose T = 1 *s*. Any other value would affect only the

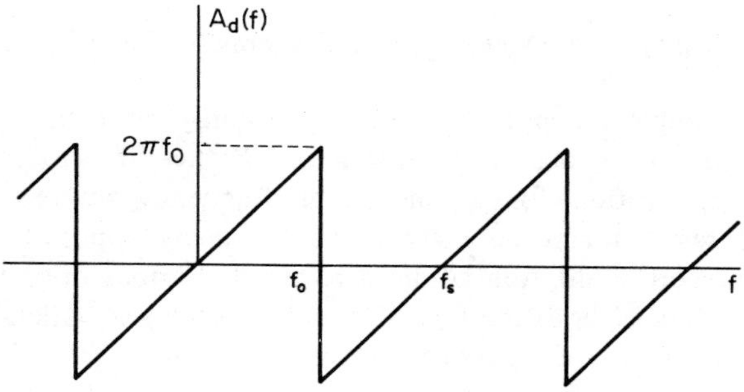

Figure 8-10 Desired amplitude response for FIR differentiator.

relative levels of the various c_m coefficients, but it would not affect the shape of the resulting response. The non-causal basic coefficients are then

$$d_m = \frac{(-1)^{m+1}}{m} \quad \text{for } m \neq 0 \text{ and } -6 \leqslant m \leqslant 6 \tag{8-58}$$

The Hamming window function coefficients are obtained from (8-48) with $t = n\mathrm{T}$ and $\tau = 12\mathrm{T}$. We have

$$\mathrm{w}_m = 0.54 + 0.46 \cos \frac{m\pi}{6} \quad \text{for } |m| \leqslant 6 \tag{8-59}$$

After multiplication of the w_m coefficients by the d_m coefficients, the final coefficients a_i of the transfer function are obtained by the procedure outlined in (8-37) through (8-40) with c_m replaced by d_m in these equations. The coefficients before and after multiplication by the window function are listed in Table 8-2. The actual amplitude response is shown in Fig. 8-11.

	Original Coefficients	Modified by Hamming Window
$a_0, -a_{12}$	-0.16666667	-0.01333333
$a_1, -a_{11}$	0.20000000	0.02832566
$a_2, -a_{10}$	-0.25000000	-0.07750000
$a_3, -a_9$	0.33333333	0.18000000
$a_4, -a_8$	-0.50000000	-0.38500000
$a_5, -a_7$	1.00000000	0.93837169

Table 8-2 Digital filter coefficients for Ex. 8-3.

This example was not intended to necessarily represent any particular optimum design for a digital differentiator. Rather it was selected as a representative application for a sine series frequency response expansion. However, this result might be satisfactory for many applications in which approximate numerical differentiation is required. Various optimum differentiating digital filters of both the recursive and nonrecursive varieties have been developed by Rabiner and Steiglitz (ref. 7).

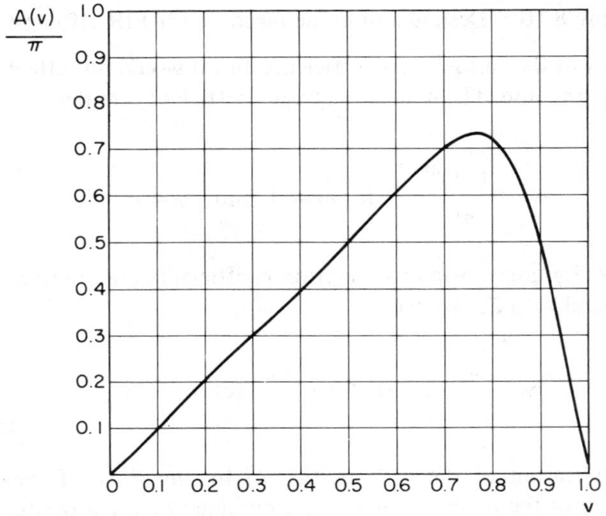

Figure 8-11 Actual amplitude response for 12th order FIR differentiator using Hamming window function.

PROBLEMS

8-1 Derive equation (8-9).

8-2 Derive equation (8-19).

8-3 Verify that equations (8-14) and (8-15) are correct.

8-4 Verify that equations (8-25) and (8-26) are correct.

8-5 The transfer function of a certain FIR filter is given by

$$H(z) = \frac{1}{10}[1 + 2z^{-1} + 4z^{-2} + 2z^{-3} + z^{-4}]$$

(a) Determine the frequency response of the filter. Express in the form of an amplitude response and a phase response. (Hint: The amplitude response can be expressed as a cosine series in this case.)
(b) Determine the impulse response $h(n)$.

8-6 The filter of Prob. 8-5 is excited by the discrete-time step function

$$x(n) = u(n)$$

(a) Determine the response $y(n)$ using the transfer function approach.
(b) Determine the response using direct convolution. Carry out the convolution far enough so that the steady-state condition is reached.

8-7 Show that both the phase and group delay functions for a causal FIR filter derived from a *cosine* series are identical and are constant.

8-8 Show that the phase and group delay functions for a causal FIR filter derived from a *sine* series are different. Furthermore, show that the group delay is constant, but that the phase delay is not.

8-9 The desired amplitude response of a certain low-pass FIR filter can be stated as

$$\begin{aligned} A_d(f) &= 1 \text{ for } 0 \leqslant f \leqslant 500 \text{ Hz} \\ &= 0 \text{ elsewhere in the range } 0 \leqslant f \leqslant f_0 \end{aligned}$$

The sampling rate is 2 kHz, and the impulse response is to be 30 ms long. Using a rectangular window function, determine the transfer function.

8-10 Repeat Prob. 8-9 if the desired amplitude response is

$$\begin{aligned} A_d(f) &= 1 \text{ for } 0 \leqslant f \leqslant 50 \text{ Hz} \\ &= 0 \text{ elsewhere in the range } 0 \leqslant f \leqslant f_0 \end{aligned}$$

All other quantities are unchanged.

8-11 A Hanning window function is to be used to smooth the coefficients in Prob. 8-9. Determine the modified transfer function.

8-12 A Hamming window function is to be used to smooth the coefficients in Prob. 8-10. Determine the modified transfer function.

8-13 The desired amplitude response of a certain band-pass FIR filter can be stated as

$$\begin{aligned} A_d(f) &= 1 \text{ for } 250 \leqslant f \leqslant 750 \text{ Hz} \\ &= 0 \text{ elsewhere in the range } 0 \leqslant f \leqslant f_0 \end{aligned}$$

The sampling rate is 2 kHz, and the impulse response is to be limited to 30 delays. Using a Hamming window function, determine the transfer function.

8-14 Repeat Prob. 8-13 if the desired amplitude response is

$$\begin{aligned} A_d(f) &= 1 \text{ for } 450 \leqslant f \leqslant 550 \text{ Hz} \\ &= 0 \text{ elsewhere in the range } 0 \leqslant f \leqslant f_0 \end{aligned}$$

All other quantities are unchanged.

8-15 The Fourier transforms of window functions containing trigonometric terms such as the Hanning and Hamming functions can be most easily derived by the procedure that follows: Consider that $w(t)$ is expressed as the product of a periodic trigonometric function $g(t)$, which extends to infinity in both directions, and a non-periodic pulse $p(t)$ of width τ; i.e.

$$w(t) = p(t)g(t)$$

Assume that $g(t)$ can be expressed as

$$g(t) = \sum_n c_n e^{j2\pi n f_1 t}$$

Show that $W(f) = F[w(t)]$ can be expressed as

$$W(f) = \sum_n c_n P(f - nf_1)$$

where

$$P(f) = F[p(t)]$$

8-16 Derive the Fourier transform of the triangular window function, i.e., equation (8-45).

8-17 Derive the Fourier transform of the Hanning window function, i.e., equation (8-47). Hint: Consider the result of Prob. 8-15.

8-18 Derive the Fourier transform of the Hamming window function, i.e., equation (8-49). Hint: Consider the result of Prob. 8-15.

8-19 Show that when the quantity under the radical in equation (8-51) is negative, the function may be expressed as

$$W(f) = \frac{\tau}{I_0(\theta)} \frac{\sinh\left[\sqrt{\theta^2 - (\pi f \tau)^2}\right]}{\sqrt{\theta^2 - (\pi f \tau)^2}}$$

8-20 The Blackman window function is defined by

$$w(t) = 0.42 + 0.5 \cos \frac{2\pi t}{\tau} + 0.08 \cos \frac{4\pi t}{\tau} \qquad |t| \leqslant \frac{\tau}{2}$$

Using the results of Prob. 8-15, show that the Fourier transform $W(f)$ is

$$W(f) = \tau \frac{\sin \pi f \tau}{\pi f \tau} \left[0.42 + \frac{0.5(f\tau)^2}{1 - (f\tau)^2} - \frac{0.08(f\tau)^2}{4 - (f\tau)^2} \right]$$

REFERENCES

1. R. B. Blackman and J. W. Tukey, *The Measurement of Power Spectra from the Point of View of Communication Engineering*. New York: Dover, 1959.

2. B. Gold and C. M. Rader, *Digital Processing of Signals*. New York: McGraw-Hill, 1969.

3. Helms, H. D., "Nonrecursive digital filters: design methods for achieving specifications on frequency response", *IEEE Trans. Audio and Electroacoustics*, vol. AU-16, pp. 336-342, Sept. 1968.

4. H. D. Helms and L. R. Rabiner, Eds., *Literature in Digital Signal Processing*. New York: IEEE Press, 1973.

5. J. F. Kaiser, "Digital Filters", in *System Analysis by Digital Computer*, F. F. Kuo and J. F. Kaiser, Eds., New York: Wiley, 1966.

6. T. W. Parks and J. H. McClellan, "A Program for the Design of Linear Phase Finite Impulse Response Digital Filters", *IEEE Trans. Audio and Electroacoustics*, vol. AU-20, pp. 195-199, August 1972.

7. L. R. Rabiner and K. Steiglitz, "The design of wideband recursive and nonrecursive digital differentiators", *IEEE Trans. Audio and Electroacoustics*, vol. AU-18, pp. 204-209, June 1970.

8. L. R. Rabiner, "Techniques for designing finite-duration impulse-response digital filters", *IEEE Trans. Comm. Tech.*, vol. COM-19, pp. 188-195, April 1971.

9. L. R. Rabiner and C. M. Rader, Eds. *Digital Signal Processing*. New York: IEEE Press, 1972.

10. J. V. Wait, "Digital Filters", in *Active Filters: Lumped, Distributed, Integrated, Digital, and Parametric*, L. P. Huelsman, Ed. New York: McGraw-Hill, 1970.

CHAPTER NINE

BASIC PROPERTIES OF DISCRETE AND FAST FOURIER TRANSFORMS

9-0 Introduction

The primary objective in this chapter is the development of the basic theory and computational procedures for evaluating discrete Fourier transforms. The particular aspect of major importance is the so-called fast Fourier transform (FFT), which is a high-speed algorithm for computing the Fourier transform of a discrete-time signal. The FFT has made it possible to compute the Fourier transforms of signals containing thousands of points in a matter of milliseconds.

The material will emphasize various transform properties both from the analytical and the computational points of view. Various signal flow graphs and computer flow charts will be presented to enhance the design of FFT processing systems. Some of the possible applications of the FFT will be discussed in the next chapter, but the material in this chapter is necessary as a basis for understanding its use.

9-1 Forms of the Fourier Transform

In describing the properties of the Fourier transform and inverse transform, it is quite convenient to use the concepts of time and frequency, even though the transformation is applicable to a wide range of physical and mathematical problems having other variables. It is very instructive to see the variety of forms that the transform takes when the time and frequency variables assume combinations of continuous and discrete forms.

The following quantities are defined:

t = continuous-time variable
T = time increment between successive components when a time function is sampled
t_p = effective period for a time function when it is periodic
f = continuous-frequency variable
F = frequency increment between successive components when a frequency function is sampled
f_s = sampling rate or frequency when a time function is sampled, i.e., the number of samples per second
N = number of samples in the range $0 \leq t < t_p$ when the time function is sampled. N is also equal to the number of samples in the range $0 \leq f < f_s$ when the frequency function is sampled.

From the previous definitions, it can be seen that when the time function is sampled and the length of the signal is limited to t_p, we have

$$t_p = NT \tag{9-1}$$

Similarly, when the frequency function is sampled and the width of the frequency function is limited to f_s, we have

$$f_s = NF \tag{9-2}$$

We will now consider four possible forms that could be used in representing Fourier transform and inverse transform functions. These correspond to the four combinations obtained from successively assuming the time and frequency variables to each be continuous and discrete. In some cases, we will encounter functions previously used, but the notation chosen will be slightly different here for the sake of comparison with the other functions. The properties of these functions will be illustrated by a series of transform pairs shown in Fig. 9-1 through 9-4. The hypothetical functions actually shown in these figures were chosen purely for clarity in illustrating various properties, and they are not intended to represent any actual transform pairs.

1. *Continuous-Time and Continuous-Frequency.* This form was encountered in Chapt. 3 and was used there for describing the continuous spectrum of a non-periodic time signal. The Fourier transform $X(f)$ of a continuous time function $x(t)$ can be expressed as

$$X(f) = \int_{-\infty}^{\infty} x(t)\, \epsilon^{-j2\pi ft} dt \tag{9-3}$$

The inverse transform is

$$x(t) = \int_{-\infty}^{\infty} X(f)\, \epsilon^{j2\pi ft} df \tag{9-4}$$

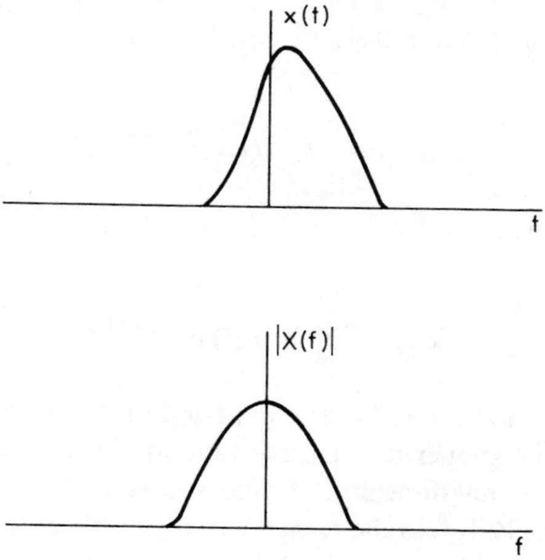

Figure 9-1 Non-periodic continuous-time function and its Fourier transform, which is a non-periodic continuous-frequency function.

The forms for the time function and the transform function are illustrated in Fig. 9-1. It is seen that *a non-periodic continuous-time function corresponds to a non-periodic continuous-frequency transform function.*

2. *Continuous-Time and Discrete-Frequency*. This is the form of the Fourier transform that is most often referred to as a Fourier series, and it was also encountered in Chapt. 3. Let $x(t)$ represent a periodic continuous-time

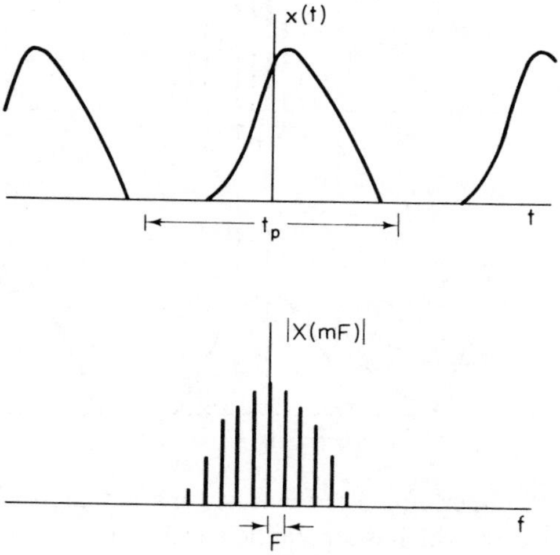

Figure 9-2 Periodic continuous-time function and its Fourier transform, which is a non-periodic discrete-frequency function.

function with period t_p. The Fourier transform of $x(t)$ is a discrete-frequency function, which we will denote here by X(mF). The transform pair is given by

$$X(mF) = \frac{1}{t_p} \int_{t_p} x(t)\epsilon^{-j2\pi mFt}\, dt \qquad (9\text{-}5)$$

and

$$x(t) = \sum_{-\infty}^{\infty} X(mF)\, \epsilon^{j2\pi mFt} \qquad (9\text{-}6)$$

The integral in (9-5) is evaluated over one period of $x(t)$.

Some of the properties of these functions are illustrated in Fig. 9-2. In giving the transform relationships, it was stated that $x(t)$ was periodic. This property automatically forces the transform to be a discrete-frequency function. On the other hand, consider the possibility where $x(t)$ is originally not periodic, which leads to a continuous-frequency transform as shown in Fig. 9-1. Then assume that the transform is sampled. In effect, the process of sampling the spectrum leads to a periodic time function upon applying the inverse transform of (9-6). Thus, in one sense, it is immaterial whether the original time function was periodic or not if the spectrum is sampled. The sampling process itself forces the time function to be periodic if inversion is performed.

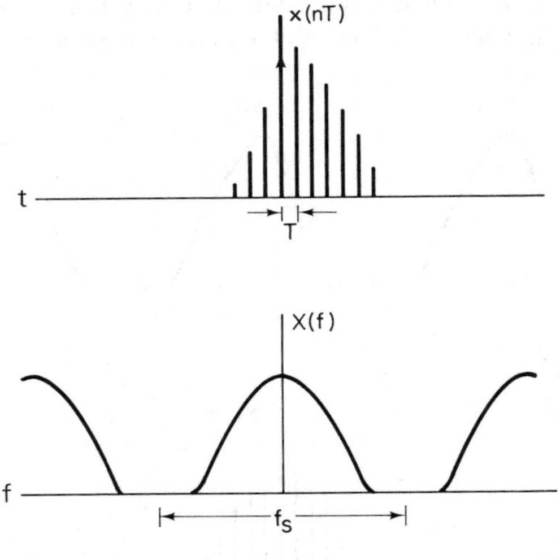

Figure 9-3 Non-periodic discrete-time function and its Fourier transform, which is a periodic continuous-frequency function.

The frequency increment F between successive spectral components is related to the time period t_p by

$$F = \frac{1}{t_p} \tag{9-7}$$

The conclusion is that a *periodic continuous-time function corresponds to a non-periodic discrete-frequency transform function.*

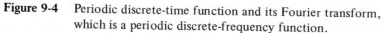

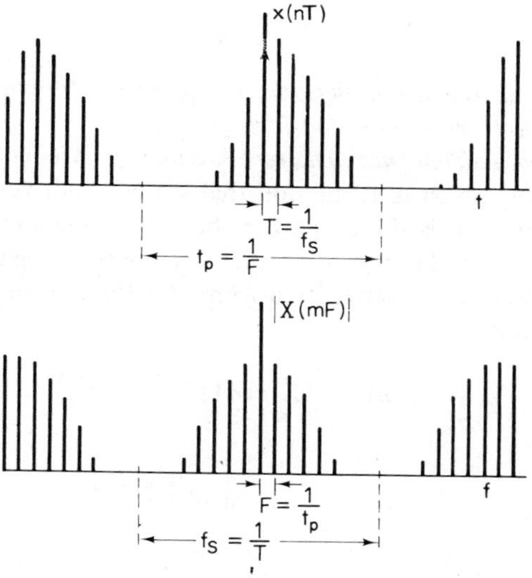

Figure 9-4 Periodic discrete-time function and its Fourier transform, which is a periodic discrete-frequency function.

3. *Discrete-Time and Continuous-Frequency.* This form of the Fourier transform is equivalent to evaluating the z-transform and inverse transform on the unit circle. The relationships may be obtained by applying this concept to the z-transform pair given in Chapt. 4. Let $x(nT)$ represent the discrete-time signal, and let $X(f)$ represent the transform. We will leave as an exercise for the reader (Prob. 9-2) to show that the pertinent Fourier transform relationships are

$$X(f) = \sum_{0}^{\infty} x(nT)\,\epsilon^{-j2\pi nfT} \tag{9-8}$$

and

$$x(nT) = \frac{1}{f_s} \int_{f_s} X(f)\epsilon^{j2\pi nfT}\,df \tag{9-9}$$

The integral in (9-9) is evaluated over one period of $X(f)$.

Some of the properties of these functions are illustrated in Fig. 9-3. Sampling of the time function produces a periodic frequency function. By the same logic, if a frequency function is specified as being periodic, the resulting time function must be a discrete-time signal.

The period of the frequency function is simply the sampling rate f_s, and it is related to the sample time T by

$$f_s = \frac{1}{T} \tag{9-10}$$

The conclusion is that a *non-periodic discrete-time function corresponds to a periodic continuous-frequency transform function.*

4. *Discrete-Time and Discrete-Frequency*. We will now consider the fourth possibility, which is a situation that we have not yet encountered in any form in this text. This is the case where both the time and frequency variables are discrete. Let $x(nT)$ represent the discrete-time signal, and let $X(mF)$ represent the discrete-frequency transform function. A suitable Fourier transform pair is given by

$$X(mF) = \sum_n x(nT)\, \epsilon^{-j2\pi mnFT} \tag{9-11}$$

$$x(nT) = \frac{1}{N} \sum_m X(mF) \epsilon^{j2\pi mnFT} \tag{9-12}$$

The summation in (9-11) is evaluated over one period of $x(nT)$, and the summation of (9-12) is evaluated over one period of $X(mF)$.

Equations (9-11) and (9-12) describe one form of the *discrete Fourier transform* (DFT) pair that constitutes an important basis for the work of this chapter. In the next section, this pair will be modified for convenience in digital computation, but for the moment, we will consider the forms as given. The basic properties of the time and frequency functions are illustrated in Fig. 9-4. Since the time function is sampled, the frequency function is periodic with a period f_s given by

$$f_s = \frac{1}{T} \tag{9-13}$$

On the other hand, since the frequency function is sampled, the time function is periodic with a period t_p given by

$$t_p = \frac{1}{F} \tag{9-14}$$

It is seen, then, that *a periodic discrete-time signal corresponds to a periodic discrete-frequency transform function.*

By reviewing the preceding steps, several general conclusions can be made. If a function in one domain (either time or frequency) is periodic, then the corresponding transform in the other domain is a sampled form, which means it is a function of a discrete variable. Conversely, if a function in one domain is sampled, then the function in the other domain becomes periodic. The period in one domain is always the reciprocal of the increment between samples in the other domain. Some of the preceding properties are summarized in Table 9-1.

Time Function	Frequency Function
Non-Periodic and Continuous	Non-Periodic and Continuous
Periodic and Continuous	Non-Periodic and Discrete
Non-Periodic and Discrete	Periodic and Continuous
Periodic and Discrete	Periodic and Discrete

Table 9-1 Comparison of forms for Fourier transform pairs.

When a function is evaluated by numerical procedures, it is always necessary to sample it in some fashion. This means that in order to fully evaluate a Fourier transform or inverse transform with digital operations, it is necessary that both the time and frequency functions be eventually sampled in one form or another. Thus, the last of the four possible Fourier pairs (DFT) is the one that is of primary interest in digital computation.

It is necessary that the implications of the sampling process in both the time and frequency domains be considered in order to ascertain that the data obtained by the discrete process represents the actual data desired. The fictitious transform pairs used for illustration in Figs. 9-1 through 9-4 were chosen to be both band-limited and time-limited within proper ranges. The sampling rate was assumed to be greater than twice the highest frequency, and the period of the time function was chosen to be longer than the time length of the signal, so no overlapping of time or frequency functions (aliasing) was observed in the illustrations. However, these properties are not always satisfied, so one must be very careful in applying discrete computational methods to evaluate the Fourier transforms of continuous functions. This problem will be discussed at some length in Chapt. 10.

9-2 Discrete Fourier Transform

In this section, the discrete Fourier transform pair introduced in the last section will be studied in more detail. Consider the transform pair introduced by Equations (9-11) and (9-12). The following modifications in notation and form will be made at this time:

(a) The time signal will be denoted simply as $x(n)$ with the sample time T understood.

(b) The frequency function will be denoted as $X(m)$ with the frequency increment F understood.

(c) The time domain interval will be shifted to the right so that the range of n corresponding to a period is $0 \leqslant n \leqslant N-1$. Note that the point $n = N$ actually corresponds to the beginning of a new period.

(d) The frequency domain interval of interest will be shifted to the right so that the range of m corresponding to a period in the frequency domain is $0 \leqslant m \leqslant N-1$. Note that the point $m = N$ corresponds to the beginning of a new period.

In addition to the preceding changes, let us inspect the arguments of the exponential appearing in (9-11) and (9-12). Using (9-1) and (9-14), the quantity FT can be expressed as

$$FT = \frac{1}{N} \tag{9-15}$$

We will now define a quantity W_N as

$$W_N = \epsilon^{-j(2\pi/N)} \tag{9-16}$$

The reciprocal of W_N can be expressed as

$$W_N^{-1} = \epsilon^{j(2\pi/N)} \tag{9-17}$$

When the subscript N is omitted from W_N, it will be understood that we are dealing with an N point signal. Thus, $W_N = W$ in many subsequent developments.

Using the relationships given by (9-15), (9-16), and (9-17), and the assumptions previously made, the discrete Fourier transform (DFT) pair can be stated as

$$X(m) = \sum_{n=0}^{N-1} x(n)W^{mn} \tag{9-18}$$

$$x(n) = \frac{1}{N} \sum_{m=0}^{N-1} X(m)W^{-mn} \tag{9-19}$$

This is the form of the DFT that will be employed in subsequent developments. In some cases, it is advantageous to express these operations in symbolic forms. The transformation of (9-18) will sometimes be denoted as

$$X(m) = D[x(n)] \tag{9-20}$$

The inverse transformation of (9-19) will sometimes be denoted as

$$x(n) = D^{-1}[X(m)] \tag{9-21}$$

Furthermore, there will be cases where the following notation is convenient in relating the various transforms pairs:

$$x(n) \longleftrightarrow X(m) \tag{9-22}$$

In studying the various properties of the DFT pair, it is convenient to think of the integers n and m as the variables rather than time and frequency (or whatever the actual physical variables are). In this sense, n represents a *time integer* and m represents a *frequency integer* whenever the physical variables are actually time and frequency. Thus, the actual time associated with an arbitrary time integer n is nT, and the actual frequency associated with an arbitrary frequency integer m is mF. As long as these points are understood, the complete problem can often be analyzed in terms of the integer variables.

Some of the properties of the transform pair in terms of these integer relationships are illustrated in Fig. 9-5. The hypothetical transform pair shown was sketched on the basis of N = 16. However, the results are labeled in terms of arbitrary N in order to make the results appear more general. Only one period of each function is shown, but both functions may actually be assumed to be periodic as previously indicated. The time function in this case is assumed to be *real*.

In the time domain, one period corresponds to N points. The point n = N actually corresponds to the beginning of a new period, and the points n = 0 though n = N-1 are the N points contained in one period.

Similar relationships hold in the frequency domain. A period may be assumed to correspond to the N points in the range from m = 0 through m = N-1. The point m = N corresponds to the beginning of a new period.

There is one important difference between the frequency and time functions when the time function is real, which is the most common case. Although the "period" in the frequency domain, as measured on a continuous-frequency scale, is f_s, the transform over half of the interval is related to the transform over the other half. Thus, the maximum unambiguous frequency range is $f_s/2$, which is the familiar folding frequency f_0. This concept is seen to be in perfect agreement with the results of earlier chapters.

In terms of the frequency integer, the maximum unambiguous integer when the time function is real is (N/2)-1 as illustrated in Fig. 9-5. Since m = 0 is the first integer, this means that there are N/2 unique transform components when the time signal has N points and is real. The point m = N/2 corresponds to the folding frequency for the given sampling rate. The components in the range N/2 $\leqslant m \leqslant$ N-1 are shown with dashed lines in Fig. 9-5.

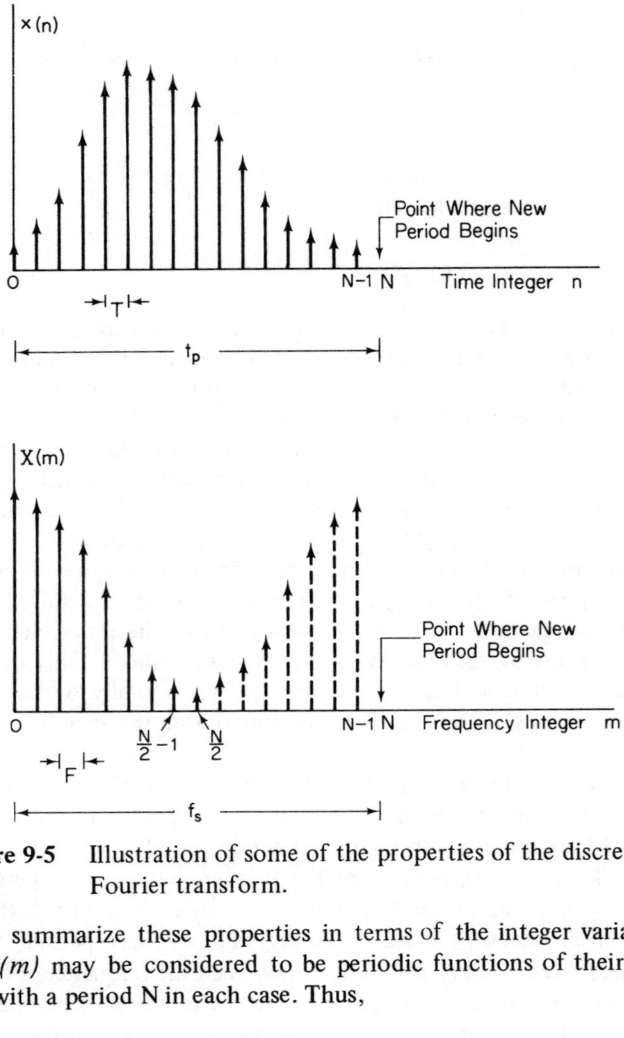

Figure 9-5 Illustration of some of the properties of the discrete Fourier transform.

To summarize these properties in terms of the integer variables, both *x(n)* and X*(m)* may be considered to be periodic functions of their respective arguments with a period N in each case. Thus,

$$x(n + kN) = x(n) \tag{9-23}$$

and

$$X(m + kN) = X(m) \tag{9-24}$$

for any integer *k*. In addition, if *x(n)* is a real function, the transform is unique at only N/2 points.

Because we have stated the range of the integer variables in terms of positive values, it is convenient to redefine the concepts of even and odd functions in this case. It can be readily shown that the behavior of either $x(n)$ or $X(m)$ over the range from N/2 to N is identical to the behavior from −N/2 to 0. Thus, we can consider the interval from N/2 to N as a sort of "negative" time or frequency range in interpreting various even or odd properties of the transform functions.

Using this type of interpretation, the following definitions of even and odd functions will be made:

even function $$x(N-n) = x(n) \tag{9-25}$$

odd function $$x(N-n) = -x(n) \tag{9-26}$$

even function $$X(N-m) = X(m) \tag{9-27}$$

odd function $$X(N-m) = -X(m) \tag{9-28}$$

From the appearance of $|X(m)|$ in Fig. 9-5, it can be seen that this function is even. The magnitude spectrum satisfies this property when the time function is real. More general relationships will be developed shortly.

9-3 Even and Odd Properties of the DFT

We will now investigate some of the even and/or odd properties of the DFT transform pair and how they relate to the real and/or imaginary parts of the transform functions. The casual reader who is interested only in using available Fourier transform programs may not need to pursue all of this section in great depth. However, it is felt that more efficient use of available programs and better interpretation of the results may be possible with a better understanding of these concepts.

As a starting point, some of the properties of W_N as defined by (9-16) will be listed. The quantity W_N^k can be readily shown to be a periodic function of k with a period N. Using this property, a number of additional properties of W_N^k can be readily derived, and these are tabulated in Table 9-2. The reader is encouraged to verify these results (Prob. 9-3.)

Assume now that we have a *real* sequence $x(n)$ with a DFT $X(m)$. Let

$$X(m) = X_r(m) + jX_i(m) \tag{9-29}$$

where $X_r(m)$ is the real part of $X(m)$ and $X_i(m)$ is the imaginary part. Using the basic definition of the DFT and the expansion of W_N into its real and imaginary parts, we can write

$$X(m) = \sum_{n=0}^{N-1} x(n) \cos \frac{2\pi mn}{N} - j \sum_{n=0}^{N-1} x(n) \sin \frac{2\pi mn}{N} \tag{9-30}$$

$$W_N^N = 1 \qquad \text{(a)}$$

$$W_N^{\frac{N}{2}} = -1 \qquad \text{(b)}$$

$$W_N^{\frac{N}{4}} = -j \qquad \text{(c)}$$

$$W_N^{\frac{3N}{4}} = j \qquad \text{(d)}$$

$$W_N^{KN} = 1 \qquad \text{(e)}$$

$$W_N^{KN+r} = W_N^r \qquad \text{(f)}$$

$$W_{2N}^K = W_N^{\frac{K}{2}} \qquad \text{(g)}$$

Table 9-2 Properties of the quantity W.

The real and imaginary parts of (9-29) can be equated to those of (9-30) to yield

$$X_r(m) = \sum_{n=0}^{N-1} x(n) \cos \frac{2\pi mn}{N} \tag{9-31}$$

$$X_i(m) = -\sum_{m=0}^{N-1} x(n) \sin \frac{2\pi mn}{N} \tag{9-32}$$

It can be seen from (9-31) that $X_r(-m) = X_r(N-m) = X_r(m)$. Similarly, it can be seen from (9-32) that $X_i(-m) = X_i(N-m) = -X_i(m)$. These results mean that when $x(n)$ is real, $X_r(m)$ is an even function of m and $X_i(m)$ is an odd function of m. Thus, *when the time function is real, the real part of the frequency function is an even function of frequency, and the imaginary part is an odd function of frequency.*

Now let $x(n)$ represent a purely imaginary sequence with a DFT $X(m)$. (The reason why the time signal is represented as an imaginary sequence will be discussed later.) Using (9-29) as the definition of the transform again, it can be shown (Prob. 9-4) that now $X_r(m)$ is an odd function of m and $X_i(m)$ is an even function of m. Thus, *when the time function is purely imaginary, the real part of the frequency function is an odd function of frequency, and the imaginary part is an even function of frequency.*

Let $x_e(n)$ be a *real even* function of n. The reader is invited to show (Prob. 9-5) that the DFT is of the form

$$x_e(n) \longleftrightarrow X_r(m) \tag{9-33}$$

where $X_r(m)$ is a *real even* function of m.

Let $x_0(n)$ be a *real odd* function of n. It can be shown (Prob. 9-6) that the DFT is of the form

$$x_0(n) \longleftrightarrow jX_i(m) \tag{9-34}$$

where $jX_i(m)$ is an *imaginary odd* function of m. (Note that $X_i(m)$ itself is a real function.)

Properties opposite to those associated with (9-33) and (9-34) apply to the cases where $x(n)$ is a purely imaginary sequence with even and odd properties respectively. All of the preceding properties are summarized in Table 9-3.

x (n)	X (m)
Real	Real Part is Even Imaginary Part is Odd
Imaginary	Real Part is Odd Imaginary Part is Even
Real and Even	Real and Even
Real and Odd	Imaginary and Odd
Imaginary and Even	Imaginary and Even
Imaginary and Odd	Real and Odd

Table 9-3 Even and Odd Properties of the DFT.

Assume now that the time function $x(n)$ is permitted to be *complex*. In effect, this means that two time sequences are represented by association with the real and imaginary parts respectively. Let

$$x(n) = x_1(n) + jx_2(n) \tag{9-35}$$

where $x_1(n)$ and $x_2(n)$ are both real sequences.

Let

$$x_1(n) \longleftrightarrow X_1(m) \tag{9-36}$$

$$x_2(n) \longleftrightarrow X_2(m) \tag{9-37}$$

It is readily shown that

$$x_1(n) + jx_2(n) \longleftrightarrow X_1(m) + jX_2(m) \tag{9-38}$$

However, it should be noted that $X_1(m)$ and $X_2(m)$ are both complex. Therefore, in the right-hand side of (9-38), the overall real and imaginary parts are not directly identifiable.

We will next evaluate $X(m)$ in the "negative" frequency range and make use of the even and odd properties of the real and imaginary parts of $X_1(m)$ and $X_2(m)$. Let $(\sim)$ denote the process of complex conjugation. We begin with

$$X(m) = X_1(m) + jX_2(m) \tag{9-39}$$

Substituting N-m for m, we have

$$X(N\text{-}m) = X_1(N\text{-}m) + jX_2(N\text{-}m) \tag{9-40}$$

By earlier developments of this section, it can be deduced that the real parts of X_1 and X_2 are even and the imaginary parts are odd. This means that the imaginary parts of X_1 and X_2 in the negative frequency range are the negatives of the corresponding segments in the positive frequency range; this is equivalent to the imaginary parts being the complex conjugates in the negative frequency range of their values in the positive frequency range.

Thus, (9-40) can be expressed as

$$X(N\text{-m}) = \tilde{X}_1(m) + j\,\tilde{X}_2(m) \tag{9-41}$$

Forming the complex conjugates of both sides of (9-41), we have

$$\tilde{X}(N\text{-}m) = X_1(m) - j\,X_2(m) \tag{9-42}$$

Now let us successively add and subtract (9-39) and (9-42) and solve for the functions $X_1(m)$ and $X_2(m)$ respectively. We obtain

$$X_1(m) = \frac{1}{2}\,[X(m) + \tilde{X}(N - m)] \tag{9-43}$$

$$X_2(m) = \frac{1}{2j}\,[X(m) - \tilde{X}(N - m)] \tag{9-44}$$

These results are rather significant in that they permit two real sequences $x_1(n)$ and $x_2(n)$ to be combined into a single complex function as indicated by (9-35). After the transform of the complex combination $X(m)$ is computed, the relationships of (9-43) and (9-44) permit the separation of the two distinct transforms $X_1(m)$ and $X_2(m)$. Thus, it is possible to obtain the transforms of two separate signals in one computational sweep using this approach.

9-4 Functional Operations with the DFT

As has been the case with all previous transform pairs considered in the text, there are a number of operations pairs that are useful in dealing with the DFT. Some of the most useful of these are summarized in Table 9-4. Several of these will be derived, while others will be left as exercises for the reader. For

$x(n)$	$X(m) = D[x(n)]$	
$ax_1(n) + bx_2(n)$	$aX_1(m) + bX_2(m)$	(DO−1)
$x(n-k)$	$W_N^{km}\, X(m)$	(DO−2)
$W_N^{-kn}\, x(n)$	$X(m-k)$	(DO−3)
$x(n)^* h(n) = \sum_{K=0}^{N-1} x(k)\, h(n-k)$	$X(m)\ H(m)$	(DO−4)
$\sum_{n=0}^{N-1} x(n) y(n-k)$	$X(m)\ \tilde{Y}(m)$	(DO−5)
$x(n)\, y(n)$	$\frac{1}{N} \sum_{K=0}^{N-1} X(k)\ Y(m-k)$	(DO−6)

Table 9-4 Discrete Fourier transform operation pairs.

clarity in presentation, the derivations given will be postponed until the end of the section and presented as example problems. Within this section, we will discuss some of the basic interpretations of the various transform pairs. In some cases, more detailed explanations will be given in later sections where they are actually applied to spectral analysis.

1. *Linearity Property.* Consider the transform pairs

$$x_1(n) \longleftrightarrow X_1(m) \tag{9-45}$$

$$x_2(n) \longleftrightarrow X_2(m) \tag{9-46}$$

Let a and b represent two arbitrary constants. Then, the following transform pair can be readily obtained from the basic definition:

$$ax_1(n) + bx_2(n) \longleftrightarrow aX_1(m) + bX_2(m) \tag{9-47}$$

This property implies that the DFT is a linear operation and thus satisfies the superposition principle.

2. *Shifting Theorem.* The process of shifting a time signal k intervals to the right (or to the left for that matter) introduces a phase shift factor similar to that encountered in other transform pairs. This theorem, which will be derived in Ex. 9-1, reads

$$x(n-k) \longleftrightarrow W_N^{km}\ X(m) \tag{9-48}$$

The factor W_N^{km} introduces additional phase shift only, and it does not modify the magnitude spectrum of the unshifted spectrum. The reader is invited to show (Prob. 9-7) that the phase introduced by this process is $2\pi km/N$ radians, which is a linear function of the frequency integer m.

3. *Modulation Theorem.* This operation will be referred to as the modulation theorem, since it corresponds to the product modulation operation obtained by multiplying a signal by a sinusoidal function. The reader is invited to derive this theorem (Prob. 9-8), and it is

$$W_N^{-kn}\ x(n) \longleftrightarrow X(m-k) \tag{9-49}$$

In effect, the spectrum is shifted to the right by k intervals when the time signal is multiplied by an exponential term of the form given.

Whenever we are dealing directly with real functions, a complex exponential in the time domain is usually accompanied by its complex conjugate. Using (DO-3), the reader is invited to show (Prob. 9-9) that two alternate forms of the modulation theorem applicable directly to cosine and sine functions may be expressed as follows:

$$x(n) \cos \frac{2\pi kn}{N} \longleftrightarrow \frac{1}{2} [X(m-k) + X(m+k)] \tag{9-50}$$

$$x(n) \sin \frac{2\pi kn}{N} \longleftrightarrow \frac{1}{2j} [X(m-k) - X(m+k)] \tag{9-51}$$

4. *Convolution in the Time Domain.* One of the most important applications of the DFT is in dealing with convolution products in the time domain. The convolution theorem will be derived in Ex. 9-2, and it reads

$$\sum_{k=0}^{N-1} x(k)h(n-k) \longleftrightarrow X(m)H(m) \tag{9-52}$$

This theorem states that discrete convolution in the time domain is equivalent to forming the product of the DFT's in the frequency domain. Thus, a discrete convolution could be evaluated by evaluating the two DFT's, forming their product at all frequency integers in the proper range, and determining the inverse DFT of the result. However, there are some possible difficulties with this process, so a rather detailed discussion will be given in the next chapter.

5. *Lagged Products.* The computation of lagged products is an integral part of determining the discrete cross-correlation or autocorrelation functions of discrete-time signals. While similar in form to the convolution operation, there are some minor differences. The development of the transform relationship for this pair is left as an exercise (Prob. 9-10), and it reads

$$\sum_{n=0}^{N-1} x(n)y(n-k) \longleftrightarrow X(m)\tilde{Y}(m) \tag{9-53}$$

Some discussion of the applications of this operation will be given in Chapt. 10.

6. *Multiplication in the Time Domain.* When two discrete-time signals $x_1(n)$ and $x_2(n)$ are multiplied in the time domain, the DFT of the product may be determined by performing a convolution between the respective DFT's. The development of the theorem is left as an exercise (Prob. 9-11). The result is

$$x(n)y(n) \longleftrightarrow \frac{1}{N}\sum_{k=0}^{N-1} X(k)Y(m-k) \tag{9-54}$$

The various properties of convolution in the time domain apply in this case, but with the concepts of time and frequency reversed. Hence, the details of convolution to be discussed in Chapt. 10 may be readily applied to this operation as long as the time and frequency variables are interchanged.

Example 9-1

Derive operation pair DO-2 of Table 9-4.

Solution

The function $x(n-k)$ is shifted to the right by k sample points (assuming $k > 0$) so that the N points are assumed in the range $k \leqslant n \leqslant N + k - 1$. Application of the DFT definition to the function yields

$$D[x(n-k)] = \sum_{n=k}^{N+k-1} x(n-k)W_N^{nm} \tag{9-55}$$

Let $n-k = i$. Substituting this change of variables, we have

$$D[x(n-k)] = \sum_{i=0}^{N-1} x(i) W_N^{(i+k)m}$$

$$= W_N^{km} \sum_{i=0}^{N-1} x(i) W_N^{im} \tag{9-56}$$

$$= W_N^{km} X(m)$$

Example 9-2

Derive operation pair DO-4 of Table 9-4.

Solution

Application of the DFT definition to the convolution definition yields

$$D[x(n)*h(n)] = \sum_{n=0}^{N-1} \left[\sum_{k=0}^{N-1} x(k) h(n-k) \right] W_N^{nm} \tag{9-57}$$

The order of summation for the indices k and n will now be reversed. At the same time, it is desirable to change the range of summation for the inner function $h(n-k)$ due to its shifted nature. We have

$$D[x(n)*h(n)] = \sum_{k=0}^{N-1} x(k) \left[\sum_{n=k}^{k+N-1} h(n-k) W_N^{nm} \right] \tag{9-58}$$

The quantity in the brackets of (9-58) has the same form encountered in Ex. 9-1 in relation to DO-2, and it is $W_N^{km} H(m)$. The quantity $H(m)$ may be factored out to yield

$$\begin{aligned} D[x(n)*h(n)] &= \left[\sum_{k=0}^{N-1} x(k) W_N^{km} \right] H(m) \\ &= X(m) H(m) \end{aligned} \tag{9-59}$$

9-5 Fast Fourier Transform

This section will be devoted to a discussion of certain special algorithms which permit implementation of the discrete Fourier transform with considerable savings in computational time. The class of such algorithms is referred to as the *fast Fourier transform* (FFT). It should be pointed out that the FFT is not a different transform from the DFT, but rather it represents a means for computing the DFT with a considerable reduction in the number of computations. Of course, the development of these FFT algorithms represented the major step in the realization of modern high-speed digital Fourier analysis equipment.

Because of the intended level of this book, we will not attempt to present a rigorous development of the underlying analytical and computational theory of the FFT. Instead, we will first present a somewhat simplified overall discussion of the general computational approach. Next we will present several signal flow charts corresponding to several versions of the FFT. The emphasis will be on forms that are easier to follow computationally rather than those that are optimally organized.

While it is possible to develop FFT algorithms that work with any number of points, maximum efficiency of computation is obtained by constraining the number of time points to be an integer power of two. In fact, most of the hardware available at the time of this writing has been designed around this concept. Consequently, this assumption will be made for all forms of the algorithms that are presented.

Let us now inspect the actual steps involved in the computation of the DFT. The operation described by (9-18) can be expressed by the array of equations

$$\begin{aligned}
X(0) &= x(0)W^0 + x(1)W^0 + x(2)W^0 + \cdots + x(N-1)W^0 \\
X(1) &= x(0)W^0 + x(1)W^1 + x(2)W^2 + \cdots + x(N-1)W^{N-1} \\
X(2) &= x(0)W^0 + x(1)W^2 + x(2)W^4 + \cdots + x(N-1)W^{2(N-1)} \\
\cdot &= \cdot \quad \cdot \quad \cdot \quad \cdot \\
\cdot & \quad \cdot \quad \cdot \quad \cdot \quad \cdot \\
\cdot & \quad \cdot \quad \cdot \quad \cdot \quad \cdot \\
X(N-1) &= x(0)W^0 + x(1)W^{N-1} + x(2)W^{2(N-1)} + \cdots + x(N-1)W^{(N-1)^2}
\end{aligned} \tag{9-60}$$

Since $W^0 = 1$, some simplification could be achieved in the array by making this substitution. However, it is conceptually convenient to leave the W^0 term in the array. With this assumption, it can be seen that the computation of any one particular spectral component requires about N complex multiplications and about N complex additions. Thus, there are about 2N complex arithmetic operations involved in computing a given frequency component. From the array, it would appear that we should compute N spectral components. However, if $x(n)$ is real, only N/2 components are unique, and a full expansion of the form expressed in (9-60) would necessitate computing only that many. This results in a minimum of about $2N \times (N/2) = N^2$ complex operations. Thus, it is convenient to state that the number of complex computations involved in obtaining the complete spectrum using the DFT is approximately N^2. For a reasonably long signal, this number can be very large, resulting in a prohibitively long computational time.

The array of (9-60) can be arranged in a matrix form as

$$\begin{bmatrix} X(0) \\ X(1) \\ X(2) \\ \cdot \\ \cdot \\ \cdot \\ X(N\text{-}1) \end{bmatrix} = \begin{bmatrix} W^0 & W^0 & W^0 & \cdots & W^0 \\ W^0 & W^1 & W^2 & \cdots & W^{N-1} \\ W^0 & W^2 & W^4 & \cdots & W^{2(N-1)} \\ \cdot & \cdot & \cdot & & \cdot \\ \cdot & \cdot & \cdot & & \cdot \\ \cdot & \cdot & \cdot & & \cdot \\ W^0 & W^{N-1} & W^{2(N-1)} & \cdots & W^{(N-1)^2} \end{bmatrix} \begin{bmatrix} x(0) \\ x(1) \\ x(2) \\ \\ \\ \\ x(N\text{-}1) \end{bmatrix} \tag{9-61}$$

This can be expressed as

$$\overline{X} = [W]\overline{x} \tag{9-62}$$

where $\overline{X}$ is the column vector defining the transform, $\overline{x}$ is the column vector defining the discrete time signal, and [W] is the N by N square matrix.

The basis for the fast Fourier transform (FFT) is an algorithm presented by Cooley and Tukey (ref. 3), and it can be thought of as a matrix factorization of (9-61) or (9-62). Assume that N is chosen as an integer multiple of 2, and define an integer L as

$$L = \log_2 N \tag{9-63}$$

or

$$N = 2^L \tag{9-64}$$

Then [W] can be factored into L matrices in the form

$$W = [W_1]\,[W_2] \cdots [W_L] \tag{9-65}$$

Each row of each of the individual matrices has the property that it contains only two non-zero terms: unity and W^k, where k is some integer.

Substitution of (9-65) into (9-62) yields the form

$$\overline{X}_s = [W_1]\,[W_2] \cdots [W_L]\overline{x} \tag{9-66}$$

where the subscript on $\overline{X}_s$ is used only to denote the fact that the components of this vector appear in a different order than assumed in the original definition of X. At the outset $[W_L]$ operates on $\bar{x}$ to yield a new vector. Each component of the new vector may be obtained by one multiplication and one addition, since all but two elements on a given row of the matrix are zero. Since there are N components of $\bar{x}$, there will be N complex additions and N complex multiplications required in this process. The new vector is then operated on by $[W_{L-1}]$, and the process is repeated until (9-66) is completely satisfied. Thus, it initially appears that the number of operations is $NL = N \log_2 N$ complex additions and $N \log_2 N$ complex multiplications. However, by taking advantage of various symmetry properties and the fact that many of the W^k terms are unity, the actual number of complex computations can be reduced by one-half or more. As an approximate worst-case bound for comparison, we will state the value $N \log_2 N$ as the number of complex computations involved in the Cooley-Tukey FFT algorithm. Approximate ratios of the number of computations required for the FFT to the number required with direct use of the DFT definition are given in Table 9-5 for several possible cases.

N	N(DFT)	N(FFT)	N(FFT)/ N(DFT)
16	256	64	0.250
32	1024	160	0.156
64	4096	384	0.0938
128	16,384	896	0.0547
256	65,536	2048	0.0312
512	262,144	4608	0.0176
1024	1,048,576	10,240	0.0098
2048	4,194,304	22,528	0.0054
4096	16,777,216	49,152	0.0029

N = Number of Points in Time Sample.

$N(DFT) = N^2$ = Approximate Number of Complex Arithmetic Operations With DFT.

$N(FFT) = N \operatorname{Log}_2 N$ = Approximate Number of Complex Arithmetic Operations With FFT.

Table 9-5 Comparison of approximate number of computations required for DFT and FFT.

There are a number of variations in the FFT algorithms indicated by (9-66), and some of these variations will be explored in Sec. 9-6. Most of these algorithms may be classified as either (a) *in-place* or (b) *natural input-output*. An in-place algorithm is one in which a given component of any intermediate vector may be stored in the same location occupied by the corresponding component of the preceding vector, thus reducing the total storage required. Unfortunately, most of the in-place algorithms result in either the output spectrum appearing in an unnatural order, or they require that the input data be rearranged before entering the computational array. The natural input-output algorithms, on the other hand, require more internal memory in order to maintain this natural order. Thus, if memory size is extremely critical, it would be desirable to use an in-place algorithm even though the input or output data has to be reordered. This reordering process will be referred to as a *scrambling* operation, and it will be discussed next.

The *scrambled value* of a given integer m will be denoted as $\widehat{m}$. Assume that m can be represented in binary form as

$$m = m_{N-1} m_{N-2} \cdots m_1 m_0 \tag{9-67}$$

The scrambed value of m will be defined as

$$\widehat{m} = m_0 m_1 \cdots m_{N-2} m_{N-1} \tag{9-68}$$

Thus, the scrambled value of a given integer is a new number obtained by reversing the order of all the bits in the binary representation of the given number. Note that if m is scrambled twice, the original value is obtained again, i.e.,

$$\widehat{\widehat{m}} = m \tag{9-69}$$

For the sake of illustration, values of m and $\widehat{m}$ for N = 8 and 16 are given in decimal and binary form in Table 9-6.

N = 8

m (decimal)	0	1	2	3	4	5	6	7
m (binary)	000	001	010	011	100	101	110	111
$\hat{m}$ (binary)	000	100	010	110	001	101	011	111
$\hat{m}$ (decimal)	0	4	2	6	1	5	3	7

N = 16

m (decimal)	0	1	2	3	4	5	6	7	8	9	10	11	12	13	14	15
m (binary)	0000	0001	0010	0011	0100	0101	0110	0111	1000	1001	1010	1011	1100	1101	1110	1111
$\hat{m}$ (binary)	0000	1000	0100	1100	0010	1010	0110	1110	0001	1001	0101	1101	0011	1011	0111	1111
$\hat{m}$ (decimal)	0	8	4	12	2	10	6	14	1	9	5	13	3	11	7	15

Table 9-6 Integers and their scrambled values for N = 8 and 16.

With some of the in-place algorithms, the data must either be scrambled before or after processing. Using the output as a reference for discussion, assume that the output registers are arranged in a natural order ranging from 0 to N-1.

Then, at a particular location m, the component appearing at the output is not $X(m)$, but rather $X(\widehat{m})$. In this case, it would be necessary to go to location $\widehat{m}$ to obtain the component desired for the index m. The computer flow chart of an algorithm for performing the scrambling operation will be shown and discussed later in the chapter (Fig. 9-16).

9-6 Survey of Algorithms

At this point, we will inspect some of the variations of the basic FFT algorithm and their various computational structures. It must be stressed at the outset that the collection presented is not intended to be a complete set of such algorithms. Indeed, there have been many additional modifications depending on the particular requirements, the limitations of available hardware, and the ingenuity of the individual designer or programmer. Many applications of the FFT involve programming a general purpose digital computer to solve a particular problem. In these cases, the efficiency of the program organization is not always of paramount importance. On the other hand, special purpose FFT computers are rapidly increasing in appearance, and the designers of these machines must pay extremely close attention to optimum organization.

The particular layouts shown have been organized around the goal of clarity in presentation rather than optimum organization efficiency. It is a challenge for the programmer or system designer to finalize these layouts into the most practical form, subject to the particular constraints present.

For each variation of the algorithm presented, a signal processing layout referred to as a *signal flow graph* will be given. This terminology is used because of the close physical and mathematical similarity to a conventional signal flow graph as used in system theory. In all cases, the organizational layout of an 8 point system will be used to illustrate the flow graph. The general trends in each case may be observed from a close inspection of the 8 point system so that the result may be generalized to any arbitrary number of points satisfying (9-63) and (9-64).

A total of eight signal flow graphs will be shown. The first four (Figs. 9-6 through 9-9) represent variations of the original Cooley-Tukey algorithm. These algorithms have been derived by a process called *decimation in time* (ref. 5). The second form (Figs. 9-10 through 9-13) represent variations of an algorithm developed independently by Sande, Tukey, Stockham, and others. The derivations of these forms have been accomplished by a process called *decimation in frequency* (ref. 5). For convenience in discussion, we will refer to the decimation in time forms as *type 1* algorithms and the decimation in frequency forms as *type 2* algorithms. This terminology will be used in the remainder of the chapter.

In addition to the signal flow graphs, two *computer flow charts* will be presented (Figs. 9-14 and 9-15) corresponding to two particular type 1

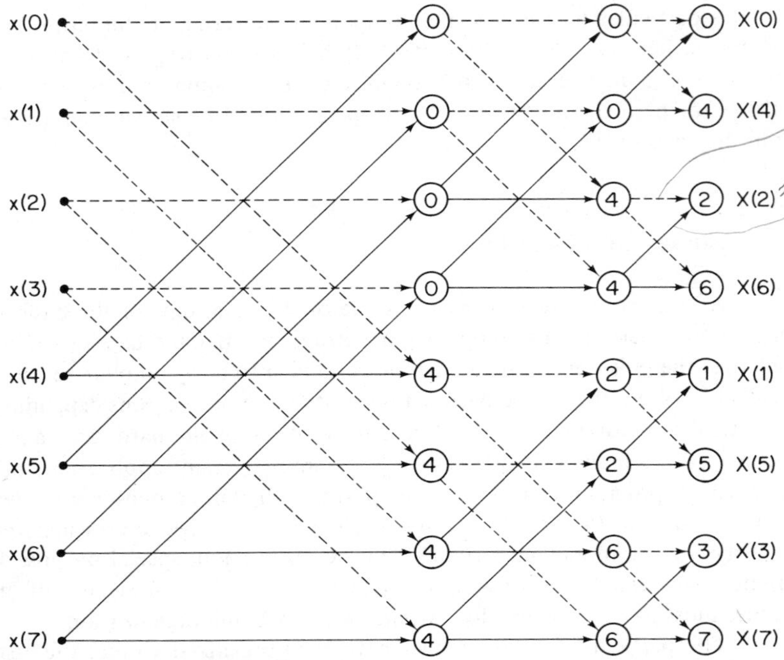

Figure 9-6 In-place algorithm with natural input and scrambled output (type 1).

algorithms. These flow charts are in forms from which computer programs can be readily written.

From the definitions of the DFT and inverse DFT as given by (9-18) and (9-19), it is seen that the only differences in form between the two functions are the presence of the 1/N factor in the inverse function and the replacement of W by W^{-1}. Actually, the exact forms given here are somewhat arbitrary as a number of possible forms have been used. One common modification is the placement of the 1/N factor in the DFT rather than the inverse DFT, and this form appears extensively in the literature.

The signal flow graphs and computer charts have been organized around the computation of the DFT using the form of (9-18). The same layouts can be used to compute the inverse DFT using (9-19) with the following simple modifications: (1) The quantity $W = \epsilon(-j2\pi/N)$ is replaced by $W^{-1} = \epsilon(j2\pi/N)$. This is achieved by reversing the signs of all the sine terms. (b) All terms must be multiplied by 1/N. This can be done at either the input or the output. (c) The input is now the transform $X(m)$ and the output is the time signal $x(n)$.

The procedure for reading the signal flow graphs will now be discussed. Refer to Fig. 9-6 for discussion. There are four columns and each column contains eight entries. For the sake of clarity, the two-dimensional variable $y(\ell,m)$ will be used to denote the value of a given node in the array, where ℓ is the

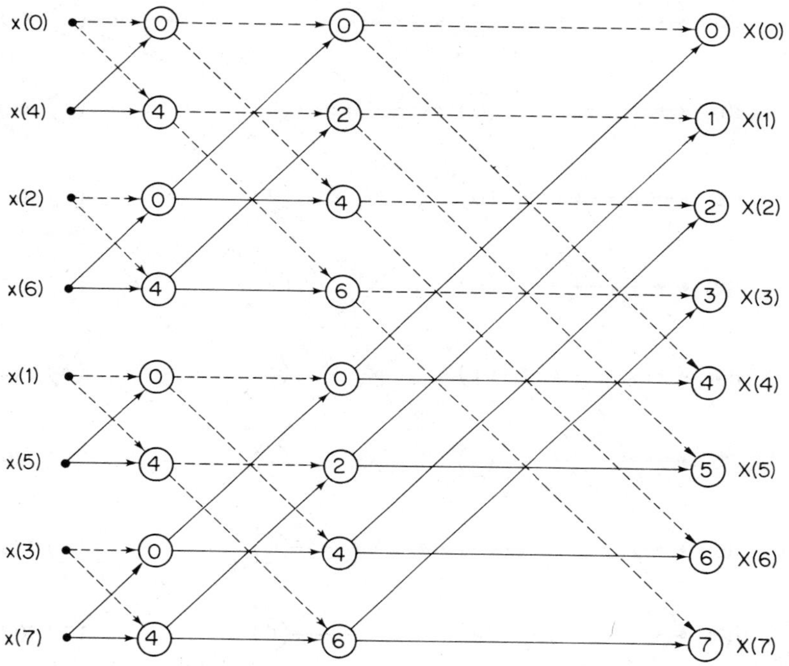

Figure 9-7 In-place algorithm with scrambled input and natural output (type 1).

number of the column and m is the number of the component within the column. Note that in general, ℓ varies over the range $0 \leqslant \ell \leqslant L$ with $\ell = 0$ at the left, and m varies over the range $0 \leqslant m \leqslant N\text{-}1$ with $m = 0$ at the top.

The preceding does *not* imply that separate storage will have to be set aside for all of the elements of the two-dimensional variable $y(\ell,m)$. Indeed, with the in-place algorithms, the column $y(\ell+1,m)$ is stored in the same array as $y(\ell,m)$. With other algorithms, it is usually necessary to maintain more internal storage, but it is rarely necessary to provide total storage for every variable in the process. Nevertheless, in our discussion it is very convenient to look at all the elements of the total array as a distinct set of variables. In this respect, the input $x(m)$ is stored in the location $y(0,m)$ when no scrambling is required there and in the location $y(0,\widehat{m})$ when scrambling at the input is required. Likewise, the output $X(m)$ is obtained in the location $y(L,m)$ when no output scrambling is required and in the location $y(L,\widehat{m})$ when scrambling at the output is required.

The procedure that follows applies to the type 1 algorithms of Figs. 9-6 through 9-9. At the node corresponding to column ℓ and row m, the variable $y(\ell,m)$ is found from an equation of the form

$$y(\ell,m) = y(\ell-1,m_1) + W^r y(\ell-1,m_2) \tag{9-70}$$

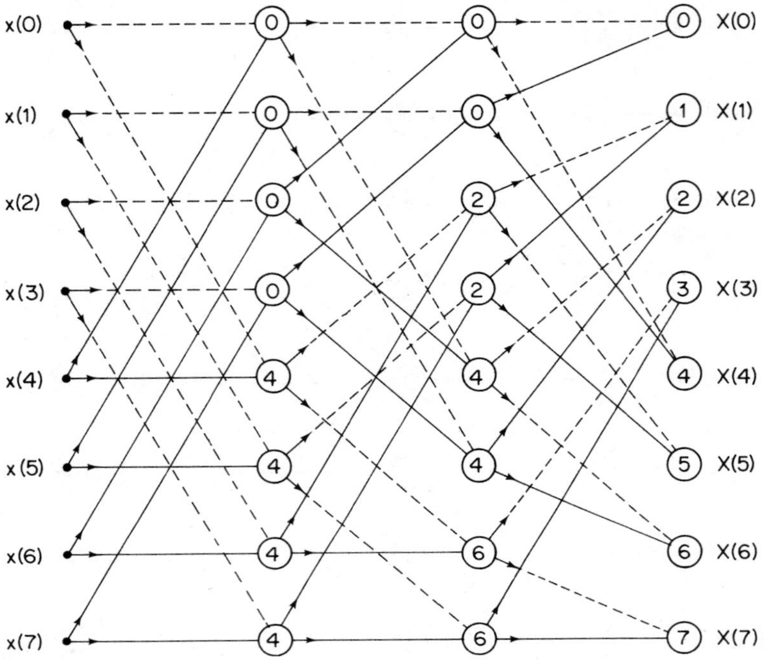

Figure 9-8 Natural input-output algorithm requiring more internal storage (type 1).

where m_1, m_2, and r are functions of the location within the array and the particular algorithm. In each case, the *dashed line* connecting the variable in row ℓ-1 with row ℓ refers to the first term on the right-hand side of equation (9-70), i.e., the *non-weighted* term. The *solid* line refers to the second term on the right-hand side of (9-70), i.e., the *weighted* term. The number in the circle is the degree of W as indicated by the integer r in (9-70). The correctness of this signal flow graph will be illustrated for a particular component in Ex. 9-3.

The algorithm of Fig. 9-6 is one of the in-place forms as will be illustrated later in the flow chart of Fig. 9-14. This means that when a particular column of data is calculated, the values can be stored in the same locations occupied by the previous column. Thus, storage for about N complex signal values is required.

In the preceding algorithm, the input signal appears in natural order and the output is scrambled. A modification in which the input is scrambled and the output appears in natural order is shown in Fig. 9-7.

The signal flow graph of a natural input-output algorithm is shown in Fig. 9-8. It can be shown that the in-place property no longer holds, so it is necessary to maintain storage for about 2N complex signal values in this case.

A rather interesting arrangement is shown in Fig. 9-9. In this form, the geometry of each stage is identical with that of other stages. This property might

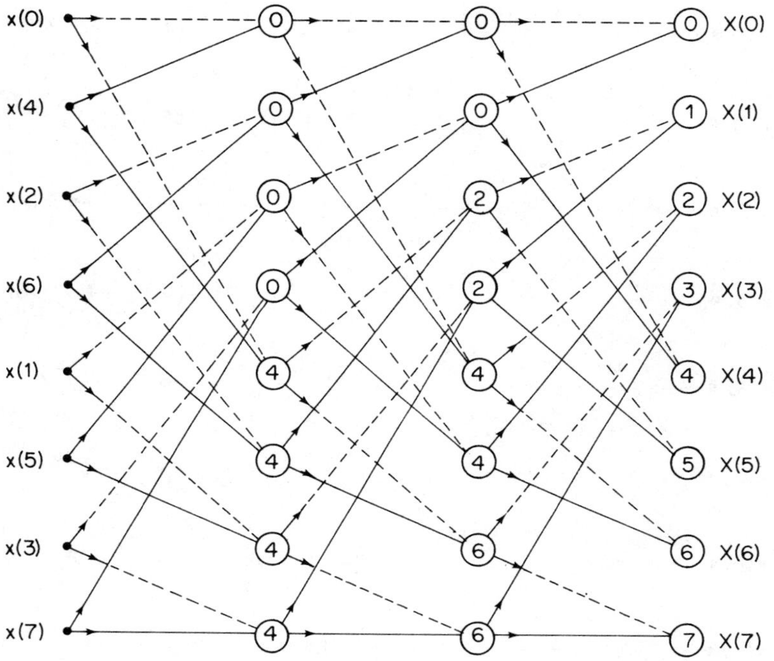

Figure 9-9 Algorithm having identical geometry in each stage (type 1).

be advantageous in the design of certain systems. However, this form requires more internal storage, and the input data must be scrambled, so that the algorithm is neither an in-place nor a natural input-output version.

The signal flow graphs shown in Figs. 9-10 through 9-13 all represent type 2 algorithms. With all of these flow graphs, the equations relating successive columns have one of two possible forms, depending on the location within the array. One form is the equation

$$y(\ell,m) = y(\ell\text{-}1,m_1) + y(\ell\text{-}1,m_2) \tag{9-71}$$

The other form is the equation

$$y(\ell,m) = W^r\,[y(\ell-1,m_1) - y(\ell-1,m_2)] \tag{9-72}$$

where m_1, m_2, and r are functions of the location within the array and the particular algorithm.

Refer to Fig. 9-10 for illustration. Components that correspond to (9-71) are those with two *dashed* lines terminating on them. Components that correspond to (9-72) are those with two *solid* lines terminating on the pertinent circle. The integer in the circle is the degree of W as indicated by r in (9-72). The

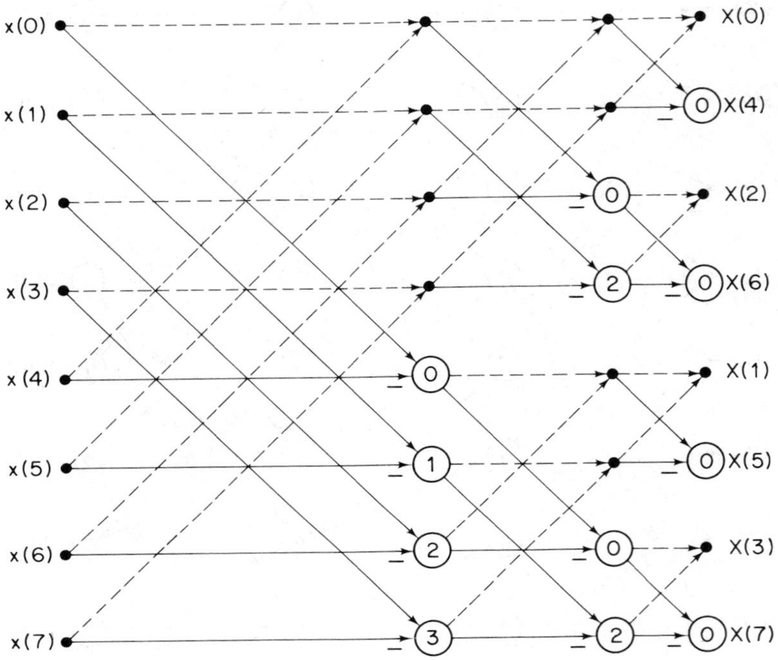

Figure 9-10 In-place algorithm with natural input and scrambled output (type 2).

(−) sign appears adjacent to the branch which is subtracted, and this is always the lowest branch terminating on the given circle.

To further illustrate this graph, the equations corresponding to the first inner column of Fig. 9-10 are written as follows:

$$
\begin{aligned}
y(1,0) &= y(0,0) + y(0,4) \\
y(1,1) &= y(0,1) + y(0,5) \\
y(1,2) &= y(0,2) + y(0,6) \\
y(1,3) &= y(0,3) + y(0,7) \\
y(1,4) &= W^0\,[y(0,0) - y(0,4)] \\
y(1,5) &= W^1\,[y(0,1) - y(0,5)] \\
y(1,6) &= W^2\,[y(0,2) - y(0,6)] \\
y(1,7) &= W^3\,[y(0,3) - y(0,7)]
\end{aligned}
\tag{9-73}
$$

The reader is invited to verify the correctness of this graph (Prob. 9-14) by writing the equations at the other columns and solving for some particular component. After a few exercises of this type, most readers will probably be content to accept the algorithms given in the text on faith!

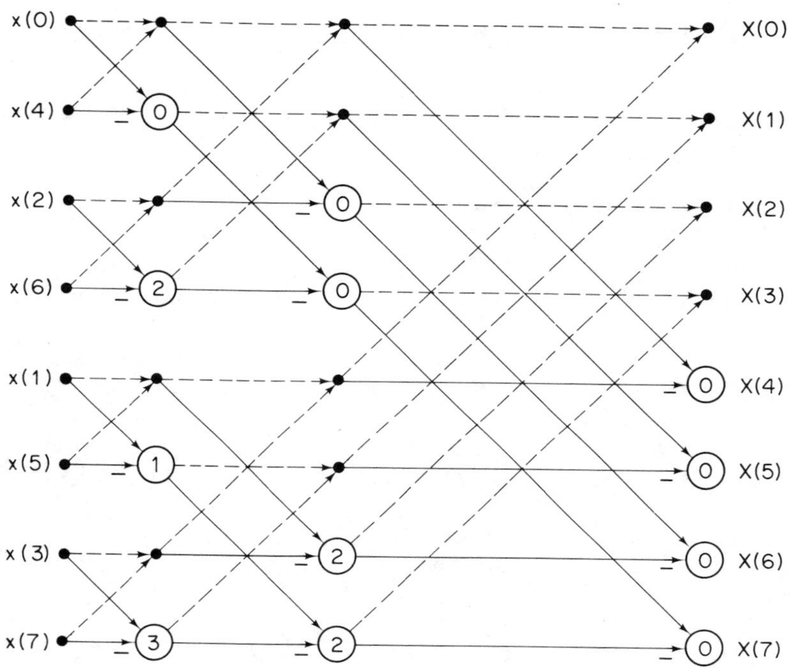

Figure 9-11 In-place algorithm with scrambled input and natural output (type 2).

The algorithm of Fig. 9-10 is an in-place form, and the output data is scrambled. A modified form in which the input data is scrambled and the output appears in natural order is shown in Fig. 9-11.

The signal flow graph of a natural input-output type 2 form is shown in Fig. 9-12. As in the case of the type 1 natural input-output version, more internal memory is required in this case. Finally, an algorithm exhibiting identical geometry in each stage is shown in Fig. 9-13.

Two computer flow charts corresponding to two particular algorithms previously given are shown in Figs. 9-14 and 9-15, and a flow chart for performing the scrambling operation is shown in Fig. 9-16. The equations appearing on these flow charts represent a sort of mixture between normal algebraic equations and equations typically used in programming languages, but with clarity in presentation sought as a primary goal. An equation of the form $x = x + y$ should be read as follows: "Add y to the value found in location x and store the result in location x." The integer m is shown on the flow chart in its natural range, i.e., $0 \leqslant m \leqslant N\text{-}1$. However, dimensioned variables in many programming languages accept only positive integers in arguments, so it may be necessary to shift such arguments by one unit in an actual program.

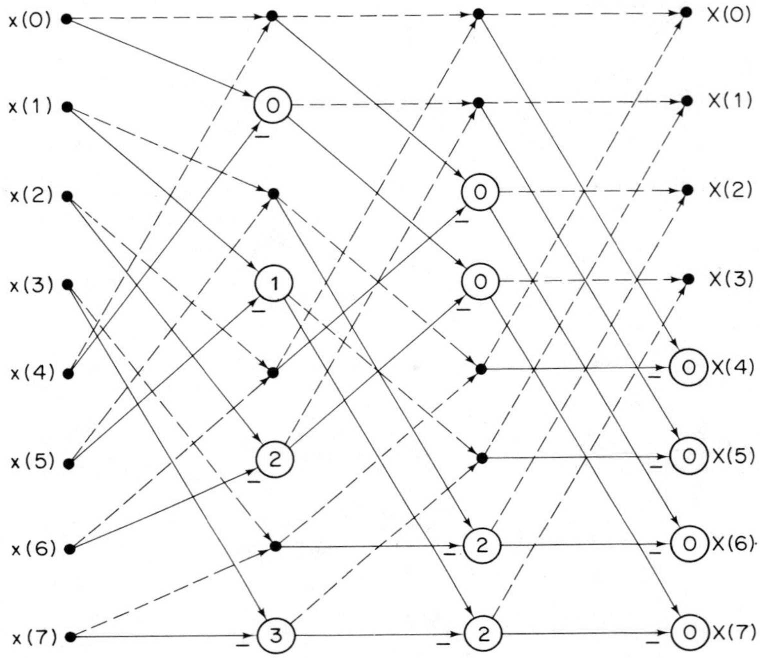

Figure 9-12 Natural input-output algorithm requiring more internal storage (type 2).

The flow chart of Fig. 9-14 corresponds to the in-place algorithm of Fig. 9-6. The integers L and N on the flow chart correspond to the definitions of (9-63) and (9-64) and are assumed to be constrained accordingly. The operation ($\frown$) over an integer refers to the scrambled value of that particular integer. A separate routine may be developed for performing the scrambling operation, and a flow chart for this purpose is shown in Fig. 9-16.

One of the operations shown in Fig. 9-14 is given by

$$I_e = \widehat{\left[\frac{I_c}{I_a}\right]} \tag{9-74}$$

The operation [ ] is defined as the "integer part" of the quantity within the brackets. This refers simply to the process of rounding off the number to the largest integer equal to or smaller than the given number. Thus, the integer parts of 2, 2.3, and 2.7 are all equal to 2. This operation is achieved in some programming languages by equating an integer variable on the left to the given quotient on the right. In the particular operation of (9-74), the resulting integer is in turn scrambled.

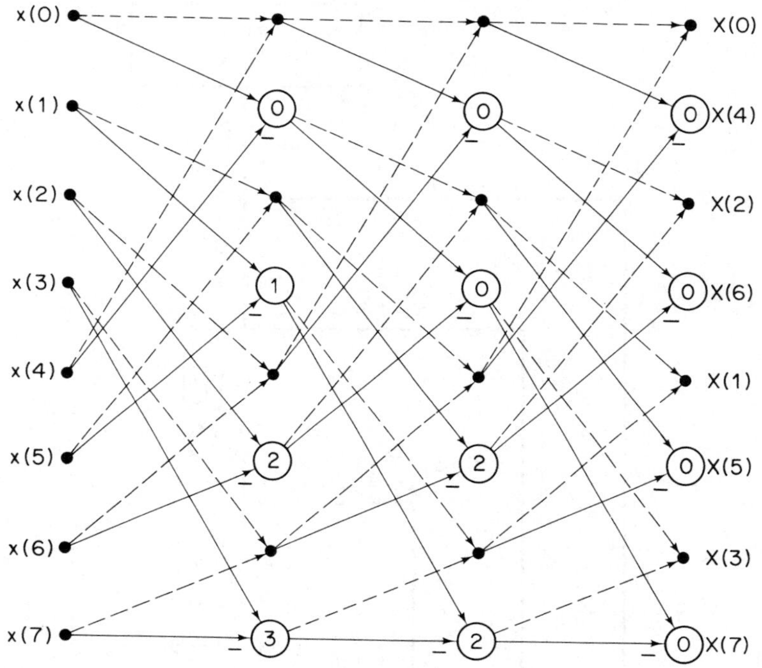

Figure 9-13 Algorithm having identical geometry in each stage (type 2).

The computer flow chart corresponding to the natural input-output algorithm of Fig. 9-8 is shown in Fig. 9-15. As expected, the amount of internal storage for this form is about twice that of the in-place algorithms, since it is necessary to maintain the separate arrays $y_1(m)$ and $y_2(m)$ in this case. However, no scrambling is required so that the overall organization is somewhat simpler.

Example 9-3

Illustrate the signal flow graph of Fig. 9-6 by solving for the particular component X(3) in terms of the input components, and verify that the result is identical to the quantity obtained by direct application of the DFT definition.

Solution

In the results that follow, use will be made of the relationship

$$W^{kN+r} = W^r \tag{9-75}$$

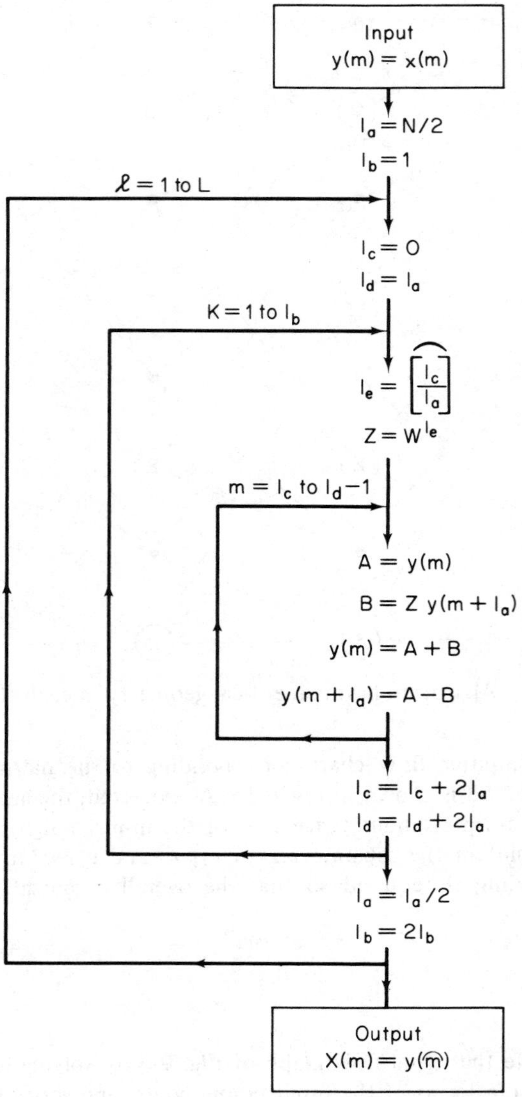

Figure 9-14 Computer flow chart corresponding to signal flow graph of Figure 9-6.

where r and k are integers. This relationship was given in Table 9-2. From Fig. 9-6, the equations of column 1 are

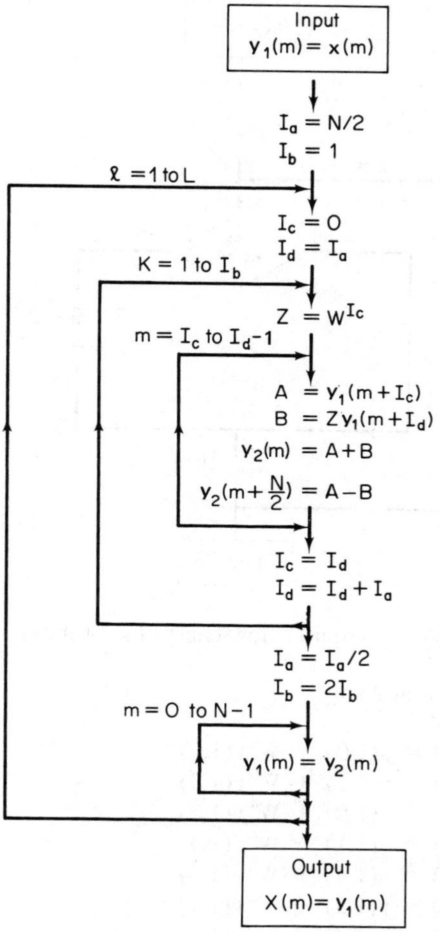

Figure 9-15 Computer flow chart corresponding to signal flow graph of Figure 9-8.

$$
\begin{aligned}
y(1,0) &= y(0,0) + W^0 y(0,4) \\
y(1,1) &= y(0,1) + W^0 y(0,5) \\
y(1,2) &= y(0,2) + W^0 y(0,6) \\
y(1,3) &= y(0,3) + W^0 y(0,7) \\
y(1,4) &= y(0,0) + W^4 y(0,4) \\
y(1,5) &= y(0,1) + W^4 y(0,5) \\
y(1,6) &= y(0,2) + W^4 y(0,6) \\
y(1,7) &= y(0,3) + W^4 y(0,7)
\end{aligned}
\qquad (9\text{-}76)
$$

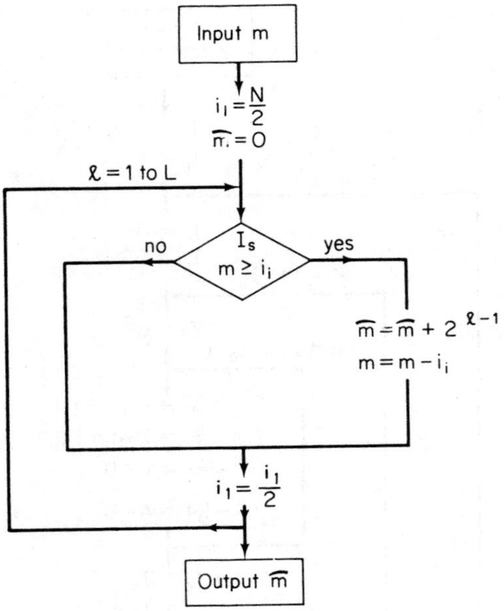

Figure 9-16 Computer flow chart of scrambling algorithm.

The equations of column 2 are

$$
\begin{aligned}
y(2,0) &= y(1,0) + W^0 y(1,2) \\
y(2,1) &= y(1,1) + W^0 y(1,3) \\
y(2,2) &= y(1,0) + W^4 y(1,2) \\
y(2,3) &= y(1,1) + W^4 y(1,3) \\
y(2,4) &= y(1,4) + W^2 y(1,6) \\
y(2,5) &= y(1,5) + W^2 y(1,7) \\
y(2,6) &= y(1,4) + W^6 y(1,6) \\
y(2,7) &= y(1,5) + W^6 y(1,7)
\end{aligned} \tag{9-77}
$$

The equations of column 3 are

$$
\begin{aligned}
y(3,0) &= y(2,0) + W^0 y(2,1) \\
y(3,1) &= y(2,0) + W^4 y(2,1) \\
y(3,2) &= y(2,2) + W^2 y(2,3) \\
y(3,3) &= y(2,2) + W^6 y(2,3) \\
y(3,4) &= y(2,4) + W^1 y(2,5) \\
y(3,5) &= y(2,4) + W^5 y(2,5) \\
y(3,6) &= y(2,6) + W^3 y(2,7) \\
y(3,7) &= y(2,6) + W^7 y(2,7)
\end{aligned} \tag{9-78}
$$

By successive elimination, we can solve for either of the variables on the left-hand side of (9-78) in terms of the input data. The particular value desired is X(3) and this quantity actually corresponds to $y(3,6)$ in the array of (9-78), as can be seen in Fig. 9-6. From the expression for $y(3,6)$, it is seen that we must substitute in $y(2,6)$ and $y(2,7)$. However, the expressions for $y(2,6)$ and $y(2,7)$ in (9-77) require that we substitute in $y(1,4)$, $y(1,6)$, $y(1,5)$, and $y(1,7)$. Finally, each of these latter variables involve all eight values of the input data as seen in (9-76). Carrying through this successive chain of substitutions, we obtain

$$\begin{aligned} y(3,6) &= y(0,0) + W^3 y(0,1) + W^6 y(0,2) + W^9\, y(0,3) \\ &\quad + W^4 y(0,4) + W^7 y(0,5) + W^{10} y(0,6) + W^{13} y(0,7) \end{aligned} \tag{9-79}$$

If this expression is correct, the result should be X(3). If we take the general DFT expression and expand it for $x(3)$ we initially obtain

$$\begin{aligned} X(3) &= x(0) + W^3 x(1) + W^6 x(2) + W^9 x(3) \\ &\quad + W^{12} x(4) + W^{15} x(5) + W^{18} x(6) + W^{21}\, x(7) \end{aligned} \tag{9-80}$$

Before comparing (9-79) and (9-80), we first note that $y(o,m) = x(m)$ and $X(m) = y(L,\overline{m})$. It can then be readily observed that the first four terms of (9-79) and (9-80) are equivalent. The last four terms are then seen to be equal by application of (9-75).

PROBLEMS

9-1 Consider that we are given a certain continuous-time signal $x(t)$ having a continuous-frequency Fourier transform $X(f)$. The time signal has a duration of 2.048 seconds. The signal is then sampled at 256 equally spaced points.
(a) Determine the increment in Hz between successive frequency components in the spectrum of the sampled signal.
(b) Determine the "period" in Hz of the spectrum.
(c) What is the highest frequency permitted in the spectrum of the signal if no aliasing is to occur?

9-2 Derive the form of the Fourier transform pair of equations (9-8) and (9-9) by evaluating the z-transform and inverse transform functions on the unit circle in the z-plane.

9-3 Verify all of the results of Table 9-2.

9-4 Prove that when $x(n)$ is purely imaginary, the real part of $X(m)$ is an odd function of m, and the imaginary part is an even function of m.

9-5 Prove that when the time function is a real even function of n, the frequency function is a real even function of m as indicated by equation (9-33).

9-6 Prove that when the time function is a real odd function of n, the frequency function is an imaginary odd function of m as indicated by equation (9-34).

9-7 Show from the shifting theorem as given by operation pair DO-2 that the amplitude spectrum is not affected by the shifting operation, but that a phase shift of $2\pi km/N$ radians is introduced in the spectrum.

9-8 Derive the form of the modulation theorem as given by operation pair DO-3.

9-9 Using the basic form of the modulation theorem as given by operation pair DO-3, derive equations (9-50) and (9-51).

9-10 Derive the DFT of a lagged product as given by operation pair DO-5.

9-11 Derive the DFT of the product of two signals as given by operation pair DO-6.

9-12 A certain long signal contains about 100,000 points. Assume that zeros are added to the end of the signal to make the total number of points be an integer power of two. Assuming that a program is available to transform the entire signal as a unit, determine the approximate ratio of the time required with the FFT to the time required for a direct DFT evaluation.

9-13 Compute a table of the forms given in Table 9-6 for N = 32.

9-14 The equations for the first column of Fig. 9-10 were outlined in (9-73). Write similar equations for the remaining columns on the right, and solve for X(3) in terms of the input data. Verify that this result is correct by solving directly for X(3) using the DFT definition.

REFERENCES

1. G. D. Bergland, "A guided tour of the fast Fourier transform", *IEEE Spectrum,* vol. 6, pp. 41-52, July 1969.

2. E. O. Brigham and R. E. Morrow, "The fast Fourier transform", *IEEE Spectrum*, vol. 4, pp. 63-70, Dec. 1967.

3. J. W. Cooley and J. W. Tukey, "An algorithm for the machine computation of complex Fourier series", *Math. Computation*, vol. 19, pp. 297-301, April 1965.

4. W. M. Gentleman and G. Sande, "Fast Fourier transforms for fun and profit", *1966 Fall Joint Computer Conference, AFIPS Proc.*, vol. 29, pp. 563-578. Washington, D.C.: Spartan Books.

5. B. Gold and C. M. Rader, *Digital Processing of Signals*. New York: McGraw-Hill, 1969.

6. H. D. Helms and L. R. Rabiner, Eds., *Literature in Digital Signal Processing*. New York: IEEE Press, 1973.

7. Hewlett-Packard, Inc., *Fourier Analyzer Training Manual*, Application Note 140-0.

8. L. R. Rabiner and C. M. Rader, Eds. *Digital Signal Processing.* New York: IEEE Press, 1972.

CHAPTER TEN

APPLICATIONS OF THE DISCRETE FOURIER TRANSFORM

10-0 Introduction

The basic properties of the discrete Fourier transform (DFT) were introduced in the last chapter. It was shown that this operation could be implemented by a fast Fourier transform (FFT) algorithm, which permits a considerable reduction in the number of computations required for evaluating a discrete spectrum. Some of the basic relationships and the computational procedures were discussed.

Possible applications of the FFT appear in almost all of the general areas of engineering, science, and mathematics. The variety of applications includes the analysis of mechanical and structural vibrations, the extraction of vital information from radar and sonar signals, analysis of statistical data, digital filtering, and many other applications.

The primary emphasis in this chapter will be on the consideration of the various properties of the DFT (or FFT) when utilized for general applications. The approximations involved when using the DFT in the analysis of continuous-time systems must be carefully understood. There are problems that arise in the process that may lead to erroneous results unless proper precautions are taken. These problems and means for alleviating them will be discussed, and some of the general applications will be considered.

10-1 Approximation of Continuous-Time Transforms with the DFT

We have seen that the DFT pair can be considered as the combination of a periodic discrete-time function and a periodic discrete-frequency function, which are related through the processes of finite summations. Such summations can be performed on a digital computer with the special assistance of an FFT algorithm, which provides the means for high-speed spectral analysis.

While the mathematical properties of the DFT are exact, the DFT is seldom of interest as the end goal in most digital signal processing applications. Rather, it is usually employed to transform data which may arise from either an actual continuous-time process or perhaps a discrete-time process which is being analyzed from a continuous-time system approach. In this sense then, the DFT is usually employed to approximate the Fourier transform of a continuous-time process, and it is necessary to understand some of the limitations inherent in this process. In studying some of these various limitations, we will frequently refer back to the properties and equations developed in the preceding chapter.

By inspecting the differences between the continuous Fourier integral transform pair and the DFT pair, it can be deduced that the DFT pair has the form (but not the magnitude) of a zero-order approximation for the continuous integral pair. While this observation provides some qualitative insight, it does not tell us anything about the nature or magnitude of the error in the spectrum.

Assuming that the primary goal is to use the DFT to approximate the Fourier transform of a continuous-time signal, we will investigate three possible phenomena that result in errors between the computed and the desired transform. These three phenomena are (a) *aliasing*, (b) *leakage*, and (c) *the picket-fence effect* (ref. 1). These properties will be investigated individually.

(a) *Aliasing.* The phenomenon of aliasing has been discussed in some detail in earlier chapters but will be reviewed here in reference to the DFT. Consider the continuous-time signal $x_1(t)$ shown in Fig. 10-1. The transform $X_1(f)$ is assumed to be bandlimited to $0 \leq f \leq f_h$ as shown. Assume now that the time signal is sampled at a rate f_s which is less than $2f_h$, and let $x_2(n)$ represent the sampled signal. Its transform $X_2(f)$ is characterized by spectral overlap or aliasing, as can be seen. In effect, frequencies in the overlap region may be mistaken for other frequencies, so that it is impossible to recover the original signal. For example, if $f_h = 4$ kHz and if $f_s = 5$ kHz, a 4 kHz component could be mistaken as a 1 kHz component.

The only solution to the aliasing problem is to ensure that the sampling rate is high enough to avoid any spectral overlap. This means that some prior knowledge of the nature of the spectrum is often required before the exact sampling rate is determined. In some cases, the signal may be filtered with a low-pass analog filter before sampling to ensure that no components higher than the folding frequency appear.

(b) *Leakage.* This problem arises because of the practical requirement that we must limit observation of the signal to a finite interval. To illustrate, consider the discrete-time signal $x_1(n)$ shown in Fig. 10-2, which is presumed to be infinite in extent. Assume for the sake of argument that the spectrum is of the form illustrated by $X_1(f)$. (Only a portion of one cycle of the periodic

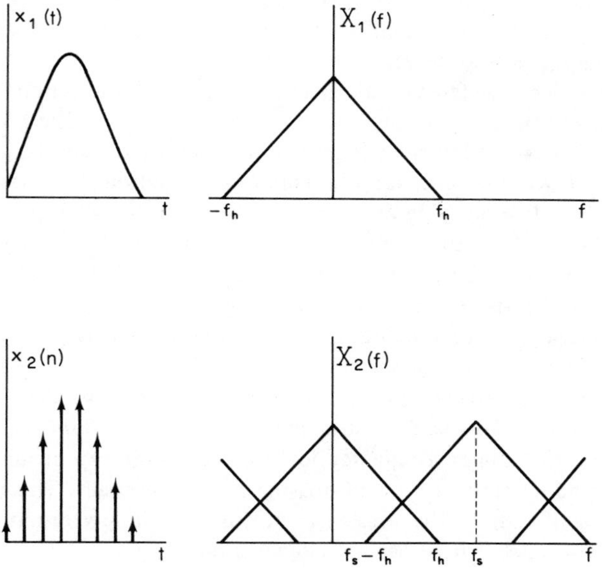

Figure 10-1 Illustration of how aliasing error arises when sampling rate is too low.

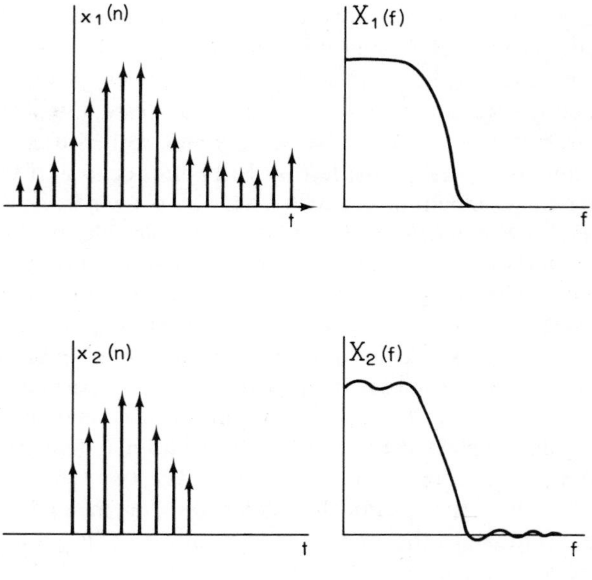

Figure 10-2 Illustration of leakage effect produced by abrupt termination of signal.

spectrum is shown.) Since we do not possess the capability nor can we wait long enough to sum an infinite number of terms, it is necessary to select a finite segment of the signal to observe.

The process of terminating the signal after a finite number of terms is equivalent to multiplying the signal by a *window function*. The problem is the same as was encountered in the design of finite impulse response digital filters in Chapt. 8. If the window function is a rectangular function, the series is abruptly terminated without modifying any coefficients within the window, as illustrated by $x_2(n)$. The resulting transform can be considered as the convolution of the desired spectrum with the spectrum of the rectangular window. The net effect is a distortion of the spectrum, as illustrated by $X_2(f)$. There is a spreading or leakage of the spectral components away from the correct frequency resulting in an undesirable modification of the total spectrum.

The leakage effect cannot always be isolated from the aliasing effect because leakage may also lead to aliasing. Since leakage results in a spreading of the spectrum, the upper frequency of the composite spectrum may move beyond the folding frequency, and aliasing may then result. This possibility is particularly significant in the case of a rectangular window function, since the tail of the window spectrum does not converge rapidly.

While the rectangular window may be acceptable in some applications, the best approach for alleviating the leakage effect is to choose a suitable window function that minimizes the spreading. The problem of selecting an appropriate window function is essentially the same as was encountered with FIR filter design, so the material in Sec. 8-3 and the Appendix are directly applicable to spectral analysis. To apply the notation of Sec. 8-3 and the Appendix for spectral analysis, the length τ should be interpreted as the length of the signal for which the window is to be applied. In each case, the window function should be centered on the signal to be transformed, so it is necessary to either momentarily shift the signal to the left by $N/2$ points or to shift the window to the right by the same amount before multiplying by the window coefficients.

(c) *Picket-Fence Effect*. This effect is produced by the inability of the DFT to observe the spectrum as a continuous function, since computation of the spectrum is limited to integer multiples of the fundamental frequency F. In a sense then, observation of the spectrum with the DFT is analogous to looking at it through a sort of "picket-fence" since we can observe the exact behavior only at discrete points. It is possible that the major peak of a particular component could lie between two of the discrete transform lines, and the peak of this component could not be detected without some additional processing.

One procedure for reducing the picket-fence effect is to vary the number of points in a time period by adding zeros at the end of the original record, while maintaining the original record intact. This process artificially changes the period, which in turns changes the locations of the spectral lines without altering the continuous form of the original spectrum. In this manner, spectral components originally hidden from view may be shifted to points where they may be observed.

When zeros are added to a signal record for the purpose of artificially changing the period, the width of any window function used should *not* be changed. In other words, the window function should be selected around the true length of the data record rather than the longer length obtained from adding additional zeros.

Apart from the differences in the spectra of continuous-time and discrete-time functions previously discussed, a minor additional point of consideration is the manner in which the relative magnitudes are defined. There have been a number of variations appearing in the literature for continuous-time Fourier transforms and series, so this problem is nothing new.

For the sake of this discussion, assume that the definitions of the transforms of continuous-time nonperiodic signals are those given by (9-3) and (9-4) and that the definitions of the Fourier series for periodic signals are those given by (9-5) and (9-6). Computation of the DFT could be done as either an approximation to (a) the Fourier transform of a nonperiodic signal according to the definition of (9-3) or (b) the Fourier coefficients of a periodic signal according to the definition of (9-5).

If it is desirable to determine the Fourier transform of a nonperiodic signal, the approximation employed must involve sums of areas in the time domain. Assume that the basic DFT definition of (9-18) is used. The proper magnitude level of the spectrum can then be obtained by multiplying all the components by T. This completes the process of representing the DFT as a zero-order integration approximation of the true integral.

Suppose now that we have a transform computed by the true integral transform definition of (9-3) or as computed by the DFT and modified by multiplying all components by T as indicated in the last paragraph. Assume that we wish to compute the time signal by an approximation to (9-4) obtained by using (9-19) with the 1/N factor included. In this case, the approximation must involve sums of areas in the frequency domain. The proper magnitude level is obtained by multiplying all of the resulting time signal components by $NF = f_s$. Note that in the whole cycle from time to frequency and back again as discussed here, we have multiplied by $T \times NF = 1$, so the magnitude level of the complete cycle has, of necessity, not been affected.

Slightly different forms for the scaling constants are required when it is desired to use the DFT to determine the approximate coefficients for the Fourier series of a periodic function. The usual expression for the coefficients of a Fourier series as given by (9-5) involve determining the average value of the integrand. The corresponding magnitude level using the DFT could be obtained by multiplying by T and dividing by t_p. However, $T/t_p = 1/N$. This suggests that the 1/N factor would be best associated with the transform rather than the inverse transform for this purpose. Hence, if it is desired to use the DFT for computing regular Fourier series using the standard definitions of (9-5) and (9-6), it is recommended that the DFT definitions be modified by placing the 1/N factor with the direct transform rather than with the inverse transform.

The process of scaling the levels may not really be necessary in many applications. In fact, the actual levels of the transform components are often not important, but it is the *relative* levels between different components in the spectrum that determine the most significant properties, and these are preserved independent of the overall levels. This fact is illuminated by the variations in the literature concerning the magnitude levels of continuous-time transforms.

To summarize this section, the DFT algorithm can be used to approximate the transform of a continuous-time function, subject to the following limitations and difficulties.

(a) The signal must be band-limited, and the sampling rate must be sufficiently high to avoid aliasing.

(b) If it is necessary to limit the length of the signal for computational purposes, the spectrum will be degraded somewhat by the leakage effect. Leakage is most severe when the simple rectangular window function is used.

(c) Components lying between discrete frequency lines are subject to error in magnitude due to the "picket-fence" effect.

(d) The magnitude level may be different from that of the continuous-time transform due to the variation in definitions. This problem is readily resolved by multiplying all of the components by a simple constant as discussed earlier, if it is necessary to force the levels to be compatible with those of the continuous-time definitions.

10-2 Selection of DFT (or FFT) Parameters

The purpose of this short section is to summarize the important parameter relationships that must be considered in using the DFT. It is assumed that the actual discrete-time signal is either derived from a continuous-time function or at least referred to such a function for analysis purposes. The major parameters of interest will be reviewed here and are as follows:

T = increment between time samples (in seconds)
f_s = sampling rate (in hertz) = $1/T$
F = increment between frequency components (in hertz) = frequency resolution
t_p = record length (in seconds) = effective period of time signal = $1/F$
f_0 = folding frequency = $f_s/2$ (in hertz)
f_h = highest possible frequency in spectrum (in hertz)
N = number of samples in record

Assume that the function to be analyzed is a *baseband* signal. Such a signal is one in which the spectrum is primarily concentrated at lower frequencies and in which no translation of the spectrum has been performed.

In order to avoid aliasing, it is necessary that

$$f_s \geqslant 2f_h \tag{10-1}$$

This result implies that T must be selected according to

$$T \leqslant \frac{1}{2f_h} \tag{10-2}$$

The increment between spectral components F can also be thought of as the *frequency resolution*. For a desired frequency resolution, the minimum record length t_p must be selected according to

$$t_p = \frac{1}{F} \tag{10-3}$$

A study of (10-2) and (10-3) leads to the conclusion that there is a tradeoff between the high-frequency capability and the frequency resolution between successive components. To increase the high-frequency capability, it is necessary that T be reduced. For a given N, this would shorten the record length and, thus, decrease the frequency resolution. Conversely, to increase the resolution, it is necessary to increase t_p. For a given N this would increase T, which would decrease the high-frequency capability.

The only way in which either the high-frequency capability or the frequency resolution can be increased while holding the other constant is to increase the number of points N in a record length. If f_h and F are both specified, N must satisfy

$$N \geqslant \frac{2f_h}{F} \tag{10-4}$$

The preceding relationships are minimum conditions that should be satisfied with a basic DFT (or FFT) processing algorithm with no special data modification techniques applied. Modifications in the basic procedures could alter these conditions. For example, the use of a special window function will broaden the widths of spectral components, so the frequency resolution may be degraded somewhat in this case. Consequently, it may be necessary to increase the record length in order to maintain a fixed resolution when a special window function is employed.

Example 10-1

An FFT processor is to be employed in the spectral analysis of a random real signal. Assume that the number of points permitted by the processor must be an integer power of two, and assume that no special data modifications are used. The following specifications are given: (1) resolution between frequencies $\leqslant$ 5 Hz, (2) highest frequency in signal $\leqslant$ 1.25 kHz. Determine the following parameters: (a) minimum record length, (b) maximum time between samples, and (c) minimum number of points in a record.

Solution

(a) The desired resolution determines the minimum record length.

$$t_p = \frac{1}{F} = \frac{1}{5} = 0.2 \text{ seconds}$$

The record length t_p must then satisfy the equation

$$t_p \geqslant 0.2 \text{ seconds} \tag{10-5}$$

(b) The highest frequency determines the maximum sample time.

$$T \leqslant \frac{1}{2f_h}$$

$$\frac{1}{2f_h} = \frac{1}{2 \times 1.25 \times 10^3} = 0.4 \times 10^{-3}$$

The sample time T is constrained by

$$T \leqslant 0.4 \text{ milliseconds} \tag{10-6}$$

(c) The number of points must satisfy

$$N \geqslant \frac{0.2}{0.4 \times 10^{-3}} = 500$$

The minimum number is seen to be 500, so an appropriate number for the processor is

$$N = 512 \tag{10-7}$$

10-3 Convolution with the FFT

One of the most important applications of the FFT is that of *high-speed convolution*, a process made possible by the simplicity of the corresponding relationships in the transform domain. The convolution of two signals $x(n)$ and $h(n)$ is denoted by $x(n)*h(n)$, and it is defined as

$$x(n)*h(n) = \sum_{k=0}^{N-1} x(k)h(n-k) \tag{10-8}$$

By the use of DFT operation pair DO-4, this expression is equivalent to

$$x(n)*h(n) \longleftrightarrow X(m)\,H(m) \tag{10-9}$$

If $x(n)$ and $h(n)$ are relatively long functions, the number of computations required to perform a direct convolution can become excessively large. However, according to (10-9), this operation is equivalent in the transform domain to simply multiplying the DFT's of the two signals.

There are actually three basic steps involved in using the DFT to perform high-speed convolution: (a) The DFT's of the two signals are computed using an FFT algorithm. (b) The transforms of the signals are multiplied together at all pertinent frequency points. (c) The inverse transform of the product is computed, again using an FFT algorithm.

Among the many possible applications of this concept is that of digital filtering as illustrated in Fig. 10-3. It is desired to filter a certain input signal which may be in either analog or digital form. (If it is analog, it must first be converted to digital form with an A/D converter.) The DFT of the input signal $x(n)$ is first computed. Next, the DFT is modified by the desired frequency response directly in the frequency domain. The inverse DFT $y(n)$ is then computed, and the result represents the filtered signal. This concept represents a rather interesting approach to digital filtering in the sense that frequency response functions completely unattainable with rational transfer functions may be applied directly to the spectrum.

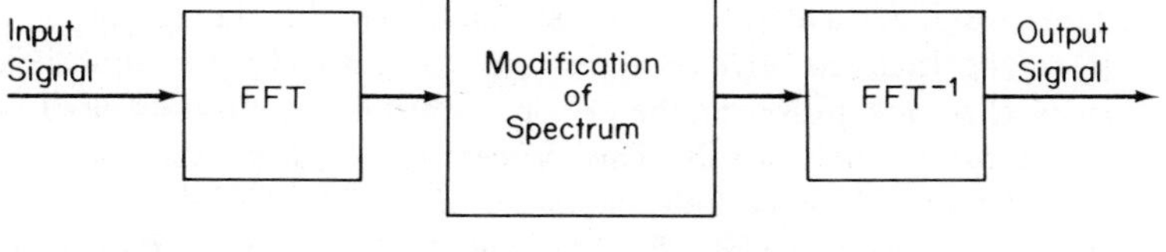

Figure 10-3 Digital filtering using the FFT.

Before concluding that high-speed convolution is so straight-forward, we must point out that there are some serious problems that must be considered, and it is necessary that these be understood before operation DO-4 can be blindly employed. In addition to the possible difficulties discussed in Sec. 10-1, which are always present in DFT analysis, there are some special problems which arise when transforming a convolution using the DFT. Finally, there are certain limitations concerning the type of frequency response weighting that can be applied to a spectrum when the DFT is used for digital filtering.

Discrete convolution may be applied directly to a purely discrete system, or it may be used as an approximation for a continuous-time convolution. For the moment, let us consider the latter case, since the nature of the approximation must be considered. Let $x_c(t)$ and $h_c(t)$ represent two continuous-time signals for which we desire a convolution, and let $y_c(t)$ represent the result. Assume that all of the signals are zero for $t < 0$. The desired response can be expressed in the form

$$y_c(t) = \int_0^t x_c(u) h_c(t-u)\, du \tag{10-10}$$

The use of operation DO-4 to evaluate this operation is equivalent to approximating the area under the integrand curve by a zero-order numerical summation process. Assuming that the approximation is reasonable, let $x(n)$, $h(n)$, and $y(n)$ represent the discrete-time functions corresponding to the three continuous-time functions. Assume that N samples of $x(n)$ and $h(n)$ are used. The differential du in (10-10) becomes T, and the required function at sample points can be approximated by

$$y_c(n\mathrm{T}) \approx y(n) = \mathrm{T} \sum_{k=0}^{n} x(k) h(n-k) \tag{10-11}$$

In effect, the desired continuous-time convolution has been approximated by a discrete-time convolution summation, which could be evaluated with the help of the DFT according to operation DO-4.

Everything up to this point appears in order, but there is one important point that may not be evident yet. In general, the input signal $x_c(t)$ and the impulse response $h_c(t)$ of the continuous-time system are not periodic. However, we have previously seen that the inverse DFT operation, resulting from sampling the spectrum, produces a periodic time signal. From the standpoint of using DO-4, this means that the inverse transform of $\mathrm{X}(m)\,\mathrm{H}(m)$ is equivalent to having formed the convolution of the *periodic* versions of $x(n)$ and $h(n)$ rather than their true nonperiodic forms. This process is called *cyclical convolution*, and it is a direct result of the periodic character of the DFT.

Before discussing means of alleviating this difficulty, let us present a numerical example to clarify the concepts involved. For illustration, we will choose some functions far too simple to warrant use of the DFT, but appropriate for explaining the process. Consider the two 4-point non-periodic functions $x(n)$ and $h(n)$ shown in Fig. 10-4, for which the convolution is desired. Using impulse notation, the two signals can be written as

$$x(n) = 2[\delta(n) + \delta(n-1) + \delta(n-2) + \delta(n-3)] \tag{10-12}$$

$$h(n) = \delta(n) + 2\delta(n-1) + 3\delta(n-2) + 4\delta(n-3) \tag{10-13}$$

The operation which we desire is

$$y(n) = x(n)*h(n) = \sum_{k=0}^{n} x(k)h(n-k) \tag{10-14}$$

Whether or not (10-14) represents a reasonable approximation to some continuous-time process is unimportant for this illustration.

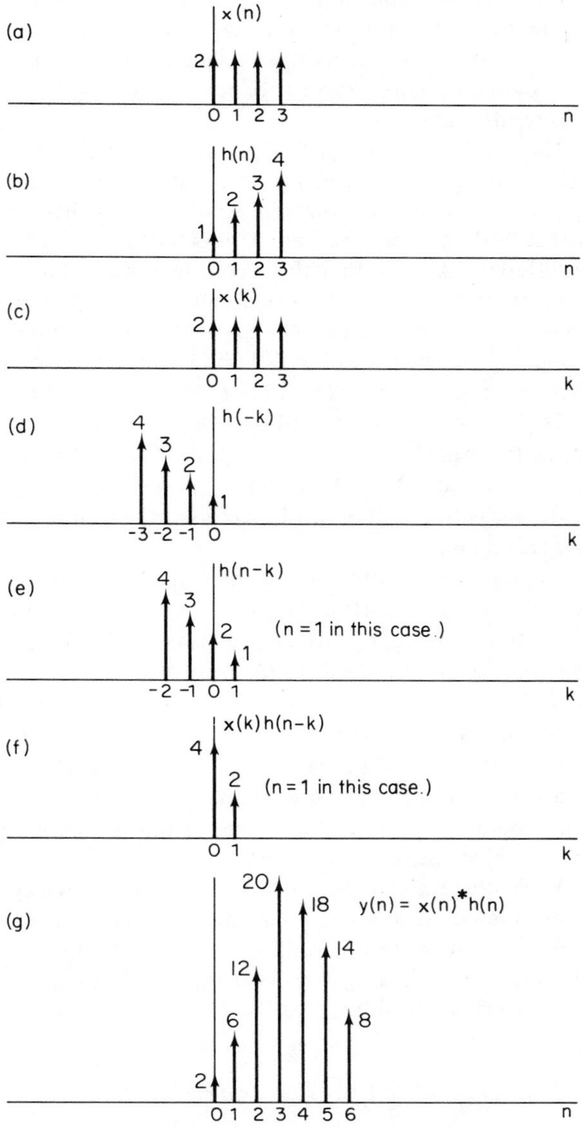

Figure 10-4 Convolution of two non-periodic signals.

The various steps involved with this convolution are illustrated in Fig. 10-4. The actual discrete variable n is first replaced with a dummy variable k in $x(n)$ as shown in (c). The quantity $h(n-k)$ is generated by first replacing n by $-k$ as shown in (d) and then replacing $-k$ by $n-k$ as shown in (e). In theory, it would be necessary to consider a separate figure for each value of n, but with proper insight to the process, this need not be done. The particular case shown is for $n = 1$. Next, the product function $x(k)h(n-k)$ is formed as shown in (f). Finally, the sum of the product terms is computed to yield $y(n)$ for that particular value of n. This process is repeated for all pertinent values of n. Note that the product function is zero for $n < 0$ and for $n > 6$, so only a finite number of terms is involved.

The preceding function is the result that would be obtained if a direct convolution summation were performed, and it is the result that we would like to obtain using the DFT. However, what actually happens is that the DFT assumes that both $x(n)$ and $h(n)$ are periodic, and the resulting convolution may be quite different. Assume that the record length for both $x(n)$ and $h(n)$ is held to the four points previously indicated and that no additional points are added. This means that the two signals are equivalent, as far as the DFT is concerned, to the periodic signals $x_a(n)$ and $h_a(n)$ shown in Fig. 10-5. (Note that we will interpret $x_a(n)$ to have a period of 4 because of the way it is defined.)

To illustrate what the inverse DFT would produce, we will actually convolve the two signals. The various steps involved are shown in (c) through (g). Note that in (f) and (g), we have shown the output over one period only, but these results are periodic. It is clearly seen that the resulting function is not what we had hoped to obtain.

The significant difference in the convolution process here as compared with Fig. 10-4 is that a portion of a different cycle of $h_a(n-k)$ moves into the summation interval as $h_a(n-k)$ is shifted to the right. This phenomena is called *wrap-around error*, and this leads to the incorrect results.

A different way of explaining this process is related to the fact that the convolution of two non-periodic signals yields a function whose width is approximately the sum of the widths of the two functions being convolved. If both signals are assumed to be periodic, with a period equal to the record length, there is no room to spread in this sense, so that the resulting convolution will not be able to have the required width.

While there are different ways of resolving this type of difficulty, we will concentrate on some simpler schemes. Assume that both $x(n)$ and $h(n)$ are of equal length and have N points each. The period of each function may be artifically doubled by adding N zeros at the end. Let $\hat{x}(n)$ and $\hat{h}(n)$ represent the two new functions defined by

$$\begin{aligned} \hat{x}(n) &= x(n) \quad 0 \leqslant n \leqslant N-1 \\ &= 0 \qquad N \leqslant n \leqslant 2N-1 \end{aligned} \tag{10-15}$$

$$\hat{h}(n) = h(n) \quad 0 \leqslant n \leqslant N-1$$
$$= 0 \quad N \leqslant n \leqslant 2N-1 \tag{10-16}$$

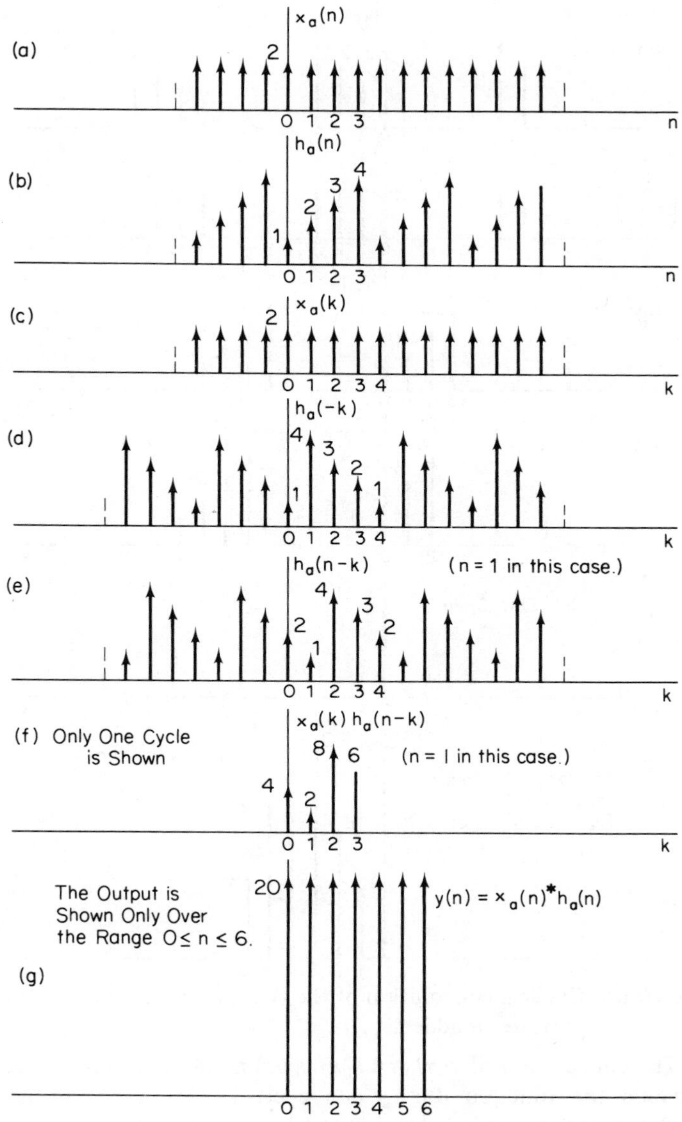

Figure 10-5 Cyclical convolution of the two signals of Figure 10-4.

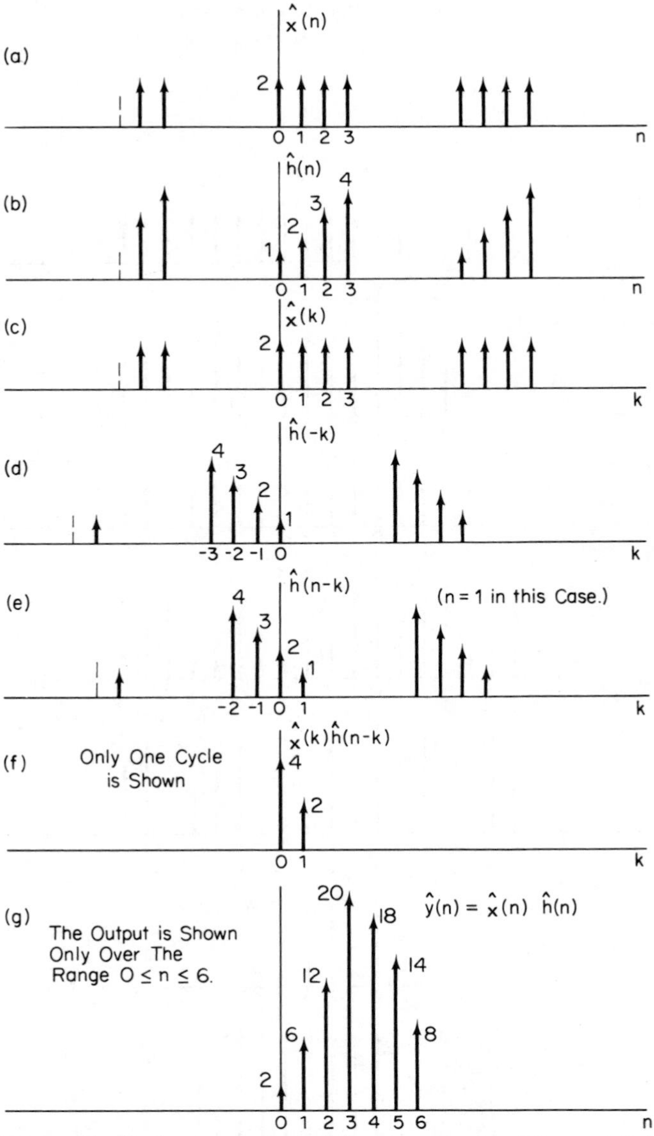

Figure 10-6 Cyclical convolution of the two signals of Figure 10-4 with extra zeros added.

The convolution of $\hat{x}(n)$ and $\hat{h}(n)$ is a function $\hat{y}(n)$ having a period 2N, but in which the function during one cycle is equivalent to the original non-periodic convolution of $x(n)$ and $h(n)$. This process is illustrated in Fig. 10-6 for the functions considered earlier. Only one period of the quantities shown in (f) and (g) is shown. The result in (g) during this period is clearly seen to agree with the result of Fig. 10-4. Thus, if the DFT process were applied to the functions $\hat{x}(n)$ and $\hat{h}(n)$, the desired convolution would be obtained.

It should be recognized that in eliminating the wrap-around error, we have been forced to double the required capacity of the DFT or FFT algorithm. The quantity N should be replaced by 2N in the various DFT expressions. Placing N zero values at the end of each function provides an effective total period of 2N, which is sufficient for the convolution of two functions with N points each.

The discrete convolution of two non-periodic functions with N points each yields a new function with 2N-1 points. When N zeros are added to the original functions, the resulting cyclical convolution has a period of 2N, which is one more point than is required for the original non-periodic convolution. The one additional point in each cycle has a value of zero.

If the two functions are reasonably close, but not equal, in length, additional zeros may be first added to the shorter signal so that the resulting signals are equal in length before adding additional zeros. This means that more than N zeros would be added to the shorter signal overall.

To summarize the highlights discussed so far, the process of high-speed convolution can be achieved as follows:

(a) Modify $x(n)$ and $h(n)$ by adding zeros so that wrap-around error will not appear. The modified functions are $\hat{x}(n)$ and $\hat{h}(n)$.

(b) Compute $\hat{X}(m)$ and $\hat{H}(m)$, the DFT's of the two modified functions, using an FFT algorithm or processor.

(c) Determine $\hat{Y}(m) = \hat{X}(m)\hat{H}(m)$ by multiplying the values of $\hat{X}(m)$ and $\hat{H}(m)$ together at all frequency integers.

(d) Compute $\hat{y}(n) = D^{-1}\ [\hat{Y}(m)]$ using an FFT algorithm or processor. One cycle of this function is the desired convolution.

(e) Multiply the result by any additional constants required, such as the factor T in (10-11) when the convolution represents an approximation to a continuous-time process.

The method just described becomes rather inefficient when the two functions to be convolved differ appreciably in length. This method also breaks down when one or both of the functions are so long that they exceed the capacity of the FFT processor available. A method referred to as "select-saving" can be employed for such cases.

Consider the functions $h(n)$ and $g(n)$ shown in Fig. 10-7. For the sake of clarity, these quantities are shown as continuous curves, but they are assumed to be discrete-time functions. The function $h(n)$ is assumed to be of relatively short length with N points. The function $x(n)$ is assumed to be very long and could, in fact, represent a random signal of indefinite length.

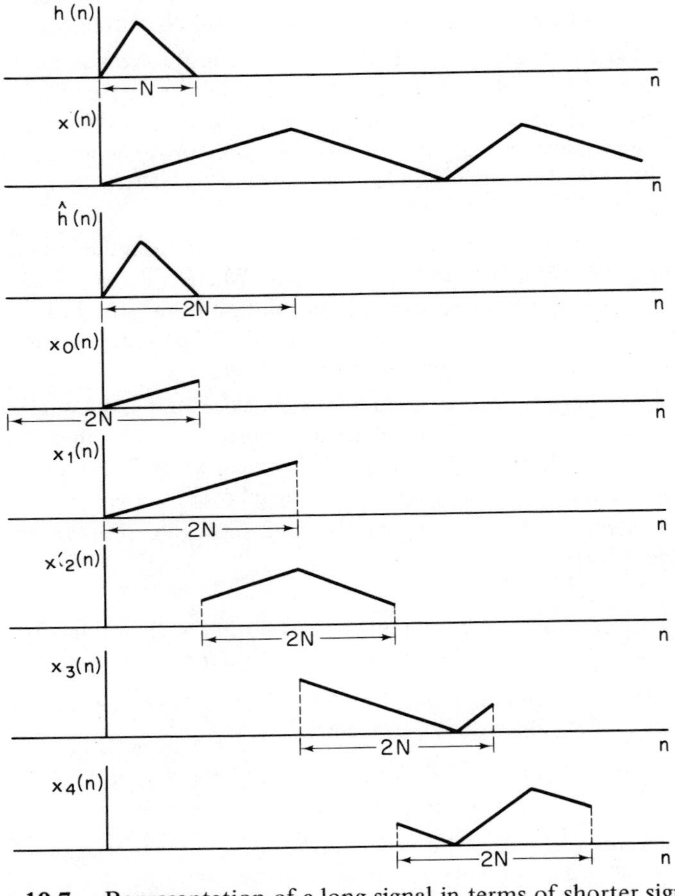

Figure 10-7 Representation of a long signal in terms of shorter signals in order to use the "select-saving" method.

The period of the function $h(n)$ is increased to 2N by adding N zeros according to the scheme previously discussed. Letting $\hat{h}(n)$ represent this function, we have

$$\begin{aligned} \hat{h}(n) &= h(n) \quad 0 \leqslant n \leqslant N-1 \\ &= 0 \quad\quad N \leqslant n \leqslant 2N-1 \end{aligned} \tag{10-17}$$

Assume that $x(n) = 0$ for $n < 0$. This function is then sectioned into an arbitrary number of 2N point signals $x_i(n)$ in which the first N points are used to establish the proper "history" of the signal required in the convolution process, and the last N points actually determine the required output. The sections are defined by the relationships

$$x_0(n) = x(n-N) \quad \text{for} \quad 0 \leqslant n \leqslant 2N-1 \qquad = 0 \quad \text{otherwise} \tag{10-18}$$

$$x_1(n) = x(n) \quad \text{for} \quad 0 \leqslant n \leqslant 2N-1 \qquad = 0 \quad \text{otherwise} \tag{10-19}$$

•
•
•

$$x_i(n) = x(n+iN-N) \quad \text{for} \quad 0 \leqslant n \leqslant 2N-1 \qquad = 0 \quad \text{otherwise} \tag{10-20}$$

This process is illustrated in Fig. 10-7. The point $n = 0$ is assumed to be redefined at the beginning of each segment of $x_i(m)$.

The convolution of $h(n)$ with all of the sections $x_i(n)$ yields a set of 2N point periodic signals. The verification of some of the properties will be left as an exercise (Prob. 10-3), but the results will be stated here. The major properties of each of the signals are as follows: (a) The first N points in the convolution corresponding to $0 \leqslant n \leqslant N-1$ represent either incorrect data due to inadequate history or, in the case of the point $n = N-1$, a correct value which has already been computed in the preceding convolution. Thus, this data can be discarded. (b) The next N terms corresponding to $N \leqslant n \leqslant 2N-1$ are the correct values of the convolution corresponding to the second half of $x_i(n)$. Letting $y_i(n)$ represent the set of convolved functions, the desired function $y(n)$ can be expressed as

$$y(n) = y_0(n+N) \quad \text{for} \quad 0 \leqslant n \leqslant N-1 \tag{10-21}$$

$$y(n+N) = y_1(n+N) \quad \text{for} \quad 0 \leqslant n \leqslant N-1 \tag{10-22}$$

•
•
•

$$y(n+iN) = y_i(n+N) \quad \text{for} \quad 0 \leqslant n \leqslant N-1 \tag{10-23}$$

Note again that the beginning of each segment $y_i(n)$ is defined as $n = 0$ as far as the convolution is concerned.

Let us now turn our attention briefly to the possibility of using the DFT for digital filtering by operating directly on the spectrum. At first glance, it would seem that an ideal block filter characteristic could be readily applied to the spectrum, which would result in an infinitely sharp amplitude response. The difficulty arising with this concept is that the resulting impulse response in the time domain would have a sin x/x type of response with infinitely long tails in both directions. Since the frequency function can be sampled only at a finite number of points, the time response would exhibit an aliasing effect analogous to frequency-domain aliasing when a time function is sampled at too low a rate. The solution to this problem is to choose a filter function whose impulse response can be truncated to a finite range without introducing intolerable errors in the frequency response. (See refs. 6 and 7.)

10-4 Power Spectrum

We have seen that when a time series $x(n)$ is transformed by an FFT algorithm, a complex transform $X(m)$ is obtained. For reasons that will be clear shortly, we will refer to $X(m)$ as a *linear* spectrum. Since the linear spectrum is complex, it has both real and imaginary parts. These individual parts are each dependent on the position of the signal, but the resulting magnitude is, of course, independent of the position.

While the linear spectrum is sufficient for many purposes, there are applications in which the square of the magnitude is of primary importance. Since the square of the magnitude is proportional to power, the term *power spectrum* is widely used in reference to this function. Let $S_{xx}(m)$ represent the power spectrum. (The signficance of the double subscripts will be seen in the next section. At that point, the adjective "auto" will also be used in the definition.) The power spectrum can be expressed as

$$S_{xx}(m) = \frac{|X(m)|^2}{N} = \frac{X(m)\widetilde{X}(m)}{N} = \frac{X_r^2 + X_i^2}{N} \tag{10-24}$$

From the last term on the right of (10-24), it can be seen that the power spectrum is readily calculated from $X(m)$ by squaring the real and imaginary parts and adding the results. Many FFT processors have a direct provision for determining some form of the power spectrum.

The function $S_{xx}(m)$ may or may not actually represent true power in watts as this would depend on what physical variables are involved and in what manner the signal is used. However, it is conceptually useful to think of this quantity as representing the power in a general sense.

Additional insight into this concept can be gained by a modified form of Parseval's theorem as applied to discrete-time signals. This theroem, which will be derived at the end of the next section in Ex. 10-3, reads

$$\sum_{n=0}^{N-1} x^2(n) = \sum_{m=0}^{N-1} S_{xx}(m) \tag{10-25}$$

The expression on the left of (10-25) is proportional to the energy represented by the signal in one time-domain cycle. According to this theorem, the same result may be obtained directly from the spectrum by summing the terms of the power spectrum over a frequency-domain cycle.

Example 10-2

(a) Determine a closed form expression for the DFT of $x(n) = 1$, for $0 \leq n \leq N-1$. (b) Verify Parseval's theorem for this function.

Solution

(a) The DFT of $x(n)$ is given by

$$X(m) = \sum_{n=0}^{N-1} (1) W_N^{mn} \tag{10-26}$$

The series of (10-26) constitutes a finite geometric series and can be expressed as

$$X(m) = \frac{1 - W_N^{Nm}}{1 - W_N^m} = \frac{1 - \epsilon^{-j2\pi m}}{1 - \epsilon^{-j(2\pi m/N)}} \tag{10-27}$$

The expression of (10-27) is zero for all integer values in the range of $0 \leq m \leq N-1$ except for $m = 0$, where the expression initially has an indeterminate form. Application of L'Hospital's Rule for $m = 0$ results in

$$X(0) = \lim_{m \to 0} \frac{Nj2\pi\epsilon^{-j2\pi m}}{j2\pi\epsilon^{-j(2\pi m/N)}} = N \tag{10-28}$$

(b) The "energy" contained in the time signal is readily determined as

$$\sum_{n=0}^{N-1} x^2(n) = \sum_{n=0}^{N-1} (1) = N \tag{10-29}$$

Since there is only one term in the power spectrum, we have

$$\sum_{m=0}^{N-1} S_{xx}(m) = \frac{|X(0)|^2}{N} = \frac{N^2}{N} = N \tag{10-30}$$

Comparison of (10-29) and (10-30) verifies the theorem for this case.

10-5 Correlation and Statistical Analysis

The concept of lagged products was introduced in Chapt. 9 in conjunction with transform pair DO-5. There are two primary operations in which this form is used: (a) *crosscorrelation* and (b) *autocorrelation*. These functional operations are used extensively in signal and statistical analysis, both in continuous-time systems and in discrete-time systems. Many of the correlation applications previously performed with analog circuits for continous-time signals can now be achieved with either a general purpose computer or with a special purpose digital processor using discrete-time techniques.

Treatment of the statistical theory serving as a basis for correlation theory is covered extensively elsewhere (e.g. refs. 2, 14, 15). We will concentrate here on applying these concepts to possible applications using the FFT and related numerical techniques.

For the sake of simplicity, the basic correlation relationships will first be discussed in terms of their continuous-time forms. Let $x(t)$ and $y(t)$ represent two random continuous-time signals. The *crosscorrelation* function $R_{xy}(\tau)$ of the two signals over an interval t_p can be defined as

$$R_{xy}(\tau) = \overline{x(t)y(t-\tau)} = \lim_{t_p \to \infty} \frac{1}{t_p} \int_0^{t_p} x(t)y(t-\tau)dt \tag{10-31}$$

The quantity τ represents a *delay* or *lag* variable. The integral represents the area of the product of the two signals expressed as a function of the amount by which one signal is delayed. The line above the product $\overline{x(t)y(t-\tau)}$ is used to denote a time average of the quantity involved.

The relative value of $R_{xy}(\tau)$ indicates how well the two signals are correlated for that particular value of delay. If the correlation function peaks for a particular value of τ, this would indicate a very good correlation, which means that the two signals match each other very well. Conversely, a very small or zero value of the correlation function indicates little or no correlation.

The *autocorrelation* function $R_{xx}(\tau)$ can be considered as a special case of the crosscorrelation function with $y(t) = x(t)$. The definition for continuous-time random signals reads

$$R_{xx}(\tau) = \overline{x(t)x(t-\tau)} = \lim_{t_p \to \infty} \frac{1}{t_p} \int_0^{t_p} x(t)x(t-\tau)dt \tag{10-32}$$

This operation is simply the average of the product of the signal and a delayed version of the signal as a function of the delay.

The Fourier transforms of the cross and autocorrelation functions often provide useful interpretations of the nature of the signals. It can be shown that the Fourier transform of the autocorrelation function is the square of the magnitude of the Fourier transform $X(f)$ of the signal $x(t)$. This function is called the *auto power spectrum*, and it will be denoted by $S_{xx}(f)$. Hence,

$$S_{xx}(f) = F\,[R_{xx}(\tau)] = X(f)\widetilde{X}(f) = |X(f)|^2 \tag{10-33}$$

In a similar fashion, the Fourier transform of the crosscorrelation function can be calculated. This function is called the *cross power spectrum*, and it will be denoted by $S_{xy}(f)$. It can be shown that the cross power spectrum can be expressed as

$$S_{xy}(f) = F\,[R_{xy}(\tau)] = X(f)\widetilde{Y}(f) \tag{10-34}$$

Note that while $S_{xx}(f)$ is a real function, $S_{xy}(f)$ is, in general, complex.

One of the primary applications of crosscorrelation is in determining the delay of a signal which has been hidden in additive noise. For example, this operation arises in radar and sonar systems where a known signal is transmitted and reflected from a target at some later time. Measurement of the exact delay will provide information regarding the range of the target. Let $x(t)$ represent the transmitted signal and let $u(t)$ represent the additive noise. Although the transmitted signal will undergo some distortion, we will neglect this effect in this discussion. The received signal $y(t)$ will then be of the form

$$y(t) = x(t-T_d) + u(t) \tag{10-35}$$

where T_d represents the total two-way delay of the signal.

A crosscorrelation can now be made at the receiver between a stored version of the transmitted signal $x(t)$ and the received signal $y(t)$. This operation yields

$$R_{xy}(\tau) = \overline{x(t)y(t)} = \overline{x(t)x(t-T_d)} + \overline{x(t)u(t)} \tag{10-36}$$

The second term in (10-36) represents the correlation between the transmitted signal and the noise. In general, there is no correlation between these quantities, so the expected value of this function is zero. The first term in (10-36) is actually an autocorrelation if any distortion of the received signal is neglected. The function $R_{xy}(\tau)$ can be expected to show a peak for $\tau = T_d$, which would provide an accurate measure of the delay time. Using these methods, it is possible to measure the delay of a signal which has been virtually buried in noise.

The reader is invited to verify (Prob. 10-5) that the autocorrelation function of a periodic time signal is a periodic function of τ, and the resulting period is the same as that of the original time signal. This concept leads to a very useful application of autocorrelation. Consider the situation where an unknown periodic signal is buried in noise, but in which a measurement of the period is desired. If the signal is correlated with itself, the resulting autocorrelation function will display the desired period.

Certain statistical parameters can be related to the autocorrelation function. Let $p(x)$ represent the *probability density function* of the variable x. The function $p(x)$ is characterized by a number of useful statistical parameters, of which some of the most important are (a) the mean value $\overline{x}$, (b) the mean-squared value $\overline{x^2}$, and (c) the variance σ^2.

The mean (or dc) value is defined as

$$\overline{x} = \int_{-\infty}^{\infty} x p(x) dx \tag{10-37}$$

The mean-squared value is defined as

$$\overline{x^2} = \int_{-\infty}^{\infty} x^2 p(x) dx \tag{10-38}$$

Finally, the variance is defined as

$$\sigma^2 = \int_{-\infty}^{\infty} (x - \bar{x})^2 p(x) dx \tag{10-39}$$

It can be readily shown from (10-39) that σ^2 can be expressed as

$$\sigma^2 = \overline{x^2} - \bar{x}^2 \tag{10-40}$$

Assume that the process under consideration is an *ergodic* random process. This means that the *ensemble* averages given in the preceding few equations are equivalent to appropriate *time* averages taken from the same process.

The mean-square value is determined from

$$\overline{x^2} = \lim_{t_p \to \infty} \frac{1}{t_p} \int_0^{t_p} x^2(t) dt = R_{xx}(0) \tag{10-41}$$

If the process contains a dc value, it would appear as a long-term constant in $R_{xx}(\tau)$. Assuming the absence of any periodic components, the square of the mean can be expressed as

$$\bar{x}^2 = \lim_{t_p \to \infty} \frac{1}{t_p} \int_0^{t_p} x(t) x(t - \tau) dt = R_{xx}(\infty) \tag{10-42}$$

Finally, the variance is readily expressed as

$$\sigma^2 = R_{xx}(0) - R_{xx}(\infty) \tag{10-43}$$

It is seen then that for an ergodic process, some of the most important statistical properties may be determined from the autocorrelation function.

Having considered some of the basic definitions and properties of correlation and the associated statistical concepts, we will now investigate the possible digital implementation of these operations. In order to keep the notation as simple as possible, we will continue to use the same basic symbols established in this section for continuous-time functions, but with the arguments replaced by integers for the discrete-time case.

Consider that we are given two discrete-time signals $x(n)$ and $y(n)$. The discrete *crosscorrelation function* will be denoted by $R_{xy}(k)$, and a suitable definition is

$$R_{xy}(k) = \overline{x(n)y(n-k)} = \frac{1}{N} \sum_{n=0}^{N-1} x(n)y(n-k) \tag{10-44}$$

The *discrete autocorrelation function* will be denoted by $R_{xx}(k)$, and it can be expressed as

$$R_{xx}(k) = \overline{x(n)x(n-k)} = \frac{1}{N}\sum_{n=0}^{N-1} x(n)x(n-k) \tag{10-45}$$

Using the DFT operation pair associated with lagged products, (DO-5), the DFT of (10-45) is readily determined as

$$D[R_{xx}(k)] = \frac{X(m)\tilde{X}(m)}{N} = \frac{|X(m)|^2}{N} = S_{xx}(m) \tag{10-46}$$

where $S_{xx}(m)$ is the *discrete auto power spectrum* of the signal as defined earlier in (10-24). The inverse DFT of the power spectrum is the autocorrelation function as expressed by

$$D^{-1}[S_{xx}(m)] = R_{xx}(k) \tag{10-47}$$

The *discrete cross power spectrum* $S_{xy}(m)$ can be readily expressed as

$$D[R_{xy}(k)] = \frac{X(m)\tilde{Y}(m)}{N} = S_{xy}(m) \tag{10-48}$$

The inverse DFT of the cross power spectrum is the crosscorrelation function

$$D^{-1}[S_{xy}(m)] = R_{xy}(k) \tag{10-49}$$

The various relationships associated with the discrete cross-correlation function are illustrated in Fig. 10-8. The crosscorrelation function of two signals $x(n)$ and $y(n)$ may be calculated directly as shown on the left. However, an alternate procedure is to use an FFT algorithm to compute the spectra of the two signals and then multiply one spectrum by the conjugate of the other. The result of this operation is the cross spectrum which can then be inversely transformed with the FFT to yield the crosscorrelation function. All of the operations apply to the autocorrelation function when the two signals are the same. Other computational combinations are possible depending on what functions are known in a given case.

When either of the correlation functions are computed by these DFT procedures, it is necessary to apply the same types of precautions discussed in Sec. 10-3 for convolution computation. In fact, inspection of operation pairs DO-4 and DO-5 reveals that the major difference between the two operations is that one of the functions is reversed in direction for one operation as compared with the other. Thus, the techniques discussed in Sec. 10-3 are generally applicable to correlation, as long as the basic differences are understood. More advanced developments of various procedures for both convolution and correlation are given in the literature (e.g. refs. 1, 5, 6, 7, 16).

Use of the FFT and discrete-time techniques necessitates that the interval of analysis be restricted to a finite length having a finite number of sample points. When the composite signal is composed of a desired signal plus additive random noise, the effect of the noise is to reduce the certainty in both the time and spectrum measurements. The spectrum computation can be improved considerably by taking a number of different spectra and then performing an average of the corresponding frequency components on a point by point basis.

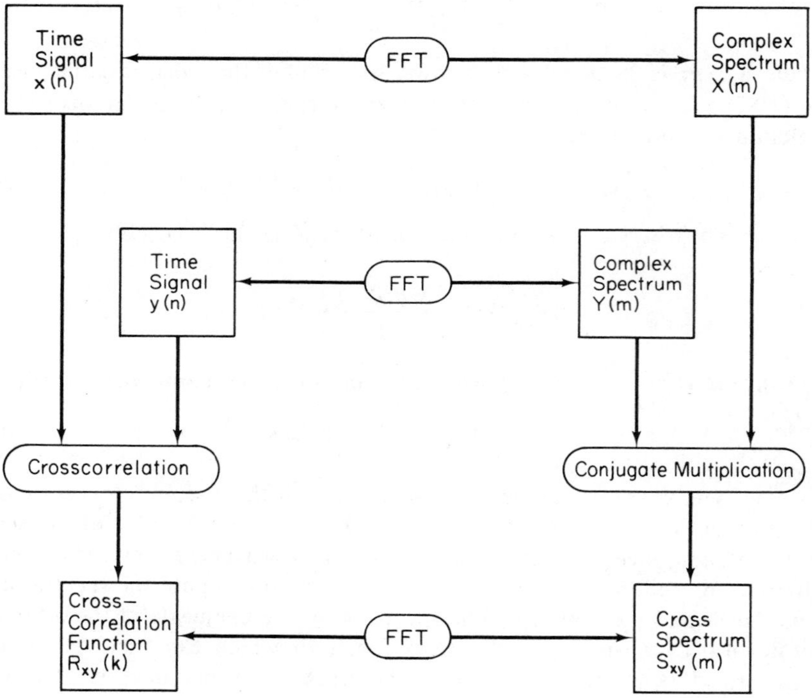

Figure 10-8 Various cross correlation relationships.

The basis for this concept is the fact that the components of the signal are correlated from one spectrum to the next, whereas the noise components are uncorrelated. The variance of the measurement is inversely proportional to the number of spectra averaged together, so that a considerable improvement in accuracy can be obtained by this process.

Example 10-3

Derive Parseval's theorem for discrete-time signals as given by equation (10-25).

Solution

The sum of $x^2(n)$ can be expressed as the discrete autocorrelation function evaluated at $k = 0$ from (10-45). Hence,

$$\frac{1}{N}\sum_{n=0}^{N-1} x^2(n) = R_{xx}(0) \tag{10-50}$$

In general, $R_{xx}(k)$ can be expressed as

$$R_{xx}(k) = \frac{1}{N}\sum_{m=0}^{N-1} S_{xx}(m)W^{-km} \tag{10-51}$$

The value of $R_{xx}(0)$ is readily expressed as

$$R_{xx}(0) = \frac{1}{N}\sum_{m=0}^{N-1} S_{xx}(m) \tag{10-52}$$

Comparing (10-50) and (10-52), the desired result is readily obtained.

10-6 Frequency Sampling Filters

In this section we will show how the DFT may be used to assist in the design of FIR filters. In particular, we will discuss a special class of FIR functions called *frequency sampling filters* due to the manner in which they are designed.

It will be recalled from Chapt. 8 that one of the major steps required in the design of FIR filters is the determination of the coefficients of the time domain impulse response. These coefficients are determined by evaluating the Fourier series associated with the periodic frequency response. These coefficients are normally determined by an integration process.

Instead of actually performing the integration, consider the possibility of using the DFT (actually the *inverse* DFT or IDFT) for this purpose. In order to utilize the IDFT in this manner, the frequency response can be specified at N equally spaced frequencies in the range $0 \leq f < f_s$ or, equivalently, in the integer range $0 \leq m \leq N-1$. Let $H(m)$ represent the complex form of the desired frequency response function, and let $A(m)$ and $\beta(m)$ represent the amplitude and phase functions respectively. The frequency response can then be expressed as

$$H(m) = A(m)\epsilon^{j\beta(m)} \quad 0 \leq m \leq N-1 \tag{10-53}$$

The guidelines for selecting the values of $A(m)$ and $\beta(m)$ are somewhat involved, and they will not be given here. The interested reader may refer to some pertinent journal articles (refs. 10, 11, 12). We will concentrate on some interesting aspects of the realization and implementation properties. Thus, for our purposes we will assume that $H(m)$ as expressed by (10-53) is given.

The desired transfer function $H(z)$ can be expressed as

$$H(z) = \sum_{n=0}^{N-1} a_n z^{-n} \tag{10-54}$$

The coefficients a_n are determined from the IDFT as

$$a_n = \frac{1}{N} \sum_{m=0}^{N-1} H(m) W^{-nm} \tag{10-55}$$

Substitution of (10-55) in (10-54) yields

$$H(z) = \sum_{n=0}^{N-1} \left[\frac{1}{N} \sum_{m=0}^{N-1} H(m) W^{-nm} \right] z^{-n} \tag{10-56}$$

If the order of summation is reversed in (10-56), the function $H(z)$ can be expressed as

$$H(z) = \frac{1}{N} \sum_{m=0}^{N-1} H(m) \sum_{n=0}^{N-1} W^{-nm} z^{-n} \tag{10-57}$$

The summation on the right-hand side of (10-57) can be expressed in closed-form as

$$\sum_{n=0}^{N-1} W^{-nm} z^{-n} = \frac{1 - W^{-Nm} z^{-N}}{1 - W^{-m} z^{-1}} = \frac{1 - z^{-N}}{1 - W^{-m} z^{-1}} \tag{10-58}$$

Substitution of (10-58) in (10-57) yields

$$H(z) = \frac{1 - z^{-N}}{N} \sum_{m=0}^{N-1} \frac{H(m)}{1 - z^{-1} W^{-m}} \tag{10-59}$$

$$= \frac{1 - z^{-N}}{N} \sum_{m=0}^{N-1} \frac{H(m)}{1 - z^{-1} \epsilon^{j(2\pi m/N)}} \tag{10-60}$$

Each term in the series of (10-60) contains one of the poles of $H(z)$. The various poles p_m are located at

$$p_m = \epsilon^{j(2\pi m/N)} \tag{10-61}$$

It is convenient at this point to use the normalized frequency $\nu = f/f_0$, which has been used extensively in earlier parts of the book. Let

$$\nu_m = \frac{mF}{f_0} = \frac{2m}{N} \tag{10-62}$$

The values ν_m represent a set of normalized frequencies occurring at integer multiples of the fundamental frequency F. The poles can be expressed as

$$p_m = \epsilon^{j\pi\nu_m} \tag{10-63}$$

We will now represent $H(z)$ as the product of two functions of the form

$$H(z) = H_1(z)H_2(z) \tag{10-64}$$

where

$$H_1(z) = \frac{1 - z^{-N}}{N} \tag{10-65}$$

and

$$H_2(z) = \sum_{m=0}^{N-1} \frac{H(m)}{1 - z^{-1}\epsilon^{j\pi\nu_m}} \tag{10-66}$$

Observe that the notation of (10-62) has been used in (10-66).

The poles of $H(z)$ corresponding to (10-62) are now associated with $H_2(z)$. It can be readily shown that the zeros of $H_1(z)$ are located at the same position as the poles of $H_2(z)$. The reader is invited to show (Prob. 10-6) that the amplitude response $A_1(\nu)$ corresponding to $H_1(z)$ is given by

$$A_1(\nu) = \frac{2}{N} \sin \frac{\pi}{2} N\nu \tag{10-67}$$

This function is called a *comb filter*. There are N zeros of $A_1(\nu)$ in the range $0 \leqslant \nu < 2$. The form of $|A_1(\nu)|$ for a particular value of N (N = 16 in this case) is shown for the range $0 \leqslant \nu \leqslant 1$ in Fig. 10-9.

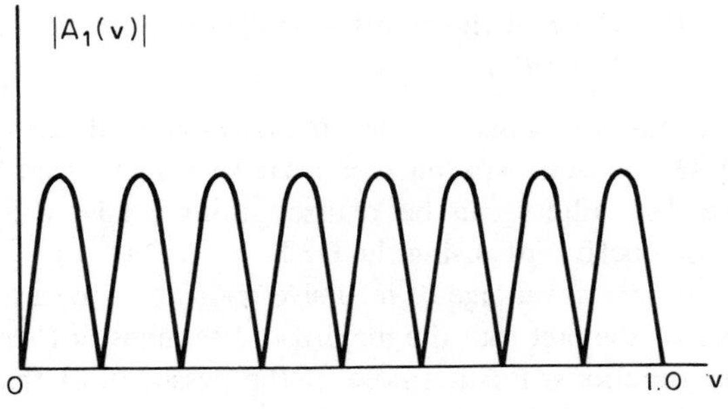

Figure 10-9 Form of the amplitude response of a comb filter (N=16).

Each term in $H_2(z)$ can be considered as a complex resonator in whicn the amplitude response would be infinite at a particular frequency ν_m. However, when $H_1(z)$ and $H_2(z)$ are connected in cascade, the various zeros of $H_1(z)$ can be shown to cancel the effects of the poles at the frequency values ν_m. In fact, it canbe shown (Prob. 10-7) that the overall amplitude response at $\nu = \nu_m$ is $H(m)$ as originally specified.

This concept suggests a possible recursive realization in which a comb filter is connected in cascade with a bank of resonators as shown in Fig. 10-10. In practice, the various terms in $H_2(z)$ can be combined in pairs having complex conjugate poles plus single terms involving the real poles. Thus, a given resonator would either be a second-order or a first-order function with real coefficients. For the combination of any particular resonator with the comb filter, the frequency response will be zero at all discrete values of frequency satisfying (10-62), except the one or two corresponding to the pole (or poles) of the given resonator, at which the response will be as specified. The combination of all of the various resonators then produces the required overall response at the set of sampling frequencies specified. Hence, the term *frequency sampling filter* is quite appropriate.

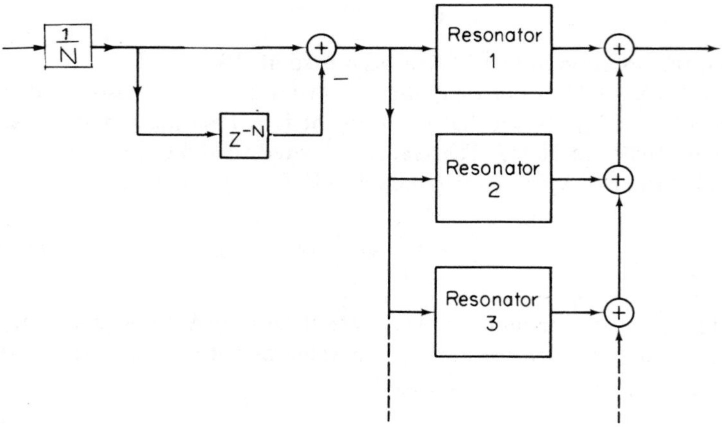

Figure 10-10 Form of the recursive realization of a frequency sampling FIR filter.

It was stated in Chapt. 8 that recursive realizations of FIR filters were possible, and the present approach is seen to achieve that result. Of course, frequency sampling filters can be realized nonrecursively by solving for the impulse response coefficients using the DFT.

The primary advantage of recursive realization for a frequency sampling filter is related to the fact that the majority of samples of $H(m)$ are either 1 or 0 for most filter functions. Furthermore, if the passband of the filter is relatively narrow, the majority of the values are zero, corresponding to the stopband. This means that only a relatively few non-zero values of $H(m)$, corresponding to the passband and transition band, are present. Consequently, only a limited number of resonators are required, so that a very efficient design may be achieved.

In theory, the zeros of the comb filter cancel the poles of the resonators. In practice, there may be slight differences which could result in instability problems. This problem can be avoided by moving the zeros and poles very slightly inside the unit circle without degrading the nature of the response.

Filters designed using the frequency sampling method will always achieve the response specified at the frequency values ν_m. If the designer simply specifies the value one in the passband and zero in the stopband without providing any transition band, the response may display significant ripple between frequency sample points. This difficulty can be minimized by providing a sufficiently wide transition band. Unfortunately, it is not intuitively clear as to how much of a transition band should be used in a given case. This uncertainty has led to computer-aided methods for design using optimization criteria. (See refs. 3, 10, 11.) Many future designs for finite impulse response filters will probably be obtained from these computer-aided optimization techniques.

PROBLEMS

10-1 An FFT processor is to be used to estimate the spectrum of a real signal. Assume that the number of points must be an integer multiple of two, and assume that no special data modifications are used. The specifications are: (1) resolution between frequencies $\leqslant$ 0.5 Hz, (2) highest frequency in signal $\leqslant$ 250 Hz. Determine the following parameters: (a) minimum record length, (b) maximum time between samples, and (c) minimum number of points in a record.

10-2 A certain FFT processor has a maximum capacity of 2048 points, and the maximum time required to load and compute a complete spectrum is 200 ms. The unit is to be operated in real-time, and sufficient auxiliary storage is used to permit one record to be stored while the previous one is transformed. Determine (a) the highest frequency that can be resolved and (b) the frequency resolution. Assume that no special data modifications are used.

10-3 Using Fig. 10-7 and the definitions of the various segments indicated by equations (10-18), (10-19), and (10-20), verify the properties of the "select-saving" method leading to equations (10-21), (10-22), and (10-23).

10-4 Consider the signal defined over eight points as

$$x(n) = 1 \quad 0 \leqslant n \leqslant 3$$
$$= 0 \quad 4 \leqslant n \leqslant 7$$

(a) Determine a closed-form expression for the DFT of $x(n)$, i.e., $X(m)$.
(b) Verify Parseval's theorem for this function.

10-5 Prove that the autocorrelation function of a periodic time signal is a periodic function of τ.

10-6 Show that the amplitude response of the comb filter of equation (10-65) is of the form of equation (10-67).

10-7 Show that the amplitude response of $H(z)$ for the frequency sampling filter at $\nu = \nu_m$ is $H(m)$.

REFERENCES

1. G. D. Bergland, "A guided tour of the fast Fourier transform", *IEEE Spectrum*, vol. 6, pp. 41-52, July 1969.
2. A Bruce Carlson, *Communications Systems.* New York: McGraw-Hill, 1968.
3. B. Gold and K. L. Jordan, "A direct search procedure for designing finite duration impulse response filters", *IEEE Trans. Audio and Electroacoustics*, vol. AU-17, pp. 33-36, March 1969.
4. B. Gold and C. M. Rader, *Digital Processing of Signals.* New York: McGraw-Hill, 1969.
5. C. L. Heizman, "Signal analysis with digital time-series analyzers", *General Radio Experimenter*, pp. 3-7, July/Sept. 1970.
6. H. D. Helms, "Fast Fourier transform method of computing difference equations and simulating filters", *IEEE Trans. Audio and Electroacoustics*, vol. AU-15, pp. 85-90, June 1967.
7. H. D. Helms, "Nonrecursive digital filters: design methods for achieving specifications on frequency response", *IEEE Trans. Audio and Electroacoustics*, vol. AU-16, pp. 336-343, Sept. 1968.
8. H. D. Helms and L. R. Rabiner, Eds., *Literature in Digital Signal Processing*. New York: IEEE Press, 1973.
9. Hewlett-Packard, Inc., *Fourier Analyzer Training Manual*, Application Note 140-0.
10. L. R. Rabiner, B. Gold, and C. A. McGonegal, "An approach to the approximation problem for nonrecursive digital filters", *IEEE Trans. Audio and Electroacoustics*, vol. AU-18, pp. 83-106, June 1970.
11. L. R. Rabiner, "Techniques for designing finite-duration impulse-response digital filters", *IEEE Trans. Comm. Tech.*, vol. COM-19, pp. 188-195, April 1971.
12. L. R. Rabiner and R. W. Schafer, "Recursive and nonrecursive realizations of digital filters designed by frequency sampling techniques", *IEEE Trans. Audio and Electroacoustics*, vol. AU-19, pp. 200-207, Sept. 1971.
13. L. R. Rabiner and C. M. Rader, Eds. *Digital Signal Processing.* New York: IEEE Press, 1972.

14. P. R. Roth, "Digital Fourier Analysis", *Hewlett-Packard Journal*, vol. 21, pp. 2-9, June 1970.

15. Mischa Schwartz, *Information Transmission, Modulation, and Noise*, 2nd Ed. New York: McGraw-Hill, 1970.

16. T. G. Stockham, "High-speed convolution and correlation". *1966 Spring Joint Computer Conf.*, AFIPS Proc., vol. 28. Washington, D.C.: Spartan Books, pp. 229-233.

APPENDIX

The window functions given here are all assumed to be even functions of t with a width τ. However, only half of the function, corresponding to the range $0 \leq t/\tau \leq 0.5$ is shown in each case.

Let $w(t)$ represent the continuous-time form of any window function as given in the equations or as shown on the curves. The discrete-time window function is determined by replacing t by nT and evaluating the function for integer values of n.

Let $W(f)$ represent the Fourier transform of $w(t)$, and let W(0) represent the dc value of the transform. The amplitude response for each window function is presented in decibel form as defined by

$$W_{db}(f) = 20 \operatorname{Log}_{10} \frac{|W(f)|}{W(0)} \tag{A-1}$$

The amplitude response curves are presented as a function of f/F, where F is defined as

$$F = \frac{1}{\tau} \tag{A-2}$$

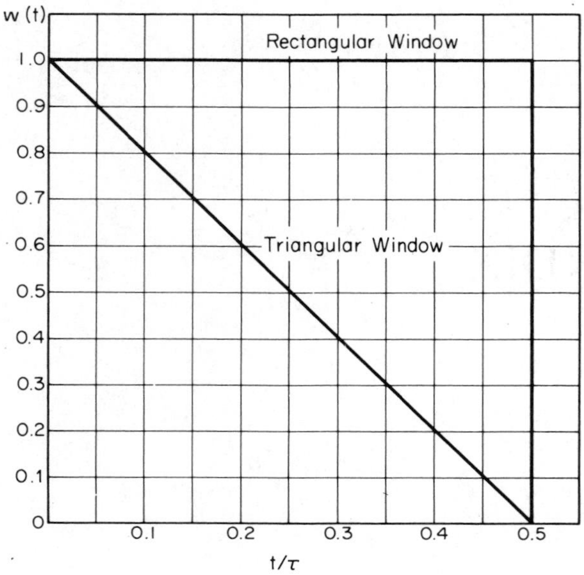

Figure A-1 Rectangular and triangular window functions.

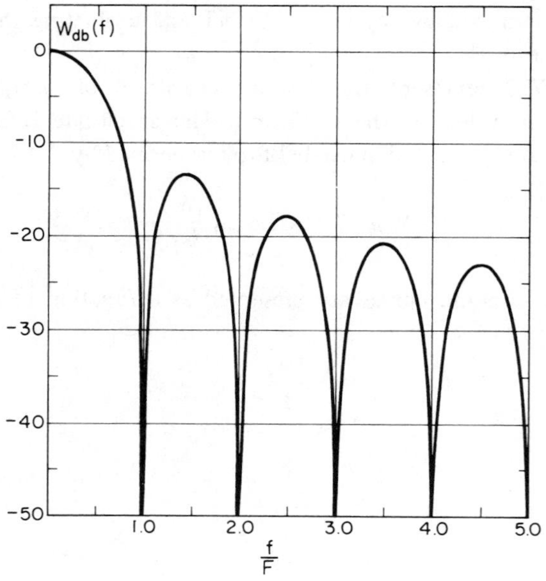

Figure A-2 Decibel amplitude response of rectangular window function.

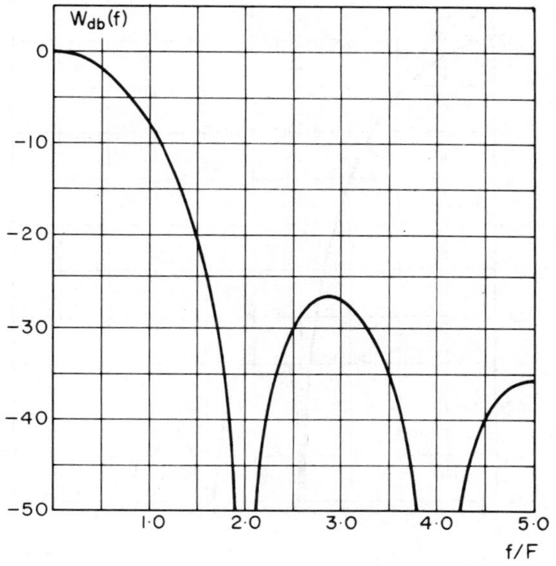

Figure A-3 Decibel amplitude response of triangular window function.

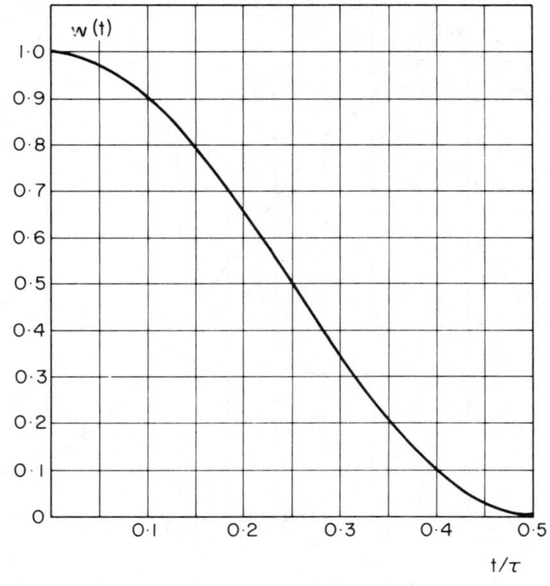

Figure A-4 Hanning window function.

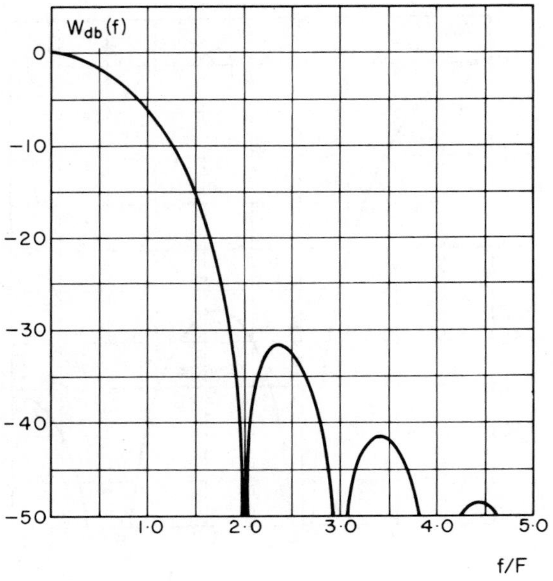

Figure A-5 Decibel amplitude response of Hanning window function.

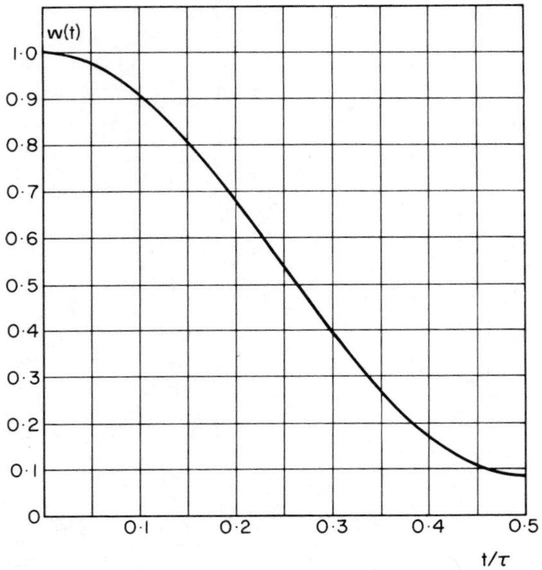

Figure A-6 Hamming window function.

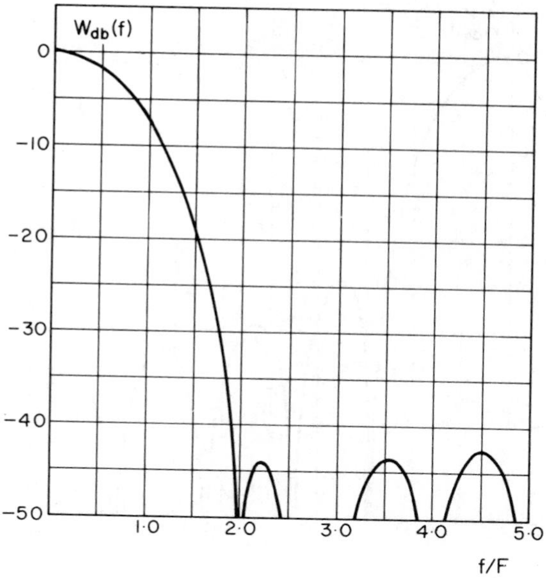

Figure A-7 Decibel amplitude response of Hamming window function.

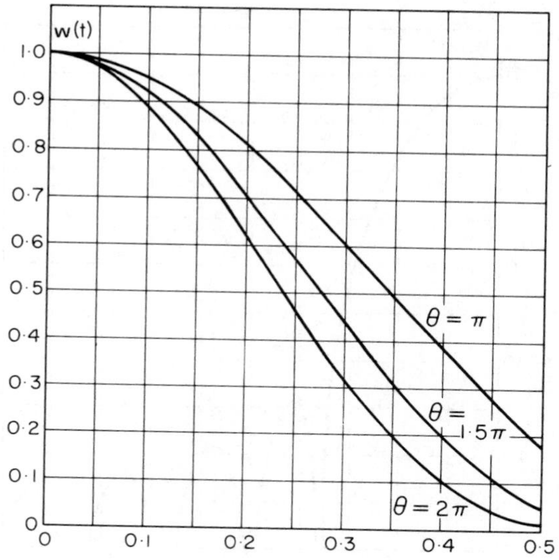

Figure A-8 Typical Kaiser window functions for three values of θ.

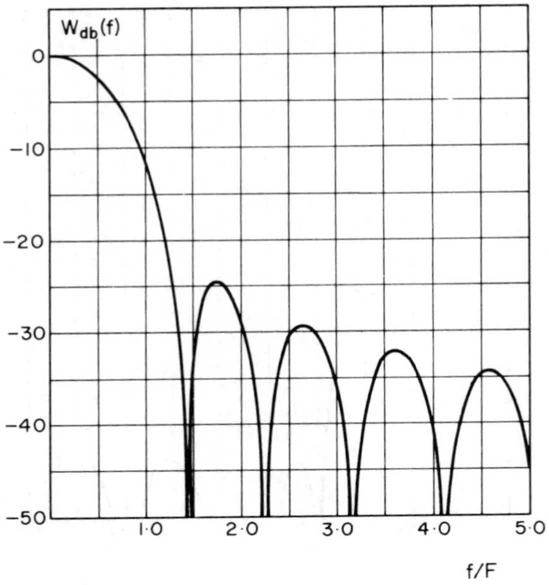

Figure A-9 Decibel amplitude response of Kaiser window function with $\theta = \pi$.

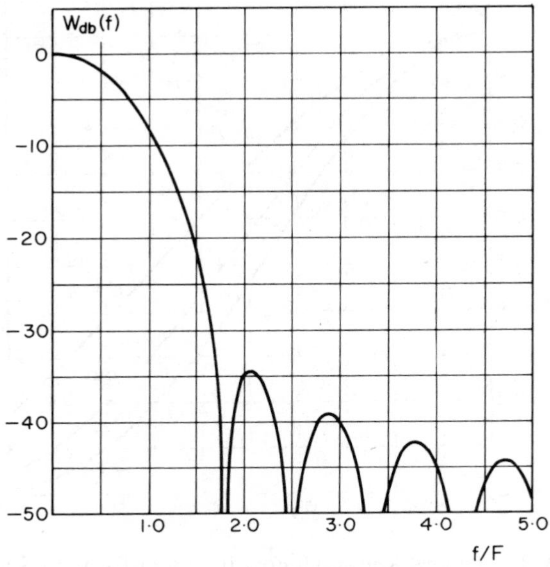

Figure A-10 Decibel amplitude response of Kaiser window function with $\theta = 1.5\pi$.

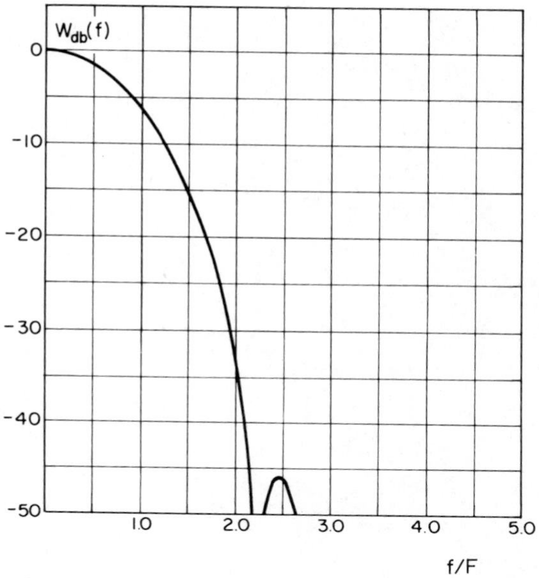

Figure A-11 Decibel amplitude response of Kaiser window function with $\theta = 2\pi$.

INDEX

A

Aliasing, 5, 47, 188, 191, 278, 279
Amplitude response of continuous-time system, 30, 123-126
Amplitude response of discrete-time system, 102-113
Analog, 1, 2, 117
Analog filter design data, 136-139, 151-157
Analog filters, 117-161
Analog-to-digital conversion, 4
Autocorrelation (*See* correlation.)

B

Band-pass digital filter, 194-202
Band-rejection digital filter, 202-204
Bilinear transformation, 168-186, 205, 206
Bit, 3
Blackman window, 228, 237
Butterworth filter (analog), 126-218, 133, 136-139, 143, 144, 147, 148, 150, 151, 155-157

C

Cauchy's residue theorem, 63, 73
Cauer filter, 135
Chebyshev filter (analog), 128-133, 136-139, 152-157
Chebyshev inverted filter, 134, 160
Comb filter, 303
Continuous-time signal, 2
Continuous-time systems, 2, 11-35
Convolution integral, 12, 14-15, 286
Convolution of discrete-time signals, 79-81, 212, 213
Convolution theorems for DFT, 253-255
Convolution with FFT, 284-295
Cooley-Tukey algorithm (*See* Fast Fourier transform.)
Correlation, 295-301
Crosscorrelation (*See* correlation.)

D

Decibel amplitude response, 104
Decimation-in-frequency, 261

Decimation-in-time, 261
Demultiplexer, 7
Difference equation, 66, 67
Differential equation, 11-14, 19
Digital filter, 7, 8, 164
Digital filter design, 163-238
Digital signal, 2
Digital-to-analog conversion, 4
Digital transfer function, 164
Discrete Fourier transform (*See* Fast Fourier transform)
Discrete-time signal, 2, 60
Discrete-time systems, 2, 59-115
Dolph-Chebyshev window, 228

E

Elliptic function filter, 135
Envelope delay (*See* group delay.)

F

Fast Fourier transform, 7-9, 166, 239-307
FFT (*See* Fast Fourier transform.)
FFT algorithms, 261-273
Finite impulse response digital filter, 166, 167, 211-238
Folding frequency, 47, 48, 102, 247
Forced response of continuous-time system, 16, 25
Forced response of discrete-time system, 77
Fourier series, 37-41, 213-221, 241-245, 281, 282
Fourier transform, 41-44, 239-245, 281, 282
Fourier transform, fast (*See* fast Fourier transform.)
Frequency sampling filters, 301-305

G

Group delay, 30, 104, 119-121

H

Hamming window, 227, 230, 231, 233, 234, 312, 313
Hanning window, 226, 230, 311, 312

High-pass digital filter, 205, 206
Holding circuit, 51-54, 191, 209

I

Impulse invariance, 187-189
Impulse response of continuous-time system, 12, 14-15
Impulse sampling, 48-51
Infinite impulse response digital filter, 166-210
Inverse z-transform, 69-78

K

Kaiser windows, 227, 231, 232, 313-315

L

Lagged product theorem for DFT, 253, 255
Laplace transform, 16-19
Leakage with DFT, 278-280
Linear system, 2
Low-pass to band-pass transformation, 139-144
Low-pass to band-rejection transformation, 144-148
Low-pass to high-pass transformation, 148-151
Lumped system, 2

M

Magnitude response (*See* amplitude response.)
Maximally-flat amplitude approximation, 126, 159, 160
Maximally flat time-delay filter, 133
Mirrow-image polynomial, 112
Modulation theorem for DFT, 253, 254
Multiplex, 3

N

Natural response of continuous-time system, 16, 25
Natural response of discrete-time system, 77

Nonrecursive realization, 166, 167, 212, 213
Nyguist frequency, 48

P

Partial fraction expansion of z-transforms, 69-72
Phase delay, 30, 104, 119-121
Phase response of continuous-time system, 30
Phase response of discrete-time system, 102-110
Picket-fence effect with DFT, 280-282
Poles of continuous-time system, 22
Poles of discrete-time system, 68
Power spectrum, 294-301

Q

Quadrantal symmetry, 123
Quantization, 2, 6, 91, 92, 213
Quantization noise, 5, 6

R

Realization of discrete-time systems, 85-91, 93-100, 166, 167, 212, 213
Rectangular window, 226, 228, 229, 310
Recursive realization, 166, 167, 304, 305
Residue, 24

S

Sampled-data signals, 2, 44-51, 59
Shannon's sampling theorem, 47
Shifting theorem for DFT, 253, 254
Stability of continuous-time system, 22-27
Stability of discrete-time system, 77-79
Statistical parameters, 297, 298
Steady-state frequency response of continuous-time systems, 28-32
Steady-state frequency response of discrete-time systems, 101-113
Steady-state transfer function of continuous-time system, 29

Steady-state transfer function of discrete-time system, 102
Step-invariance, 190-194

T

Time-invariant system, 2
Transfer function of continuous-time system, 19-22
Transfer function of discrete-time system, 66-69
Transient response (*See* natural response.)
Triangular window, 226, 228, 229, 310, 311

W

Window functions, 221-234, 309-315

Z

Z-transform, 61-66
Zeros of continuous-time system, 23
Zeros of discrete-time system, 68